Neo-Pentecostalism

Neo-Pentecostalism

A Post-Colonial Critique of the Prosperity Gospel in the Democratic Republic of the Congo

NELSON KALOMBO NGOY

Foreword by Brian Stanley

WIPF & STOCK · Eugene, Oregon

NEO-PENTECOSTALISM
A Post-Colonial Critique of the Prosperity Gospel in the Democratic Republic of the Congo

Copyright © 2019 Nelson Kalombo Ngoy. All rights reserved. Except for brief quotations in critical publications or reviews, no part of this book may be reproduced in any manner without prior written permission from the publisher. Write: Permissions, Wipf and Stock Publishers, 199 W. 8th Ave., Suite 3, Eugene, OR 97401.

Wipf & Stock
An Imprint of Wipf and Stock Publishers
199 W. 8th Ave., Suite 3
Eugene, OR 97401

www.wipfandstock.com

PAPERBACK ISBN: 978-1-5326-6468-7
HARDCOVER ISBN: 978-1-5326-6469-4
EBOOK ISBN: 978-1-5326-6470-0

Manufactured in the U.S.A.   MAY 23, 2019

To God be the Glory!

Contents

Foreword by Brian Stanley | ix
Abstract | xi
Preface | xiii
Acknowledgements | xv

1. Introduction | 1
2. Overview of the Historical Development of Neo-Pentecostalism in the Kongo Kingdom | 27
3. Translation | 51
4. A Congolese Critique of the Prosperity Gospel | 77
5. The Rise of Televangelism: A Historical Assessment | 103
6. Western Influence and Its Enculturation | 122
7. An Analysis of Selected Passages: The Prosperity Gospel Hermeneutic | 151
8. Prophetic Voices in the Twenty-First Century: A Congolese Context | 185
9. Conclusion | 209

Appendix 1: Interview Questions | 223
Appendix 2: Oral Interviews | 229
Appendix 3: Systematic Analysis of Materials | 244
Bibliography | 245
Index | 257

Foreword

FORMS OF NEO-PENTECOSTAL CHRISTIANITY that emphasize the material blessings promised by God to the individual believer are perhaps the most prominent feature of contemporary African Christianity. While in many cases tracing their origins to American prosperity gospel teachers, these expressions of African Neo-Pentecostalism are also profoundly African in their insistence that the point of spiritual power is to transform everyday material realities. They thus raise disturbing questions for Christian theology. Is a pronounced emphasis on the ability of the power of God to enhance the prosperity of believers to be understood as a welcome recovery by African Christians of a holistic understanding of salvation, and as a healthy corrective to the other-worldly preoccupations of Western mission Christianity? Or is it in fact a retreat from holism into a highly individualized and commercialized gospel, in which God becomes the automatic dispenser of health and wealth in contractual response to the financial sacrifices of the individual?

Scholarly literature on African Pentecostalism by historians and social scientists continues to expand at a phenomenal rate. However, theological critiques of the prosperity gospel written by African Christian authors remain very rare. Evaluations by northern-hemisphere theologians of African versions of the prosperity gospel can have only limited impact in Africa itself, for they can too easily be dismissed as culturally ill-informed or as manifestations of a continuing neo-colonial mindset. The distinctive interest of Nelson Ngoy's book is that it is written by a Congolese Christian. The Democratic Republic of the Congo has had one of the most tragic and fractured histories of any modern African state, and it is no accident that the prosperity gospel has exerted a powerful appeal to its long-suffering people. It is highly appropriate, therefore, that this book comes from a Congolese source.

Nelson Ngoy's provocative thesis is that the prosperity gospel is itself a form of neo-colonialism, perpetuating North American religious and indeed capitalist hegemony in Africa in the most subtle of ways. By clothing itself with the appearance of African authenticity, the prosperity gospel succeeds in persuading countless Africans that the unbridled pursuit of personal enrichment is entirely congruent with biblical Christianity as well as with their own cultural frameworks. In reality, its rampant individualism is contrary to the deepest instincts of both Judeo-Christian and African tradition. In both the Hebrew Bible and the New Testament the many-sided blessings of God are promised in covenantal response to the faithfulness of the people of God, who are themselves responding to the prior initiative of divine grace. They are not to be understood as a contractual reward for the individual.

This book will provoke debate and disagreement, but that is healthy and indeed necessary. Questions of where the boundary lies between authentic enculturation and inauthentic syncretism, or between a holistic gospel and a materialistic gospel, are not simple ones. Christians have the collective responsibility of seeking to provide answers to these questions, and in each regional context, the onus must fall primarily on indigenous Christian scholars to take the lead in seeking such answers. That is why this book is worth reading.

BRIAN STANLEY
Professor of World Christianity
University of Edinburgh

Abstract

THE AMERICAN-EXPORTED EXPRESSION OF the prosperity gospel to the post-colonial Congo is a different gospel. Prosperity theology is a betrayal of authentic proclamation of the biblical Gospel, a betrayal rooted in neocolonial progressive and materialistic endeavors which do not offer quality of life to adherents. The prosperity theology and the gospel-sanctioned effects of an incomplete holism have left a vacuum in the domestication and assimilation of faith.

The first chapter is an introduction discourse that identifies strategic methodological metrics as a roadmap of the research. The second chapter explores the social-historical, theological, and missiological milieu of the traditional Kongo kingdom. The third chapter examines the effects and impact of Bible translation. The fourth chapter serves as a critical analysis of the Congolese prosperity gospel. The fifth chapter critiques the Congolese prosperity gospel.

The sixth chapter explores how the rise of televangelism, socialnetworks, globalization, and modernity are reshaping Congolese Christendom. The seventh chapter investigates the hermeneutics of the theologies of prosperity case studies of selected biblical passages. The eighth chapter articulates the prophetic voice in a twenty-first century Congolese context. The ninth chapter is the concluding section that sums up the prosperity gospel and Neo-Pentecostalism by restating the original thesis and providing recommendations for further research.

NELSON KALOMBO NGOY, Ph.D.

Preface

NEO-PENTECOSTALISM AND THE PROSPERITY gospel have increasingly become forces in the twenty-first century because of neo-liberal progressive and excessive capitalistic features. Pentecostalism and the prosperity gospel have been domesticated, adopted, and reinvented within a Congolese society. These expressions have reshaped the Congolese religious landscape. Missionary approaches and a hermeneutic pedagogy had little or no impact on evangelization. The recipients failed to discard their pre-Christian roots and belief systems, which led to the surge in the prosperity gospel. Did missionaries fail to ask critical questions for a transformative contextualized holistic evangelism to alter pre-existing patterns of spirit-worlds? The failure of the state or government to meet the needs of the population and a systematic collapse of the economy due to bad governance and mismanagement of resources are underlying issues prosperity preachers seek to alter.

Furthermore, preachers tend to engage their members by providing opportunities to develop skills, secure employment, and receive investment possibilities. The social crisis and lack of affordable healthcare systems are quandaries the prosperity culture seeks to address; therefore, deliverance through spiritual encounters was developed. The adherents of this Christian expression are drawn to the practices of anointing oil, exorcism, cure for confessing witches, ritual bathing, and drinking of blessed water. This is the basis of syncretism and the integration of traditional Congolese beliefs into Christianity.

Neo-Pentecostalism assessed from the vantage of the margins, those who have been exploited by their apostles and prophets. This is a pathway to negotiating a literal translation of the Bible in the Post-colonial Congo..

The motivation to study this subject matter was born from the writer's interest in evangelism and missions. Having lived in the context of the margins, he felt the weight of accountability to voice his concerns and critique the sanctioned mechanism that impoverishes, through a pattern of systematic exploitation, some of the poorest adherents of the Christian faith. He recognized that exploited victims were voiceless because of their lack of freedom of speech. This project will be utilized as a pedagogy and model to newer, growing generations of evangelists, church planters, teachers, and academicians in the Congo to benefit a model for translating the gospel through a biblical hermeneutic. A literal translation of the biblical gospel can assure a profound transformation and authentic discipleship.

This writer is compelled by Christ's mandate, as articulated in the Great Commission (Matt 28:18-20) and Great Compassion (Matt 25:35-39), to take the gospel to the seven million unreached people groups around the planet and tell them about Jesus and His gift of salvation. A passion for evangelism and missions through reaching a lost and broken world with the message of the gospel of Christ, including a heart for those in the margins are the primary motivations of this writer, leading him to pursue this adventure.

Nelson Kalombo Ngoy
Franklin Square, New York
May 2018

Acknowledgments

I EXPRESS HEARTFELT GRATITUDE to myriads of scholars and colleagues for their selfless collaboration. I could not have made it without their support. Moreover, it is with sincere gratitude, I thank Dr. Brian Robertson for his editing endeavors and contribution to my academic quest. My most profound appreciation goes to the editing services at Wipf and Stock for their professionalism.

Besides the editors, gratitude goes to professors Brian Stanley, Amos Yong, and Nimi Wariboko for endorsing and forwarding this book. Many thanks to Professor Stanley Brian for writing the foreword of this book. Also, thanks to professors David Nelson Persons, Katherine Hill-Miller, and Daniel R. Sanchez for their insightful comments and encouragement throughout the process of writing. This book in its initial format was a Ph.D. dissertation that I expanded and refined due to the high demand of readers who requested its use in both academic and church settings. I am grateful for the many questions and comments which challenged me to broaden my research and directed me to various sources.

My sincere thanksgiving goes to my children: Angel, Francis, Arcel, John, Charles, and Lisa who provided unconditional love, wisdom, and inspiration. I owe many thanks to my congregation the Wesley United Methodist Church in Franklin Square New York for their support. My sincere appreciation and many thanks go to my wife Lucie Tshama for her selfless support, encouragement, and wise advice. Finally, I express heartfelt gratitude to my academic supervisor Keith Eitel for supervising my Ph.D. dissertation.

1

Introduction

FOR OVER A CENTURY, Pentecostalism has played a critical role in the life of formerly colonized people of Africa as an instrument of oppression, corruption, and exploitation. Nevertheless, Pentecostal efforts continue to sustain the socio-spiritual political and economic manipulation which sanctions systemic structures of inequality within certain segments of African societies. African Pentecostal trends have sanctioned the effects of prophecies resulting in human exploitation and left a vacuum in the assimilation of faith within the paradigm shift of the twenty-first century missional engagement.

Moreover, the dramatic shift of Christianity's center of gravity emerging from the Global North to the Global South that appears as a twenty-first-century phenomenon is characterized by an appropriation of the American prosperity gospel.[1] Neo-Pentecostalism and the prosperity gospel have altered the face of Christianity in the Congo. However, neo-Pentecostalism's resurgence is a Congolese response to the gospel of Christ with additions from local traditions. The pre-Christian primal cultural tradition, or heritage, is rooted in an appropriation and integration of an African worldview with Christian expressions. The African worldview is central to the expansion of the religion. As a result, the Congolese religious consciousness is a matrix of the paradigm shift leading to a massive resurgence of faith.

---

1. Kalu, *Interpreting Contemporary Christianity*, 1. Also, Anderson, "The Pentecostal Gospel and Culture in Africa: Charismatics of the Pentecostal Full Gospel," 17.

This writer observes that in post-colonial Congo[2] (1960–2018), Neo-Pentecostals and charismatic groups have propagated a "different gospel."[3] The American prosperity gospel found a home and has been appropriated and adopted within Congolese cultural expressions based on the concept of a life force. The life force concept is an African expression rooted in a traditional man-centered religion. Besides, the conventional African promotes the very concept of a life force, which is an acquisition of possessions that will enrich someone physically and materially.

These traditional worldviews include ritual sacrifices and occult invocations of ancestral spirits. In his book *Bantu Philosophy*, Placide Tempels argues, "The Bantu say, in respect of a number of strange practices in which we see neither rhyme nor reason. That their purpose is to acquire life, strength or vital force, to live strongly, that they are to make life stronger, that force remains perpetually in one's posterity."[4] For Tempels, "*Whole* is the theory of vital force."[5] The Congolese relate the wholeness of life to these transcendent spiritual powers and forces.

As a result, African Christianity is reshaping Christianity in the twenty-first century. Africa has increasingly become one of the new heartlands of a Christian worldview. Andrew F. Walls argues: "This means that we have to regard African Christianity as the representative Christianity of the twenty-first century."[6] The church's role in society has caused an expansion of Christianity as a final push for the next Christendom. These traditional worldviews are the basis for the fundamental turning point in re-transmitting the gospel.

---

2. The terms "Neo-Pentecostalism, post-colonial, and prosperity gospel" are used objectively in this research. The term post-colonial denotes a time delimiting phenomenological shift in religious, socio-political, and economic life after Congolese independence and theoretical approaches. Neo-Pentecostalism is a charismatic trend based on a spiritual baptismal experience similar to Peter's community in Acts 2. These trends are based on speaking in tongues, healing, and prophecies. The prosperity gospel distorts the biblical gospel by articulating that God's blessings are available to those who exhibit faith, obedience, health, wealth, and financial giving to specific ministries.

3. The term "different gospel" means distorted or twisted doctrine. In the present project, the term is used to prove that the prosperity gospel is distinct from the gospel of Christ. To attain this goal, the writer will interpret a biblical and historical analysis rooted in Galatians 1:6–9. The gospel is free and a life-giving experience. However, the prosperity gospel movement tends to exploit more impoverished adherents.

4. Tempels, *Bantu Philosophy*, 43–45.

5. Tempels, *Bantu Philosophy*, 99

6. Walls, *The Cross-Cultural Process in Christian History*, 85.

The majority consensus of African religious scholarship argues that Christianity's emergence within a Congolese context is a typical product of the locals' involvement in re-translating and re-transmitting the gospel. For instance, "The church of our Lord Jesus Christ in the World, known as Red Star after the church's symbol. This movement started in 1949 in the Western Congo in a decisive Pentecost of its own, with trembling and speaking in tongues."[7] Allan H. Anderson documents that the movement headed by the prophet Simao Toco, "had in the1950s 82 followers; by 1965 the movement claimed 10,000 adherents and had become multiethnic, thanks to the Portuguese practice of exiling Tocoists to distant provinces."[8]

Neo-Pentecostal patterns of a post-colonial re-transmission of the prosperity gospel are rooted in traditional evangelism's efforts and missional impact.[9] Unlike classical Pentecostalism, which is based on

7. Anderson, *African Reformation*, 135.
8. Anderson, *African Reformation*, 135.

9. The term "post-colonial" represents a period pointing to the remarkable shift in 1960 that occurred after the Congo's independence from Belgium. This period marks the beginning of the religious transformation of the Congo. Post-colonization inaugurated a new era in nearly all levels of Congolese life: religious, social, economic, political, and cultural. Religion took a new approach as the Congolese religious landscape shifted with the rise of neo-Pentecostalism and charismatic preaching. Also, African religions rooted in traditional evangelism diffused a gospel of prosperity. However, the term or theory which uses "post" as its prefix is not easy to pinpoint, and its definition remains unsettled. The term "post-colonial, has both historical and theoretical nuances: (a) It examines and explains social, cultural, and political conditions such as nationality, race, and gender before and after colonialism. (b) It interrogates the often-one-sided history of nations, cultures, and nationalities, and peoples. (c) It engages in a critical revision of how the other is represented." See Sugirtharajah, *Exploring Postcolonialism*, 12–13. Biblical scholars and feminist liberationist theologians tend to use the term "postcolonial" to describe modern imperialism, beginning with the process of colonization, the struggle for political independence, and the emergence of the neocolonial globalization era. See Dube. *Postcolonial Feminist Interpretation of the Bible*, 4.

The term "re-transmission" is used to explain how the gospel is retransmitted over and over within local Congolese expressions. For example, prosperity teachings have taken a new shape within Congolese society. The gospel is being reinvented, domesticated, and appropriated within an African expression. Missionaries evangelized and sowed seeds; however, at present, many locals have become missionaries to their people and land. On the one hand, the movement of prosperity theology within neo-Pentecostalism and the charismatic movements are proof of the emergence of Christianity and the socio-structural development within the Global South communities. On the other hand, it affects its recipients due to its mechanisms of exploitation, inequality, and false hope. Walls, *The Cross-Cultural Process in Christian History*, 9, 26.

the Western holiness movement of the nineteenth century, Neo-Pentecostalism is one of the fastest growing brands of religion or streams of Christianity in twenty-first century Congo. For instance, Matthews A. Ojo notes, "These churches constituted the fastest growing phenomenon in West Africa during the 1980s and 1990s."[10] African-initiated churches and Neo-charismatic types are proliferating and igniting proliferations of various forms of Christianities.

As a result, the Congo has developed into one of the new heartlands of Christianity in the twenty-first century. The receiving nation understood the gospel, translated it into its terms, and fashioned it to reflect cultural patterns of the twenty-first century. Pentecostal churches are devoted to re-inventing their version of an idealized prehistoric Christianity. Donald E. Miller stresses that Pentecostal churches are reshaping, reinventing, and transforming Christianity.[11] As a result, the Congolese have appropriated the gospel and domesticated it within local

---

The terms "traditional evangelism" and "missional impact" were brought about by missionaries who established a chain of the mission station in Congo and adopted a policy to penetrate the gospel in Zaire. Peter Falk argues, "This was the beginning of Christian ministry in Zaire and of the effort to penetrate the country with the gospel and establish a chain of mission stations along Zaire River . . . In 1886 it established a separate ministry Nils Westlind, a capable linguist, translated the New Testament into Kikongo in 1891. The society soon began a ministry at Matadi on the northern bank of Zaire River. A mission press was established at Matadi in 1892 and began publishing Minsamu Miayenge, the first periodical of Zaire. They adopted this policy to diffuse the gospel rapidly into the interior of the continent and as many tribes as possible. They also wished to open the internal to contacts with outside world and counteract the devastating activities of the slave traders." Falk, *The Growth of the Church in Africa*, 175–77. This traditional evangelistic effort describes the original intent of the Christian mission in the Congo that fueled an incomplete holism. The church in the Congo was birthed by European and American missionaries who evangelized the region known as the Belgian Congo (1885), later Zaire (1971), and finally, the Democratic Republic of the Congo (1997). Churches were planted, hospitals built, and schools established that taught reading, writing, and Bible knowledge. Throughout the colonial period, these parochial schools were the only ones available to the poor. Congolese clergy were trained in primary or elementary Bible schools, and the material taught was primarily taken from a Western worldview. Many Congolese recognize that the churches established by the missionaries no longer resonate with or adequately address their daily realities. The hymns they sing do not correspond to their internal longings and cries. As a result, revivals and prosperity-gospel churches have sprung up and attracted large followings.

10. Ojo, "Transnational Religions Networks and Indigenous Pentecostal Missionary Enterprises in the West African Coastal Region," 17.

11. Miller and Yamamori, *Global Pentecostalism*, 17–18.

cultural expressions. Philip Jenkins observes that the center of gravity for Christianity is no longer the West, but it has shifted to the non-Western world and southern hemisphere.[12] Africa has increasingly become one of the leading voices within the Judeo-Christian religion, and its role is critical to reshaping faith in the world. Currently, there has been a remarkable change in the mission field. The United States and Europe used to send missionaries to Africa, but today, Africa can supply missionaries to the Western world. In, *The Mission of the Church Today in the Light of Global History*, Walls reveals, "The Christian story is serial; its center moves from place to place. No church or place or culture owns it. At different times different people and places have become its heartlands; its chief representative. Then the baton passes on to others."[13]

Additionally, he says, "Christian progress is never final, is never a set of gains to be plotted on the map."[14] New converts are not required to travel to Jerusalem to interact with Christ or other Christians. The gospel is already translatable as a universal medium for the salvation of humanity. Therefore, one is not required to acquire a visa or a laissez-passer to cross the border or frontiers and have access to God's saving grace. Jesus is available and accessible to any culture, village, and people group.

The traditional and primal belief systems influence the methods of translating and re-transmitting the gospel of Christ. Therefore, Christianity loses its flavor of holistic commitment to impact life change and transformation. A critical contextual translation of the biblical gospel might be transformative for discipleship within the Democratic Republic of the Congo.

---

12. Jenkins, *The Next Christendom*, 1–2. He argues, "Christianity has in very recent times ceased to be a Euro-American religion and is becoming thoroughly global: in 1900, 83 percent of world's Christians lived in Europe and Latin America. In 2050, 72 percent of Christians will live in Africa, Asia, and Latin America, and a sizable share of the remainder will have roots in one or more of those continents." In 1900, there were over 9 million Christians in Africa. According to Barrett, *World Christian Encyclopedia*, the year 2000 revealed that African Christians numbered more than 300 million. "Presently, the total number of Christians in Africa and Latin America outnumbers that in Europe and North America." See Park, "Journey of the Gospel," 3. Also see Jenkins, "The Next Christianity," 60. Also Sanneh, *Whose Religion is Christianity?*, 10. Also see Bediako, *Christianity in Africa*, 3.

13. Walls, "The Mission of the Church Today," 18–19.

14. Walls, "The Mission of the Church Today," 18–19.

THESIS

Practiced through the lens of Sub-Sahara African primal religious belief systems, Pentecostalism translates into a deceiving gospel rooted in a syncretized super-structure of an underlying worldview that has not been radically transformed by the biblical gospel. This investigation attempts to demonstrate that the non-Christian's view of the transformation of Christian thought is a hindrance for effective evangelism and missions. Have the cultures transformed the gospel, or are the cultures transformed by the gospel? To achieve its primary goal, this study compares and contrasts selected Neo-Pentecostal practices with specific Congolese primal religious worldviews and belief systems regarding prosperity and appeasing ancestors.

The research explores the hypothesis that the translated gospel, as rendered, failed to be a prophetic voice. In other words, the way the gospel was translated was unable to be a prophetic voice or vessel at the time of its translation. A prophetic reading of the gospel allows recipients of faith and members of the body of Christ to discontinue or discard their prehistoric belief systems rooted in animistic worldviews of consulting ancestors' spirits.[15]

Moreover, the study will critically engage case studies of Neo-Pentecostal thoughts, practices, belief systems, and influences contributing to the surging paradigm shift within the Congolese Christian worldview. Authentic evangelism based on a post-colonial prophetic translation of the biblical gospel is critical for holistic discipleship and change. Such translation can be a transformative, life-changing phenomenon for the Congolese social fabric. A literal translation of the gospel becomes a force to ignite Congolese revivals, holistic development, and empowerment.[16]

---

15. The phrase, "prophetic translation of the gospel" is used to illustrate the significance of an interpretation of the biblical gospel, and the "Bible that is prophetic" means engages the recipients and leads them to Christ without exploiting them. Prophetic leadership and prophetic imagination are the essences of the Gospel and Christ's mission. This model allows recipients or Christians to discard traditional belief systems and syncretism for the sake of eternal life and salvation through Christ.

16. "Holistic development" is a term the writer uses to demonstrate that the gospel of Jesus Christ is a life-changing phenomenon. The life-changing aspect implies that whenever one receives this gospel of Jesus Christ, it affects the receiver's lifestyle. The encounter with the Christian gospel engages a complete transformation of the whole person. The change is not limited to spiritual, mental, physical, and social factors, but applies to the whole person.

INTRODUCTION

Ronald J. Sider and others advocate a "biblical mandate and efficient, holistic evangelism and social outreach."[17]

DEFINITION OF KEY TERMS

Expressions or syntax terminologies play a crucial role in a comprehensive study of the phenomenon or subject matter. "Neo-Pentecostalism" refers to both charismatic and neo-charismatic churches. "Pentecostalism" is a renewal movement within the broader arena of Christianity. The phenomenon can be understood as a continuation of a series of renewal movements that extends to the earliest days of the church.

Pentecostalism is rooted in the Acts 2 community of spiritual baptism and speaking in tongues. "Pentecostalism is defined most conveniently as an extensive but loosely tied global Christian missionary and revivalist movement with origins in international holiness movement of the late 19th and early 20th century, emphasizing themes like baptism in the Spirit, healing, and glossolalia."[18] Moreover, "Neo-Pentecostals/Neo-Pentecostal churches are terms associated with the charismatic revival from the 1960s and onwards."[19] These revivalists are Pentecostal Holiness groups with a grassroots character.

In its modern form, Pentecostalism is dated from the beginning of the twentieth century, with its immediate roots going back to the nineteenth century into revivalist Methodism, holiness offshoots of Methodism, Pietism, international missions, and protagonists of divine healing.[20] Nevertheless, according to Torbjorn Aronson, "The term Pentecostal is derived from Pentecost, a Greek term describing the Jewish Feast of

---

17. Sider et al., *Churches That Make A Difference*, 17. The authors surmise, "A holistic congregation results: a church that practices both evangelism and social ministry; balances nurture and outreach, knows and loves its community, clearly communicates its theology and particular vision for holistic mission; integrates the holistic vision into the internal life of the church; builds its ministry on a base of spiritual maturity and healthy, loving relationships; and equips its members to action" (17).

18. Aronson, "Community in Charismata," 33. Aronson argues, "Today the umbrella term Pentecostalism covers both the earlier and the later forms of movements, numbering about 500 million adherents with a stronghold in Latin America, USA, sub-Saharan Africa and East Asia. The earlier forms of Pentecostalism are commonly labeled classical Pentecostalism, consisting of denominations, organizations and local churches with their roots in the revival of early 1900s" (33).

19. Aronson, "Community in Charismata," 34.

20. Kay, *Pentecostalism*, 1.

Weeks. For Christians, this event commemorates the descent of the Holy Spirit upon the followers of Jesus-Christ, as outlined in the second chapter of the book of Acts."[21] The Congo has increasingly become a Pentecostal religious landscape.

"Neo-Pentecostals" refers to those Pentecostal groups who have taken root within the Congolese expressions since the 1970s and 1980s and represent the new face of African Christianity. Neo-Pentecostals are part of charismatic renewal progressive movements that proliferate the prosperity gospel. In his dissertation, "Pentecostalization: The Changing Face of Baptists in West Africa," Randy Ray Arnett conveys that Neo-Pentecostals "typically attract the upwardly mobile middle-class, preach a health and wealth message, and associate with the Word-Faith movement."[22] These groups systematically preserve a global network and connection. The nondenominational groups include, but are not limited to, "A. Adeboye's Redeemed Christian Church of God, Mensa Otabil's International Central Gospel, David Oyedepo's Winner's Chapel, and a myriad of Independent groups."[23]

Candy Gunther Brown discusses, "The underlying Pentecostal conviction that the gifts of the Holy Spirit are ongoing, that they did not cease after the apostolic period. This belief is what gives the name Charismatic (Charisma means gift)."[24] This group refers to a type of Christianity that stresses the importance of spiritual gifts and a manifestation of personal experience and power such as healing, speaking in tongues, and prophecies.

"Neo-charismatic" is a movement that refers to a sect of evangelical churches that emphasizes spiritual gifts of the Holy Spirit. It is a mixture of Western, especially American, Christianity and local expressions of the host culture. Furthermore, Maija Penttila states, "Neo-Charismatic is indigenized when churches distance themselves from what is viewed as Western values and adapt localized rituals, reconstruct the usable

21. Aronson, "Community in Charismata," 33.

22. Randy Ray Arnett argues that the Word-Faith movement is known under diverse names, such as the Word of Faith Movement, Health and Wealth, Prosperity Theology, Positive Confession, and Name It and Claim It. Arnett, "Pentecostalization," 27. Some Pentecostal scholars deny the Word-Faith movement is a variation of Pentecostalism. See, for example, McConnell, *A Different Gospel*. This variation of Neo-Pentecostalism is a strong movement in the Congo, and according to Arnett's research, the movement appears to have a strong presence in West Africa.

23. Arnett, "Pentecostalization," 27.

24. Brown, *Global Pentecostal and Charismatic Healing*, xix.

narratives of history, and work to alleviate social problems."[25] This movement is the third wave, which includes broader Pentecostal groups that originated from the first wave and second waves of classical Pentecostal Holiness movements.

A "Missions and Mission" Christian begins with the Great Commission—the final words of Jesus to his disciples before His ascension, sending them out into the world to make disciples of all nations.[26] Christopher J. H. Wright discusses that the mission has a sense of sending and being sent.[27] However, the mission is a cross-cultural experience of churches engaged and responding to missionary work, including evangelism and church planting. Missions are not only a humanitarian charity or relief system of caring for the poor, homeless and the needy, but also, they are an expression of God's purpose and saving plan for lost and broken humanity. God has called people to participate in His mission. Wright avers, "Mission arises from the heart of God, and it is a global outreach of the global people of a global God."[28]

"Missional" is the process of engaging others with the gospel of Jesus Christ. Therefore, a missional church it is one that engages or evangelizes other people groups and cultures with the message of the gospel. The missional initiative involves connecting ministries and establishing relationships and partnerships with other communities across the globe. Wright argues, "Not everything is cross-culture evangelistic mission, but everything a Christian and a Christian church says and does should be missional in its conscious participation in the mission of God in God's world."[29] A "missionary" is a Christian who responds to the highest calling to go into a home or foreign mission field to serve people in the name of Christ and share the gospel. Some missionaries are engaged in the social development, education, medical, and other humanitarian activities.

"Evangelism" begins with the good news which is the essence of this transformative force. A Christian's mission is to impact the world with the specific intent of living out the good news or pointing someone to Christ, and the desire to advance that cause. Whenever one is engaged in missions, he is already evangelizing at the same time. The person who

---

25. Penttila, "Saint Peter's New Churches," 19.
26. Wright, *Biblical Theology for Life, The Mission of God's People*, 23.
27. Wright, *Biblical Theology for Life, The Mission of God's People*, 23.
28. Wright, *Biblical Theology for Life, The Mission of God's People*, 24.
29. Wright, *Biblical Theology for Life, The Mission of God's People*, 26.

is involved in evangelism is already fulfilling his mission. Wright states, "World evangelization requires the whole church to take the whole gospel to the whole world."[30]

"Renewalists Renewal Churches" are characterized by Pentecostals, Charismatics, and Third Wave Christians. These types refer mainly to groups within Global South churches. These movements emphasize the gifts of the Holy Spirit, speaking in tongues, prophecies, and spiritism. Often, they feel crushed by economic, social, and political systems, so they seek renewal and social lift, which is a desire for upward mobility through religious experiences.

The "gospel" is the good news of Jesus Christ. It is a message concerning the life, ministry, and death of Jesus Christ. According to the Apostle Paul, the gospel is an orally proclaimed message about salvation through Christ alone.

"Post-Colonialism" is a problematic term which refers to both an era of colonialism and a set of critical attitudes taken toward colonialism. The design of postcolonial discourse is region-specific and employs Western, as well as native, modes of expression.[31] Sugirtharajah suggests, "Post-colonialism is seen no longer as recovering distorted and defamed histories and injustices, but as reframing and recovering the cultural soul in the widening global market."[32] The chief task of post-colonial discourse is to write and listen to the stories of the host culture in their own terms and languages. However, this writer uses the term to indicate a historical shift within Neo-Pentecostalism.

"African Traditional Religion" [ATR] refers to African conventional indigenous belief systems and practices based on oral traditions. The Congolese handed down the traditional pattern from one generation to another. The traditional religion has a syncretistic character. According to John Mbiti, "ATR plays a holistic role in an African understanding of his/her origin and purpose."[33] ATR is a way of life in Africa. However, Mbangu Anicet Muyingi, an African scholar, insists, "It is a unified system of beliefs that gives an anchor to human life; religion becomes an important signifier, a framework for identification, a basis of membership,

---

30. Wright, *Biblical Theology for Life, The Mission of God's People*, 26.

31. Castle, *Postcolonial Discourses an Anthology*, 508.

32. Sugirtharajah, *Exploring Postcolonial Biblical Criticism, History, Method, Practice*, 25.

33. Mbiti, *Introduction to African Religion*, 5.

and a potent tool for mobilization."[34] The syncretistic character of Christianity is the mix of traditional belief systems and Christian worldviews.

"African Initiated Churches" [AIC] are also called, interchangeably, African Instituted Churches or African Independent Churches. These types of churches are rooted in pre-Christian beliefs systems and practices. Some broke from mission-established churches and mainline denominations such as Anglicans, Lutherans, Presbyterians, Baptists, and Methodists as a resistance to colonial and Western models of Christianity.

For instance, Kimbanguism is one of the major traditional independent religions. Arnett asserts, "The AIC cluster is composed of churches that beginning in the late-1800s, broke away from mission churches or were founded independently by Africans."[35] According to Arnett, these groups include, but are not limited to, "The Ethiopian, Aladura, Zionist, Kimbanguist Harriste, and *Christianisme celeste* movements."[36] These groups are the prototypes of older AICs, which are different from the newer, independent Neo-Pentecostal churches. "New Generation Churches" are independently founded churches by African prophets and apostles. After gaining their independence in the 1960s, with the collapse of the economy and social structure, common Congolese took the Bible seriously, and the gospel became a means of survival. New Generation churches are growing sects and house churches. Some use government buildings and public squares. They emphasize deliverance, healing, and prosperity messages.

---

34. Muyingi, *African Traditional Religion* 89. Muyingi concludes, "Given this definition, it can be understood that religion plays a holistic role in determining a person's understanding of his/her origin and purpose." "According to the definition above, it would be true of ATR as well as those religions that have their origin outside the continent. ATR is the religion of the African people before the coming of Western missionaries. ATR can be defined as the indigenous religion of the Africans. It is the belief that has been handed over down from generation to generation by the forebears of the present generation of Africans. It is not a fossil religion (something of the distant past rather than a religion that Africans have made theirs by living and practicing it in the twenty-first century. However, Western missionaries succeeded in converting some African people to the new religions (Christianity and Islam), which made them lose their identities. The ATR was condemned by the new religions to be not a religion, and ATR was called by many names like magic, sorcery, animist, witchcraft, etc" (89).

35. Gilliland, "How Christian Are African Independent Churches," 259–72. For further study, see also Anderson, "The Newer Pentecostal and Charismatic Churches," 167–84. He discusses newer AICs.

36. Arnett, "Pentecostalization," 26.

"Classical Pentecostalism" refers to the holiness movement originating from the Azusa Street Revival (1906) in the United States. However, according to Arnett, the term "Classic Pentecostals" refers to historic Pentecostal denominations, such as Assemblies of God, the International Church of God, the Church of the Foursquare Gospel, the Apostolic Church, the Church of Pentecost, and the Church of God.[37]

REVIEW OF RELATED LITERATURE

The review of the literature will focus on certain aspects of prosperity theology: church growth, social gospel, healing and deliverance, economic collapse, foreign prosperity influence, and social lift.

Prosperity Theology

Prosperity theologies and Neo-Pentecostalism are the basis of the proliferation of Congolese forms of Christianity. These theologies attract millions of people. Attanasi and Yong pose the question: "Why has their preaching been so well received. Is it a betrayal of the gospel or a retrieval of one of its vital overlooked dimensions?"[38] These questions are crucial to achieving a comprehensive and qualitative analysis of the phenomena as a global concern.

Attanasi and Yong's study explores the socio-economic implications of the prosperity gospel in Pentecostal/charismatic Christians. They discuss and define the function of prosperity theologies within local communities around the globe. The population Attanasi and Yong used was based on a cross-cultural study of a quantitative research analysis of the prosperity gospel and satisfied random sampling techniques of case studies across the globe. The authors' case studies of the socio-economic implications of the prosperity gospel clarify Congolese prosperity theology in the wake of poverty facing the population.

Hermen Kroesbergen's approach of using theological skills to examine and assess the prosperity gospel from an African Sub-Saharan perspective is significant to this research. "Renewalists" (a term including both Pentecostals and Charismatics, according to a 2006 Pew Forum on religion and public life) believe that when a person sows seed, he or

---

37. Arnett, "Pentecostalization," 27.
38. Attanasi and Yong, *Pentecostalism and Prosperity*, 265.

she is entitled to God's physical and material blessings. The prosperity gospel poses a challenge to churches in the twenty-first century. A proliferation of the movement in post-colonial Congo presents challenges and potentially frightening developments. Congolese scholars need to address and adequately document these trends. Congolese prosperity preachers preach physical health such as good food, clothing, and beautiful children. They also teach that motor vehicles and homes are given to Christians because Christians have within themselves the power to create reality by speaking a word.[39] Power and Spirit-filled are critical to renewalists and their devotion to deities.

Kroesbergen used the population of impoverished groups. He employed theological skills and surveys to examine and assess relevant topics from an African Reformed perspective. Moreover, these African scholars posed critical questions worth consideration: Is the prosperity gospel biblically sound? Where did it originate? What is the prosperity gospel, and how should we evaluate it? Does it represent an incorrect way of looking at health and wealth, or can we learn something from it?[40] These writers used both qualitative and quantitative research approaches to study the phenomenon. Their treatment of the subject of prosperity from a Sub-Saharan African viewpoint and their assessments are pertinent to this hypothesis.

Ogbu U. Kalu, an African theologian, bridges the complex fabric of Africa and traces the story of various Pentecostal forms of Christianity. His elaboration does not exclude the effects and influences of the prosperity gospel among the Congolese. He suggests that the expression of prosperity goes beyond material wealth to embrace spiritual renewal. These terms characterize "the rebuilding of the forms of brokenness, the provision of health, the reversal of economic desolation, and the political and the social well-being of individuals and communities."[41] He uses quantitative methods to study the statistics behind the phenomenon. His unique perspective as an African voice allows for a holistic understanding of Pentecostalism and the prosperity gospel event.

---

39. Walker, *The Concise Guide to Today's Religion and Spirituality*, 347.
40. Kroesbergen, ed., *In the Search of Health and Wealth*, ix.
41. Kalu, *African Pentecostalism*, 213.

Church Growth

Philip Jenkins investigates various forms of Christianity in the Global South, revealing what they mean for the future. He asserts that Africa has become the new heartland of Christianity, and believers are now reading the Bible with fresh eyes. Jenkins posits that Christians in the Global South connect with a New Testament (NT) agricultural society marked by famine, plague, poverty, demons, and exile.

Jenkins critiques the prosperity gospel and suggests it is "something like a superstitious cargo cult from an anthropology text: if we follow these rituals, divine forces will bring us rich gifts."[42] Anthropological methods and approaches attempt to adapt or fit into the new cultural expressions or host cultures without challenging them. Promises of prosperity theology underlie the success of major or mega Congolese churches. Jenkins argues, "The prosperity gospel is an inevitable by-product of a church containing so many of the very poorest."[43] His use of quantitative and qualitative methods to interpret the dramatic shift and the changing face of Christianity is vital to this research. His approach is useful to understanding the surge of the prosperity gospel.

David Tonghou Ngong says, "The recent spread of neo-Pentecostal/charismatic Christianity in Africa is usually credited to the ability of this expression of Christianity to address the religious needs of the people in light of African traditional cosmology."[44] Ngong interprets the significance of the Holy Spirit as enabling a critical philosophical rational development of science and technology in Africa. He posits that the Holy Spirit is the power that overcomes the malevolent spiritual forces which deprive many Africans of a fuller life.

As Kalu puts it, "Pentecostalism is the fastest growing stream of Christianity in the world today; the movement is reshaping religion in the twenty-first century."[45] Proponents of Neo-Pentecostalism are devotees and "born again"[46] adherents of new revival churches. Anderson sur-

---

42. Jenkins, *The New Face of Christianity*, 91.
43. Jenkins, *The New Face of Christianity*, 97.
44. Ngong, *The Holy Spirit, and Salvation in African Christian Theology*, 140.
45. Ngong, *The Holy Spirit, and Salvation in African Christian Theology*, 339.
46. These born-again Christians are evangelical and charismatic renewal groups that identify themselves as having undergone spiritual rebirth or regeneration. Adherents to these groups prioritize a personal relationship with Jesus Christ. The term "born again" has biblical roots in John 3:3 as Jesus spoke unto Nicodemus, a Pharisee

mises, "This born-again conversion experience . . . Identified them, even with outsiders."[47] Presently, as one of the largest nations in Sub-Sahara Africa, the Congo is crucial to Neo-Pentecostalism's surging prosperity theologies in Africa.

Social Gospel

Prosperity preachers interpret cosmological experience as longevity (having long life) and material prosperity such as children, good health, and wealth. This link of prosperity to spirituality is crucial to this research in determining the roots and effects of Neo-Pentecostalism in the Congo, along with the role of the Holy Spirit and prophecies.

Robert Reese suggests that Christian missions have planted growing churches in many lands, but the prominent model was a "form of Western Christianity that failed to spark vital local expressions of faith."[48] Reese's argument is proof that an incomplete holism has fueled a Neo-Pentecostal re-transmission of the prosperity gospel in Africa, especially in Zimbabwe. Imported Western methods of worship, organization, and the administration of these elements developed a dependency syndrome.

Moreover, the prosperity gospel is a mechanism of dependency. Preachers hold their listeners hostage. As a result, recipients (i.e., poor and needy) of prosperity theologies are often fed with false promises of healing, wealth, and spiritual power. The author's insights are significant in studying this sanctioned mechanism of impoverishment.

Wesley Granberg-Michaelson and James H. Billington present a survey of the emerging face of Christianity. They interviewed four hundred churches in the Global South. Renewalists advocate a progressive Pentecostalism engagement and effort to develop education, health clinics, housing, food assistance, community development, microenterprises, loans, job training, drug and alcohol rehabilitation, anticorruption efforts, and election monitoring, among others.[49] Progressive Pentecostalism is like a neo-liberal systematic prosperity gospel, and it has become a neo-colonial movement influenced by Western-imported

---

seeking the truth, "Very truly I tell you no one can see the kingdom of God without being born-again."

47. Anderson, "The Pentecostal Gospel and Culture in Africa," 20.
48. Reese, *Roots of Remedies of Dependency Syndrome in World Mission*, 1.
49. Granberg-Michaelson and Billington, *From Times Square to Timbuktu*, 143.

patterns of capitalism and the ideology of progress. The writer's critique of the holistic re-transmission of the gospel is significant to this study.

Isaac Phiri and Joe Maxwell critique the rise of the prosperity gospel in Sub-Sahara Africa by focusing on Nigeria. The phenomenon is connected to the "belief that God will provide money, cars, houses, and even spouses in response to believer's faith."[50] They examine how Renewalists move beyond traditional Pentecostal practices of speaking in tongues, prophesying, and healing.

Naomi Haynes assesses the Zambian development of the prosperity gospel movement and its implications from a sociological and anthropological vantage point. The author explores the phenomenon as it ignites a social lift in the Zambian community. She studies the changing nature of the prosperity gospel: "How Pentecostalism embeds believers in social relationships that often extend beyond their religious cohort."[51] Neo-Pentecostals aim to use the gospel as a vehicle to holistic renewal.

Pentecostalism, for some, has become a way of life beyond the congregational space of the church. Their experiences shape social economies and political systems along with a theology of success, wealth, and entrepreneurship. The sociological shift in views and practices of the prosperity gospel in Zambian society demonstrates this form of Christianity has been informed by the expressions of neoliberal forms of Christianity. Haynes avers, "Pentecostalism meets neoliberal enterprise as adherents pursue a wealth and prosperity gospel whose confidence in divine wealth pushes them onto the market place."[52] To her, the Zambian prosperity gospel is proof of an incomplete holism where people are pointed to materialism rather than the biblical gospel, which points to a life-giving experience in Jesus Christ. The author's socio-anthropological treatment of the phenomenon will help discern the Congolese spread of the prosperity gospel and the rapid growth of Neo-Pentecostalism from a theological and missiological vantage point.

Healing and Deliverance

Pentecostals emphasize and promise divine healing, deliverance, and miracles. This experience resonates with African traditional religions.

---

50. 50 Reese, *Roots of Remedies of Dependency Syndrome in World Mission*, 1.
51. Haynes, "Pentecostalism and the morality of money," 19.
52. Haynes, "Pentecostalism and the morality of money," 125.

Kalu argues, "The emphasis of African Independent churches on healing, and their worldview of mystical causality in etiology and diagnosis are retained in the healing and deliverance sectors of African Pentecostal ministries and churches."[53] Also, he asserts, "The ministries of healing and deliverance have thus become some of the most important expressions of Christianity in African Pentecostalism."[54] These matrixes of innovation are reinventing and reshaping the face of Christianity in the Congo.

Economic Collapse

Nevertheless, due to an economic collapse and socio-political instability, Neo-Pentecostal expressions of Christianity remain dominant within the Congolese religious landscape. The degradation and collapse of economies and infrastructures, along with the failures of leadership and entrepreneurship, are issues which have led numerous Congolese people to believe the prosperity message. Paul Gifford suggests that the greatest factor in the emergence of these new churches was the collapse of African economies by the 1980s. Gifford sees this new phenomenon as a type of neo-colonialism propagated by American preachers.[55]

Moreover, Marie Rose Mukeni Beya, a Congolese scholar, states, "The Congo's official economy has collapsed in the previous decades due to hyperinflation, mismanagement and corruption, war conflict and general instability, political crisis, and economic dislocation."[56] In this context, a United Nation report suggests that the "Congo is still a fragile post-conflict country . . . halting declining trends on social and economic issues."[57] Moreover, the prosperity gospel is also associated with the Word-Faith movement.[58] As a result, economic inflation is a long-term effect which does not do justice to the Congolese struggle. Pentecostalism systematically feeds the sanctioned mechanism of adverse outcomes.

---

53. Kalu, *African Christianity*, 340.
54. Kalu, *African Christianity*, 346.
55. Gifford, *Christianity, and Politics in Doe's Liberia*, 196–99, 294, 314–15.
56. Beya, "Socio-Economic Collapse in the Congo: Causes and Solutions," 1-2
57. Beya, "Socio-Economic Collapse in the Congo: Causes and Solutions," 1-2.
58. Kroesbergen, *In the Search of Health and Wealth*, 4.

Foreign Prosperity Influence

Some American television programs and broadcasts influence the Congolese religious worldview. Joel Osteen, T. D Jakes Ministries, and Joyce Meyer broadcasts are the most-watched telecasts. These Western trends and religious worldviews are imported, and they are presently shaping Christianity in the Congo. For example, the "Word of Faith-Force," "Name it and Claim it," or "Wealth and Health Gospel of Success" philosophies are imported foreign initiatives.

Andrew Perriman states, "The phenomenon is a movement that arose in the United States after World War II."[59] Faith-healing prosperity gospel preachers assure adherents that if they confess verbally, they will enjoy both health and wealth. These movements practiced by Neo-Pentecostals have become acculturated into a Congolese religious worldview.[60] The word of faith force phenomenon is not exclusively a foreign initiative. The movement is a mixture of foreign and local expressions of Christianity reproduced in a brand-new approach. Therefore, the movement is both global and local. For instance, the Nigerian prophet Joshua sells an aggressive prosperity gospel through the ministries of prophecy and healing. These African expressions of Christianity become intercontinental and global phenomena because they are being reproduced all over the world.

Social Lift

There is resistance to superstition, pagan beliefs, and neo-paganism among hundreds of ethnic groups where clannish attitudes and tribalism hinder original translation. The social economic, moral, and political shift of the nation has been marked by superficial readings of the gospel

---

59. Andrew Perriman, *Faith Health and Prosperity: A Report on Word of Faith and Positive Confession Theologies by the Evangelical Alliance (UK) Commission on Unity and Truth Evangelicals* (Waynesboro, GA: Paternoster Press, 2003), xviii.

60. Proponents of the prosperity message argue that God created human beings in His physical appearance as deities. Before the Fall, humans had the potential to call things into existence by using the faith force. After the Fall, humanity took on Satan's nature and, as a result, lost the ability to call things into existence. To remediate this situation, Christ offered Himself, forwent His perfect form, became human, died spiritually, took Satan's nature upon Himself, went to trial, was born again, and rose from the dead with a divine nature. After this, Jesus sent the Holy Spirit to replicate the Incarnation in believers, so they could become the little gods He had initially intended.

and poverty. The neo-charismatic way of proclaiming the good news encourages a proliferation of prosperity gospels aimed at social lift and entrepreneurship.

The phenomenon of social lift can be viewed as a sanctioned form of capitalism. This phenomenon authorizes selfish intentions of distorting Scripture, sanctifying greed, and importing Western televangelism trends. In 1971, Mobutu Seseseko, the late President of Zaire, issued a philosophical decree against foreign influences: "*Le retour à l'authenticité.*"[61] Mobutu's rhetorical ideology of *retour à l' authenticité* influenced the

---

61. In 1971, the Congo was renamed Zaire. Christian names were banned, and cities were renamed (Leopold became Kinshasa, Elisabethville became Lubumbashi, and Stanleyville became Kisangani). In 1885, the region fell into the hands of Leopold II of Belgium Congo. He named it the Etat Independent du Congo (He named Etat-Independent du Congo translated as the Congo Free State), commonly referred to in the Dutch language as Congo-Vrijstaat. In 1908, in the virulent criticism at home and abroad, he transferred his holdings to the Belgian state. It would continue to be called the Belgian Congo until 1960 when it became an independent country, the Republic of Congo. In 1965 Joseph Désiré Mobutu carried out a coup that kept him in power for thirty-two years. During that period the country received a new name, Zaire. In 1997, when Laurent – Désiré Kabila dethroned Mobutu, it was renamed the Democratic Republic of Congo. The Democratic party required some patience, however, for it was only in 2006 that the first free elections were held in more than forty years. See Van Reybrouck, *Congo*, 11. These measures weakened the authority of the church. Mobutu designed a large-scale cultural policy under the slogan, "Use authenticity!" Western names were banned, and genuine Zairians became the opposites of those who loved from a colonial influence. The phrase, "Le retour à l authenticité," is translated, "The return to authenticity," or reclaiming Congolese traditional roots or values and a belief system. This view of returning to traditional values was revolutionary and marked a shift in the social, economic, political, and religious landscape. The zairianization or consciousness led to a return to African authenticity concerning places, names, and surnames, removing all that sounded Western. This political move was the turning point of Christian emergence and social crisis.

See Bulu, *Refonder l'idéal panafricaniste à l'aune de l'intellectualité symbolique de la musique* [archive]. Conférence commémorative du trentième anniversaire de CODESRIA. Kabanda, *L'interminable crise du Congo-Kinshasa*, 103–05, 119–22. Mobutu, the father of the nation, became a "myth," and a unique multiparty democratic system was seemingly disintegrated and forgotten. In these changes, the Congo became Zaire, and almost all European names were changed. Several strategies were put into place to secure the society of the many nationals who had been deprived of education, food, were impoverished, and without health care. As a result, African Initiated Churches emerged so that Christianity was inundated with a new viewpoint. Mobutu even forced the citizens of Zaire to forgo their baptismal names because they tended to possess a different connotation and ideal. As a result of these "reforms," the locals developed new trends of spirituality, prophecy, and overcoming disease through occult forces or mystical powers.

Zairian's social-political and religious landscape. Seseseko's speech and political propaganda in 1971 inaugurated the turning point in the history of the Republic of Congo. As a result, Christianity became indigenized, and the Congolese reclaimed ancestral traditional patterns and belief systems. Consequently, the Congolese proliferated indigenous traditional belief systems. Neo-Pentecostalism emerged with a new outlook.

Pentecostals tend to have a materialistic view of salvation based on the belief that God provides the faithful with physical healing.[62] Congolese are often attracted to prosperity messages as a means of survival and solution to their physical, spiritual, and emotional needs. Their vulnerable socio-political and economic states are the causes that attract many Christians to the prosperity message. Nevertheless, during the decades of evangelism in the late twentieth century (1965–1989), common Congolese were drawn to the Pentecostal phenomena and received physical aid, but some missed Christ.

THEORY

To achieve a holistic change, an authentic translation of the biblical gospel must be considered. Prophetic translation suggests pointing people to Christ without exploiting them. Therefore, translation is the pinnacle of missional evangelistic success. Translation is the pinnacle, or heart, of this venture in investigating how the vernacular translation impacted the Congolese religious worldview. In *Translating the Message: The Missionary Impact on Culture*, Lamin Sanneh's thesis argues that translation is the process of entering the vernacular and allowing the gospel to find its own voice within the host culture. He rightly asserts, "Missions should proceed by a translation which requires that one institute the recipient culture as a valid and necessary locus of the proclamation, allowing the religion to arrive without the requirement of deference to the originating culture."[63]

The gospel's ability to be translated through this theoretical approach echoed acceptance or adoption of pre-Christian patterns, yet, it warrants no potential for a lasting transformation. In other words, the literature advocates for a process of assimilation which supports the continuity of the host cultural trends. Christ's gospel as the incarnate word

---

62. Kabanda, *L'interminable crise du Congo-Kinshasa*, 4.
63. Sanneh, *Translating the Message*, 33.

must penetrate the host cultural expressions or individuals and transform them into brand new cultural disposition or lifestyle.

The phenomenon of continuity of primal belief systems regarding Christian consciousness is an essential paradigm that is foreign to the recipients of the gospel in a time and place.[64] These continuities imply, "The desire to indigenize, to leave as a Christian yet as a member of one's society, to make the church a place to feel at home" is a challenge for real transformation and efficient discipleship in the Congo.[65]

Furthermore, Andrew Walls suggests the "Vernacular nature of Christian faith, which rests on a massive act of translation, the Word made flesh, God translated into a specific segment of social reality as Christ is received there. Christian faith must go on being translated, must continuously enter into the vernacular culture and interact with it, or it withers and fades."[66] On the other hand, Sanneh posits that a vernacular paradigm enabled new Christians to obtain the ability of vernacular *literacy* which is the capacity to read and write in one's native tongue. This vernacular gave self-assurance to the new converts during the first century in the process of transmitting the gospel to diverse communities. As a result, Christianity expanded from Jerusalem to Antioch and then to Athens and Rome.[67] The gospel validated the natives' cultural expressions; Jewish civilization was and is no longer a prerequisite standard to connect with Christ.

Sanneh's counterargument proposed a continuous possibility of translating the gospel and does not suggest a deep transformation of the host cultural trends or diffusion. It does, however, deal with the issue of identity. Walls advocates an in-depth translation that can be experienced through the act of the incarnation. He discusses "the appropriation of Christian gospel, culture, down to the very roots of identity."[68] The gospel becomes critical for transforming culture. According to Walls, Christ is God translated into humanity, and conversion is a human response to God's saving activity. Thus, "Conversion is turning to Christ."[69] Sanneh

---

64. Walls, *The Missionary Movement in Christian History*, 7.
65. Walls, *The Missionary Movement in Christian History*, 7.
66. Walls, *The Cross-Cultural Process in Christian History*, 29.
67. Walls, *The Cross-Cultural Process in Christian History*, 29.
68. Burrows et al., *Understanding World Christianity*, 132.
69. Walls, "The Mission of the Church Today," 20.

and Walls both advocate for the translated gospel as the medium of the proliferation of Christianity across the planet.

Yet the Congolese emergence of the Christian faith presents a lack of a contextualized discipleship. The failure to abandon traditional belief systems and practices suggests syncretism. Hence, the missionaries missed to adequately address the critical problems facing the locals. For instance, the issues of consulting traditional doctors, spirits, and ancestors remain part of the Congolese religious activity. The translation of the gospel failed to be contextualized.

In the Congo, during the translation of the gospel, natives were taught a basic knowledge of Christian ethics. This basic knowledge included, but was not limited to, stewardship, worship, the significance of offering, and membership as the body of Christ expanded. However, a holistic translation of the gospel was lacking. Confession of faith in Christ alone is not enough, but equipping discipleship is critical. Paul says in Romans 12:2, "Do not conform to the pattern of this world but be transformed by the renewing of your mind. Then you will be able to test and approve what God's will is—his good, pleasing and perfect will."

In the case of the Congolese, the recipients received part of the translation of the gospel but lacked the growth of profound transformation. Pentecostalism and evangelicalism focused on Biblicism and eschatology but failed to question the real problems. Thus, the missionary enterprise failed to address the dualistic practices of mixing Christianity with traditional religious trends. This reality resulted in increasing the local expressions of Christianity instead of the true gospel.

Neo-Pentecostalism systematically abused pre-Christian cultural expressions. The prosperity gospel has been a dominant force of the Neo-Pentecostal/charismatic movement in the Congo. Therefore, what kind of gospel needs to be preached within a Congolese spiritualized worldview? The prosperity gospel is seen as a remedy to the various existing economic and social issues, political miscarriages, or the failures of systems. The worship of ancestral spirits is an often-used practice within the renewal movements.

As a result, the Pentecostal gospel of prosperity became a local phenomenon. The gospel's encounter with the Congolese cultural worldviews engaged a different approach to missions and evangelism. For example, the foreign Pentecostal model of healing and deliverance practices grew amidst fertile soil in the Congo because these trends resembled traditional practices.

RESEARCH PROBLEM

Neo-Pentecostalism has both negative and positive impacts. First, concerning its positive impact, a Neo-Pentecostal/charismatic diffusion contributes to the dramatic shift in the center of gravity and resurgence of faith. These trends of Neo-Pentecostal patterns have become a new force for evangelism and discipleship among the Congolese. The Congolese are taking the gospel to other nations and becoming missionaries to Africa and the Global North.

Second, as a different gospel, prosperity theology is the basis of an incomplete holism in the Congo. This movement tends to diminish and overlap the content, or the tenets, of the prophetic character of Jesus' gospel. Jesus' gospel is free. It is the good news. The impact, affect, and practices of the prosperity gospel and Neo-Pentecostalism phenomenon have not been adequately critiqued academically. As a result, the recipients of this theology are exploited because they are not prepared to discover its lack of biblical authenticity. This writer acknowledges the scholarship of several who have written about and voiced opinions on the subject from both African and global perspectives. The aspects and dimensions of Neo-Pentecostalism that have never been studied are the misinterpretations of Scripture by the Congolese prosperity gospel movement. This research seeks to discover an authentic hermeneutic in preaching the prosperity gospel and prophecies without exploiting the adherents and provide a life-giving experience.

Proponents of prosperity theology misuse the biblical gospel to exploit and impoverish others. However, one can appreciate that their economic advance depends upon good leadership, trade, and education. Therefore, the re-transmission and translation of the Christian message through Neo-Pentecostalism does not practice biblical integrity and justice but proves to be a vehicle to perpetuate the exploitation of the most vulnerable adherents. Biblical integrity and justice are the tenets of the Christian Gospel that stand on equity. A theology of prosperity neither does justice to the evangelized nor allows for the integrity of the Christian Gospel. It exploits the poor adherents. For example, many Congolese preachers own cars, outlandish homes, and even private jets, while their adherents remain impoverished.

The prophets and apostles sustain the effects of neo-colonialism by narrowing their focus on the accumulation of wealth, materialism, and dependency patterns. Kirbyjon H. Caldwell posits, "God wants you to be successful! God has literally laid all the bountiful gifts of the universe at your feet."[70] This trend is an entrepreneurial gospel claiming that the faithful can maximize God's given potential in their lives in the here and now; He provides rewards, financial wealth, and physical health to believers who have sufficient faith.

METHODOLOGY AND VANTAGE POINT

This research discusses the missiological and theological backgrounds of the phenomenon of the prosperity gospel and Neo-Pentecostalism from the vantage point of World Christianity. The chief method, attraction, and problems of the prosperity gospel are defined. Moreover, primary and secondary literature, firsthand experiences, and oral interviews are utilized to illustrate the prosperity gospel. This writer's interest is to investigate the dramatic shift in re-transmission pedagogy. Post-colonial methods will help to discover how the translated gospel might be a holistic and transformative life-changing phenomenon in a multicultural religious worldview.

To accomplish this goal, this writer will critique and expose biblical, missional, and theological patterns that encompass the prosperity movement. For an adequate interpretation of the biblical gospel, the topic will be built on the knowledge of literature and findings by understanding its concepts, methods, and measures. Prophetic or authentic re-transmission are neither exploitative nor manipulative; it is rather empowering.

This research will suggest a comprehensive contextual hermeneutical procedure useful in sharing effectively the biblical gospel of Jesus Christ. Therefore, a biblical hermeneutic will inform and discover the Congolese voice. Several pieces of literature have been written within a Western context and cultural patterns. However, the Congolese can tell their story and rewrite it in their own terms. Therefore, these comprehensive case studies enable them to prove that hearing a post-colonial native's voice is beneficial for the evangelized.

A post-colonial holistic hermeneutic can help retrieve the biblical gospel from its colonial patterns. This writer suggests that the gospel is incomplete in its presentation to the Congolese society. Therefore, an authentic and holistic interpretation can be liberating and useful for

---

70. Caldwell et al, *The Gospel of Good Success*, 11.

discipleship. The methodology used in this study will include data collection, scope and limitation of the study, and research questions.

DATA COLLECTION AND RATIONALE

Research is conducted using several sources of contextual hermeneutics, personally focused oral histories, and a biblical theological hermeneutic based upon primary and secondary resources. The research schedule includes international travel and use of governmental and local sources of information. The data collected will benefit the opportunities for authentic evangelism and prophetic voices both within Congolese churches and the West.

The research will analyze the various sources of information used for authenticity and contribution to the mission field. This writer will translate the data received into useful information. The integrity and originality of the data will enable him to achieve a high level of scientific and scholarly work that contributes to the field of World Christian studies. Furthermore, the missionaries and heroes of evangelism in recorded missionary works are useful and relevant practical examples which will strengthen this research.

Therefore, the rationale of this thesis is to provide a systematic examination of the Neo-Pentecostal movement to understand the prosperity gospel. Growing generations and readers in the twenty-first century and years to come in the Global South and North will be able to appreciate the effects of Neo-Pentecostalism's revolutions and its missional impacts. It is also imperative to alter the hermeneutic that seems manipulative and exploitative and instead, develop an authentic, comprehensive model for evangelism and discipleship for the Congolese.

SCOPE AND LIMITATIONS
AND UNIQUENESS OF THE STUDY

The thesis will be critical for new, emerging generation churches. A reason why the subject is essential for further assessment is so that the growing Congolese generations, emerging churches and leaders, scholars and academic bodies, pastors and evangelists will be able to appreciate the opportunity for a hermeneutic that is prophetic and helpful to its adherents. As a result, a deep discipleship and translation of the biblical gospel will be transformative and life-changing.

Hence, the articles and research from this writer treat the subject of prosperity from both a sociological and anthropological vantage point. In other words, the authors consulted tend to use socio-economic and anthropological viewpoints to observe the problem of the prosperity gospel. However, this writer will address and document the problem from a theological and missiological approach. He will present a theological voice and biblical perspectives that enhance the topic of the prosperity gospel.

The uniqueness of this thesis is evident because the subject has never been adequately critiqued from an academic worldview. As a result, the Congolese religious landscape has been informed by mistranslations and misinterpretations of the biblical texts which generate syncretism and reinforce the sanctioned mechanism of exploitative models. This research project presents two limitations and delimitations. This writer is limited in access to gray data, and, as a result, will travel and conduct research in the original context.

RESEARCH QUESTIONS

This research asks critical questions worth consideration. The following are four key questions which this thesis attempts to investigate:

1. Is the attraction to the prosperity theology and the rise of Neo-Pentecostalism an indication of the failure of enculturation and contextualized Christianity?
2. Is Neo-Pentecostalism a syncretized super-structure or underlying worldview that has not been radically transformed by the biblical gospel?
3. Has the culture transformed the gospel or is the culture changing the gospel?
4. How can the biblical gospel be released from its neo-colonial disposition and traditional patterns?

2

Overview of the Historical Development of Neo-Pentecostalism in the Kongo Kingdom

INTRODUCTION

THIS SECTION EXPLORES THE historical milieu of the *Kongo* kingdom and places the context for the Congo's story within its context (not on a designed politico-geographical map) by seeing it through the lens of a socio-historical, theological, and missional scope and overview. The discussion engages the development of Christianity in Congolese society and the rise of specific selected Neo-Pentecostal-prosperity theologies. The data and research will prove that the North American social gospel movements and classical Pentecostal trends are the basis for the rise of the prosperity gospel and Neo-Pentecostalism in the twenty-first century post-colonial Congo. As a result, there are multiple factors which constitute the cause of the rapid growth of these forms of Neo-Pentecostal Christianity in post-colonial Congo.

Subsequent factors have systematically contributed to the rise of the Neo-Pentecostal gospel: sociopolitical, theological, cultural-economic, spiritual, and historical elements. Moreover, these dynamics serve as the turning point of Christianity in the Congo that channeled or fueled the effects of the rise of African traditional religions and historical trends. Though the pre-historic trends preceded the arrival of Western Christianity on the African continent, Western imported trends contributed to the expansion of a renewed emphasis on African expressions and worldviews. Mark Shaw argues there are causes and implications of the shifts: "There were missionaries everywhere, Evangelicals called for conversion. National Christians eagerly shared the good news in words and deed. Bibles were translated into vernacular languages. Christianity became indigenized into new people groups. It became enculturated into new worldviews."[1] These factors and expressions were the basis of the turning point in the history of religion in post-colonial Congo.

Are the African expressions, or traditional belief systems, the basis of the current awakenings embedded in grassroots and syncretistic movements? Local expressions paved the way for the current development and Congolese quest for spiritual powers and traditional practices. These shifts, factors, and systems include sacrifice, ancestral veneration, prophecies, curative occult rituals, and deliverance.

As David A. Shenk asserts,

> Throughout the twentieth century, the Western missionary factor was certainly of extreme importance in Africa for the growth of the Christian movement. However, even more significant was the African factor set within a spirit world where meditation and sacrifices were dominant. Moreover, central to that factor has been the emergence of African–Initiated Churches (AICs) by the thousands, found virtually everywhere throughout the sub-Saharan region of the continent.[2]

As a result, these local expressions of Christianity have been the forces and voices that influenced the socio-political, religious, and economic arena.

---

1. Shaw, *Global Awakening*, 11.

2. Shank, *Mission*, 2. Shank argues, "Tens of millions of Africans are today living out their faith in AIC communities, totally independent of Roman Catholic, Protestant, Evangelical or sectarian churches and denominations planted by Western missions" (1). Thus, certain Western movements named themselves "Ethiopian churches after the biblical term for Africa. Similarly, certain movements in the West Africa, such as the spiritual churches of Ghana, emerged in response to specific spiritual needs felt by Africans—needs related to spirit powers, healing, trances, possession, witchcraft, dreams, visions and prophecy. Among the Yoruba of western Nigeria, where the substantial accent was placed on the healing power of God and where prayer largely replaced the traditional practices of sacrifice, new movements called themselves the *aladura* or praying churches. Elsewhere, particularly in southern Africa, the newly emerging churches preferred the name Zionist, inspired by the imagery surrounding the biblical Zion-Place of God's abiding presence and eternal promise" (2).

At the same time, over the centuries, the Congo has experienced numerous wars and ethnic conflicts, post-war trauma, socio-economic and political collapse, bad leadership styles, poverty, and lack of affordable health care systems. Consequently, there has been a shift in religion resulting from acceptance of various forms of the prosperity gospel phenomenon.

HISTORICAL BACKGROUND

Within an historical context, this research will explore the Congo before the arrival of Christianity. It will analyze the early arrival of the missionaries and the modern missionary period.

Pre-Christian Period

Theoretically, the Congo has an extensive history and a complex narrative. A twenty-first century historian, Marie Rose Mukeni Beya, traces its origins to the "waves of Bantus' migrations moving into [the] Congo River basin from 2000 BC to AD 500 [who] then gradually started to expand southward."[3] According to Mutwale Ntambo Wa. Mushidi, "A Congolese is someone who lives in the center of the continent of Africa but came from the North. There are Pygmies still found within the Nord-Ouest Africa in the provinces of Katanga and Kivu and other states."[4] Pygmy cultures are nomadic; they enjoy hunting, communal life, dancing, nature, singing, and polygamy. They believe in a Supreme Being who controls everything.

Placide Tempels, a Belgian missionary to the Congo, asserts that, for the Bantu, the "supreme value is life, force, to live strongly, or vital force."[5] The idea of *Vital force* is critical for shaping the religious landscape within the Congolese tribes.[6] Prior to the arrival of missionaries and the Con-

3. Beya, "Socio-Economic Collapse in the Congo," 1.

4. Mutwale Ntambo Wa Mushidi is an active Congolese Missionary and United Methodist Minister based in Tanzania. He is among the pioneer Congolese missionaries who planted United Methodist churches. Mushidi, "United Methodist Church and Mission," interviewed by author July 15, 2015.

5. Tempels, *Bantu Philosophy*, 44.

6. Tempels, *Bantu Philosophy*, 44. According to Tempels, "The Bantu say, in respect of a number of strange practices in which we see neither rime nor reason. In fact, their purpose is to acquire life, strength or vital force, to live strongly, that they are to

golese encounter with the Western gospel, local people prayed and had a notion of God. The natives directed their invocations and veneration to the supreme force.[7] As Tempels points out, "God, the Bantu would say, possesses or He is THE supreme, complete, perfect force. He is the strong One, in and by Himself. He has existential cause within Himself."[8] In other words, God is regarded by the Bantu as the causative agent and sustainer of these resultant forces.

According to Tempels, man, by the divine force, is a living force.[9] This philosophic theory of vital force equals the idea of a life force, a man-centered idea that explains why the Bantu venerate their ancestors. When the Bantu face adversities such as sickness, starvation, lack of rain, or socio-political or economic crises, they consult the supreme force.

Prior to the arrival of Western civilization and missionaries, the Congo was stable and prosperous. For instance, in several places or areas within the nation, local people lived in solidarity and shared their wealth with equity. Even though there were some tribal and remote ethnic conflicts and isolated alienation, the Congolese kingdom was peaceful and sustainable. Diane B. Stinton describes this situation: "They lived in communal and collective organized life."[10] At that time, oral tradition was the strongest form of communication. Before the arrival of technology in the late nineteenth century, there were no phones. The sound of drums or

---

make life stronger, or to assure that force shall remain perpetually in one's posterity. Force, the potent life, vital energy are the project of prayers and invocations to God, to spirits and the dead as well as of all that is usually called magic, sorcery or magical remedies. The Bwanga (which has been translated magical remedy) ought not to say to be applied to the wound of the infected limb. It does not necessary possess local therapeutic effects, but it strengthens it increases the vital force." Tempels, *Bantu Philosophy*, 44–45

7. Tempels, *Bantu Philosophy*, 44–45. Tempels, writing from the perspective of the Luba of Katanga Bantu language, defines the term "Vital Force: it signifies the creator and owner of everything that exists. Traditionally, the Congolese have believed in a Supreme Being who made the nature, stars, moon, and people. Their deity has the power to control the well-being of his creations. These terms reflect that God is creator and owner of all. Originally the Congolese had a notion of a creator, but their understanding of God was further developed by the gospel of Christ, which is the good news of saving grace that transcends cultural realities and belief systems. So, the Congolese had a vague notion of the biblical creator until they received the light and Savior of the world Jesus Christ."

8. Tempels, *Bantu Philosophy*, 99.

9. Tempels, *Bantu Philosophy*, 99.

10. Stinton, *Jesus of Africa, Voices of Contemporary African Christology*, 55.

rhythms announced or alerted the people of neighboring villages about news or occurrences.

For instance, if a person died, or a significant event took place—such as a festival or an ethnic conflict—one way to communicate the message or reach out to the neighboring villages was to play the drums. The sound or tone of the drum being played determined the level of the matter or problem at hand. As a result, neighboring villages might decide to join the event, regardless of whether it was a tragedy, death, or banquet celebration. Even during times of war, the melody of the drum dictated the state of freedom or liberty, while at the same time serving as a warning to prepare for war and face one's enemies. The same instrument was used to spread the good news in churches or to outsiders.

Since there was neither an adequate means of communication nor literacy, people trusted oral communication and retranslated it to others. They wrote no agreements, but rather shook hands and agreed verbally on something they wanted to achieve. However, when the Belgians, through *la mission civilizatrice*, introduced literacy, some chiefs in the ancient *Kongo* kingdom signed agreements in their quest for freedom. As David Van Reybroucck opines, "Around 1900 even his leader has died of it, Nfmu Makitu, the big chief of Mbanza-Gombe. In 1884 he had been one of the first chieftains to sign an agreement with Stanley."[11] The signed agreements were either out of or against their will because most chieftains were unable to read, write, and understand the weight and meaning behind the language they signed. Due to their lack of literacy and the language barrier, some Congolese believed that Belgians came to set them free during the "early years of the colonial regime."[12] Moreover, their oral belief systems and tendency to be trusting were fertile soil for Pentecostal success.

---

11. Van Reybrouck, *Congo the Epic History of a People*, 101–02.

12. Van Reybrouck, *Congo the Epic History of a People*, 101. "On March 26, 1884, along with several other chieftains, he put his mark at the bottom of a sheet of paper which read: We the undersigned chiefs of Nzungi, agree to recognize the sovereignty of the association international Africaine, and in sign thereof adopt its flag blue with a golden star . . . We declare that from henceforth we and our successors shall abide by the decision of the representatives of the Association in all matters affecting our welfare or our possessions."

The Early Arrival of Missionaries

Preceding the arrival of missionaries and explorers on Congolese soil, the locals viewed God as the creator of all forces. Peter Falk, an American scholar and missiologist, asserts, "Except for Ethiopia, the Congo is the only African country south of the Sahara that had intimate and prolonged relations with the Christian faith prior the missionary activities of the last century."[13] Their response and exposure to the gospel of Christ warrants or justifies the current explosion or awakening of Christianity. The Congolese's religious predisposition is a force to understand their massive adhesion to Christianity and their reception of the gospel within the paradigm of the present rapid growth of their churches.

Philomena Njeri Mwaura, an African feminist scholar, states, "Ever since the encounter of Western Christianity and culture with African religion and culture in the nineteenth century, there has developed a variety of responses to the gospel that have created different Christianities."[14] The encounter between the gospel and the local cultures proliferated Western Christianity into a new brand of religion in the Congo.

In, *The Global Awakening: How 20th Century Revivals Triggered a Christian Revolution*, Shaw relates the factors serving as the causes and effects that have radicalized the emergence of Christianity. Christianity's explosion and the rise of the prosperity gospel within Neo-Pentecostal/charismatic renewal movements in the Congo have contributed to the global renaissance of faith across the planet.

The first Protestant missionaries to come to the Congo were British Baptists from the Baptist Missionary Society (BMS) in January 1878.[15] Their presence influenced social reform in at least the following ways: vernacular translation, an educational system, economic transformation,

---

13. Falk, *The Growth of the Church in Africa*, 77.

14. Mwaura, "Gendered Appropriation of Mass Media in Kenyan Christianities," 274.

15. Falk, *The Growth of the Church in Africa*, 374–75. These missionaries did not intend to start a mission (i.e. the Communauté Baptiste du Fleuve Congo); they were missionaries to Cameroon. A British Christian wanted missions to continue the work of David Livingstone (who died in 1871 just east of Lubumbashi in Zambia). He gave the BMS a large sum of money to explore the Congo River as a possible route for Christian missions and commerce for economic development which he argued was necessary to allow Africans to adopt Christianity. Henry Morton Stanley arrived in the Congo from Maniema, traveling from Zanzibar by caravan, so the world became aware that the Congo River had a large navigational portion upstream from Kinshasa.

OVERVIEW OF THE HISTORICAL DEVELOPMENT 33

and spiritual revolution. Moreover, the translation of the Bible into the vernacular gave authority to local religious expressions.

Shaw explains, "Bibles were translated into vernacular languages, Christianity became indigenized into new people groups. It became enculturated into new worldviews."[16] Shaw believes that globalization was at the heart of the Christian awakening. This idea of globalization was central in the resurgence of faith. Pentecostalism fit the context of the Global South and responded well to the felt needs of locals such as spirituality, social-cultural shift, infrastructure, and civilization. Also, Pentecostalism reflected the languages of the cultures in Africa because of its ability and power to adapt the gospel to audiences. Shaw argues, "Pentecostalism seemed to speak everybody's language. Moreover, then there was God, at work behind the scenes orchestrating the great symphony of religious revolution."[17] In this context, Pentecostalism was successful and efficient in outreach to a larger public.

Falk states, "[In] 1491, the first party of missionaries arrived on Congolese soil. Besides the Catholics, Franciscans, Holy Father and missionaries' presence, the king of Portugal sent 'masons, carpenters, and other skilled craftsmen, who were to construct a part of the capital.'"[18] As a result, Alphonso the Congolese king, his wife, and oldest son were baptized.[19] Following these conversions, many churches were built. In "1412, Manuel, King of Portugal, sent five ships with masons, carpenters, and building materials to construct churches in the Congo."[20] However, because of their work, several Catholic missionaries died from a tropical disease in their first attempt to evangelize the people.

Falk records, "As a result of the tropical diseases, the death rate among the Catholic missionaries was very high, while others returned to Europe because of ill health."[21] The Jesuits arrived in the Congo about 1548 with three priests and one brother. During this time, they baptized over five thousand people in three months.[22] However, they were unable

---

16. Shaw, *Global Awakening*, 11.

17. Shaw, *Global Awakening*, 11.

18. Falk, *The Growth of the Church in Africa*, 78. Leopoldville is presently known as Kinshasa.

19. Falk, *The Growth of the Church in Africa*, 78.

20. Falk, *The Growth of the Church in Africa*, 78.

21. Falk, *The Growth of the Church in Africa*, 79.

22. Even though several Congolese were baptized and adhered to the Christian faith, there was little impact and influence on discipleship. People were taught basic

to follow up, instruct, and encourage these believers in a NT manner. As a result, many left the faith and returned to their previous ways and practices of life.[23] Traditional evangelism, which pointed to both African practices and biblical evangelism, was thus somewhat successful; however, it made few lasting changes.

The Modern Missionary Period

The "modern missionary period" was a second attempt of missionary evangelization in the Congo that can be traced to 1913.[24] Along with the Second Great Awakening (1787–1843) and the Azusa Street Revival of 1906–1915, the gospel encountered the Congolese people in a fresh way. Christians in Europe and the US proclaimed the gospel to the Congolese, but its translation resulted in a conflicted reality due to the complexity of the Congolese cultures connected to idolatry and animistic ceremonies as well as *syncretism*.[25] Consequently, the locals retranslated the gospel into their own cultural experiences.

Falk states, "The establishment of Christian ministry in Zaire owes much to David Livingstone who drew the world's attention to Central

---

principles of Christian ethics and faith but lacked deep transformation. Falk states, "Even though *Alphoso* energetically supported the Christian mission and many people were baptized, little evidence of radical change among the population could be noted." Falk, *The Growth of the Church in Africa*, 79. Traditional evangelism in the Congo and beyond was based on asking locals to repeat the Lord's prayer and be baptized in the name of Jesus.

23. Falk, *The Growth of the Church in Africa*, 79.

24. Hoover, interview by author, February 10, 2015.

25. The term "syncretism" refers to a mixture of the African traditional animistic belief systems and practices with Christianity. For instance, demonic realities, sorcery, and witchcraft or the non-Christian religions' encounter with the Christian gospel created a paradigm shift or radical thinking about these realities; especially when a Christian combines African traditions to justify a Christian lifestyle. Rommen discusses, "Western missionaries came from societies in which witchcraft, sorcery, magic, omens, divination, spirits of the dead, and spirits of other kinds, are—or have been until recently absent from the cultural discourses of everyday life." See Rommen, *Spiritual Power, and Missions Raising the Issues*, 10. Some missionaries, however, ignored the presence of these spiritual forces and phenomenon and viewed them as superstitious and animistic. According to the author, "Animism originally referred to belief in spirit beings and was intended to characterize all religion, including Christianity. Animism, however, has come to be used as a synonym for tribal or folk religion as over against the major world religion" (12–13).

Africa."²⁶ Livingstone's purpose was to establish a chain of mission stations and penetrate the country with the gospel. The presence of missionaries influenced both society and a spiritual explosion resulting in revival. However, the locals' spiritual discourse surprised the Western missionary enterprise.

In short, the recipients' spiritual worldview and cosmic cultural realities influenced and shaped their understanding of Christianity. The evangelized adapted the gospel to their cultural patterns so that it ignited revival and an African awakening. As a result, the sanctioned Spirit-filled and power were the causes of the current developments and awakenings of a massive presence of Christians on Congolese soil.

In this context, locals who contributed to the drama of the resurgence and emergence of Christianity in the Congo are to be credited with this expansion. Western scholars and historians tend to bestow credit for the growth of Christianity on foreign missionaries alone, but local evangelism and missions efforts have proven effective on Congolese soil, as well. Missionary enterprises and the locals' efforts are to be recognized and appreciated equally.

Falk points out that the locals became the messengers of the gospel by contributing to the growth and organization of the church in the Congo. He states, "The Zaire Christians have taken the gospel to their people. The catechists have made an inestimable contribution in proclaiming the gospel in the villages and teaching the children."²⁷ Due to local participation, chapels were erected in thousands of villages. Missionaries' efforts to train local leaders paved the way for revivals, which served as the turning points in Congolese Christianities as the emergence of new Christian expressions.

THE NEO-PENTECOSTAL MOVEMENT

This research will now explore the arrival of the Neo-Pentecostal movement in the Congo along with the contextualization of the movement within a Congolese context.

---

26. Falk, *The Growth of the Church in Africa*, 374.
27. Falk, *The Growth of the Church in Africa*, 374.

Arrival of the Neo-Pentecostal Movement in Congo

Historically, world Christian scholars identify three waves of Pentecostalism that are classified as "Renewal" movements: Classical Pentecostalism, the Charismatic movement, and Neo-Pentecostalism. These Renewal movements are the fastest growing areas within world Christianity. Katherine Attanasi and Amos Yong argue that Neo-Pentecostals are part of newer churches associated with the prosperity gospel.[28] However, the Charismatic movement of the 1960s occurred in mainline Protestant denominations. They share similar characteristics, such as speaking in tongues or spirit power.

The movement crossed the borders with the waves of the nineteenth and twentieth century missionary enterprise movement from the United States to the Congo. As Shaw discusses,

> In the twentieth century American folk rituals packed up their tents and sawdust trails and went global. They learned to speak Spanish, Portuguese, Yoruba, Korean, Mandarin, and Gujarati. They crossed the equator. As they traveled abroad, they grabbed hold of dictionaries, Bible translations, national evangelists, globalization, and *glossolalia* and turned them into a religious revolution.[29]

Religious revolution often means Christian awakening in post-colonial Congo.

Besides local expressions, there are imported foreign patterns and practices from the classical Pentecostalism of Azusa Street, which have contributed to the surging phenomenon. Shaw posits, "Azusa Street . . . Sent it to witness throughout the Americas, Africa, and Asia in the decade after 1906."[30] Moreover, the philosophy of the "American Dream"

---

28. Attanasi and Yong, *Pentecostalism and Prosperity*, 2. Classical Pentecostalism traces its roots to the Azusa Street Revival of 1906–09.

29. Shaw, *Global Awakening*, 12.

30. Ibid. Shaw argues, "Africa experienced several waves of revival during the century. In southern Africa the violent eschatology of Watchtower Society trigged a cluster of apocalyptic revival movement in South Africa, the Rhodesians (now Zimbabwe and Zambia) and as far north as Congo. The rise of prominent prophet figures like William Wade Harris, Simon Kimbangu and Joseph Babalola in the first thirty years of the Twentieth century saw new churches formed out of powerful movements of the Spirit. The East Africa revival of the 1930s and 1940s stayed largely in the mission churches but brought an evangelical depth and characteristic openness that breathed new life into aging structures. These earlier waves of the revival paved the way for the

has been imported to the Congolese through social media and Western Neo-Pentecostalism through connectional ministry partnerships. For instance, Joel Osteen's prosperity gospel and theology in America are being imported to the Congolese through broadcasting as a model of Neo-Pentecostalism.

Both African and Western scholars believe the prosperity gospel trend is an imported phenomenon to Africa.[31] Lovemore Togarasei argues, "The gospel of prosperity was started by American preachers like E. W. Kenyon, Oral Roberts, and Kenneth Copeland. In Africa, one of the earliest inspirers and promoters of the gospel of prosperity is the late Nigerian Archbishop Benson Idahosa."[32] One of the prominent founders of the prosperity faith movement was William Kenyon (1867–1948), founder of Bethel Bible Institute. He was an ordained Methodist minister.[33] Also, the prosperity gospel appears to have started in the West as a contextualized gospel. Furthermore, Allan Anderson asserts,

> Paul Gifford has become a leading exponent on this subject. He suggests that the biggest single factor in the emergence of these new churches is the collapse of African economies by the 1980s and the subsequent increasing dependence of the new churches on the USA. Gifford argues that it is Americanization rather than the African quality of the prosperity message that is responsible for the growth of these churches. He sees this new

---

largest cluster of revivals, those associated with the neo-Pentecostal churches that have arisen and proliferated since the mid-1970s."

31. Schieman and Jung, "Practical Divine Influence," 739. These scholars argue, "Although it is beyond the scope . . . to provide a comprehensive overview of the origins of prosperity gospel, some scholars identify its roots in North America, especially in evangelical Protestantism and Pentecostal denominations in the United States. From the 1940s to the 1970s, a Charismatic or neo-Pentecostal movement developed as roving Pentecostal preachers sought to promote the faith, in part by stressing the importance of spiritual healing. These preachers laid the foundation for the broader 'Faith Movement,' out of which beliefs in the prosperity gospel emerged." See Zink, "Anglocostalism in Nigeria," 235. Zink discusses, "One aspect of the intensification of the revival movement in the 1980s and 1990s is the growing influence of American and European televangelists and preachers, People like Jim and Tammy Bakker, Pat Robertson, Jimmy Swaggart, and others began to work more closely with African Christian leaders. One result was that these new religious movements began to preach what is often called the prosperity gospel." Zink, "Anglocostalism in Nigeria," 235.

32. Togarasei, "The Pentecostal Gospel of Prosperity in African Contexts of Poverty," 339.

33. Togarasei, "The Pentecostal Gospel of Prosperity in African Contexts of Poverty," 5.

phenomenon as a type of neo-colonialism propagated by the American prosperity preacher.[34]

Moreover, Kroesbergen opines, "The origin of the prosperity movement can be traced to the US in the early twentieth century."[35] Also, Asamoah-Gyady avers, "There is undeniable foreign, mainly North American influence and inspiration on African Neo-Pentecostal Christianity."[36]

Contextualization of the Neo-Pentecostal Movement

The prosperity gospel and Neo-Pentecostal movements have been revolutionized, enculturated, and remade within a Congolese context. The belief systems and philosophies of Neo-Pentecostalism's teachings feed the Spiritism of the prosperity gospel. As Deacon and Lynch aver, "Neo-Pentecostal narratives help ordinary people assert some control over their lives. However, the control provided often represents defensive mechanisms or coping strategies that can assist survival and rarely offers socio-economic or political transformation."[37] These new renewals or Neo-Pentecostal/charismatic churches and their leaders are responding to the systematic failure of the government in addressing social and economic concerns and altering the mechanism of impoverishment.

In 1971, post-independence, some missionaries left the Congo due to troubled relationships, unrest, and conflict. Pentecostalism appealed to the Congolese because of its entrepreneurial and social characteristics. Because of Pentecostalism's trends and emphasis on spiritual forces, the Bible became a Congolese book, and the chapter on the Holy Spirit was written by Congolese. Furthermore, these cosmic realities connected to spirit encounter and their understandings of the prosperity gospel are essential to Neo-Pentecostalism's development in the Congo today. The missionary enterprises' premature departure caused many Congolese to take the gospel in personal directions. For many, Christianity was remade, and Pentecostalism reinvented.

Congolese pastors and evangelists promoted television broadcasting systems and entrepreneurship as they built enterprises, newspapers,

---

34. Anderson, "The Pentecostal Gospel and Culture in Africa," 17. Paper read at the History of Religion Seminar, University of Oxford, 29 May 2000, 17.

35. Kroesbergen, *In the Search of Health and*, 4.

36. Asamoah-Gyadu, "Anointing Through the Screen," 20–21.

37. Deacon and Lynch, "Allowing Satan?," 109.

clinics, and educational institutions. The church attempted to respond to the systematic failure of the government by addressing social and economic concerns and by altering the sanctioned mechanism of impoverishment. As a result, the gospel was practiced and understood within traditional cultural patterns; thus, the history of Christianity in a Congolese worldview shifted.

Soon after the colonization of the 1960s and 1970s, African-initiated churches proliferated or promoted this different gospel of socio-economic exploitation. Therefore, a different gospel was introduced that developed theologies of social-economic differences and an incomplete holism within the Congolese religious worldview. Neo-charismatic Pentecostals see these trends as a way to resist colonial heritage. However, the transmission also notes that a transformation has taken place because the sending culture met the receiving nation with the gospel.

The prosperity movement attracted millions of adherents because it fit the Congolese context. In the 1980s, Reinhard Bonnke, a charismatic German Pentecostal preacher, launched an evangelistic crusade, thereby leading to a dramatic shift in Zairian Christianity and the birth of televangelism. As Bonnke puts it, "For the first time I witnessed thousands running forward to respond to the call of salvation. God opened my eyes, and I saw an invisible, mighty wave of Holy Spirit power active in the stadium. A mass baptism in the Holy Spirit accompanied by many healing miracles took place."[38] His ministry promised divine healing and restoration. In June 1982, the soccer stadium in Lubumbashi in Katanga Province was packed with people—some in wheelchairs expecting deliverance and miracles. Many who attended were people challenged by physical, emotional, and spiritual needs. A prosperity message of hope was promised: sight to the blind, the lame would soon walk, and demons that possessed people would be cast aside in Jesus' name.

Regrettably, the vulnerable men, women, and children remained unhealed and disillusioned. Neither a physically disabled person nor one who was possessed was physically or spiritually healed. No one who was blind recovered sight as promised. Bonnke argues, "We come to Bukavu first visited by missionary C. T. Studd, and still remote, we saw seventy thousand people respond to the call of God's love."[39] Healing miracles were at the heart of Bonnke's prophetic vision to evangelize Africa.

---

38. Bonnke, *Evangelism by Fire*, 3.
39. Bonnke, *Evangelism by Fire*, 3.

In the 1990s, a Catholic Priest, L'Abbé Kasongo, started revival services that transformed the religious landscape in Lubumbashi and other provinces. Utilizing traditional animism, or African religious practices, a Christian holistic experience, exorcism, and anointing oil, L'Abbé Kasongo promised supernatural healing to the Congolese. However, most survivors remained in their physical and spiritual situations. Congolese believers practiced syncretism as they mixed Christianity with traditional practices. Prophetic healers known as "Ngangas"[40] used biblical literature mixed with traditional paganism and animism to cure people. The process was never free of charge.

The traditional values and spirit-worlds are connected to materialistic achievements or successes within the Congolese traditions. However, Tempels objects, "The Bantu ideal will be a vital force exclusively earthly and materialistic."[41] For instance, many of the residences of these traditional healers have been transformed into houses of worship, and traditional healers have become self-proclaimed prophets or apostles. Traditional instruments used for ancestor invocations have also been used in churches. The African tradition of venerating ancestors for occult practices is an acceptable religious practice like the Christian invocation of the saints. Therefore, are the Ngangas' practices the basis for the easy spread of Neo-Pentecostalism and the prosperity gospel in the twenty-first century Congo?

For example, during L'Abbé Kasongo's ministry, the barren were promised children, wealthy husbands, and decent homes, while the poor were promised promotions, jobs, and cars, among other materialistic items. Many desperate and vulnerable women were required by healers to drink palm oil. Instead of receiving healing, they became ill. Incidences of mixture between Christian principles and animism are examples of an incomplete holism within Neo-Pentecostalism.

---

40. The term "Nganga" refers to a traditional spiritual mediator. According to the Congolese religious worldview, this person is skilled in interpreting the causes of malevolent spirits and forces that bring about sickness and social misfortune. This person possesses a supernatural ability to communicate with other worlds and provide remedies for healing and prosperity. Sometimes, they practice natural medicine for spiritual forces to protect individuals from malevolent spirits. Therefore, these Ngangas, who once practiced professional mystical occult magical forces, have been transformed in the twenty-first century to apostles, prophets, and healers. Their houses are often spaces of worship and miracles.

41. Tempels, *Bantu Philosophy*, 187.

Neo-Pentecostalism and the prosperity gospel have been contextualized, adapted, and appropriated within Congolese religious worldviews. This shift in Christianity's center of gravity affects how the story of Jesus and the gospel are presently told, translated, or re-transmitted. Furthermore, Neo-Pentecostalism in the twenty-first century has grown into a transnational version of the prosperity gospel. The transnational character of the prosperity gospel implies that the prosperity movement exceeds or goes beyond the Congolese nation to cross geographical borders. Congolese preachers are now taking the new expression of the American brand of the prosperity gospel to other African nations.

CONTRIBUTING FACTORS TO THE EXPANSION OF NEO-PENTECOSTALISM

The following factors require further exploration as they have contributed to the expansion of Neo-Pentecostalism in the Congo: historical, spiritual, economic, worldview and theological.

Historical Factors

In 1885, King Leopold II of Belgium took control of the *Kongo* kingdom and named it the "Congo Free State."[42] He ruled over it as his personal or private property from 1877–1908. The Belgium Congo achieved its freedom and sovereignty from Belgium's Imperial system on June 30, 1960. Several decades ago, the nation of the Congo experienced a remarkable shift in its name from the Free State to the Republic of Congo 1877, (Belgian Congo) and Zaire in 1971, to the Democratic Republic of the Congo in 2007. The missionary enterprise is understood to be the basis of la mission civilizatrice the idea of Free States. The Free State is now recognized or known as the Democratic Republic of the Congo. This *mission civilizatrice* is not peculiar to modern scholars of religion though it functions as a secularized activity. Leopold promised a mission to civilize or develop the nation, and he exploited the locals and their resources.

---

42. The term "Free State" is a name given to the *Bakongo* kingdom. This is in connection to the primal people who dwelled in the land of the *Kongo* kingdom. The term "Kongo" means river or literally translated "by the river of the bakongo." The Free State originated under Leopold II in 1885 after the Berlin Conference. He convinced the Western world that he was involved in a humanitarian effort to sustain the local people. He exploited the people, their land, and resources.

Classical Pentecostalism and political realities influenced the rise of the prosperity gospel.

Spiritual Factors

Christians are connected with the holiness movement, spiritual forces, and a cosmological worldview. These philosophies of spiritual forces and holiness movement equate the argument of "the Kenyan theologian John Mbiti who argued that the pre-Christian Africa has a coherent worldview characterized by the search for the power to be in a spiritualized cosmology."[43] Spirituality is part of an everyday life experience and maintains a clear social order. African evangelical belief systems are often associated with spirit powers such as witchcraft, demonic forces, and sorcery as real phenomena that hinder people's wellbeing. Thus, the converts interpret the Gospel as a shield against these demonic forces that prevent people from enjoying true freedom.

African-initiated (indigenous) traditional elements are often mixed with biblical principles and practices, thus, reinforcing the idea of syncretism. Neo-Pentecostalism's practices of surging spiritual forces are a response to the forces perceived responsible for the social and economic struggle. As Chris Wright asserts, "Neo-Pentecostal beliefs stress the need for God's power as an effective force in the believers' life against the evil of the world."[44] Spirit-filled is a central feature of the Neo-Pentecostal movement and the prosperity gospel in the context of the Congo today.

Christianity has become for many not only a religion, but also a refuge against paganism and demonic oppression. This pagan tactic constructs a pattern of fear for adherents and reinforces the needs for Congolese to join Neo-Pentecostal movements. Rommen states, "Paradigm-shift experiences are being formulated, systematized, publicized,

---

43. Ngong, *The Holy Spirit and Salvation in Africa*, 5. Ngong argues, "Africa's primal religions, as the Edinburgh World Missionary Conference of 1910 held, contained no preparation for Christianity. It has therefore been the task of post-colonial African theology to show that African pre-Christian traditional religions prepared Africans to receive the gospel." This project was given a boost especially by the works of the Belgian missionary Placide Tempels, and the Rwandan philosophers, Vincent Mulago, and John Mbiti.

44. Wright, "Lausanne Theology Working Group Statement on Prosperity Gospel," 100.

accredited, and institutionalized in mainstream evangelical and missionary institutions."[45]

Therefore, spirit power, spiritual warfare, and animism are vehicles that have fueled the resurgence of Christianity in the Congo. As a result, revivals occur mechanically and spontaneously. This implies that these revivals happen automatically. As Shaw puts it, "Revivals restore the spiritual dynamic of Christianity and lead to new movements or renewed institutions."[46] The prosperity gospel, Neo-Pentecostalism, and charismatic movements are successful because they associate the traditional practices of animism or pagan practices with biblical scriptures.

In this sense, Jesus is depicted as "Nganga Mukata," the great doctor or physician in Neo-Pentecostalism.[47] Congolese are attracted to these renewal movements because they mix both Christian scriptures and spirit power. Additionally, the lack of efficient health care systems has spiritualized the Congolese religious worldview. Many adhere to these movements to seek power, healing, protection against malevolent spirits, and prosperity.

Spirit encounter is an essential feature that has ignited revivals in the twenty-first century Congo. Moreover, the Holy Spirit is also a critical factor for the growth of renewal churches or new generation churches within Pentecostalism. Pentecostalism found fertile soil in the Congo through practices used to invoke spirits or spiritual forces. These practices are similar to Pentecostal experiences in the Acts 2 community.

Animistic ceremonies consist of elders' sacrifices of material elements or animals to their ancestors. This is like biblical stories of sacrifice in Leviticus and the NT. When Neo-Pentecostals give, it is a sacrificial act. As a result, they cannot live in fear of any demonic attack or oppression from evil spirits because they are protected or covered. So, charismatic Pentecostal preachers view the sowing of seed as a sort of sacrifice for one's protection, growth, success, and power.

In the wake of a calamity such as continuous mortality in a traditional village, the elders of the village offer sacrifices. The mortalities often relate to epidemic or endemic maladies or sickness, misfortune, or

---

45. Rommen, *Spiritual Power and Missions Raising the Issues*, 10.

46. Shaw, *Global Awakening*, 27.

47. "Nganga Mukata." Jesus is often expressed through songs of deliverance as individuals recite the name of Jesus as the healer and restorer of their plight, deliverer, and sustainer of all things. The songs imply that the great physician's name is Jesus. He is present and will see them through despite their current pain and suffering.

natural disasters which occur within the social fabric, causing massive deaths. The locals have limited or no resources to redress the problems. The rapid solution is to inquire from the ancestors. The concepts of invoking spiritual forces are equivalent to prayer and worship in Christianity. The Congolese of Katanga province, for example, believe that the spirits are powerful enough to solve their many problems. Syncretism is one of the reasons the Congolese have become a spiritualized society and adhere to Christianity. They believe the power of the Holy Spirit can solve all their societal problems.

Economic Factors

The new expression of Pentecostalism is a radical force that combines Pentecostal worship, aggressive evangelism, and grassroots efforts to provide education, social-political development, and health services. These evangelical ministerial developments have been critical to African Christian worldviews in relation to the ongoing Congolese religious awakenings. Bryant L. Myers asserts that in the "1980s and 1990s in Sub-Sahara Africa and the other part of the Global South, neo-Pentecostalism was the good news for the poor."[48] His argument shows that Neo-Pentecostalism and charismatic movements emerged in poor urban slums in Africa, Latin America, and parts of Asia because of foreign influences.

The proliferation of the prosperity gospel movement was a self-generating expression of Pentecostalism that emerged from the grassroots and was deeply contextual since it responded well to the felt needs of Africans.[49] Myers argues, "Pentecostal churches began providing basic services in health, education, and economic development whose ability to provide these services by the impact of the Washington Consensus."[50] Imported neoliberal policies were seen as a reliable anti-poverty prescription for the Global South that influenced the Congolese culture.

Extreme poverty and economic inflation are factors as to why many choose Christianity in the twenty-first century post-colonial Congo. The economic collapse and systematic failure of the government to answer

---

48. Myers, "Progressive Pentecostalism, Development, and Christian Development NGOs," 115.

49. Myers, "Progressive Pentecostalism, Development, and Christian Development NGOs," 115.

50. Piot, "Pentecostal and Development Imaginaries in West Africa," 113.

the issues confronting the population is one reason the prosperity gospel is a dominant culture today. For example, the lack of an affordable and decent health care system, jobs, along with both public and social services have led some to practice syncretism to cure the sick and give hope to the vulnerable. Beya states, "The country's official economy has collapsed in the last few decades due to hyperinflation, mismanagement and corruption, war conflict and general instability, political crisis, and economic dislocation."[51] Moreover, poverty is a critical problem for this surging reality and shift within Christianity in the Congo.

Consequently, African independent and renewal movements attempt to offer responses to people's everyday living experiences of broken systems as well as people's struggle for survival and life. It stands to reason that the lack of employment opportunities, the Congolese growing intellectual community, and young adults tend to lean towards the prosperity gospel. Some identify themselves as ambassadors of Christ sent for a special mission. Pentecostals create prayer groups. There are tent and house churches on almost every street corner. Hence, Christianity in the Congo is a phenomenon beyond the congregational and denominational platform due to economic hardships. The philosophy of the liberalization and centralization of trade revenue fueled economic inflation and resulted in instability in high exchange rates within the marketplace of the Congo.

Economic inflation and the systematic collapse of lifestyles are the reasons the church has engaged in missional and social actions. Some missional realities and factors contribute to the development of the prosperity gospel and Neo-Pentecostalism. For instance, the translation of local languages into the vernacular contributes to the surging phenomenon of the prosperity gospel and Neo-Pentecostalism. These factors—spiritual, historical, and economic—have contributed to the shape of African Christianity. On the other hand, missionary efforts are to be appreciated as they built clinics, vocational schools, roadways, provided an education infrastructure, and introduced new technology. For instance, increased education opened doors for local people to connect with the outside world.

---

51. Beya, "Socio-Economic Collapse in the Congo," 2.

Worldview Factors

African necrology is at the center of Congolese culture as people aspire to eternal life. The role of ancestral incarnation is essential to Congolese religious life and experience. For instance, in their worldview, when persons die, they do not die completely, but they relocate from their physical address to an ideal or invisible place. Therefore, the deceased are expected to be reborn somewhere else. Moreover, ancestors, even though they may no longer be present in the physical world, are still alive somewhere in the memories of the living. The Congolese belief systems and cultural practices, which are based on ancestral appeasement and aspiration to perpetual life, cause Congolese to adhere to Neo-Pentecostalism.

In several Congolese tribes, the deceased go to *Kalunga Nyembo*, translated in Lingala as *Lola*, an expression meaning "eternity." The term *Kalunga Nyembo* is translated as an eternal place of rest or life eternal. The prefix *mu* is a definite article insisting or pointing to the location or place of eternity. Therefore, the dead are not dead but are believed to be alive and have relocated to *Kalunga Nyembo* or *Lola*. In other words, locals aspire to live with no limits. As Stinton puts it, "They believe life is central and it is a sacred gift for all Congolese."[52] The dead are not dead or lifeless. They are believed to dwell among the realms of the living. For instance, when a child dies, he or she is buried behind the house, instead of a regular cemetery, because the people believe the child is not gone forever. He or she will come back through rebirth. Therefore, the deceased sustain the natural order and have the capacity to advocate, speak, eat, and even walk among the living. Therefore, Christian eschatology is relevant and appealing.

Many Congolese Christians believe they are surrounded by real ancestral spiritual forces and powers able to carry out divine miracles. This philosophy is parallel to the biblical understanding of eschatology and a secularized metaphysical worldview. Christians believe, as the Bible says, that when a person dies, he or she still has life. It is the physical body which dies even though the spirit disappears. However, the soul does not die and awaits the return of Jesus to attain its full resurrection and life eternally.

The Congolese philosophies of eternal life suggest that people die physically, while spiritually they remain because even if one dies, he or she still exists in the netherworld or invisible world. These traditional

---

52. Stinton, *Jesus of Africa, Voices of Contemporary African Christology*, 55.

practices influence concepts of Neo-Pentecostalism and the gospel of prosperity which attempt to address socio-economic issues and metaphysical worldviews. The concept of having an afterlife as well as a perpetual or limitless life relates to the idea of abundant life. Congolese long to have a limitless life. This is one reason why they adhere to the prosperity gospel movement.

Theological Factors

Several theological factors are critical paradigms to understand the rise of African Christianities. John Binti poses a critical question as to whether Christianity is suited to the average African. As Binti puts it, "The Christian way of life is in Africa to stay certainly for the foreseeable future."[53] The challenge of African Christianity is an attempt to appropriate and integrate various pre-Christian traditions. The attempt to Christianize pre-Christian religious traditions is a theological challenge within Neo-Pentecostalism and charismatic movements in the Congo.

Kwame Bediako also argues that "appropriating and integrating primal-Christian cultural traditions was perhaps the most important achievement of African theology. Africanization was the process of indigenizing the Christian faith and the gospel."[54] African primal religions are the matrices of the fertile soil rooted in the current Christian expansion. The critical theological question is how can the Christianization of African religions establish a credible basis for evangelism?

The Pentecostal gospel of prosperity not only encourages a social lift and entrepreneurial spirit to sustain social development, but it contributes to the rapid growth of Christianity in Sub-Sahara Africa. Togarasei suggests that the gospel of prosperity is not uniquely about materialism, but it is holistic because this trend encourages the growth of individual life. Furthermore, the theological philosophy that affirms materialism or "wealth" as essential models of translating the gospel seems irrational or ineffective. This writer suggests that God's "blessings" are often obtained by oppression, deceit, greed, and corruption. This implies that God's blessings are limitless without prejudice or precondition. While some individuals accumulate wealth through hard work, others navigate the systems using deceptive techniques such as corruption, greed, and

---

53. Bediako, *Jesus and the Gospel in Africa, History, and Experience*, 3.
54. Bediako, *Jesus and the Gospel in Africa, History, and Experience*, 4.

oppression to gain wealth. The Congolese theology of God's providence seems contrary to the philosophy which affirms poverty, sickness, or an early death as a sign of God's curse, lack of faith, or human fault.

The theology of the prosperity gospel tends to be individualistic, greedy, and lack appropriate attention for Congolese belief systems and its deepest need for community accountability. This theology has damaged traditional features of African society which were committed to caring for the extended family and wider social community. On the other hand, the Africanization or indigenization of the Christian faith and gospel is essential for a proper theological understanding of African Christianities.

In 1971, in the wake of the struggle for African identity through the theological affirmation of indigenous religions, an African council of churches was convened in which African religious leaders met in Kinshasa and discussed strategies to lead churches in preparation for "a new millennium of World Christianity."[55] Due to the past African theological framework, today the Congo is witnessing firsthand the revelation of the 1971 ecumenical declaration that paved the way for the current proliferation of Christian expressions within Neo-Pentecostalism. The theological factor is an essential metric of indigenizing the Christian gospel and its proliferation.

CONCLUSION

Neo-Pentecostal charismatic networks offer pastoral care and support to vulnerable groups in the Congo. Adherents are attracted to the message of prosperity because of the mechanism of hope and social improvement, especially in third world countries. Hope is the metaphor people live by every day. Spiritual power and social lifts are the leading causes of current revivals in Africa, particularly in the Congo. Many Christians live anxiously in areas where prophecies and spirituality sustain them. These Christians take the Bible seriously and read the Scripture literally. These instances and proceedings have become part of the rapid expansion of Neo-Pentecostalism and the attraction to the prosperity gospel in the Congo.

Therefore, the reasons behind the rise of the prosperity gospel in Africa are based on the following theologies of mission: (1) The failure

---

55. Kato, *Theological Pitfalls in Africa*, 198.

of contextualization and enculturation of the gospel are missiological and theological dynamics. (2) The process of translating its transmission and re-transmission generate an incomplete holism. (3) The mixture of traditional cultures with the biblical heritage creates a new face of Christianity. (4) The importation of Western cultural ideas such as progress, materialism, and neo-capitalism and neo-socialism serve as foundations for classical Pentecostalism. Thus, African Christianity has become a syncretized religious worldview.

Furthermore, Neo-Pentecostalism tends to meet the felt needs of its members associated with globalization and structured reforms. The prosperity gospel, including the theology of progress, social lift, and entrepreneurship, are key ingredients used by Neo-Pentecostals. For example, the Full Gospel Fellowship Church in the town of Lubumbashi Katanga Province of the Congo appeals to its followers because of the social, spiritual, and economic perspectives which it presents. Also, new generation churches or renewals such as African Initiated Churches and Neo-Pentecostals/ charismatics have understood the felt needs of the larger population. Consequently, they offer social-spiritual support and pastoral care. This is due to the networks of healing and support used by Neo-Pentecostal churches in urban settings to contribute to social reform and structural agendas.

However, their use of the prosperity gospel seems manipulative and selfish given the fact that the messages tend to make preachers richer. As the Lausanne Theology working group Statement on the Prosperity Gospel asserts,

> It vastly enriches those who preach it but leaves multitudes no better than before, with the added burden of disappointed hopes. While emphasizing various alleged spiritual or demonic causes of poverty, it gives little or no attention to those causes that are economical and political. Including injustice, exploitation, unfair international trade practices. It just tends to victimize the poor by making them feel that their poverty is their fault which the Bible does not do so while failing to address and denounce those whose greed inflicts poverty and others. Some prosperity streams are not really about helping the poor at all and provide no sustainable answer to the real causes of poverty. However, we are distressed that much use of the Bible is seriously distorted,

selective, and manipulative, we call for a more careful exegesis of texts, and more holistic biblical hermeneutic.[56]

Paul's gospel was, however, free of charge (1 Cor 9:18a). People cannot purchase or work their way to heaven. The idea of prosperity is biblically and theologically sound, but its misuse as a theology associated with greed and materialism poses critical challenges to the body of Christ. The prosperity theology fails to be an effective biblically prophetic voice of the twenty-first century.

As Hanjorg Dilger suggests, "The practices of healing and rebuilding of communities originated by the legacy of Pentecostalism which contribute to the rise of neo-Pentecostalism as a result Full Gospel Bible Fellowship is the biggest neo-Pentecostal churches in Tanzania."[57] Similarly, the Full Gospel Pentecostal church in Lubumbashi Township "viens-et-vois is an influential religious movement in the Congo."[58] The movement has expanded not only within the Congo but also across neighboring countries where it has become a global phenomenon influenced by globalization. It has become a trans-continental, intercontinental, and global movement. The church sends missionaries and preachers all over Africa and beyond the colonial geographical borders to Europe, the US, Asia, and Latin America.

---

56. Wright, "Statement on the Prosperity Gospel," 100–01,

57. Dilger, "Healing the Wounds of Modernity," 59.

58. The expression *viens-et-vois* literally means "come and see." The words originally were pronounced by Jesus (John 1:39). Christ's disciples wanted to follow Him and to know their Lord's residence or place He stayed. The Full Gospel Fellowship in the town of Lubumbashi adopted this saying and made it their own by describing the space where Jesus operated miracles and wonders. As a result, many have joined this neo-Pentecostal character but are identified as non-denominational.

3

Translation

THIS SECTION EXPLORES THE effect and impact of Bible translation on the vernacular cultures within the context of cross-cultural religious systems. Missionary evangelistic activities, vernacular adoption, as well as cultural pluralism, resulted in a paradigm shift of the gospel and Christian mission within the Congo. The change to a missional model allowed for the fusion of the Christian religion into local traditions that have been regarded as the basis for the proliferation of Neo-Pentecostal expressions. This writer tests Lamin Sanneh's[1] scholarly discourse in connection to translatability and an indigenous assimilation of the gospel, along with

---

1. Sanneh surmises, "Missions also arrived in Africa from the need to spread the gospel, a need that now found new justifications and fresh means. However, much missionary may have been conceived as the arm of European political expansion, missionaries still had to rely on indigenous languages to preach their message, and this created a distinction between European culture and native traditions. Consequently, however, much mission tried to suppress local populations, the issue of the vernacular helped to undermine its foreign character. By the same token, the new interest in creating vernacular Scriptures for societies that had no Scriptures of their own ushered in a fundamental religious revolution; with new religious structures coming into being to preside over the changes." See Sanneh, *Translating the Message*, 159. Sanneh states, "One of the most dramatic changes was undoubtedly the popular, mass participation of Africans in this process. It began to dawn on African populations that the missionary adoption of vernacular categories for the Scriptures was in effect a written sanction for indigenous religious vocation. The God of ancestors was accordingly assimilated into the Yahweh of ancient Israel and the God and Father of our Lord Jesus Christ. The exclusive notion of Western Christianity was replaced with the inclusive rule of African religions, an inclusiveness that helped deepen the pluralist ethos of the gospel" (159–60).

the place and role of pre-Christian traditions as the matrices which prepared Africans to receive Christianity.

Does Sanneh's assessment do justice to the evangelized, whose responses to Christianity reshaped and reinvented the religion, or do his findings accurately justify foreign missionary enterprise vis-à-vis imperialism? Missionaries translated the gospel into an African context so that this setting reflected their own Western cultural patterns. In the Congolese context, however, although primal belief systems prepared locals to access God's revelation and domesticate the gospel, the encounter facilitated continuity with primal religious systems and syncretism.

This chapter will be divided into four sections. The first will deal with missionary efforts and vernacular translation. The second will address the paradigm shift of the Congolese worldview. The third section encompasses Pentecostalism and Neo-Pentecostalism. The fourth will deal with the appropriation of prosperity theology.

MISSIONARY EFFORTS AND VERNACULAR TRANSLATION

This section encompasses the following: the negative aspects of the missionary effort, the positive dimensions of the missionary effort, the translation effort, and the results of the translation effort.

The Negative Aspects of the Missionary Effort

During the colonial period, Belgian leadership attempted to control the missionary effort. For example, King Leopold II's 1920 speech urged Belgian missionaries in the Congo to promote solely the interests of Belgium: "Your role as evangelists, pastors in the land of Congo, is to facilitate the interests and benefits of Belgium."[2] He continued, "Your role as pastors is to interpret the Bible in a manner that protects the interests of the metropolitans."[3] It seems that the role of colonial interpretation was to exploit natural resources and keep the minds of local people weak,

---

2. Discours du roi des belges, accessed July 17, 2013, http://www.youtube.com/watch?v= zf86zTBmoHg.

3. Discours du roi des belges, accessed July 17, 2013, http://www.youtube.com/watch?v= zf86zTBmoHg.

so they would be incapable of reacting against the abusive systems of the government and society that were being practiced and put into place.

Leopold said to the missionaries:

> Your knowledge of the Bible will help you to find the texts that sanction poverty . . . use in your sermons texts such as blessed are the poor in spirit for theirs is the kingdom of God (Mt. 5:3). It is hard for someone who is rich to enter the kingdom of heaven: It is easier for a camel to go through the eye of a needle than for someone who is rich to enter the kingdom of God' (Mt.19:23–24).[4]

Leopold instructed the missionaries to teach the local people to be faithful and irrational. He clearly stated, "Teach them to obey, to be physically strong for labor, to forgive but not to retaliate."[5]

Robert B. Edgerton relates, "The missionaries put the local chiefs of the Luba people in chains because these chiefs refused to build for them. The Superior Priest of Luluabourg caused Congolese women who had voluntarily left the mission station to be bound and brought back from the nearby government station because these women were not free."[6] In the wake of the colonial settlement in the Congo, a number of Christian missionaries posed no direct challenge to colonial exploitation. In fact, there were few distinct differences between the colonial enterprise and Christianity.

David Livingstone asserted, "Civilization-Christianity and Commerce should never be separable."[7] This comment suggests that Christian missions were essential in the quest and implementation of European economic agendas. "Presbyterian missionaries William Sheppard and William Morrison faced trial in 1909 for exposing the atrocities perpetrated on rubber gatherers in the Belgian Congo."[8]

Elizabeth Isichei, a feminist scholar and historian, believes that the promotion of education on the land of Africa was to perpetuate colonialism and imperial expressions. Western settlers needed elite locals for a high quality of labor and achievements. Isichei deduces,

4. Discours du roi des belges, accessed July 17, 2013, http://www.youtube.com/watch?v= zf86zTBmoHg.

5. Discours du roi des belges, accessed July 17, 2013, http://www.youtube.com/watch?v= zf86zTBmoHg.

6. Edgerton, *The Troubled Heart of Africa*, xiv.

7. Dube, *Postcolonial Feminist Interpretation of the Bible*, 6.

8. Robert, "Shifting Southward," 50.

The construction of roads railways, and the increased security of travel, meant that it became easier to spread the Christian message—but it was near monopoly of education that was the single most effective way of attracting Christians. White hegemony was only one form of social stratification; it was an enduring paradox of Christian life that mission education created new inequalities.[9]

The historic pattern of Congolese worldviews records instances in which certain politics of translation were enforced that seemed to support imperial propaganda and colonialism. J. Kabamba Kiboko, a Congolese biblical scholar and feminist theologian, argues, "These ideological forces have attempted to exert an extra-biblical monologic authoritarian view of divination in the Hebrew Bible in order to serve their own Christian imperial-colonial and missiologist interests, all of which have been problematic in African mission contexts."[10] The imperial translation of vernacular cultures seemed to have motivated the current spiritism of divisive character reflecting the Congolese religious pluralistic worldviews. It seems like the Bible and its messages supported the colonizers' efforts to exercise control, power, and dominion while extracting raw material resources. According to Mulimbe, "Christianizing, colonizing, civilizing, as well as enslaving become part of the mission effort to save."[11]

The Positive Aspects of the Missionary Effort

Missionary efforts are to be credited and appreciated as they built clinics, vocational schools, roadways, provided an education infrastructure, and introduced new technology. For instance, increased education opened

---

9. Isichei, *From Antiquity to the Present*, 229.

10. Kiboko, *Divination in 1 Samuel 28 and Beyond*, ii. Her thesis asserts, "Much of the vocabulary of divination in 1 Samuel 28:3–27 and beyond has been misinterpreted in authorized English and other translations used in Africa and scholarly writings." She continues, "I argue that the woman of Endor is not a witch, it is a label that has a long negative social history and often led to violence against those so labeled. The woman of Endor is rather a diviner, much like other Ancient Near Easterner and modern African diviners. She resists an inner-biblical conquest theology and monologic authoritarian to assist King Saul by various means, including invoking the spirit of a departed person. The translators steeped in such ideology whether consciously or unconsciously translated what is fundamentally a heteroglossia, polyvalent, dialogic text that seeks to undermine any authoritarian voices regarding divination" (2).

11. Mulimbe, *The Idea of Africa*, 30.

doors for the local Congolese to connect with the outside world. Besides the translation of the gospel into local vernacular cultures, this writer argues that education was one of the best projects offered by missionary enterprises to the locals.

The historic, innovative revolution of universalized printing presses, the birth of technology, and the autonomy of vernacular translations have inaugurated a new era, thereby suggesting a new Christendom within the Congolese religious worldview. Bible translation in local languages and literacy were the final stages that enabled the spread of the gospel during social-political and economic alteration.

This writer argues that even though the translation of vernacular cultures allowed the proliferation of the gospel, its mistranslation of biblical texts, along with a narrow interpretation, caused an incomplete holism. Moreover, the causal effects of the modern resurgence brought about a different gospel of prosperity. The Christian message's mal – interpretations within Neo-Pentecostal and charismatic churches have changed the face of Christianity in post-colonial Congo. At the same time, the act of translating the biblical message verbatim caused the authenticity of God's voice to become relevant and fit the context of the recipients as they were able to hear God speaking to them in their own language. The translation was, therefore, a successful tool for the new Christendom.

Moreover, a translation phenomenon has to be evangelistic, liberating, and empowering rather than exploitative. As Elaine Heath states, "Real evangelism is not colonialism, nationalism, or imperialism. Evangelism rightly understood is a holistic initiation of people into the reign of God as revealed in Jesus Christ."[12] Bible translation and vernacular linguistic phenomena ignited religious revivals and signaled a turning point in the history of religion. The process of translating the Christian message was critical to empowering local leadership, sustaining political independence and social development in the 1960s Congo, and rendering possible the process of decolonization and the construction of educational systems.

Education has been necessary for Christian awakenings and decolonization in post-colonial Congo. Dana L. Robert posits, "Mission education, which combined vernacular literacy with Western learning, clearly played a vital role in equipping nationalist leadership."[13] As a result of

---

12. Heath, *The Mystic Way of Evangelism*, 13.
13. Robert, "Shifting Southward," 51.

the availability of literacy education, ordinary Congolese, through the channels of missionary enterprises, received the gospel and translated it into their cultural approaches that best suited or fit their worldviews and met their spiritual needs, cultural expressions, and contexts. Moreover, as Robert puts it, "The process of decolonization and independence began to sever the connection between Christianity and European imperialism. The repudiation of missionary paternalism, combined with expanding indigenous initiatives, freed Christianity to become more at home in local situations."[14] Christian missions contributed to the freedom of the Congolese society due to the indigenous phenomenon.

Literacy vernacular translation was a roadmap to freedom and exchange with the civilized world and a successful initiative of church growth. Robert states, "It is evident that even during the colonial period, indigenous Christians—Bible women evangelists, catechists, and prophets—were all along the most effective interpreters of Christianity to their own people. The explosion of non-western Christianity was possible because Christianity was already indigenized before the colonizers departed."[15] Neo-Pentecostal trends and charismatic models of Christian expressions developed because of the meeting between Western and local religions.

The Translation Effort

Kwame Bediako, an African theologian from Ghana, says: "[The] vernacular mother tongue was an essential vehicle of religious tradition. The gospel is translatable into vernacular, for God speaks Twi, Swahili, and Setswana."[16] The Gospel's translation into the vernacular allowed God to speak to people's innermost feelings and hearts and the locals to hear His voice directly through revelation from the text.

Sanneh agrees with Bediako and puts it this way:

> The missionary linguists who shouldered the burden of translation grappled with numerous technical issues of the alphabet, script, tone, orthography, grammar, semantics, usage, culture, and currency, matters of great importance to specialists; it has to be stressed. It was the indigenous reception and appropriation

14. Robert, "Shifting Southward," 51.
15. Robert, "Shifting Southward," 53.
16. Bediako, *Jesus and the Gospel in Africa, History, and Experience*, vi.

of the gospel in the post-colonial era that the magnitude and scale of what was achieved was finally revealed.[17]

Therefore, hearing the Word of God and understanding Jesus in the vernacular as those at Pentecost (Acts 2) is crucial to igniting revival in the twenty-first century Congo. Because of translation, Congolese can hear in their own languages the great things that Jesus has done. Furthermore, Bediako advocates, "Christianity is a universal religion because it is translatable and able to be at home in every cultural context without injury to its essential character."[18]

He states, "The Christian belief that the Bible in the vernacular remains in every aspect the Word of God, has its basis in what took place on the Day of Pentecost when the Holy Spirit through the first Christian witnesses, spoke at one and the same time to people who had come from every country in the world" (Acts 2:5). Each participant at Pentecost heard the gospel in his own language, allowing them to hear the great things God has done in Jesus Christ (Acts 2:1–12).[19]

However, Andrew Walls views the concept of translation as an act of "a divine embodiment, or Incarnation, wherein God is translated into humanity. The cross-cultural spread of the gospel leads to Christ being received by faith in other cultures and retranslated into the customs and languages of those people."[20] Translation is not merely a manuscript or word printed on a sheet of paper; it is instead a change of life. When Christ's gospel encounters people or culture, or a community transforms it, the gospel becomes a life-giving phenomenon.

Results of the Translation Effort

As a result, a vernacular translation of the Bible and its message has been heard by the Congolese in their language using their own terms. As Franz Fanon asserts, "Language has the power to name and, therefore to construct the lens through which understanding takes place."[21] The translation was a step towards liberation and a certain degree of freedom. The

---

17. Sanneh, *Whose Religion*, 106.
18. Bediako, *Jesus and the Gospel in Africa, History, and Experience*, 32.
19. Bediako, *Jesus and the Gospel in Africa, History, and Experience*, 32.
20. Walls, "The Mission of the Church Today in the Light of Global History," 19.
21. Edwards, *Postcolonial Literature*, 30.

Congolese not only have heard or received the gospel, but also the gospel has become their story.

The current phenomenon of church growth in the Congo justifies the shift of the center of gravity that the world's Christian scholars, missiologists, historians and religious leaders advocate. Moreover, the shift has been the panacea of social-economic, political, and religious development within the Congolese social fabric. In his book *Whose Religion Is Christianity? The Gospel beyond the West*, Sanneh says, "As it happened, in the centuries of ferment and expansion, Christians became pioneers of linguistic development with the creation of alphabets, orthographies, dictionaries, and grammars. The resulting literacy, however limited, produced social and cultural transformation."[22] The linguistic phenomenon of the written text and alphabetization caused the celebrated freedom, social equality, and several local awakenings.

Sanneh says, "Without translation, there is no Christianity or Christians. Translation is the church's birthmark as well as its missionary benchmark: the church would be unrecognizable or unsustainable without it."[23] In other words, outside translation, there are no missions by which to evangelize, and missions without evangelism are meaningless. Translation produced Christian expressions, civilization, social-economic, political, and spiritual development, as literacy enabled locals to read, write, and interact with the outside world. Shaw asserts that translation "discovered contextualization and fought injustices around the world."[24] Language has encouraged spiritual renewal, awakenings, and social revo-

---

22. Sanneh, *Whose Religion Is Christianity?*, 99. In this paradigm of literacy's role, Sanneh believes, "The religion was a translated faith right from the start: the Gospels are not a verbatim of the preaching and acts of Jesus. The Bible of Christianity is not a Qur'an, the untranslatable scripture of Islam. Through the Western missionary movement, this linguistic fact about Christianity turned it into an active translation force, resulting in the production of grammars, dictionaries, and primers of local languages for Bible translation and religious instruction. Where it was undertaken, Bible translation became the vehicle of indigenous cultural development and the basis of establishing churches." See Sanneh and Carpenter, *The Changing Face of Christianity*, 214. Sanneh argues, "Bible translation into mother tongue has opened the way for the worldwide Christian renewal and for the diverse cultural expressions that have become the vintage mark of the religion of a global phenomenon, suggesting the need for a fresh theological outlook to take in the changes. The translated gospel into local cultures caused sweeping rivals in lieu of appeasing ancestors' spirits and veneration." Sanneh, *Whose Religion Is Christianity?*, 106.

23. Sanneh, *Whose Religion Is Christianity?*, 97

24. Shaw, *Global Awakening*, 11.

lution as a comprehensive reconciliation against ethnic conflicts and civil war within Congolese society.

As Robert deduces, "English vernacular Bible translation sowed the seeds of broad-based English culture of personal initiative, rather than control by a wealthy, Latinized elite."[25] Robert's assessment is connected to a medieval perspective and is a compelling example of the significance of vernacular culture translation. The translation was a doorway to the freedom of the press, a liberating force for social network development, and a universalization of faith. Moreover, the translation and retranslation of vernacular cultures and languages have increasingly become the fundamental basis of the spread of the prosperity gospel and Neo-Pentecostalism expressions of Christianity in the twenty-first century post-colonial Congo.

As a result, ordinary Congolese have been able to access God's revelation. Sanneh points out, "Bible translation put the power of religion into the hands of ordinary people, yes especially women and children, so that they might realize their highest potential."[26] In addition, the evangelized were able to read the Bible in their own mother tongues and hear directly from Christ's voice through the Scriptures explaining the great things (the good news of salvation) God had done for them.

As Bediako shares, "In matters of religion, no language speaks to the heart, mind and inner-most feelings as does our mother-tongue. For Christianity is, among all religions, the most culturally translatable, hence the most truly universal, being able to be at home in every cultural context without injury to its essential character."[27] In other words, Bediako asserts, "Christianity has developed as a vernacular faith."[28] Africans' possession of Scripture in their mother tongues was essential to access the original sources of Christianity which empowered them to plant and establish their own local churches.

The Bible's translation into the vernacular, along with missionary efforts in the Congo, has been instrumental in impacting the current paradigm "shift."[29] Translation into vernacular languages has shaped

25. Robert, *Christian Mission*, 35.

26. Sanneh, *Whose Religion is Christianity?*, 117.

27. Bediako, *Jesus and the Gospel in Africa, History, and Experience*, vi. Also see Walls, *The Missionary Movement in Christian Story*, 32.

28. Walls, *The Missionary Movement in Christian Story*, 32.

29. Shaw, *Global Awakening*, 11. Shaw insists that "The fact of Christianity's Global comeback is undeniable. Africa went from ten million Christians in 1900 to four

primal religious trends and validated the Christian message. Besides, the translation was strategic for people of different places and cultural trends within Congolese societies to connect to the outside world. God's voice and the message of the gospel penetrated the recipients' hearts and minds.

As Robert argues:

> Widespread literacy and printing along with Renaissance intellectual impulses stimulated an unprecedented development of individuality and the formation of individual consciousness. It was this development of individual self-awareness through literacy—with the availability of printed Bibles in local languages – that initiated the next road phase in the spread of Christianity.[30]

Moreover, translation became a force that transformed traditional religions and belief systems rooted in ancestor worship and appeasement. Contextualization of the biblical gospel into the Congolese worldview was a step towards the globalization of Christianity.

In "The Horizontal and the Vertical in Mission: An African Perspective," Sanneh states, "The subject of Western missions needs to be unhinged from narrow colonial context and placed in a much wider setting of African culture, including the religious background of African societies."[31] His argument is a wake-up call for emerging African scholars and readers of the Bible to appreciate the missionaries' efforts in translating the gospel into vernacular languages instead of viewing missionary efforts to present the idea of Christianity as a Western product. The gospel came as good news to the Congo when it was uncovered by its foreign translators. This good news has been the reason the gospel was embraced, appropriated, and domesticated within a Congolese religious worldview.

Sanneh's philosophy is critical for the twenty-first century missional church and the new Christendom. The translation of vernacular languages has proven to be the heart of the massive explosion of Christianity and its awakenings in Africa, particularly in the Congo. Nevertheless,

---

hundred million in 2000. Pentecostalism went from a handful in 1906 to half a billion worldwide by century's end. The center of Christianity shifted from North America and Europe to Africa" (11). The center of gravity as advocated by missiologists is realistic in Congolese Christian expression through neo-Pentecostalism and prosperity gospel movements. These movements are transforming the religion worldwide.

30. Robert, *Christian Mission*, 35.
31. Sanneh, "The Horizontal and the Vertical in Mission," 161.

the indigenizing character of the gospel has been a pathway to globalize Christian efforts. This effort to indigenize Christianity is the essence of the gospel because God accepts people as they are with their traditional expressions; this includes languages and cultures (along with their mores).

Because of Bible translation, people of different places and cultures can gather and form the body of Christ. For instance, in Acts 2, people from different places and cultures experienced the power of God through the Holy Spirit. Different tribes and ethnicities heard God's message communicated to them in their own languages (Cf. Acts 2:6–7). Andrew F. Walls traces the history of the Christian movement from its origins to demonstrate that the heartland of Christianity has shifted from the Western world to Africa.[32] Jerusalem is no longer seen as the heartland of Christianity. Bible translation has been one of the strongest components of cross-cultural and missional expression that facilitated the spread of the gospel.

Though there were recorded cases in which some missionaries participated consciously or unconsciously in colonial efforts, others made a significant impact in spreading the gospel through spirituality, education, and social development. For example, missionary schools helped equip national leaders and end systematic imperialism. Robert states, "Mission schools promoted literacy in both European languages and vernaculars, and they spread Western ideas of democratic government, individual rights and educability of women and girls. Despite their limitations through education provided leadership with the tools it needed to challenge foreign oppression."[33] Yet, in contrast to Robert's position, some contemporary post-colonial scholars believe that education was a tool utilized to colonize the mind of the colonized.

Seen from this point of view, the Christian message must be uncovered by colonial heritage and distinct cultures. So, a post-colonial

---

32. Walls, "The Gospel as Prisoner and Liberator of Culture," 136. Walls states, "In 325 C.E. Christians were Jews. Not only Jerusalem the main Christian centers lay in the Eastern Mediterranean, and the key language for Christians was Greek. By 600 C.E. the balance had shifted westward, and growing edge of Christianity was among the northern and western tribal and semi-tribal peoples—and Ireland was a power center. In the 1840s Great Britain would certainly be among notably associated with the expansion of the Christian faith. By 1980, the balance had shifted again southwards; Africa is now the continent most notable for those that profess and call themselves Christians" (136).

33. Walls, "The Gospel as Prisoner and Liberator of Culture," 51.

method of reading the Bible with an eye towards the margins is critical. Regretfully, recorded missions history is incomplete and has to be reread, retold, and rewritten afresh from a post-colonial perspective. For Fanon, a text written from the perspective of the European culture cannot be relevant to Africans. He argues, "The post-colonial voice can decide to resist imperial linguistic domination in two ways by rejecting the language of the colonizer or by subverting the empire by writing back in the European language."[34] Many African believers, however, are grateful for the missionaries' "work, dedication and great sacrifice."[35] Some missionaries died in foreign lands for the sake of spreading the gospel of Christ.

PARADIGM SHIFT

This section will discuss the Congolese Christian worldview, primal religious trends, the transmission and retransmission of the gospel, the face of Christianity reinvented, and the mechanism, hope, and survival.

Congolese Christian Worldview

The surging paradigm shift within the Congolese Christian worldview has been the final push and force resulting in the massive presence of Christians and spiritual awakenings. The paradigm shift has caused post-colonial readers of the Bible to reimagine new approaches for discipleship, evangelism, and missions. The cross-cultural efforts of twentieth-century missionaries and their translation of the Bible into the vernacular were the basis which motivated the emergence of the African religious worldviews. Their cross-cultural character resulted in a Christian revolution that was a transformative initiative for Congolese primal religions.

However, today, most Christians live in the Global South. Third world country theologies, pluralistic cultural dynamics, and religious realities of the context are to be taken seriously to translate the gospel. Dana L. Robert, quoting Andrew F. Walls in his book, *The Missionary Movements in Christian History Studies in the Transmission of Faith*, deduces, "As Christianity shifts southward, the nature of Christianity itself evolves. The movement of faith from one culture to another typically has caused a significant change in the self-understanding and cultural

---

34. Dube, *Postcolonial Feminist Interpretation of the Bible*, 6.
35. West and Dube, *The Bible in Africa, Transactions, Trajectories and Trends*, 74.

grounding of the Christian movement."[36] A pluralistic character of faith and its interpretations within the Global South has caused a paradigm shift.

Robert asserts, "Christianity throughout the non-Western world has in common an indigenous, grassroots leadership, embeddedness in local cultures and reliance on a vernacular Bible."[37] Christianity's shift southward is sustained by local traditional interpretations. The reality proves that the current developmental awakening and growth of the religion in Africa, particularly in the post-colonial Congo, is a local expression of Christianity. As Sanneh insists, "By virtue of its use of vernacular in speaking of God and in spreading the Scriptures, Christianity has translated or incarnated itself into local cultures."[38] The local trends are the matrices of the religion.

Furthermore, unlike the 1910 Edinburgh World Missionary Conference that marked the beginning of ecumenical spirit in which the majority of representatives were Westerners, the 1938 International Mission Council of Madras, India, marked the beginning of a new era. Africans affirmed their theological contributions through the lens of AIC Churches. In this context, there has been a,

> Transformation of world Christianity since the Second World War—a massive cultural and geographical shift away from Europeans and their descendants toward people of the Southern Hemisphere. The shift southward began in the century, and the 1938 missionary conference was vivid proof of powerful indigenous Christian leadership in both church and state, despite a missionary movement trapped within colonialist structures and attitudes.[39]

The phenomenological paradigm shift is realistic and permanent because of the relationship between the primal religion and Christian worldview which creates a cycle of continuous syncretism. There is also a primal paradigm shift of spiritual trends. An act of reciprocity concerning give and take, the gospel in the hands of the locals was a changing force at the same time the gospel was indigenized and modified by the recipients' response to fit their spiritual needs and primal trends.

36. Robert, "Shifting Southward," 56.
37. Robert, "Shifting Southward," 56.
38. Robert, "Shifting Southward," 56.
39. Robert, "Shifting Southward," 50.

Primal Religions Trends

Primal religious traditions are the matrices and fertile ground for the massive rise of Neo-Pentecostal trends of Christianity within the postcolonial Congo. Traditional belief systems were the vehicles of the religious awakening in the twenty-first century. Nevertheless, there are substantially deep connections and affinities between primal religions and Christianity. The relationships indicate a new shape of theological discourse, enabling the spread of Christian faith in the Congo beyond its geographical borders. Harold Turner states that, "It is the people of the primal religions who have made the greatest response to the Christian faith."[40] These local religious enterprises of traditional belief systems have made a significant contribution to the emergence of Christian expressions.

Moreover, Sanneh avers,

> There seem affinities between the Christian and primal traditions, an affinity that perhaps appears in the common reactions when Christian missions first arrived. (this is what we have been waiting for) and that is further evident in the vast range of new movements born from the interaction between the primal religions and Christianity and in no comparable degree in the reaction of primal religions to their meeting with the other universal religions.[41]

Consequently, trends in mediation, sacrifices, and occult practices are few among the factors and methods which resemble Christian expressions or Judeo-traditions and biblical narratives. For example, Jesus is viewed in Christianity as the mediator between people and God (1 Tim 2:5–6), but traditional Congolese use ancestors as mediators. Seeing these phenomena from a broader perspective, the emergence of AICs in Sub-Saharan Africa, especially in the Congo, has transformed the face of Christian faith radically. Traditional primal religious trends are the basis for the rise of the Neo-Pentecostal Gospel of prosperity within the Congolese worldview.

As David A. Shank puts it: "Since the 1960s, with the phasing out of the European colonial empire and its official recognition of Western mission efforts, this spontaneous African-initiated religious phenomenon

---

40. Bediako, *Christianity in Africa*, 95–96.
41. Bediako, *Christianity in Africa*, 96.

has only increased as more and more Africans are reading the Bible for themselves in their own languages, and offering their own interpretations and applications."[42]

For Sanneh, translation is a

> Sine qua non of witness and divine presence that validates the mission. Through the process of Scripture translation, the central categories of Christian theology, God, creation, Jesus Christ, and history are transposed into their local equivalents suggesting that Christianity has been adequately anticipated. The gospel communication neither requires the Western missionary transmitter to be at the center of the picture nor does that Africa pre-Christian religion have a theological significance in the whole process.[43]

Furthermore, Sanneh asserts, "The centrality of Scripture translation points to the significance of local religions for providing the idiom for Christian apprehension."[44] Sanneh's description of this whole process is found in the comprehensive term *Missio-Dei*, encompassing the divine initiative through the pre-Christian tradition. Bediako calls this "the historical missionary transmission and the indigenous assimilation."[45]

"*Missio-Dei* sustained the traditional religious enterprise by bridging a convergence with Christianity . . . so that the *Missio-Dei* was activated by the stimulus of African historical contact with the West; it has now fused with the local religious enterprise and acquired a concrete reality."[46] However, the concrete reality is a local reality, achieved by indigenous assimilation and African religious agency through the critical role of the Scripture in African languages. Local adaptation made a greater impact than the external agencies of the missionary enterprises. Alan H. Anderson shares, "Through the vernacular Bible, Africans had an independent source of authority abounding in symbolic healing practices and exorcisms not unlike their own. The Bible seemed to lend much more support to traditional African customs than to the imported cultural customs of

---

42. Shank, *What Western Christians Can Learn from African-Initiated Churches*, 3.
43. Bediako, *Christianity in Africa*, 120.
44. Bediako, *Christianity in Africa*, 120.
45. Bediako, *Christianity in Africa*, 121.
46. Bediako, *Christianity in Africa*, 121.

the European missionaries."[47] The African enterprise was greater than that of the foreigners.

African primal religions original to salvific discourse were a seedbed for the Christian awakening. However, as Sanneh argues, the foreign missionary efforts "stimulated the emergence of a genuine indigenous Christian tradition in terms of *Missio-Dei* in the local setting, a fresh cultural incarnation of faith."[48] For Sanneh, the indigenous character sustained the *Missio-Dei* because of the translation ability of the religion which resulted in a resurgence of the Christian faith. The encounter between Christianity and African primal religious traditions has produced a paradigm shift which World Christian scholars identify as a surprise. The surprise factor is that Africa is now one of the Christian heartlands on earth.

The problem is not animism, witchcraft, or ancestral worship. On the contrary, Christianity was sustained by these primal religions. Also, the problem is not colonialism or the failure of the missionary enterprise but their willingness to take the gospel to the nations where sacrifice matters most. Christianity was reborn into a non-Western religious character, suggesting that the interaction between the two had a lasting impact. As Bediako states, "By becoming a non-Western religion, Christianity has also become a true world faith, and in the African context, the depth of the inter-penetration between Christianity and Africa's primal religions points to the significance of the Christian factor of Christian transmission and retransmission of the gospel."[49]

Translation and Retransmission of the Gospel

The gospel is engaged in a continuous process of being retranslated and retransmitted within the Congolese worldviews. A few centuries ago, the missionary enterprise introduced the gospel, or Christianity, to the Congolese, but today, the Congolese are retransmitting the same message to

---

47. Anderson, *African Reformation*, 33.

48. In Bediako, *African Christianity* (122), Sanneh argues, "If it is translatability which produces indigeneity, then a truly indigenous church should also be a translating church, reaching continually to the heart of the culture of its context and incarnating that translating Word. . . . Word who took flesh and dwelt among us, not only exegetes (and so translates) God (John 1:18), but also exegetes the human predicament (John 4:29), bringing the two together in a mutually intelligible communication."

49. Bediako, *Christianity in Africa*, 265.

their own people. This re-transmission process has been a useful and successful tool of evangelism. The recipients have made the gospel their own and adapted it to their local expressions. The gospel is being retransmitted over and over within local expressions and has aided in the shaping of African expressions and cultures.

The domestication of the Christian gospel suggests that the retransmission of the gospel in post-colonial Congo is an endless process. The recipients had access to the life-saving message of the gospel translated into their own mother tongues. Walls views this transmission of the gospel as one culture bringing another culture to a particular nation. Sanneh refers to this action of translation, which a persona translated in life or resulted from the transformation of one's life, not merely as a translation of the printed text, but a life changing phenomenon.

This change, as a result of translation, implies that the receivers have not only heard, but have also understood the gospel. Then, something extraordinary happened to their lives, as well as "ordinary Congolese" in the streets of Kinshasa, Kisangani, Bukavu, Lubumbashi, Kananga, Bas-Congo, Mbuji Mayi, and other towns. The Bible was being read and interpreted literally and seriously, while, at the same time, it was taken out of context. For instance, the number of people who participate in night prayer meetings, house churches, and mobile preachers' ministries is increasing in number. As a result, nearly ninety percent of the population profess to being Christian; this means the Congo has become one of the most Christianized nations in the world. In other words, the gospel has been diffused, appropriated, domesticated, and retranslated into Congolese cultural patterns. As a result, the Congolese have reinvented the face of Christianity. However, this retransmission has not been adequately a transformative force, translating into genuine discipleship, as well as social-political and spiritual change.

The Face of Christianity Reinvented

The face of Christianity has not only been reinvented, but it has also been altered, redressed, and revolutionized within the Congolese religious worldview. Western missionaries' encounter with the African traditional religious belief systems has radicalized the invention of the religion and its expressions. Sanneh and Joel A. Carpenter argue, "The missionary impulse and religious itinerancy of an earlier age have coalesced with indigenous reception and adaptation to field Christianity in new cultural contexts and idioms."⁵⁰ The reinvention means that the Congolese pluralistic characteristics of cultural expressions and religious worldviews have been a fertile soil for the gospel's reception.

Ogbu Kalu and Alaine Low report that African traditional churches, such as *Zionist spirit churches* founded by a prophet and their *pneumatic* emphases and literal uses of biblical narratives as well as "innovative gender ideology, were significant for the emergence of African religion and culture."⁵¹ They state, "These churches changed the face of Christianity in Africa by their enlarging of religious space for women and their reclaiming of a pneumatic and charismatic experience, which had been suppressed by mainline Christianity but resonated well with African spirituality."⁵² Furthermore, the authors assert, "These churches have certain distinctive characteristics, for example, the prominent role of women and youth; the appropriation of the American prosperity gospel in the 1980s; and riveting to holiness and intercessory traditions in 1990s."⁵³ For instance, since the 1920s, Kimbanguism promoted the role of women and youth; the promotion of women was one of the reasons Kimbanguists were successful in their evangelistic initiatives.

The Christian message was translated into local trends and cultural expression, and the gospel found a home in the Congo. This happened because Congolese cultural patterns colored the gospel. For example, traditional ceremonies, chants, invocations of ancestors, or occult activities were incorporated into Christianity during worship. The overnight ceremonial prayer of invoking spiritual powers and ancestors was replaced with Christian night prayers. It revealed that when people accept Christ, they bring with them their cultural mores which are part of their DNA. The cultural mores are the basis of the challenge to read the syncretistic character of the Christian faith.

---

50. Sanneh and Carpenter, *The Changing Face of Christianity*, 214.

51. Kalu and Low, *Interpreting Contemporary Christianity: Global Processes and Local Identities*, 275.

52. Kalu and Low, *Interpreting Contemporary Christianity: Global Processes and Local Identities*, 275. Kalu further explains, "These churches have also been influenced by North American neo-Evangelical and Pentecostal Christianity. They adopt a faith-gospel focused on a *this-worldly* blessing and deliverance theology, which though built on African traditional conceptions, is expressed strongly in terms of modern western charismatic thinking" (176).

53. Kalu and Low, *Interpreting Contemporary Christianity: Global Processes and Local Identities*, 275.

Nevertheless, the Congolese have adapted Christianity by enculturating and appropriating it to fit the needs of the recipients. This writer argues that the transmission of the gospel and Christianity never successfully redeemed traditional belief systems from their roots. However, it was a mechanism of adaptation and contextualization to fit the spiritual needs of the evangelized when the encounter took place. The recipients were unprepared to learn; therefore, their embrace of the Christian faith had to mature enough for authentic conversion and discipleship.

A new form of Christianity was born in terms of Neo-Pentecostalism, neo-Charismatic, and prosperity gospels that had less influence on true discipleship development. Translation has enabled the phenomenological changing face of Christianity within the post-colonial Congo. Locals are now able to read, write, decipher the alphabets, sing, and understand grammar and dictionaries. The message of Christ was no longer a mystery or coded language; it became an open secret for the Congolese. Also, it preserved their languages and cultural worldviews and patterns. As a result, today most adherents to the faith are people of the Global South.

Mechanism, Hope, and Survival

Hope is the metaphor people live by in the Congo. Tomorrow is significant in the minds of the locals due to their pre-imagined belief systems based on an eschatological phenomenon. Many Congolese Christians believe in this utopia of the future or tomorrow: "No matter what is going through right now, we shall overcome." Okunboh Hadeyemo contends, "In Africa, people use the expression, 'by the grace of God' to explain how it is 'they survive when they live on less than the one dollar a day designated by the United Nations as the absolute minimum for survival.'"[54] They also use the expression "*on ne sais jamais*," a Swahili expression translated in French, "You never know," because they are not certain when and how they will afford or obtain access to their next meal.

For instance, during the apartheid era, South Africans chanted in the street a song of hope that, "Freedom shall come tomorrow." The longing for a better tomorrow leaves people with little or no choice than to seek alternative ways to meet their physical, spiritual, and emotional needs. As

---

54. Hadeyemo et al., *Africa Bible Commentary*, 1144.

a result of these belief systems, the Neo-Pentecostal gospel of prosperity has gained much of the heart of the Congolese religious landscape.

Neo-Pentecostal and charismatic preachers seized the opportunity due to a lack of resources, social, and economic dysfunction to preach a message of hope and promise to the most desperate and vulnerable selected groups or adherents. These adherents were promised success, promotions, beautiful children, houses, husbands, wives, and a better life The rhetoric behind these phenomena is that by faith, adherents sow seeds today for tomorrow's decent life, surprises, successes, and overflowing blessings. These misconstrued, unbiblical hermeneutics of biblical literature tend to make people depend on their prophets, apostles, preachers, or pastors. Nevertheless, many of these exploited adherents are poor, uneducated, unemployed, and alienated. Despite the adverse effects and forces of this mechanism of hope, Christianity is rapidly growing in these regions.

Sanneh relates it this way:

> These are forces that have pushed world Christianity forward and shaped its reigning convictions of promise and destiny. In spite of the vagueness enjoyed by the phenomenon of the prosperity gospel, a good proportion of the world's Christians is poor, young, and uneducated. According to the statistics of membership, new converts are characterized by extraordinary persecution and suffering. In spite of that, the rate of conversion to Christianity is greatest among these populations, and for a good reason.[55]

Consequently, the mechanism of hope is a model of survival to maintain despite one's current misery and extreme poverty. The problem with this tactic of survival is that it is a temporary fix. People are emotionally temporarily relieved, but their wounds are not healed, and their initial problems persist or remain unsolved. Instead, people deal with symptoms in lieu of curing their plight. The mechanism of hope and survival is an imported Western Pentecostalism trend in Congolese society which has translated into Neo-Pentecostalism.

---

55. Sanneh and Carpenter, *The Changing Face of Christianity*, 219.

PENTECOSTALISM AND NEO-PENTECOSTALISM

Pentecostalism is one of the fastest growing trends of Christianities in the world. The reality is that Neo-Pentecostal expressions of Christianity continue to grow and expand within non-Western and previously non-Christian societies. In the case of the post-Congo, Pentecostalism was well received and embraced by the Congolese population due to some affinities and resemblance between African traditional cultures and Pentecostalism. Pentecostalism as a movement has played an important role and impact in reshaping religion in twenty-first century Africa. This theological approach emphasizes personal salvation and pneumatic experience by attracting many adherents.

As Kalu argues, "Speaking in tongues, prophesies, visions, healing, miracles, signs, and wonders are sought, accepted, valued, and consciously encouraged among members as evidence of the active presence of God's spirit."[56] Pentecostalism and charismatic emphases on spiritual gifting have been appropriated within the Congolese society because their primal disposition systems are spirit-worlds. Leslie Newbigin sees Pentecostalism as a "third force" that has dramatically influenced African Christianity.[57] Overall, the North American classical Pentecostal or neo-Evangelical denominations fueled the AIC's mystical causality and emphasis on healing that was imported and domesticated in Congolese worldviews.

Neo-Pentecostalism is a product of new Pentecostal trends developed in Africa through renewal and charismatic churches. Christianity has experienced growth since the beginning of the twentieth century in Africa; however, for the last six decades, Neo-Pentecostal churches have been a dominant force that ignited revival and spiritual awakenings. As Kalu and Low argue, "Their chief characteristics are a theology of health, wealth, deliverance, and healing. They also knew their use of mass media in evangelism, and women play a fundamental role as founders, leaders, and participants."[58] As a result of a mixture of the primal belief from the

---

56. Kalu, *African Christianity*, 340.

57. Kalu, *African Christianity*, 340.

58. Kalu and Low, *Interpreting Contemporary Christianity: Global Processes and Local Identities*, 294. These authors insist, "There is a gender dynamic in the AIC's that is evident in preaching and ministry. The fact that women predominate in leadership in churches with pneumatic orientations suggests that Charismatic/spiritual churches are more gender-friendly than others. Women are able to use their special resources for the growth of the church." This observation is significant in terms of how Africa

AICs and North American Christian trends, the phenomena are a new Christianity, in which, though it appears syncretistic in nature, adherents attempt to reject or denounce some pre-historic belief systems.

APPROPRIATION OF PROSPERITY THEOLOGY

The theology of prosperity has been appropriated within the Congolese society. As a Euro-American imported trend and expression, this gospel of prosperity has changed the face of Christianity in the post-colonial Congo. "In this context, the prosperity gospel introduced by North American missionaries was reinterpreted to reflect opportunities for a vast accumulation of wealth by those with education, capital and political connections, and the wishful aspirations of those without."[59] Besides, the American Dream philosophy based on a philosophy of a spiritually self-made man was imported and interacted with the Congolese cultural system of life force, or man-centered and vital force, to live longer, to be stronger in the land of the ancestors, and to have strength and prosperity.

Nevertheless, the appropriation of the gospel has systematically affected the Congolese traditional belief system and religious worldviews. It seems that there is continuity between the Western culture and traditional belief systems. Prosperity, or the abundant life gospel practiced by Neo-Pentecostals, has been regarded as an attempt to appropriate the biblical message of salvation to suit the contemporary socio-economic and religious state of the Congolese. Congolese traditional belief systems and religious goals relating to the search for paradise, abundant life, salvation, wealth, and prosperity connect with the American Dream philosophy.

The appropriation of Western Christian expressions into the Congolese culture echoes the benefits of translating the gospel into the vernacular. The result has been that recipients' lives have been altered as they have made the Gospel their own possession. That is because the gospel is a transforming power over the life-patterns and systematic values of the traditional Congo. Christianity has arrived at a stage of rendezvous

---

has historically been known as a hierarchical and patriarchal society where women are voiceless and silenced. Neo-Pentecostalism has systematically contributed to gender balance and equality. This echoes the egalitarian character of the religion. This is unique and one of the reasons why the new Christianity attracts a massive following because of a liberalization and radicalization of faith.

59. Deacon and Lynch, *Allowing Satan toward a Political Economy of Neo-Pentecostalism in Kenya*, 110.

due to the mechanism of an appropriation of faith. However, the challenge is to realize an authentic spiritual transformation and growth in the wake of the economic turmoil and poverty that confront the Congolese population.

Christianity has increasingly become a religion of the developing nations or third world countries. There is a disconnect, however, between the current development of Christianity's growth in the Congo vis-à-vis the deprivation of human life and struggles. Poverty and systematic failure make it difficult to come to a comprehensive and authentic assessment of the current trend of spiritual awakenings in the Congo. Nevertheless, the poorest nations of the Global South (i.e. Sub-Saharan countries) are experiencing politico-economic powerlessness, corruption, and civil wars. As Bediako says, "Curiously, therefore, the poor, underdeveloped or developing nations of South, which have become the lands of Christians are, the two-Thirds World' being a term preferred by residents of these new lands of the Christians, which are marked by economic poverty, political powerlessness, but religious pluralism."[60] These expressions of Christianities are shaping Christian thought and action on a global scale.

This writer argues that despite Congolese Christianity's substantial increase in numbers, it must engage in a holistic missional engagement and authentic evangelism. Mathematical or numerical statistics alone are not scientifically reliable methods to assess the rapid growth of Christianity in the Congo. Locals still practice traditional belief systems and engage in social splits, civil wars, ethnic conflicts, corruption, and greed. However, as Bediako says, "The significance of this event lies in more than the weight of numbers: it has to do also with what has happened to the gospel in the minds of Christians of the Two-Thirds World, since they have received the gospel and sought to appropriate it in their contexts of poverty, powerlessness, and religious pluralism."[61]

The holistic missional engagement requires a holistic transformation or complete and authentic regeneration of the whole person, physically, spiritually, morally, socio-politically, and economically. Bediako asserts, "There has been the recognition that the gospel is essentially holistic and directed at the whole person—physical as well as spiritual, corporate as well as individual—and therefore requires a corresponding

---

60. Bediako, *Christianity in Africa*, 128.
61. Bediako, *Christianity in Africa*, 128–29.

holistic missionary engagement."⁶² Jesus' ministry was holistic, and it affected or transformed whole persons and communities. For example, the blind received sight, the hungry were fed, and the demon-possessed were delivered. Jesus said, "Come to Me, all you who labor and are heavy laden, and I will give you rest" (Matt 11:28). Healthy churches and ministries have to participate in holistic ministries for successful discipleship and evangelism following the footprint of Christ's vision. As Ronald J. Sider and others discuss,

> A holistic congregation results: a church that practices both evangelism and social ministry; balances nurture and outreach; knows and loves its community; clearly communicates its theology and specific vision; interacts the holistic vision into internal life of the church; builds its ministry on a base of spiritual maturity and healthy; loving relationships; and calls and equips its members to action.⁶³

The emergence of the third world and two-thirds churches due to the appropriation of Christian trends has changed the face of Christianity. Therefore, the translated Gospel has been appropriated by Congolese through Neo-Pentecostal expressions and the rise of prosperity teachings.

CONCLUSION

Missionaries' efforts at vernacular alphabetization and the democratization of the printing press were the bases of human civilization and social empowerment. Their success is to be appreciated and credited to the foreign missionary enterprises and vernacular translation.⁶⁴ Rather than

---

62. Bediako, *Christianity in Africa*, 129.

63. Ronald J. Sider, Philip N. Olson and Heidi Rolland Unruh, *Churches that Make A Difference: Reaching Community with Good News and Good Works* (Grand Rapids: Baker Books,2002),17. These authors argue, "The holistic church: teaches a ministry vision that integrates discipleship, evangelism, and social action, and works toward both spiritual and social transformation. Support a spectrum of social action that includes clarity, compassion, community development, public policy, and justice advocacy, addressing both individual and systematic sources of human problems. Sees ministry as fundamentally rational, seeking to develop long-term relationships with ministry recipients and welcoming them into church fellowship. Views mission as both local and global in scope." Also, see page 16.

64. Robert, *Christian Mission*, 35–36. Robert states, "But in the course of the history, it was the vernacularization process itself that laid the foundations for modern missions. The idea that each person should read the Bible in his or her own language,

placing the weight on the negative effects of imperial propaganda and colonial effects, it is worth appreciating the constant efforts and roles of Euro-American men and women who dedicated or risked their lives for the sake of spreading the gospel and the kingdom of God to the people of Africa.

The lasting impact of the missionary presence is that the recipients (Congolese) received or embraced the story of Christ, which altered their lifestyles and religious landscapes. Consequently, Congolese have engaged in the mission to witness God's saving grace and share it with others. The proclamation, or *kerygma*, is an act which brings about not only a paradigm shift but also a surprise to the original *Mission Dei*. The missionaries sow seeds; due to their presence, a diffusion and transformation have taken place. The surprise is due to what happened as the locals shared their belief systems non-strategically, unintentionally, and spontaneously at a micro-level.

However, Leslie Newbigin's concept of domestication is critical to understand why the prosperity gospel has been domesticated into the Congolese cultures through the development of Neo-Pentecostal and charismatic trends. Spontaneity is one of the qualities and natural abilities most Congolese preachers possess. Within Neo-Pentecostal churches, preachers do not spend time preparing their sermons, but they trust the power of the Holy Spirit to reveal to them prophetic words and visions rather than theological insight. Some African religious leaders belonging to the new Pentecostal weave ignore theological training because Jesus and many of His disciples were illiterate and uneducated men who received the power of the Holy Spirit. Hence, there is more to learn from Neo-Pentecostal and Charismatic trends. Classical Pentecostal paradigms failed to engage the gospel as a transformative force in the Congo. Pentecostals mistranslated the gospel and failed to be a prophetic

---

and that its readers could interpret the Bible than by educated elites, was a Reformation – era version of early church's emphasis on hearing the gospel in different languages are the time of Pentecost in Acts 2. The Protestant principle of literacy vernacularization embodied what mission historians Sanneh and Walls call 'translatability.' In the line of the idea that the translation process itself guarantees that each culture infuses its own meaning into the words of the Bible. Unlike Islam, in which Arabic is seen to be the very word of God, and the translation of the Koran is technically forbidden, Christianity delights in the translation of the Bible into languages that represent a multicity of cultural identities." See "Vernaculars and Volunteers," 450, in Robert, *Christian Mission*, 35–36.

voice to overcome the traditional belief systems of spiritism, syncretism, and appeasing ancestors.

Sanneh suggests that African traditional religions prepared locals to receive the gospel. This analysis is right if viewed from the perspective of the current growth of Neo-Pentecostalism expressions of Christianity. However, the idea of continuity indicates the failure of locals to disconnect with their pre-Christian practices and belief systems. Sanneh's silence in critiquing these effects leaves a void in the history of World Christianity and missiology. The idea of continuity presents both challenges and benefits in the center of gravity and paradigm shifts. On the one hand, it sustains the rise of Neo-Pentecostalism, which facilitates the rapid growth of Christianity in Africa. On the other hand, the appropriation of the theology of the prosperity gospel seems manipulative.

The Pentecostal Gospel has failed to disconnect or discontinue the pre-Christian practices. The challenge to prove this theory is that both the Bible and ATRs are used to support the continuity because of affinities. Therefore, if the pre-Christian belief systems are the deciding factors of Congolese worldviews that translate the biblical literature to fit the needs of the culture, it then becomes compelling to speak prophetically. That is exactly what Sanneh attempts to avoid when critiquing African Spirit-world and foreign missions.

4

A Congolese Critique of the Prosperity Gospel

PROBLEMS TO ADDRESS

Giving to Receive

THE NORTH AMERICAN EXPRESSION of the prosperity gospel has been retranslated into a *quid pro quo* corporation in post-colonial Congo.[1] As a result of its appropriation and domestication into Congolese expression, God is rendered a cosmic transaction analogous to banking systems. Nevertheless, prosperity theology that is rooted in Western models, as well as an African worldview of Christianity, has transformed the face of the global church. Neo-Pentecostals hold to the belief that, "Giving, being obedient to God's voice and having faith are seen as prerequisites for prosperity and to secure an assurance of economic security. Also, God's will is that every believer to be materially successful and wealthy."[2]

---

1. The term *quid pro quo* is an English expression meaning reciprocity, a favor for a favor, or give and take. In this pericope, this writer uses the term to indicate the characteristic of the prosperity gospel's philosophical framework.

2. Gbote, "Prosperity Gospel," 1. Gbote, an African missiologist, sustains, "The basic teaching of the prosperity gospel is that God wants believers to get rich or wealthy, but he cannot bless them unless they first send money known as seed faith to their spiritual leader or pastor who tells them about the plan. This approach was popularized by the American televangelist Oral Roberts in Tulsa Oklahoma in the United States USA it has now spread to other parts of the world, including Africa" (1).

A Congolese voice and scholarship can be legitimately useful to alter the sanctioned mechanism of the theology of prosperity.

Due to the increase in the prosperity gospel and its teachings in post-colonial Congo, the question arises, "Will the biblically defined gospel of Jesus Christ survive in the wake of the proliferation of prosperity gospel teachings in post-colonial Congo?" David Allen Bledsoe argues, "Prosperity theology clearly received its inspiration from North American proponents, but it finds the most fertile soil in two-thirds nations. The discourse, however, alters (i.e. Glocalization) for a significantly different setting than of the North America."[3] This factor of *Glocalization* implies that the prosperity phenomenon is not solely an imported expression of Christianity but a hybrid and transnational dynamic.

Neo-Pentecostal and charismatic pedagogies that encourage sowing seeds through aggressive solicitation of tithes may be one of the fundamental theological sources of incomplete holism. The prosperity theology poses a challenge to Evangelicalism as it mixes the biblical Gospel with African traditional belief systems. Bledsoe states, "Prosperity preachers exploit the poor, distort the Scriptures, and partake in and promote greed."[4] These pedagogies are the basis of the exploitation of the poor and sanction a socio-economic inequality.

David Ogungbile, an African scholar, states:

> The poor social, economic situation caused by the failure of African governments to cater to their citizens, leading to considerable uncertainty, economic disruptions, and social unrest, has inspired the theology and message of prosperity gospel of the African Pentecostals. As one speaking from the voice of considering the development and growth of prosperity gospel in Africa; discovers that the African Pentecostals have cashed in on poverty state of those communities and developed a survival and economic theology.[5]

In addition, Bledsoe believes that Neo-Pentecostalism has been a principal carrier of prosperity theology, but it poses additional and more

---

3. Bledsoe, "Prosperity Theology, Mere Symptom of Graver Problems in Neo-Pentecostalism," 302.

4. Bledsoe, "Prosperity Theology, Mere Symptom of Graver Problems in Neo-Pentecostalism," 302.

5. Ogungbile, "African Pentecostalism and Prosperity Gospel," 137.

complex challenges to evangelical missions beyond the prosperity message.[6] Moreover, Ogungbile reveals "Prosperity has become an indicator of African Pentecostals in contemporary times."[7] Evangelical missions emphasize spiritual prosperity in Africa, which is part of traditional evangelism. While the method of transmitting the gospel through evangelicalism was suited to African worldviews; the American prosperity gospel overshadows the evangelical vocation. However, as Ogungbile puts it, "The awareness and craving for material prosperity and wealth have become very influential in contemporary Africa. Several contemporary groups have developed a prosperity theology that is materialistic in content and context."[8] The mission of evangelicals is not limited to spreading the gospel and making disciples of Jesus Christ.

Sellers of the Faith

French journalists have used the phrase *"Les vendeurs de la foi"* to describe this phenomenon. This is a French expression meaning "sellers of faith." In the recorded story, the journalists explain how Bishop has become a millionaire through prosperity gospel teaching. According to the video, Bishop manipulates the consciousness of believers, especially the poor. He was a former boxer in Kinshasa and founded one of the largest *Eglise de reveilles*, or revival churches. He inter-mixed a magical healing initiative to gain the hearts of vulnerable poor communities. This is a serious concern to non-Western Christianity and is especially true of Sub-Sahara Africa due to its poverty and lack of adequate resources. Biblical faith should not be for sale or gain (Cf. Acts 8:9–24).

Bishop Mukuna and other self-proclaimed apostles demand or require their clients to pay consultation fees similar to medical physicians or surgeons. Many people are attracted to this movement because of the lack of affordable health care systems. They are required to pay fees to receive prayers and be seen by these pastors and prophets. One recorded scenario was the death of a ten-year-old girl named Merveille. Her parents trusted in the bishop's miraculous healing promises, so they brought their child to him for healing and deliverance. However, Merveille died

---

6. Bledsoe, "Prosperity Theology, Mere Symptom of Graver Problems in Neo-Pentecostalism," 302.

7. Ogungbile, "African Pentecostalism and Prosperity Gospel," 134.

8. Ogungbile, "African Pentecostalism and Prosperity Gospel," 135.

due to a lack of medical attention. One question posed was why the millionaire bishop failed to support Merveille's parents with financial assistance toward medical bills? Her death has challenged people to examine the movement which has bankrupted them for decades.

Maman Olangi's healing ministry is another case that reflects the spread of false teachings, theologies, and pedagogies. Olangi has become a multi-millionaire from the monies she receives from her clients. The heart of her message is the prosperity gospel: God will change your life. He will give you beautiful children, a husband, wife, car, house, and meet both your material and spiritual needs if you sow seeds and put Him to the test. It is also significant to note that in some instances, these prophets use black magic and rituals to cure patients from malevolent spirits and remove demonic substances from the bodies of clients.

The magical force becomes a counter force to overcome demonic spirits of the dead, witchcraft, and sorcery, which hinder people from living better and joyful lives. The number of these self-proclaimed prophets, apostles, and bishops within *Eglise the reveille* is increasingly visible while attracting emerging middle-class and business people who seek healing promotions and social lifts. These groups organize spiritual crusades and evangelistic gatherings, but in many cases, adherents are scammed.

Moreover, many Ngangas have transformed their profession from diviner to rising religious star, or self-proclaimed prophet to one who operates magical miracles and syncretizes the biblical gospel in the city of Kinshasa. The dynamics discussed are the basis of incomplete holism. The mixture between Christian worldviews and traditional belief systems are the causes of syncretized Christianity.

Consequently, many Congolese have failed to discard or discontinue their pre-Christian belief systems rooted in the practices of appeasing ancestors' spirits. The mistranslation and misreading of the biblical Gospel have led the body of Christ and the recipients to continue mixing traditional belief systems and Christian worldviews. Consequently, adherents are abused, exploited, and bankrupt. The underlying worldviews relate to which structural primal religions have not been transformed by the biblical gospel and syncretism; and the non-Christian, failure of classical Pentecostalism, evangelism and mission are emerging problems to address and to rethink theologically. In many cases, the gospel is being shaped or transformed by culture rather than culture being transformed by the gospel.

The Social Aspect of the Gospel

The social dimension of the gospel has inflicted severe damage to the body of Christ within Congolese societies. Christ's salvific message tends to be ignored, while greater emphasis and attention are drawn toward humanitarian concerns and social lifts. However, Amos Yong and others test the implication of the prosperity gospel as a tool to address social-economic solutions within the global scale. Nimi Wariboko, an African scholar with a keen interest in economic ethics and Pentecostalism, insists, "The most existential task facing Africans is economic development. Poverty and acceleration of economic development will be important for the flourishing of humanity in Africa."[9] This writer contends that a more balanced critique of the prosperity gospel is critical to understanding the prosperity gospel phenomenon.

As a result, Neo-charismatic and Pentecostal trends of Christianity, translated into a Western worldview, fail to provide transformative voices in Congolese society. Will post-colonial voices and theological worldviews within the paradigm shift of emerging Congolese scholars be able to alter problems of prosperity theology? Will the syncretistic character of Christianity in the Congo be redressed as new voices within the paradigm of emerging Congolese scholarship? These questions are central to this research as the author bridges a cross-cultural perspective of a liberating theology that is empowering to the recipients of the gospel rather than exploitative.

CONTENT OF THE CHAPTER

This chapter will bring a Congolese voice to the broader conversation of a global prosperity gospel within Neo-Pentecostalism and charismatic phenomenon. As a native of the Congo and survivor of the effects of mistranslating the biblical Gospel, this writer seeks to raise a concern that has been ignored within the paradigm of global Christianity. Compelled by the weight of accountability, this writer suggests a contextual hermeneutic that can be both a liberating and transformative force to alter the sanctioned effect of impoverishment. As Gbote discusses, "It is imperative therefore that the gospel is preached in its context, explained

---

9. Attanasi and Yong, *Pentecostalism and Prosperity*, 35.

well, and the application of the message in line with the actual text."[10] The outcome anticipated in this study is that the recipients will be able to hear the voice of Jesus from the text rather than mistranslated and misread voices and literature.

Given the implications and negative impacts of the prosperity gospel within the context of post-colonial Congo, this writer recognizes the pressing issues confronting his society. This personal responsibility has motivated him to engage the matter critically and seek answers to the prevailing concerns facing his community. These problems include syncretism, incomplete holism, schisms, hunger, economic and political instability, social injustice, inequality, and lack of accountability. Therefore, as a native of the Congo, a product of post-colonialism, an eyewitness and an offspring of the survivors of colonialism, this writer holds himself accountable and is resolved to engage the situation in a critical and prophetic hermeneutic by translating the text in a way that is liberating.

Therefore, in this section, the writer argues that the prosperity gospel is linked to materialism and spiritism and seen through syncretistic and anti-Christian beliefs because it bankrupts adherents both spiritually and materially. Self-proclaimed apostles, prophets, pastors, and evangelists claim to have been divinely empowered with apostolic authority and revelatory vision from God. This is due, in part, to their misreading and misinterpretation of the Bible, which allows them to manipulate their victims. On the contrary, for the gospel to be a transformative force, it must be separated from its Western character of progress and capitalism. Also, it must be different from traditional pre-Christian belief systems. The gospel must be authentic, prophetic, and a life-changing phenomenon.

In analyzing the root of the problem, it is worth noting that the Western imported materialistic gospel of the prosperity gospel systematically makes the weight of religion ineffective to alter the systematic issues which confront the Congolese. The emerging issues facing the Congolese are not limited to spiritual worldviews of demonic forces, theological deficiencies, sociological inadequacies, or cultural and philosophical dynamism. For instance, the US cultural worldview during the late nineteenth to early twentieth centuries of attempting to use the gospel to redress social-economic crises or issues has not been productive within Congolese Christianity. Also, the method of mixing Christian religion with the ethics of social science has not been useful in the Congolese context. In

---

10. Gbote, "Prosperity Gospel," 9.

other words, applying Christian ethics to social problems as they existed within the US in the twentieth century is not beneficial in the twenty-first century Congo.

The social gospel movement advocated by Walter Rauschenbusch and other social gospel proponents in the US failed to respond to the central problems facing people. The social gospel resonates with those Congolese longing for spiritual relief and material prosperity. In other words, the translated gospel in a Congolese worldview has perpetuated the Western-sanctioned structures of materialism, progress, and capitalism. Second, the Congolese post-missionary translation or retransmission of the biblical gospel has created a different Christianity. This is to argue that the current development of Christianity in the post-colonial Congo is a Congolese appropriation. This appropriation has been one of the bases for a perpetuation of the misuse of the gospel to meet people's physical, spiritual, and material needs. As a result, the tenets of the Gospel and Christianity in Africa have undergone an alteration. Despite its rapid growth, Christianity has failed to be a transformative force in the Congo.

This writer insists that the American-imported gospel has failed to sustain a radical transformation of nurturing discipleship within a Congolese religious worldview. Despite the rapid rise of Neo-Pentecostal and charismatic expressions of Christianity igniting the current center of gravity in the new Christendom, the syncretized gospel, as preached or spread in the post-colonial Congo, is not a transformative force. The announcement of the gospel of Christ must bring new awakenings that are transformational and pertinent to the holistic life of the recipients in terms of socio-political, economic, spiritual, cultural, and educational systems. Mixed methodologies of qualitative and quantitative approaches will inform an authentic translation of the biblical Gospel.

A SYNCRETIZED GOSPEL

The syncretized gospel within the Congolese religious worldviews is a missiological underlying issue emerging from multi-cultural and diverse religious worldviews. The systematic misreading of a translated gospel has syncretized Christianity in Africa. As a result, the body of Christ has failed to forgo its traditional rituals and belief systems rooted in mixing and blending religions. Syncretism is a global religious problem that needs to be altered for nurturing discipleship. One of the greatest challenges of syncretism is incomplete holism and a lack of authentic discipleship within the body of Christ. Nevertheless, concepts of syncretism, including animism, are imported Western terms utilized as African phenomena. These phenomena have been placed into a context of polytheistic religious worldviews in post-colonial Congo. The syncretized domesticated gospel fails to impact Christ's mission and salvific goals for the church in a twenty-first century context.

Missionaries' failure to address, redress, or alter spiritual cosmological issues faced by the Congolese is a critical missiological problem. This issue requires a solution. Though people are baptized and confirmed within missional established churches, they are still affiliated and active in their traditional gatherings, and people remain engaged with their primal belief systems. One critical question is whether one can be Congolese and at the same time Christian?

Missionaries' efforts to contextualize the gospel failed to impact a comprehensive model of discipleship and desired change in post-colonial Congo. Western missionaries' efforts to discontinue or discard traditional belief systems were unsuccessful. On the one hand, the locals' grassroots AICs' voice of social lift has appealed to Congolese believers. But the Western-imported expression of a contextualized and domesticated prosperity gospel lacks adequate metrics to ask critical questions to solve issues confronting adherents in Africa. Yet contextualization tends to place religion into a larger context rather than tolerating or accepting secular practices into Christianity.

INCOMPLETE HOLISM

Missionaries' efforts to evangelize the Congo were never, therefore, *la mission accomplie*. The syncretized gospel as a missional dilemma sanctioned incomplete holism. This Western-authorized phenomenon associated with the importation of Western Christian liberal expressions of the social gospel progress and capitalism have been the heart of a mal-translation of the gospel. For instance, the ministry of anointing cloth for healing miracles is often practiced due to a misreading of James 5:14 and Acts 19:11–12. Luke is writing in the context of a physician's mind, testifying about how God used Paul. This formula was never life-giving. It is the name of the Lord Jesus Christ that gives eternal salvation and justification through the blood of the Lamb. However, these practices of anointing clothes do not heal the sick as some still die from their sicknesses, such as cancer, malaria, and other afflictions.

Fusion and a combination between Christian worldviews and African belief systems have syncretized Christian religion in post-colonial Congo. A complete holistic and Christ-centered holism is critically needed because holistic and prophetic ministries are roadmaps to equipping genuine disciples and followers of Christ. However, incomplete holism means that the recipients of the gospel and Christianity receive half-truths. Missionary enterprises failed, therefore, based on the evidence of incomplete holism, to impact radical theology-sustaining change and authentic discipleship within a Congolese Christian context.

THE MISSIOLOGICAL AND THEOLOGICAL WEIGHT OF NEO-PENTECOSTALISM

There are not enough academic works written from the context of African worldviews capable of altering or addressing the theological issues facing the church in Africa. The underlying issues advocated by Neo-Pentecostals are spiritism, animism, syncretism, and demonic or spiritual power forces. The insufficiencies of contextualized theologies, scholarship, or exegesis are the fundamental foundation of inadequate solutions to address the ecclesiastic challenges facing the local contexts of the Global South churches.

Missiologist scholars and historians, as well as theologians, have recorded the impact and transformation of global Christianity with its multi-cultural and racial pluralities. African theological and missiological discourses give light to the emerging phenomenological reality of the rapid growth of Neo-Pentecostal and charismatic movements within the post-colonial Congo. Craig Keener suggests, "The global conversation about the Christian faith has begun in earnest in evangelical missiological and theological circles."[11] The authors stress the importance of multiethnic global readings of the Bible. This implies that the academic communities in the Global North must recognize the new emerging voices and church of the Global South. In other words, academic institutions and writings have to recognize God's move or revelation in the twenty-first century.

11. Keener and Carroll R., eds., *Global Voices*, 7–8.

The contribution to the scope of broader reality of the center of gravity and the shift in Christian mission and theology are critical. There is a need for shaping a globalized theology for a globalized church. The time has come when the mother church in both the US and Europe must recognize that the baton has been passed to the fastest growing region, that is, the Global South. Africans, until recently, were at the foreground of conversations. Today, they are eligible to take the stage, participate, and their voices to be heard. The strategy for a more global and multicultural church is to be inclusive within academic settings so that voices that were once ignored are given prominence and resources.

The syllabus to students in African seminaries across denominations must reflect African realities, African theologies, cultures, and mores. Neo-Pentecostals and charismatic misreadings and misuses of the Scripture took place because of a lack of African theological discourse or academic foundation. However, in the twenty-first century, some missional, connectional, and global churches such as the United Methodist Church and other denominations are struggling to overcome the global nature of its denominational character. For example, at the 2016 United Methodist General Conference held in Portland, Oregon, participants representing different regions, continents, and theological discourses wrestled to address theological differences over the issues of human sexuality. As a result, will the denomination succeed in maintaining its global face and unity, or cease to exist as a global church?

Craig Keener's observation is critical for a missiological and theological assessment of Neo-Pentecostals in the Congo. These authors illustrate Philip Jenkins' argument as a key to understanding the phenomenon:

> Characterizes the biblical perspective from those parts of the world as defending a high view of scriptural authority, championing literal interpretations, espousing a conservative morality, embracing the Bible's supernatural depictions of miracles and visions, and identifying closely with sociopolitical and economic realities of the OT. His point is not merely that the numbers of Majority World Christians and their new-look church cannot be ignored; it is that to take on the Bible cannot either.[12]

In addition, Craig Keener and others discuss the underlying issues related to global economic and market forces that serve as the basis of the numerical growth in the Global South. There is a great need for theological

---

12. Keener and Carroll R., eds., *Global Voices*, 7–8.

education to counter the self-theologizing character of the Congolese. Non-Western self-theologizing is key to understanding the Congolese reality of the rapid growth of Christianity. As Keener and others assert, "Professor Philip Jenkins has underscored the phenomenal growth of Christianity in the Global South (Latin America, Africa, and Asia). He has also observed that the wholehearted faith in the Bible embraced by Christians in these areas is key to this growth."[13] The theological discourse is critical to enhancing most growing Christian expressions of the Global South, particularly in post-colonial Congo.

Keener and others state, "We have a profound need for scholars from regions outside the Western world engaging the biblical text. In many cases, the social, economic and religious ethos of numerous countries outside the Western World shares significant overlaps with the world of the Bible."[14] Twenty-first century readers can, however, appreciate the African contribution to non-Western readings of Scripture. Congolese use the Scriptures and biblical stories as a shield against evil and demonic forces.

For instance, David Adamo asserts, "African Christians use Imprecatory Psalms . . . as an expression of God's righteous anger against injustice. . . . They believe that they are taking the offender or the enemies to the court of God as they repeat these imprecatory in their prayers."[15] He continues, "For many Christians in the West . . . it is done so perhaps only at a theoretical level. The African reading, by contrast, emerging as it does from powerlessness and spilled blood, provides a new dimension of conviction about the interpretation of these psalms."[16] It is crucial that Western scholars not ignore these vital contributions of African theological discourse and participation.

NEED FOR CHANGE IN THEOLOGICAL EDUCATION AND REFLECTION

Neo-Pentecostal and charismatic deficiencies, in terms of theological education or foundations, fueled the mechanism of misreading and misinterpreting the Bible. Nevertheless, Congolese self-theologizing efforts

13. Keener and Carroll R., eds., *Global Voices*, xi.
14. Keener and Carroll R., eds., *Global Voices*, 115.
15. Keener and Carroll R., eds., *Global Voices*, 116.
16. Keener and Carroll R., eds., *Global Voices*, 116.

and the theology of prosperity do not give accurate responses to the challenges facing the post-colonial Congo. A contextual and cross-cultural theology, along with an inclusive curriculum, can be empowering and transformative for Christians and readers of the Bible in an African context. Theological education is a necessity and an urgent agency in an African context.

Western scholars have written literature about Africa and the Global South in general but with little or no connection to the realities of Sub-Sahara Africa. Osvalla Padilla advocates the vital contributions brought by non-Western scholars, specifically Africans: "And yet in many of our evangelical scholarly and publishing circles, I rarely see a biblical commentary (to mention one medium of biblical scholarship) written by Africans or Hispanics or Asians. Biblical interpretation can suffer from a kind of provincialism when non-Western voices are not brought to the table."[17]

Moreover, William A. Dyrness and others opine that the twentieth century marked the birth of contextual theologies, various cultures, social conditions, and a certain way of experiencing the gospel. However, the grand task of the twenty-first century is to permit dialogue among these theologies. In other words, to appreciate the flow of the shape of global Christianity, theologians have to recognize various cross-contextual realities for constructing a global theology.

Yet, this writer observes that Christianity has become a global religion, but theological education in the US focuses on Western realities. Non-Westerners are trained within the Western culture, while their education does not match their respective contexts and needs. Even in Africa, academic fields or programs are often westernized, and methodologies of teachings are not suited to African worldviews.

As Dyrness and others put it:

> These changes would have deep reverberations within Western theological education. But outside of missions and some pastoral theology courses, not much has changed in the theological curriculum. Despite the dramatically changing character of the Christian church and global presence, the dominant theological paradigm studied in Western seminaries, and often carried by missionaries abroad, has been the received Western theological traditions.[18]

17. Keener and Carroll R., eds., *Global Voices*, 116.
18. Dyrness and Garcia-Johnson, eds., *Theology without Borders*, viii.

African theological discourse is still not discussed throughout the global Christian community. The twenty-first century Christian community and academic arena need to consider an open conversation to create new space for cross-cultural dialogue and collaboration in recognition of cultural diversity. In other words, a global theology that is deeply multicultural, transnational, and transcontinental is critical to constructing a model of the global church.

Therefore, the demographic shifts that are the basis of the changing face of global Christianity are to be appreciated and recognized. Referring to this shift in the global distribution of Christianity, Jenkins states, "We are currently living through one of the transforming moments in the history of religion worldwide."[19] Similarly, in *Globalizing Theology: Belief and Practice in an Era of World Christianity*, Harold A. Netland says, "The century has brought about numerous unprecedented transformations in the world. The pervasive impact of technology on transportation, communications, and medicine is obvious. Yet, arguably of greater significance, though certainly widely less acknowledged, is the enormous change in the demographics of Christianity worldwide."[20] These authors advocate a need to cultivate the contemporary Christian movement within the paradigm of a globalized theology and question what Christ's gospel means for a transnational global community of Christians.

In this context, Dyrness and others relate, "So it is not simply that the center of Christianity has shifted to the South (and East) as Andrew Walls argued a generation ago, but that the character of this church is undergoing massive transition: it has gone ethnic, even transnational."[21] Thus, missiological claims that stress Christianity's rapid growth without missionary presence or after missionaries left the Global South is crucial to appreciate the new look of the global church. Nevertheless, this writer argues that the church of the Global North is in crisis or great decline because Christians have discarded their roots of spirituality. As a result, the Western church no longer shapes the religion worldwide.

Dyrness and Garcia-Johnson further argue:

---

19. Ott and Netland, *Globalizing Theology*, 14–15.

20. Ott and Netland, *Globalizing Theology*, 14. Netland discusses, "Whereas, in 1900, the majority of Christians were in Europe and North America, and Christianity was identified as a Western religion, today most Christians reside in the non-Western world, and Christianity is in decline in much of Europe" (14).

21. Dyrness and Garcia-Johnson, *Theology without Borders*, vii.

The Western Church is in decline and no longer plays a significant role in defining Christianity; and that now missions will no longer be from the West to the rest, but it will be a reverse mission such as we are seeing in the Western Europe. In 2009 sociologist Robert Wuthow responded to these claims by arguing that the American church is not in decline and in fact is internationalizing itself and increasing its presence and influence in many places of the World.[22]

What does this change mean for theological education and reflection? Will the dominant voice accept and accommodate growing minority voices and theologies? Will the theological schools in the Global North change to fit the needs of the global church?

First, the Christian faith is changing. As such, there is one important thing to note: the church has become global. Christianity is not only a predominantly Western religion, but also rapid growth is taking place outside the West so that many Christians now come from places other than Europe and North America. Second, "In spite of these changes, the teaching of theology in most Western settings has not changed."[23] This writer would argue that the changing face of Christianity is a global phenomenon; therefore, its theological discourse has to be global, or universal, and inclusive. Neo-Pentecostalism has produced a different theology within the paradigm shift of the gospel of prosperity and social lifts.

A DIFFERENT GOSPEL

Neo-Pentecostals in post-colonial Congo have developed not only a different gospel but also a different Christianity based upon the theology of prosperity with a global outlook. Moreover, Congolese have contextualized and inculturated the Gospel of Christ and appropriated it into a different gospel otherwise known as a new gospel of progress and materialism. This gospel conveys a Congolese flavor that is contextually connected to primal belief systems. However, the Apostle Paul encouraged the Galatians' community not to accept a different gospel other than Christ's in his death and resurrection. The Apostle Paul asserts, "I am astonished that you are so quickly deserting him who called you in the grace of Christ and are turning to a different gospel" (Gal 1:6). Paul warns

---

22. Dyrness and Garcia-Johnson, *Theology without Borders*, viii.
23. Dyrness and Garcia-Johnson, *Theology without Borders*, ix.

the body of Christ against distortions of the gospel and false teaching enterprises that have become a dominant voice of the religion (Gal 5:4).

This writer argues that the body of Christ needs a factual, original, and orthodox gospel of Jesus Christ. This is imperative and urgent within the post-colonial Congo. This orthodox gospel includes the following fundamental basic beliefs: Jesus Christ is Lord. He was born, died, and rose from the dead for the remission of humankind's sins. Although Paul's writing seems remote from the perspective of the first century, the early apostolic community, his philosophy remains relevant for the twenty-first century global church. The globalized church, as the body of Christ, has undergone a massive mutation over the centuries. Yet, the body of Christ has struggled to alter false teachings and doctrines which are going global.

RADICAL TRANSFORMATION

The gospel of Christ has the power and full potential to transform the body of Christ. However, human cultures tend to transform the gospel. This theory of radical transformation implies that the gospel becomes a means for holistic change, altering the spiritual, emotional, physical, and economic status of believers. Radical transformation is an authentic regeneration of one's life. This radical change systemically requires engaging in a resolution by going to the root of the problem or source of the occurring challenge to create the desired change. Any culture change is always difficult because often the recipients are afraid to accept change simply because they do not know the outcomes of the change. Change is possible when the recipients are trained and equipped with the knowledge to overcome that fear.

As a result, many Neo-Pentecostal and charismatic preachers frighten believers using prophetic approaches as mechanisms to fuel fear and emotional distress within their clients. Some tell their adherents that if they do not obey and sow seeds, God's blessings and deliverance will be hindered. For instance, to address the issues of syncretism and mixing Christian practices with traditional belief systems, Christians have to be re-educated. Re-education is an extraordinary remedy to authorize radical transformation. Nurturing disciples is one step toward a radical transformation. This is the reason why a theological foundation which is fundamentally contextual to the Congolese milieu is critical for genuine renewal. An excessive emphasis on materialism, however, cannot sanction holistic and radical transformation.

In her article "Pneumatology and the Cross: The Challenge of Neo-Pentecostalism to Lutheran Theology," Cheryl M. Peterson argues, "There is a great concern about the new emphasis on material prosperity, especially since most prosperity gospel preachers do not address the structural reasons for poverty."[24] However, Congolese have moved from charismatic and Pentecostal movements, which stress the significance of speaking in tongues, spiritual baptism, visions, and dreams, to Neo-Pentecostalism trends that emphasize success and prosperity. The move has had little or no impact upon the paradigm of radically transforming the lives of locals.

The gospel is a transformative force capable of holistic change that challenges one's life. It is compelling to measure the force of African Christianity since Africa is minimized on the periphery of the global map. Nevertheless, while African expressions of Christianity have spread across the planet, there is still a long way to reach its potential in terms of radical transformation.

David Tonghou Ngong argues:

> Scholars of Christian Missions and World Christianity are swooning in celebration of the growth of Christianity in Africa suggesting that African Christianity is becoming an important player in Christian Missions and World Christianity. In fact, even some claim that African Christianity is transforming the West. However, African Christianity in the West suffers from double marginalization: the first is that it made up of those who are mostly marginalized in the Western societies and the second is that non-Africans largely shun African Christianity. Because of the marginal position of the continent in geographical map of our contemporary world, African Christianity is still a marginal element in the world Christianity, despite its rapid growth and spread around the world.[25]

Ngong's scholarship and argument suggest a careful articulation of the transformation of the Christian religion. This writer argues that despite the spread and rapid growth of African Christianity, a holistic transformation is critically or significantly needed to advance the kingdom in the new Christendom and post-colonial era.

---

24. Peterson, "Pneumatology and the Cross," 137.
25. Ngong, *The Holy Spirit and Salvation in African Christian Theology*, ix-x.

POST-COLONIALISM

A post-colonial voice can influence change upon the emerging global church. The post-colonial theory is an academic or intellectual discourse that analyzes, illuminates, and reacts to the cultural legacies of colonialism and imperialism. The post-colonial process helps to reclaim the missional and liberating side of the new Christendom, which also allows the reader to discover his voice and the sacred quality of the Hebrew Bible.

The sacred character of the prophetic post-colonial hermeneutic refers to the life-giving aspect of Jesus' gospel that liberates the poor. The post-colonial theory analyzes these elements in terms of power, wealth, race, and ethnicity. R. S. Sugirtharajah states, "Postcolonial criticism is a contextual tool to investigate the text and interpretation."[26] It is a tool to reconstruct social, political, and economic structures in the faith community as well as our own.

Sugirtharajah further asserts, "Post-colonialism examines and explains social cultural and political conditions, such as nationality, ethnicity, race and gender both before and after colonialism and it engages in a significant revision of how the "other" is presented."[27] This post-theory relates to the human consequences of controlling a country and establishing settlers for the economic exploitation of the native people and their land.[28] The postcolonial process helps to reclaim the missional and liberating sides of the gospel, which also allows the reader to discover her or his own voice and the sacred quality of the Hebrew Bible. This post-colonial effort empowers the weak and heals their plight and gives them a voice.

Post-colonial theory is a literary theory, a critical approach that deals with literature produced in countries that once colonized or are colonizing other countries. It may also deal with literature written by citizens of colonizing countries that take colonies or their peoples as its subject matter. The theory is based upon concepts of otherness and resistance.

---

26. Sugirtharajah, *Exploring Postcolonial Biblical Criticism*, 12.

27. Sugirtharajah, *Exploring Postcolonial Biblical Criticism*, 12.

28. For instance, Isichei argues, "The power and prosperity of the Europeans, and their military success meant that their religion was likely to be true. The construction of roads and railways and the increased security of travel meant that it became easier to spread the Christian message and often this was done by African laymen in the context of their ordinary avocations, but it was the missions near monopoly of education that was the single most effective way of attracting new Christianity." See Isichei, *From Antiquity to the Present*, 228–29.

Nevertheless, the essence of the theory examines the ways in which writers from colonized countries attempt to articulate or speak and even celebrate their cultural identities and reclaim them from the colonizer's perspective. The literature also examines the ways in which the history written from the viewpoint of the colonial powers or dominant voices is used to justify colonialism through the perpetuation of images of the colonized as inferior.

This post-colonial theory also enables Congolese people to discover the life-giving side of Jesus' message and its prophetic character. The life-giving and prophetic reading is a non-sanctioned theology of the Bible that promises the well-being of all. In other words, the prophetic reading is an interpretation of the Scripture that guarantees the welfare of both the evangelized and the evangelizer. It does not impoverish, exploit, or manipulate power and resources, as does the prosperity gospel. It is a theory and methodology of interpretation, especially of the scriptural text, that gives a voice and freedom to the recipients of the gospel.

Although the Post-colonial theory is a valid critique of the colonial system of exploitation, this writer first uses the method objectively to delineate the time and space in which this phenomenon takes place. Second, the objective is to alter the prosperity gospel movement within the post-colonial era of a Congolese context. A post-colonial method relates to prophetic hermeneutics because it empowers the marginalized to resist and raise their voices. Such analysis gives life to believers so that they are not exploited but are given the possibility to redress their social plights and live a normal life. It is an analysis that exposes and denounces the abuser as the accountable oppressor.

NEO-COLONIALISM

Neo-colonialism is a systemic representation of an imperialistic system in a new shape or a continuation of colonialism in a new style. It is a system which maintains and enforces policies of dominant powers and regimes of third-world countries. The neo-colonial internal oppressors walk in the footprints of former colonial powers. It is significant, however, to interrogate the socio-historical and political patterns as well as religious agencies that contributed to the colonial legacies. As Sugirtharajah surmises, "Studying legacies of colonialism extended and incarnated in the forms of neocolonialism such as globalization, free-market and multinational firms, and the media" is essential.[29] The prosperity gospel movement is one of the ways of re-colonizing internally the cosmological, spiritualized post-colonial Congo.

Moreover, the effects of the biblically sanctioned theology of poverty versus prosperity have created confusion and alienation in this formerly colonized community and contributed to the neo-colonial conflicts of the internal oppressors. The colonizer has been gone from the Congo since the 1960s, but the neo-colonizer has taken over the policies that sanctioned inequalities and social-economic and political exploitations in a new form. According to Césaire, "Colonialism is the root of real poverty because it affects both the colonized and the colonizer."[30] The former colonized have become the colonizers, and the oppressed becomes an oppressor. Hence, the methods of accommodation, negotiation, and reconciliation have had little or no impact. Some Neo-Pentecostals use biblical Scriptures to colonize their adherents.

POST-COLONIAL VOICES

Congolese writers must speak against any imperial interpretations of the biblical Gospel. Even though prosperity preachers offer hope and social lifts, their translation of Christianity causes inequalities and injustices. Therefore, prosperity preachers fail to be prophetic voices and redress the centuries of biblically sanctioned theologies of hardship. Consequently, the Congolese need a "pure gospel," an authentic gospel that is not covered or clothed by Western mores as well as African traditional worldviews.

On the other hand, the interaction between the Congolese and the rest of the world is to be credited. Civilization brought both social and spiritual enlightenment. It has helped the Congolese connect with the rest of the world. However, for such reasons, Césaire criticizes the "contact between Europe and Africa suggesting that there was a better way to interact."[31] According to him, "It is a good thing to place different civilizations in contact with each other. However, it was not the best way

---

29. Sugirtharajah, *Exploring Postcolonial Biblical Criticism*, 15.
30. Césaire, *Discourse on Colonialism*, 33.
31. Césaire, *Discourse on Colonialism*, 33.

to establish contact."[32] Human relations have to be equally and equitably shared.

Warren Carter's view of negotiating the Roman Empire is a comprehensive signal of opening a dialogue to address the underlying issues of neo-colonial power and redressing poverty. Elizabeth Fiorenza's way of critiquing the neo-liberal gospel of freedom is engaging that belief system because it has not liberated the colonized. Her approach is essential because the neo-liberal gospel is a form of social activism that suggests both liberal and conservative ways of interpreting the Hebrew Bible. The neo-liberal approach seems to be a comprehensive and prophetic, life-giving hermeneutic of Jesus' story.

On the other hand, the neo-liberal gospel resembles the prosperity gospel that is incapable of healing the wounds of those who have been oppressed for centuries. Musa W. Dube suggests there are "methods of rereading the Bible that resist both patriarchal and imperial oppression in order to cultivate a space of liberating interdependence between countries, genders, races, ethnicities."[33] Her method contradicts Carter's ideology of negotiating with the empire.

Post-colonial critical interpretations of healing and empowering the broken-hearted benefit both the recipients of the gospel of Jesus and the missionaries. In other words, the missionaries succeed in their endeavors while local people improve and develop their personal living conditions. Biblical literature read through a liberating approach helps to improve the human condition and communicate the sacred character and liberating side of Jesus' gospel. This liberating view allows the poor to move towards equality with the elites and to benefit from both material and spiritual resources.

REWRITING HISTORY

The Christian message must be uncovered by the colonial heritage and distinct cultures. Regretfully, the recorded mission history is incomplete and must be read, retold, and rewritten afresh from a post-colonial perspective. For Fanon, a text written from the standpoint of the European culture cannot be relevant to Africans. Fanon argues, "The post-colonial voice can decide to resist imperial linguistic domination in two ways by

---

32. Césaire, *Discourse on Colonialism*, 33.
33. Dube, *Postcolonial Feminist Interpretation of the Bible*, 111.

rejecting the language of the colonizer or by subverting the empire by writing back in a European language."[34] This writer suggests that rewriting the Christian story within the paradigm of the evangelized context or voice instead of the evangelizer is transformative and empowering. The indigenous voice is crucial for a productive Christian mission.

Consequently, there is a need to reread the Bible with fresh eyes and retell the sacred message of Jesus authentically. To rewrite and reconstruct the past of the people of the Congo is an urgent task. On the one hand, imperialistic strategies must be confronted, exposed, and rejected. Much literature has been written in the context of a dominant voice by those who have a monopoly and control over the printing presses and resources. Sadly, the Congolese have been misrepresented in both academic and public arenas. Finally, it is critical to reinterpret or translate the gospel with a fresh eye that inspires freedom, liberty, and economic development to improve the social and spiritual situation and promote a genuine method of reading and interpreting the scriptures. A prophetic hermeneutic is critical to reconstructing the history of missions and evangelism in post-colonial Congo.

Furthermore, a postcolonial prophetic hermeneutic serves as a tool to advocate and build up a scholarly and socio-political platform that is both intellectual and spiritual. Hence, there is a need to rewrite without leaving out the culture and contributions of people who have been historically oppressed and marginalized for decades.

RETELLING THE STORY

The story of Jesus Christ must be retold from the perspective of Congolese cultural patterns. Congolese oral tradition must be given place or priority in the exercise of transmission, retransmission, and translation of the gospel. Missionaries told the same story of Jesus Christ in the context of a cross-cultural experience. Some have translated the gospel and Christianity from the vantage point of Western worldviews because they were foreigners and received Christianity from their own indigenous cultures. The transmission and translation of the gospel and Christianity were covered by the foreigners. Although there are African translation teams who worked alongside missionaries, the native translators were not the main voices at the table by the time the translation was executed.

---

34. Edwards. *Postcolonial Literature*, 30.

There is nothing wrong with cross-cultural values, as the Apostle Paul asserts to the Roman community of believers: "How, then, can they call on the one they have not believed in? And how can they believe in the one of whom they have not heard? And how can they hear without someone preaching to them?" (Rom 10:14). God uses human agents as a resource to spread the gospel all over the world. Crossing cultural boundaries, the gospel becomes international good news or inter-continental, global, and intercultural news. In this writer's opinion, missionaries did their part; now the Congolese must take the mission of retelling the story of Christ from the vantage of Congolese worldviews while avoiding the use of syncretism.

THE GOSPEL AND SOCIAL LIFT

The prosperity gospel has served a critical role in the post-colonial Congo as a tool for social interrelation. Believers within renewal Christianity have stood in solidarity by forming networks and connections within and beyond their religious circles. This purpose is to respond to the social, economic, and political crises by working as corporate lending agencies of financial resources and capitals for social lift or elevation of standards of life among believers and beyond. In the wake of a pressing social and economic crisis and poverty, Neo-Pentecostals and charismatic Christians are committed to using the gospel as a means for social change.

Naomi Haynes asserts, "The particular approach to economic inequality and emphasis on material consumption that together characterize Copperbelt Pentecostalism work to foster social relationships both within and beyond the boundaries of this religion."[35] However, the gospel is not a predicament or a prescription for a social lift alone but a message of saving grace. Neo-Pentecostals and prosperity preachers use the gospel as a means for social lift, economic alteration, political, and social change.

The social lift phenomenon is one of the reasons this expression of Christianity attracts millions of adherents. The Pentecostal prosperity gospel is changing the nature of religion, as Naomi Haynes attempts to "show the capacity of this religion to create interpersonal relationships with a larger social world organized by a material hierarchy."[36] Even though the prosperity gospel has been used as a tool to exploit the poor,

---

35. Haynes, "Pentecostalism and the Morality of Money," 124.
36. Haynes, "Pentecostalism and the Morality of Money," 124.

it has also been used as an entrepreneurial engagement. Haynes states, "Prosperity preaching, insofar as it is part of the theological programme of these congregations, is characterized not by injunctions to give seed offerings, but by instruction in entrepreneurship . . . whose confidence in the promise of divine wealth pushes them into the marketplace."[37] The task of the gospel goes beyond the limits of religious movement.

The integration of believers into external life beyond their religious context is crucial to stressing the contributions of Pentecostalism to the economy. The prosperity gospel is not limited to material progress alone, but it includes health and spirituality as it has been altered from its transnational forms. In other words, the prosperity gospel movement has taken a local outlook. Therefore, non-Pentecostal churches have been Pentecostalized within post-colonial Africa.

THE INTEGRITY OF THE POOR

Poverty is perpetuated by a systemic culture of dependency. To overcome the phenomenon of poverty as advocated by Robert Reese, Congolese must take ownership of their churches administratively, financially, theologically, and in terms of leadership. Reese alludes to Glenn Schwartz's advice in the paradigm of Zimbabwe: "It was time for our mission to die so that local churches could be truly born with all the responsibility that we now had as foreigners."[38] This new post-colonial era in missions requires missiological independence and the freedom of non-Western churches. However, Africa is still depicted as a missionary field despite its rapid growth and role in the center of gravity.

This writer believes that to empower recipients to become self-sustaining in the long-term, missional agencies must cast durable and sustainable visions. Having a definite time frame when partners exit, the locals would enable the continuance of the missional project without depending on outside help. Partners should not do things that the locals can do by themselves. This is a problem created by short-term missions and enterprises. If Westerners continue to provide economic resources, funds, and financial aid, Africans will not be free but remain enslaved to the global church.

---

37. Haynes, "Pentecostalism and the Morality of Money," 125.
38. Reese, *Roots of Remedies of Dependency Syndrome in World Mission*, xii.

Europeans and Westerners remain the dominant voices as they have the monopoly in decision making. Dependency is an unhealthy reliance on foreign resources that accompanies the feeling that churches and institutions are unable to function without outside assistance.[39] Reese further argues that, "It is my fervent prayer that we might finally move away from dependency to healthy interdependence in the world Christian movement. I long for the day when we begin to operate in a healthy postcolonial paradigm mission."[40] Moreover, Reese believes, "Importing foreign methods of worship, pastoral training models, organizations, and administration cannot influence authentic African expressions of Christianity."[41]

Reese sustains that the dependency syndrome is the outcome of colonial legacies. In his book, *When Helping Hurts: How to Alleviate Poverty without Hurting the Poor and Yourself*, Steve Corbett suggests matrices of how believers might accomplish their mandate of Christian missions to alleviate poverty without hurting either the recipients or themselves. He suggests strategies of foundational concepts of poverty and principles of how missionaries might participate in services of relief, rehabilitation, and the development of locals and abroad. Poverty is the root of the prosperity gospel spread across a post-colonial religious landscape.

Consequently, in terms of a global perspective, the Congo has not participated in an efficient global exchange in a free market economy, including the freedom of the trade of goods and capital reported by the BBC.[42] In 1960, the Congo received political independence from Belgium. However, the economy is still controlled by the West. Western nations import and extract raw materials that are transformed into manufactured products only in Belgium. As a result, "30% of the product

---

39. Reese, *Roots of Remedies of Dependency Syndrome in World Mission*, 1.

40. Reese, *Roots of Remedies of Dependency Syndrome in World Mission*, xiv.

41. Reese suggests, "Imported methods of worship, organization, and administration. It involved foreign institutions that required foreign funding, such as schools, clinics, hospitals, seminaries, publishing houses, and bookstores. It meant foreign models of what a local church is and how it should operate." Finally, "it stood for foreign expectations for training pastoral leaders. The dependency that resulted consisted of a healthy long-term reliance on foreign funds, technology, personnel, and even theology. The ultimate tragedy of this dependency was that mission churches could not contribute to fulfilling the Great Commission but remained recipients of aid long after they should have become donors." See Reese, *Roots of Remedies of Dependency Syndrome in World Mission*, 1–2.

42. BBC WorldNews, interviewed January 17, 2013.

benefits the local people; but 70% is paid to the Europeans."[43] This writer believes that poverty is not generic or genetic. It can be redressed and addressed as well as cured by an ethical commitment and hard work. In addition, poverty is not a culture, and it can be overcome.

The integrity of the poor is to be given priority because poverty is neither an innate state nor a divine purpose. It is, instead, an intentionally and purposely created condition that results in a very prominent and unjust system. In fact, the systemic structures of capitalism that promote socio-political and economic policies between the first and third world result in economic conditions favorable to the first world and detrimental to the third world. Therefore, poverty is inhuman-made phenomenon, a complex social construct where every person who has breath possesses or has the potential to improve his or her life. When people work hard, poverty will be altered or reduced.

CONCLUSION

It is critical to re-establish and reclaim a hermeneutic that has been a foreign concept to the colonized and promote a prophetic proclamation of the gospel of Jesus Christ. That means those who receive Christ's words are to change their lives. The spiritual mission of Jesus is the need to release lower classes from their plight, redress their living conditions, and empower ordinary people, who are ignored and silenced, to raise their standard of life and inspire them to find solutions to their problems. Therefore, a strategic road map of evangelical methodologies must be developed. Among other post-colonial approaches, "enculturation" is to be given its rightful place to eliminate stereotypes that are constructed within social structures. It can be interpreted in a way that will encourage economic, social, and political liberation or release to give voice to those who are otherwise on the margins of the Republic of the Congo.

To sum up, the message of Jesus should be life-giving, liberating, and holistic. The gospel can become a potent tool for transforming lives. The gospel as good news is a welcoming message that recognizes the integrity of the poor, multicultural diversities, spiritual awareness, and the values and memories of people. People's memories shape their integral history and identity. Thus, this writer's approach to a contextual hermeneutic and

---

43. Africana Studies Course, Africa University Mutare, Zimbabwe, a course taken during the 2007–08 academic year, Mutare, Zimbabwe.

a prophetic model for proclaiming the gospel of Jesus is the path to answering the questions of poverty, as well as the misconceptions of African identity and awareness.

A post-colonial voice must be adequate, prophetic, and holistic to translate and retransmit the gospel of Christ genuinely. It is critical to recognize a theology that is deeply committed to answering the underlying issues facing the evangelized. Neo-Pentecostals, if they do not pay attention to their retransmission of the theology of the prosperity gospel, can create a dependency syndrome and a religious neo-colonialism. The African consciousness must challenge colonial and missional prejudice and the capitalistic policies that sanction poverty, social injustice, oppression, and exploitation.

5

The Rise of Televangelism: A Historical Assessment

INTRODUCTION

MASS MEDIA AND GLOBALIZATION have shaped the African role in world Christianity. Televangelism and social networks have reinvented or revolutionized Pentecostalism, radicalized charismatic expressions, and enabled the mass-mediated religion to be a globalized phenomenon in the twenty-first century. As a result, Christ's message is being retranslated and internationalized into various languages, cultures, and mores in the global village. Christ commissioned his disciples to make Him accessible to all people and received as a universal Savior in every cultural tradition. Mass-mediated trends, such as TV stations and FM and AM radios, mediate contextualizing theology as imported phenomena that have influenced the spread and resurgence of the prosperity gospel.

In short, this internationalization of religious movements is critical for a comprehensive study of the diffusion and reconstruction or revolution of the global church. Christianity's impact is being mapped as a comprehensive global and connectional religion. In his article, "Anointing Through the Screen: Neo-Pentecostalism and Televised Christianity in Ghana," Kwabena Asamoah-Gyandu sustains, "Televised Christianity plays a critical role in the process of the flow and diffusion of innovation [sic] ideas across the different religious contexts. Every neo-Pentecostal movement is thus a local expression of a global charismatic culture—they are rooted in specific local contexts and at the same time, transnational, international, or global."[1] However, the theological framework of televangelism translation categories of the prosperity gospel and social lift has radicalized Christianity in post-colonial Congo. African theologies must be given priority to engage the changing face of the emerging global church.

As Jeffrey Greenman and others assert, "If Christianity's incarnation is to succeed then, as a translation paradigm of African theology argues, our theological process must recognize African cosmology and engage in theological discourse along the lines of African categories of existence."[2] However, the appropriation of the American expression of mass-mediated Christianity, along with reproducing, selling, and trading video cassettes, sermons, gospel music CDs and DVDs, and advertisements have transformed African theological categories of "self-theorizing." These electronic expressions are imported phenomena which have been domesticated in the Congo.

David Maxwell observed, "What is new about African Pentecostalism is its recent growth, enormous vitality and its appropriation of the electronic media to the point that this has become part of Pentecostal definition."[3] In this context, mass media ministries have transnationalized Neo-Pentecostalism from the 1960s to the present within the Congolese religious landscape. The globalized Christianity of Neo-Pentecostalism, with its visual culture, has shaped the religious landscape so that Muslims and other traditional world religions have adopted and appropriated the media ministries as vital tools to reach out to millions for missions across the nations. Muslims also are doing missions and engaged in televangelism through media by giving food and clothing to the needy in the Congo.

Pentecostalization has transcended ecumenical cohorts. Even AICs, ATR, and Islam are being Pentecostalized. In her article "The Spectacular and the Spirits: Charismatics and Neo-Traditionalists on Ghanaian Television," Marleen de Witte opines, "A transnationality circulating Pentecostal program format has become paradigmatic not only for local Pentecostal groups but also for other religions seeking media success."[4] Her argument is important to understanding the impact of televangelism.

    1. Asamoah-Gyandu, "Anointing Through the Screen," 21.

    2. Greenman and Green, *Global Theology in Evangelical Perspective*, 138.

    3. Asamoah-Gyandu, "Anointing Through the Screen," 9.

    4. De Witte, "The Spectacular and the Spirits: Charismatics and Neo-Traditionalists on Ghanaian Television," 316.

Moreover, as de Witte observes, "What is so interesting about this new mass-mediated form of religion is not limited to the confines of the particular churches that produce it or to their media programming. It has become so powerful that it has become a model for the public representation of religion in general and is being taken over by other non-Pentecostal and even non-Christian religions."[5] The author argues, however, that there is a parallel between the traditional cultures of mediating the spirits and the older forms of religious mediation which relate to newer forms of the technological medium. There are similarities between traditional African practices of appeasing ancestors and technological media systems.

The only difference is that the traditional practices of sacred invocations of spiritism were done in secret wherein, only representative elders had access to communicate with ancestors and then translated the message to the people. The newer technology, visual mediation, is open to the public arena. Large Neo-Pentecostal and charismatic churches use technological means to spread the good news and make disciples of Jesus Christ. This explains the rapid growth and appropriation of televangelism, a consumeristic culture, and the transnationalization of Neo-Pentecostalism and charismatic renewals. Nevertheless, both the use of media and the prosperity gospel are the basis of the success of the new Christian expressions and self-theologizing process. The success of these newer Christian expressions is the spread of the prosperity gospel within post-colonial Congo.

In this fifth chapter, the writer assesses historic televised evangelism's impact within the paradigm of global Christianity and explores how this expression continues to shape faith in post-colonial Congo. Are electronic media technologies radically transforming the traditional expression of Christian missions or enforcing new paradigms of African theology? Religion has been used over the centuries as a survival mechanism and interventionist strategy in human affairs. Through media ministries, new churches are planted, and the gospel of Christ is spread across the planet. The revolutionary televised Christianity is a foreign import on the continent of Africa translated into African experience through an encounter with the gospel of Christ.

For example, the Congo had fewer Christian channels from the 1960s to the 1980s with the exchange of European evangelists and short-term missionaries on Congolese soil who revolutionized Christianity.

5. De Witte, "The Spectacular and the Spirits: Charismatics and Neo-Traditionalists on Ghanaian Television," 316.

For example, the arrival of Bonnke in the 1980s was the turning point of Christianity and televangelism. Satellites allowed people to hear the voices of preachers and see visual images. The post-missionary activities on Congolese soil and presence of new expressions of media ministries marked the birth of proliferated televangelism and social media, which globalized Congolese Christianity. As a result, today several television stations "promote Christian radio broadcast." This practice is established throughout the country. As a result, the gospel has gone viral and ignited revivals and revolutions within the religious enterprises.

Besides, there are foreign TV channels that import Western and European expressions of Christianity, Pentecostalism, and prosperity theologies; this includes entrepreneurial capacity. The media has both imported and exported the Congolese Christian experience. It has also translated indigenous cultures and faith in different local languages. The rapid growth and spread are the strength or golden quality of this expression. As Sanneh writes, "Not only is the Bible translatable into the languages of the world but so too the Christian faith. One does not have to become culturally Western in order to become a Christian."[6] The social media tech-culture continues to globalize Christianity and the theology of missions.

THE THEOLOGY OF SOCIAL NETWORKS

The theology of social networks is in the business of advertising the Christian message. This writer argues that advertising or promoting the message is good, but the manipulative mechanism of prosperity gospels in selling miracles in the marketplace and asking people to sow seeds corrupts the tenet of the transformative force of the Christian message. Also, these renewal expressions tend to bankrupt adherents. Western values of progress, the social gospel, and capitalism are being imported to the Congo.

On the other hand, technology and the social media network seem to be an essential means to carry out the good news of Jesus Christ and fulfill the Great Commission. Therefore, the tech digital culture approach has become a global and universal language, or way of communicating about God, along with a way to influence transformation in the social structure. In other words, with social media, the Congolese imagine the

---

6. Greenman and Green, *Global Theology in Evangelical Perspective*, 10.

ecclesiastical paradigm within the contexts of their missional and vocational perspectives.

Craig Detweiler and Barry Taylor suggest, "Getting connected is a central theme of the Christian faith—getting connected to God, to a community."[7] This connectivity relates to holistic evangelism. However, evangelism comes from having a profound and personal relationship with Jesus Christ. Detweiler and Taylor state, "We embrace pop culture because we believe it offers a refreshing, alternative route to a Jesus who for many has been domesticated, declawed, and kept under wraps."[8]

However, the great fear of religious institutions to carry online service communication includes the lack of physical contact with the audience or face-to-face interaction with the congregation. Thus, churches need to rethink how to connect digital social media and to use Western popular culture to communicate the gospel and make the church relevant. Thus, social media are a transforming force for the contemporary church much as the printing press transformed the medieval church.

Referencing Steve Jobs' "gospel" of innovation and imagination, Leonard Sweet, an American Theologian, historian and the E. Stanley Jones Professor of Evangelism, quotes Dianna L. Ciongio: "The iPhone did much more than changing the way America and the world interacted, it changed the culture."[9] People interact with each other on Facebook, Myspace, and Twitter just to be part of the global village and learn. Nonetheless, churches have accomplished work in television; thus, allowing for the gospel to be spread to millions of people all over the country. Now, with social media as a global technology, there is no doubt churches can spread the gospel of Jesus Christ through the Internet to the entire world.

AN IMPORTATION OF WESTERN VALUES

The Congolese charismatic movement has shaped new values through television ministries and the prosperity gospel. They produce and reproduce video cassettes to give to non-members. Therefore, churches in the twenty-first century need to advertise their activities and mission statements to be marketable. The church has a precious raw material to

---

7. Detweiler and Taylor, *A Matrix of Meanings*, 97.

8. Detweiler and Taylor, *A Matrix of Meanings*, 9.

9. Sweet, "Re-imagining Church: Ecclesial Mission and Ministry in a Globalized World."

sell–the good news of Jesus Christ, which heals and transforms human lives. As Craig Detweiler and Taylor posit, "Advertising has replaced spirituality as our shaping story."[10] "You can still see the religious roots of commercialism in advertising."[11] Thus, advertising for the gospel of Jesus can be a rewarding experience. Eric Liu and others assert, "It's possible to develop and cultivate imagination–at every concentric circle of human endeavor, from the personal to the global–and to show that we have no choice but to do so."[12]

Western values are transmitted alongside the gospel. When Western missionaries leave their homeland, they bring with them their mores, lifestyles, and languages. For instance, most renewal movements within charismatic and Neo-Pentecostal worship are practiced in foreign languages in the Congo. The English and French are bridging cultures to connect foreign expressions to the Congolese land. This includes partnerships with the outside world. Televangelism is an imported expression of Christianity, but it has been domesticated on the African continent.

Both local and foreign televisions, either owned by the government or private local indigenous people, have shaped Christianity in postcolonial Congo. For example, TV 5 and TBN are Christian channels that portray the lifestyle of foreign televangelists, charismatics, and prosperity preachers. These foreign styles, rooted in traditional Congolese belief systems, have systemically altered the face of Christianity. On the one hand, "The media are seen as an effective channel to spread the gospel of Christ to the masses; and to enhance an image of success, prosperity, and modernity to boost the charisma of the leader and manage his public personality. They also 'show' God's miracles to an audience outside the churches."[13] As a result, millions of people, such as politicians, successful businessmen, powerful personalities, and ordinary young people, are attracted to the movements. On the other hand, the media has shifted the focus to Christians from Christ. In other words, the media has idealized and materialized the Christian discourse.

One of the challenges of the rapid spread and adaptation of foreign expressions of Christianity has been the failure of mission-established churches to forgo traditional religious expressions. Yet the historic

10. Keener and Carroll R., eds., *Global Voices*, 65.

11. Keener and Carroll R., eds., *Global Voices*, 65.

12. Eric Liu and Scott Noppe-Brandon, *Imagination First: Unlocking the Power of Possibility* (San Francisco: Jossey-Bass, 2009), 12.

13. De Witte, "The Spectacular and the Spirits," 318.

mission churches failed to integrate the charismatic renewal phenomenon and neglected to recognize the African worldviews of mystical causality, resulting in the rise of AICs. The new expression of Christianity has been contextualized, blending traditional practices with Euro-American styles of worship. African drums have been replaced by electronic keyboards and amplified guitars. Andrew F. Walls argues that radical charismatics are African in origin. He asserts:

> Until recently the prophet-healing churches could be held the most significant and the fastest-growing sector of the indigenous churches. This is no longer so certain. Nigeria and Ghana . . . are witnessing the rise of another type of independent church. . . . Like the prophet-healing churches, they proclaim the divine power of the deliverance from disease and demonic affliction, but the style of the proclamation is more like that American Adventist and Pentecostal preaching. Gone are the drums the white uniforms of the Aladuras; the visitor is more likely to hear electronic keyboards and amplified guitars, see a preacher in elegant agbada or smart business suit and a choir in bow ties. These radical charismatics are African in origin, in leadership, and in finance. They are highly entrepreneurial and are active in radio and television and cassette ministry as well as in campaigns and conventions.[14]

Based on Walls' argument, this writer believes that televised Christianity has impacted new paradigm churches and Neo-Pentecostal streams of Christianity to redevelop a unique religious discourse and theological practices that are suited to mass media for missional efforts, enabling people to spread the gospel of Jesus Christ. This theological discourse is seen as the very core of the center of gravity and Pentecostalization of Africa. Neo-Pentecostal churches dominate the media system in the Congo, because they appeal to the broader public, and invite them to tune in and participate or watch their televised programs.

Moreover, they offer new dimensions or expressions of Christianity with promissory words such as "Impossibilities shall be turned into possibilities . . . your lack shall be turned into abundance . . . your failures shall be transformed into success." Expressions as "your life will never be the same," "come and receive your breakthrough," "God will change your destiny," and "the Spirit will meet you at the point of your need," promise

---

14. Walls, *Missionary Movements in Christian History*, 92–93.

deliverance and transformation.¹⁵ These Ghanaian examples of Neo-Pentecostal churches' practices of the "Voice of Inspiration" (hosted by Archbishop Nicholas Duncan-Williams and Bishop Charles), Agyin-Asare's "Miracle Hour," and "Your Miracle Encounter" are standard practices in post-colonial Congo. For instance, "Canal de Vie," in Lubumbashi, and "Planet Television," in Kinshasa, attract massive followings.

These four main Protestant Christian television channels spread prosperity theologies. "Sangu Malamu," meaning "good news," has many followers and spreads prosperity teachings. "Amen TV," was born out of T. L. Osborn's evangelistic ministries. Osborn was an American missionary who visited the Congo over five decades ago. He was a preacher from Tulsa, Oklahoma. He practiced healing and miracle ministries in the Congo during the 1960s. He used the media to reach millions. Megachurches were planted and birthed. As a result, his influence upon television ministry has been significant. "Assemble Chretien de Kinshasa" is another show owned by Bishop Mukuna. RTMV Radio airs this show, and the television program "Message de Vie" is broadcast to the entire country. The gospel through televised ministries promises Congolese they can make it, as God destined them to succeed and did not plan for His children to suffer fear, inferiority, or failures in life.

Media ministries in the post-colonial Congo demonstrate the African initiative and ability to appropriate Neo-Pentecostal expressions, style, techniques, strategy, and experience. At the same time, the Congolese philosophical aspirations seek whatever is Western as it is best. Many have sought to imitate North American and European lifestyles. For instance, arguing from a Ghanaian context, Asamoah-Gyadu suggests:

> This North American experience is the basis for those who conclude that the CMs are a foreign importation. Brouwer, Gifford, and Rose deny that the Christianity evolving through the CMs is a genuinely African construct, arising from African experience and meeting African needs. Contrary to this view, my contention is that the media ministries of Ghana's CMs reflect modern African ingenuity in the appropriation of Neo-Pentecostal techniques, style, and strategy in organization and expression. In Ghana's eyes, North America, with its technological superiority, military might, and material abundance, epitomizes the

---

15. Asamoah-Gyandu, "Anointing Through the Screen," 9.

aspirations of many young people, for whom what comes from the USA has great enchantment.[16]

Traditional African Christian theology holds that anything done for God must be attractive and beautiful, so Christians' lifestyles must reflect divine blessings. Also, religion serves as a survival strategy: "Africans seek for the solution to their problems in the context of religious and theological context. Televised Charismatic Christianity is popular in Ghana precisely because it offers Christian alternatives to the interventionist roles of traditional priests and priestesses from whose religions Christianity encourages people to turn away."[17] Similarly, in the Congo, televised charismatic Christianity has become a popular culture.

EVANGELISM WITHOUT FRONTIERS

This section will discuss three aspects of evangelism without frontiers or borders. They are as follows: from everyone to everywhere, the church beyond four walls, and the local expression of the gospel.

From Everyone to Everywhere

The journey of the gospel from different cultures, peoples, and places has been interpreted as the proof of its translatability, adaptability, and paradigm shift. As part of the global church or the body of Christ, the Congolese have distributed the Gospel to other nations and built churches among the Diaspora. The retransmission of the gospel and its freedom to be translated demonstrate that there are no limits for the gospel to penetrate any cultural pattern. In addition, this paradigm shift illustrates the nature of Christianity as a world religion. This paradigm shift is seen through the lens of an individual's response to the gospel of Christ.

---

16. Asamoah-Gyandu, "Anointing Through the Screen," 21.

17. Asamoah-Gyandu, "Anointing Through the Screen," 25. "In short, televangelism's popular religiosity has seriously challenged the traditional, institutional and denominational church. Televangelism has created popular expressions that have forced many pastors and denominational prelates to change the ways their churches are organized and the ways church life is practiced. Televangelism has helped introduce to congregations such things as entertainment-oriented worship, charismatic preaching, individualistic thinking, and anonymous attendance. . . . Instead of driving people away from the church, televangelism is changing their very conception of the church and its functions" (26).

Jesus has been domesticated within neo-traditional cultures, and Christianity has become a universal idiom for a global church and missions in the twenty-first century. This paradigm represents the fulfillment of Revelation 7:9, "A great multitude that no one could count, from every nation, tribe, people, and language, standing before the throne and in front of the lamb." Samuel Escobar avers, "Jesus Christ, God Son incarnate, is the core of the gospel . . . We can locate Jesus in a particular culture at a particular moment in history, for the Word became flesh and lived among us (John 1:14)."[18]

Escobar further infers that Jesus Christ's message is translatable. In this context, this means that the gospel dignifies every culture as a valid vehicle for God's revelation. People from different places and cultural backgrounds share a common faith in the global village, since the body of Christ has no frontiers or nationality but is pluralistic. People of different nationalities, places, and cultures accept each other because of Christ, and they live together in brotherhood and sisterhood. The mapping of Christianity has broadened, and the transmission of the gospel has become globalized.

Conversely, this phenomenon "relativizes every culture: no sacred culture or language is the exclusive vehicle that God might use, not even Hebrew or Aramaic that Jesus spoke because the Gospels we possess are already a translation from Hebrew or Aramaic into Greek that was the koine."[19] Translation was at the heart of Christian missions, and evangelism is the core of missions. As the writer states, "The heart of mission is the drive to share the good news with all, to cross every border with the gospel."[20] The mission of going to the other with the good news is the very reason of the existence of the global church. The theology that stresses the gospel can dignify every culture does not lead to a prioritization of traditional belief systems over Christian expressions.

---

18. Escobar, *The Global Mission*, 12. Escobar asserts, "He lived and taught in Palestine during the first century of our era. After that, the story of Jesus has moved from culture to culture, from nation to nation, from people to people. And something strange and paradoxical has taken place: though he was once an obscure peasant from Palestine, Jesus has since been welcomed and adored throughout the world, and people in all cultures and languages have come to see the glory of God the face of Jesus Christ. Moreover, men and women everywhere feel that he is theirs and artists from the past and present have proven the point by representing Jesus in their own terms" (12).

19. Escobar, *The Global Mission*, 12.

20. Escobar, *The Global Mission*, 13.

The Church Beyond the Four Walls:
An Evangelistic Approach

The reproduction of media materials and the growth of social networks are the reasons Africa is increasingly becoming the global heartland of Christianity. This social media outreach goes beyond the religious cohorts of neo-charismatics and Pentecostals, intercultural, ecumenical, and denominational lines. Despite the doctrinal alienation and organizational differences across the denominational spectrum, Pentecostalism has penetrated Methodism, Catholicism, Presbyterianism, and mission-established churches in the Congo. Pentecostalism transcends the social-religious world into incarnated spiritual worldviews. Also, the proclamation of the gospel is not limited to four walls, but it transcends cultural trends as universal good news. In the 1970s and 1980s, Jesus "movies" became popular in Zaire through missionary efforts to spread the gospel. However, the Jesus in the movie was a white man. Missionaries in many parts of Africa projected religious movies to present Jesus Christ to the locals, to whom He was unknown.

One of the challenges the church or twenty-first century congregation has had, according to Pierre Levy and others, is wrestling with the fact "that early generations decided how to evaluate and respond to cyber culture."[21] Pierre Levy defines cyber culture as the set of practices, attitudes, patterns of thought, values, and technologies (both material and intellectual) that develop, along with the growth of online connectivity in cyberspace. As a result, religious institutions around the world are questioning whether it is profitable to interact with these new technologies.

For instance, according to Leonard Sweet, "One of the professors recently began a program to offer online courses in business marketing. According to the BBC breaking news, he expected a few thousand, but, surprisingly, in less than an hour 12.000 students registered worldwide, a day later he had almost 42.000 registered students."[22] During the interview, he was asked, "How are you going to get to know your students and build relationships with them?" He replied, "The most important thing is to make a difference in those students' lives, even if I can't meet them

---

21. Levy and Bononno, *Cyber Culture*, xvi.

22. Sweet, "Re-imagining Church: Ecclesial Mission and Ministry in a Globalized World."

physically, they will be leaders and transform the world."[23] This writer believes that online courses, evangelization, or worship can touch many souls and make a difference in their lives.

Therefore, online social networks and connectivity seem to be a better choice in this global society because people interact online and have access to telephone lines, the Internet, and text messages. According to Susan G. De George, "Online social networks are web-based groups that focus on connecting people who might share the similar interests and activities."[24] In this way, the church can become a missional and connectional institute. For example, blogs, iPods, texting, Facebook, and Twitter have become part of popular culture.[25] The church as an institution needs to respond to this rapid change. As Sweet puts it, "Some religious groups continued to try to ignore the internet, closing their eyes to the changes happening in the culture around them."[26] The global church cannot avoid or ignore globalization. The church is no longer limited to four walls as people are connected online and able to be a part of the body of Christ at any distance. The disadvantage is that the body of Christ lacks intimacy and a closer relationship with one another.

Local Expressions of the Gospel

World Christian scholars acknowledge the move in the shift of global Christianity from the Atlantic North to the South. The gospel has been translated and domesticated into a local expression of second and third countries and covered by local realities or cultural trends. In other words, the gospel has taken upon itself Congolese characteristics. This shift of the missional activity rooted in the domestication of the Gospel is enabled by missionary endeavors and achievements that must be acknowledged or credited to both the recipients and those in the mission to evangelize. As Greenman and Green assert, "The great missionary movement of the

---

23. Sweet, "Re-imagining Church: Ecclesial Mission and Ministry in a Globalized World."

24. De George, "None of the Lines Outside Apply," 22.

25. A blog is also known as a weblog, a website where individuals or groups of individuals can add regular entries with comments, pictures, videos, and more.

26. Sweet, *Post-Modern Pilgrims*, 29. Sweet writes about leaders who have Alzheimer's disease: "We still love them. We remember and pass on their stories. But they're living in another world. They're totally clueless about the world that is actually out there."

nineteenth and twentieth centuries has yielded a rich harvest of burgeoning churches in the Majority World who have embraced the Word of God in their mother tongue and are now with Bible in hand, articulating Christian theology for themselves."[27] Self-theologizing is a root of the proliferation of faith in Africa.

Walls articulates the demographic shift and need to listen to the voices of the majority world who are living in minority communities. Also, he stresses the need for recipients of the gospel within the "Majority World to take the theological task on its own and in dialogue with the theological traditions they received."[28] Self-theologizing and translating the gospel into the vernacular are the basis of the development of local expressions of Christianity. The gospel of Christ is translated into local expressions that are mapped into the global church at the crossroad of multicultural and ethnic discourses. The gospel enters an interaction with the local expression and accent while it is covered with a global theological outlook so that people of different places and cultures can receive Christ at home.

Western scholars recognize that, "Western theology has a Western accent despite its claims to the contrary."[29] The gospel acculturated into the needs of the social location, or realities of the context, or the setting of the evangelized, or recipients, has become a universal message. Christ is welcomed in the Congo as a Congolese priest. Thus, the global church must be shaped by diverse theologies which are new to the former evangelizer or the missionary enterprise. The new theologies must be contextual discourses which Walls refers to as "New global theological reformation."[30] Africa has domesticated the gospel into a brand-new reformed Christianity with an African accent.

The gospel has taken the form of a local context, theological formulation, and social, political discourse. For instance, the accent of Christianity in the Congo is influenced by poverty and a longing for justice and freedom. It is critical to read the works of emerging scholars from the Global South to understand the local expressions of the global church within world Christianity from the perspective of minorities. God speaks to people within the paradigms of their socio-cultural context and

---

27. Greenman and Green, *Global Theology in Evangelical Perspective*, 9.
28. Greenman and Green, *Global Theology in Evangelical Perspective*, 9.
29. Greenman and Green, *Global Theology in Evangelical Perspective*, 11.
30. Greenman and Green, *Global Theology in Evangelical Perspective*, 12.

vernacular cultures. This generation is, therefore, witnessing "a new thing that God is doing," new accents of theological endeavors and voices arising from the land of Africa but mapped into a global form of the marginal groups who were for decades ignored.

NEO-CHARISMATIC CHURCHES

The Proliferation of Sects and the Birth of Televangelism

Mass media and technologies have enabled the proliferation of sects or renewal stream churches in post-colonial Congo. This is one of the developments of post-missionary activities resulting in self-theologizing. Tite Tienou and Andrew F. Walls argue that, "Christianity is truly a global faith because it is rooted in the multiple local realities of humankind."[31] These sects preach prosperity theologies and spread entrepreneurial versions. Timothy C. Tennent stresses, "The true matrix of Theology is not the study or the library. Theology arises from situations—social situations—where one must make Christian choices."[32] Nevertheless, the birth of televangelism fueled and proliferated this version of Western Christianity along with theological discourses in Zaire, known today as Congo. These scholars urge Western readers to rethink the church and consider the important roles that Africa, Asia, and Latin America play. They have often been regarded as a mission field, but they are now leading voices in theology. Also, Tennent states, "These continents matter theologically because they are the majority of Christians in the world today."[33] Despite the Western hegemony, the writer recognizes that theology is not determined by demographics but suggests a theological renewal. This means that Western thinkers must listen to the majority of the world. Theology is at the heart of missions, Christian choices, and decisions to engage people in their social, political, and cultural questions.

Nevertheless, mission-established churches have lost members who break away to form their own religious groups and affiliations. These are primarily offshoots, broken-off groups searching for spiritual, financial, and emotional answers and seeking to reclaim their past African traditions. They convey Pentecostal characteristics, mixed with indigenous

---

31. Tennent, *Theology in the Context of World Christianity*, xiii.
32. Tennent, *Theology in the Context of World Christianity*, xv.
33. Tennent, *Theology in the Context of World Christianity*, xiii.

expressions or heritages. The most interesting aspect of these groups is that they tend to choose to return to their traditional belief systems even though they do not entirely abandon the Western expressions or models of worship. They use technology, social media, electronic instruments, and televangelism.

Western expressions of Christianity were seen once as a gate of eternity; however, now, Christianity, or the Gospel, has crossed into a new frontier and entered new cultures which are enculturated and domesticated by locals. This is because Christian expression embedded in Western culture is the way Christianity was handed down to the Congolese. The liturgies, translated songs, theologies, and entrepreneurial spiritism dominate these sects. The mix between Western expressions and Africa is not syncretism but contextualization of the Christian expressions. Electronic churches and e-worship are succeeding in spreading the prosperity gospel movement.

ELECTRONIC CHURCHES AND EVANGELISM

Electronic churches have been the cause of the rapid growth of Christianity in Africa. The recipients are the evangelized who embrace prosperity teachings and social lifts as normative Christianities. As Walls surmises, "Witness the all-too-easy international transmission of the prosperity gospel. Through sophisticated telecommunications, in some respects the world grows smaller and smaller, making possible new ways of ongoing global theological discourse and closer connections between scattered Christian communities."[34] Electronic churches have replaced traditional methods of reaching out to people with the gospel. In some instances, couriers, missionary bulletins, and printing presses delayed taking the message across the country, but today, people are connected to the body of Christ through social networks, television, and other technological tools.

CONNECTING THE CHURCH THROUGH MISSIONS

Connecting to the church through missions is one of the core meanings of evangelism; purposely advertising church activities and creative ministry is one of the essential strategies to minister to many individuals.

---

34. Greenman and Green, *Global Theology in Evangelical Perspective*, 243.

However, the church cannot connect to the world in missions if its theological rationale is not yet globalized. This is especially true with the traditional missionary mindset that suggests the West is the ecclesiastical center of the world. As Tennent discusses, "We still see the West as the ecclesiastical center of the world, even though the vast majority of Christians in the world is located elsewhere. What African or Asian Christians are doing and writing seems so marginal to us, and it penetrates our own theological discussions only in a vague, ephemeral way."[35] This author further suggests that the Western Church has not yet fully absorbed how the dramatic shifts in global Christianity are influencing what constitutes normative Christianity.[36] If Africa and Asia are still considered mission fields, the church has not yet reached its global dimension.

One of the best approaches the United Methodist Church has taken is an initiative to create offices in other parts of the world, such as Africa, Asia, and Europe, so that theologically, these constituencies reflect the global and connectional nature and effort for self-theologizing. Yet some terms used in theological discourses and missional circles still have colonial connotations. World Christianity discovers these patterns to explain systematically the use of these terms which, in some contexts, sanction imperialism.

For instance, according to Tennent, some terms imply, "That the Western world continues to represent normative Christianity, which African Christians or Asian Christians take as their point of departure."[37] This writer suggests that when referring to churches outside the West, one should use the term, "Majority World," as per the 2004 Lausanne Forum for World Evangelization.[38] In the same spirit of attempting to deconstruct the terminologies which authorize theological inequalities, such as the terms Global South and North, Tennent states it is not

---

35. Tennent, *Theology in the Context of World Christianity*, xvii. Tennent argues, "We Westerners continue to vastly overestimate the role of our trained theologians, missionaries, denominations, and mission agencies in the actual task of global evangelism and church planting. We continue to talk about church history in a way that puts Europe at the center, and church history outside the West is received for those preparing for mission field or church historians pursuing specialist studies. We continue to think that our theological reflections are normative and universally applicable to all people from all cultures" (xvii).

36. Tennent, *Theology in the Context of World Christianity*, xvii.

37. Tennent, *Theology in the Context of World Christianity*, xix.

38. Tennent, *Theology in the Context of World Christianity*, xix.

necessary to name the rapid expansion of the church in China and refer to it as the "South."

Western missionaries had attempted to connect the church through missions when they crossed frontiers with the gospel. They were often as transformed as the indigenous people or recipients of the gospel. They were never the same because their exchange and experiences emancipated their theological endeavors and missional goals. Tennent uses Cornelius' conversion to illustrate the essence of give and take in the missionary enterprise: "When Peter brought the gospel to Cornelius's household, there is no doubt that Cornelius was transformed, but so was the apostle Peter. As he went away with some of the theological categories shaken, but in the process, he became a more globally minded Christian."[39] A cross-cultural theological framework that is global for a global church is necessary. Walls points out that, "Theological activity arises out of Christian mission and Christian living, from the need for Christians to make Christian choices and to think in a Christian way."[40]

Full Gospel Phenomenon

The term "Full Gospel" refers to the categories of Neo-Pentecostals and charismatic renewalists. When there is "full," the opposite might be half or an incomplete gospel. Self-proclaimed apostles, prophets, and bishops within the Global South prefer the term "Full Gospel" to separate themselves from the mission-established churches. These groups have domesticated Western styles of worship, electric equipment, technology, and prosperity theologies which characterize these charismatic churches.

These renewalists attract millions of adherents because of the supernatural appeal and power, warfare with the demonic world, deliverance, and miracles. For example, in many towns within the Congo, there are newly planted churches which describe themselves as "Full Gospel." These Full Gospellers have crossed frontiers, planting extensions of their religious expression. In other words, these expressions have cross-cultural aspects, so that these self-proclaimed apostles, prophets, and bishops can plant their non-denominational churches in other countries. These are national churches with an international outlook.

---

39. Tennent, *Theology in the Context of World Christianity*, xxi.
40. Greenman and Green, *Global Theology in Evangelical Perspective*, 19.

However, this is a paradox because the global church is rooted in local expression as Greenman sees: "The global church is literally next door--not over there but right here."[41] There is a critical need to consider engaging and learning global theologies as a roadmap to successful missions and evangelism. Global theologies imply the membership of people from different places and cultures who claim faith in God and belong to the body of Christ.

CONCLUSION

Televangelism has transformed Christianity as these new expressions of media and social networking continue to shape faith in post-colonial Congo. However, the electronic media technologies have transformed and altered traditional expressions of Christian missions and theology. This is one step closer to the real globalization of theologies, as Christians and scholars accept each other as a body of Christ and live in the paradigm of the identity of Christ's gospel. As Greenman states, "Western scholars can come alongside their brothers and sisters as servants, as co-laborers and fellow pilgrims without insisting on dominating the theological agenda."[42] Collaboration and dialogue are key methodologies to the success of the emerging global church.

This author suggests the internationalization of theological education to accommodate non-Western students' voices and perspectives. In other words, Christianity should provide space for non-Western theologies rather than silence them. As Walls puts it, "The discoveries about Christ that are made in the African, Asian and Latin American heartlands will belong to us all."[43] Western students and scholars should study non-Western scholarship to obtain a comprehensive picture of contemporary theological discussion.

41. Greenman and Green, *Global Theology in Evangelical Perspective*, 242.
42. Greenman and Green, *Global Theology in Evangelical Perspective*, 243.
43. Greenman and Green, *Global Theology in Evangelical Perspective*, 244. Greenman deduces, "There is no offense in working with standard thinkers of the Western canon. It is widely agreed that there is value for people of all cultures in wrestling with Aquinas or Luther or Barth on Christology. But it is now clear that working exclusively with Western figures means choosing to ignore some of the most fascinating and important theological discussions currently happening. If our investigation of Christology has overlooked the African questions about Jesus as Ancestor, the Latin American interpretation of Jesus as Liberator, or the Indian identification of Jesus as a Dalit, then our Christological horizons have been narrowed too quickly" (244).

Similarly, Craig Keener and M. Daniel Carroll R. discuss that,

> At present, Western Christians retain more resources and in academic circles often continue to focus on their own smaller constituencies to the neglect of the needs of the global church. Many experts today argue that it is time for more Western biblical interpreters to begin passing the baton, to begin partnering with emerging scholars in the Majority World for the sake of the global church.[44]

This globalizing theology results in self-theologizing, as Craig Ott and others explain in the book *Globalizing Theology: Belief in an Era of World Christianity*. These writers discuss what the gospel of Jesus Christ means for multicultural and multiethnic communities.[45] At the same time, William A. Dyrness and his colleagues make the point that,

> The Christian faith is changing: however, one frames the changes, clearly the church has gone global. Not only is Christianity no longer predominantly a Western religion, but also its most rapid growth today is outside the West so that most Christians now come from places other than Europe and North America. But second, in spite of these changes, the teaching of theology in most Western settings has not changed.[46]

Even though the church is becoming more global, the syllabi tend to reflect the narrow perspective of the Western world. Promoting honest dialogue among theologies of the global church is one of the golden tasks of the twenty-first century global church and Christianity.

---

44. Keener and Carroll R., eds., *Global Voices*, 1.
45. Ott and Netland, *Globalizing Theology*, 15.
46. Dyrness and Garcia-Johnson, eds., *Theology without Borders*, ix.

6

Western Influence and Its Enculturation

INTRODUCTION

WESTERN EUROPEAN CIVILIZATIONS AND modernity influenced African Christianity by constructing some of its missiological structure and theological discourse at the dawn of the late nineteenth and early twentieth century. Nevertheless, the same epoch signaled the rise of social gospel theologies in North America promoted by Walter Rauschenbusch. The 1910 scholars have often regarded the Edinburgh missionary conference as a historic moment, and the turning point of the current shift in the center of gravity symbolized by multicultural encounters enhanced cross-cultural diffusion and Christian awakenings.[1]

---

1. Walls, *The Cross-Cultural Process in Christian History*, 53. Walls rightly states, "The World Missionary Conference, Edinburg 1910, has passed into Christian legend. It was a landmark in the history of mission, the starting point of the modern theology of mission. The high point of the Western missionary movement and the point of which it declined, the launch pad of modern ecumenical movement, the point at which Christians began to glimpse something of what a world church would be like" (53).
  Referencing the Ephesians movement, he argues, "The purpose of theology is to make or clarify Christian decisions. Theology is about choices; it is the attempt to think in a Christian way. Moreover, the need for choice and decision arises from specific settings in life. In this sense, the theological addenda are culturally induced, and the cross-cultural diffusion of Christian faith inevitably makes creative religious activity a necessity or significant. The materials for theology are equally culturally conditioned. They are inevitably the materials at hand the situation where the occasion for a decision has arisen, in interaction with the biblical material" (79).

The twenty-first century Christian awakenings or revivals have brought about the rise of prosperity theologies and Neo-Pentecostalism in post-colonial Congo. The Pentecostalization of Africa and the indigenization of the Gospel are illustrations of the geographical shift in the center of gravity and the internationalization of the church. As a result, the global church is no longer located in the West, but it is now situated next door in local neighborhoods.[2] Pentecostalism and evangelicalism have increasingly been altered into global and fresh expressions with an innovative indigenous makeup. Despite Africa's marginal position on both the prehistoric and modern geographical map, the continent has been recognized, or seen and appreciated, as one of the leading forces and new heartlands of global Christianity.

As Jeffrey P. Greenman and others posit, "The great missionary movement of the nineteenth and twentieth centuries has yielded a rich harvest of burgeoning churches in the Majority World which have embraced the Word of God in their mother tongues and now are with the Bible in hand, articulating Christian theology for themselves."[3] The recipients, or evangelized sister churches, are better equipped and able to question the role of Christianity from their personal everyday life experiences that have, in the past, been subjugated by perpetual civil wars, tribalism, poverty, corruption, and social injustices. The majority of world Christians are now conscious of the importance of their personal interaction with the gospel concerning other cultural worldviews (Cf. 1 Cor 9:19–23).

Moreover, in his book, *Theology in the Context of World Christianity: How the Global Church is Influencing the Way we Think About and Discuss Theology*, Timothy C. Tennent asserts, "The nineteenth-century missionaries planted the seeds for a future twenty-first-century Christian harvest beyond anything they could have imagined during their lifetime."[4]

In the twentieth century, several emerging Western Pentecostals, such as Jimmy Swaggart, Reinhard Bonnke, and T. L. Osborn, exported

---

2. Greenman and Green discuss, "There is a surprise here since we discover that what we thought was global theological discourse is part of the discussion right next door. If we open the window we can hear the drum circle and the voices that exclaim Gloria a Dios; This global discourse brings us home again to a multicultural church that has also become self-theologizing." Greenman and Green, *Global Theology in Evangelical Perspective*, 10.

3. Greenman and Green, *Global Theology in Evangelical Perspective*, 9.

4. Tennent, *Theology in the Context of World Christianity*, 6.

social gospel theologies. These theological trends prepared the terrain for a massive acceptance of prosperity theologies and health and wealth teachings that penetrated the heart of Sub-Saharan Africa, particularly in the Republic of Zaire, today recognized or known as the Democratic Republic of the Congo. Nevertheless, their ministries were the turning point of the paradigm shift of Christian theologies in Africa. The 1960s-1980s foreign ministries in the Congo were the seedbed for the charismatic and Neo-Pentecostal proliferation of Western-made theologies or belief systems.

These types of Western-exported Christian expressions paved the way for the twenty-first century's resurgence of theological discourses in Africa. For instance, Oral Roberts, Kenneth Hagin, Bruce Wilkinson, Creflo A. Dollar, and Joel Osteen are printing, selling, and exporting their prosperity literature across the African continent. As a result, African Christians read the emerging North American key philosophical and Christian theologies which state that one cannot be a Christian and at the same time live in poverty. The miracle is in the power of your tongue and the spoken word of faith. Bonnke proclaimed, "Africa shall be saved" as a voice crying for liberation and reclaiming freedom.

Moreover, Bonnke's appeal was massively received in Sub-Saharan Africa as a prophetic voice in a time of socio-political uprisings and economic disaster. His prediction echoed a strategic plan not only for the liberation of Africans but also for planting "Christ for all Nations," a Neo-Pentecostal renewal branch which preached and spread prosperity gospels in the Congo and beyond. Dollar states:

> The Bible makes it so very clear: preach the gospel to the poor. You do not have to be poor anymore. Poverty is a curse. Jesus came to set us free from the curse of the law. Sin, death, sickness, and poverty are part of that curse. The Christian quest for personal success and prosperity was exalted in Bruce Wilkinson's 2001 blockbuster, *The Prayer of Jabez*, which sold some eight million copies in its first two years in print.[5]

This chapter examines how North American theologies of social and prosperity gospel movements are shaping the Congolese theological discourse and Christian worldview. People such as Swaggart, Osborne, and Bonnke's ministries in the twentieth century exported Western theologies of social gospels in the Republic of Zaire; these are regarded as

---

5. Jenkins, *The New Faces of Christianity*, 90–91.

the basis for the current surging phenomenon of the prosperity gospel movement. The social gospel movement and prosperity theologies were seen as a challenge to the evangelical mandate for a faithful translation and retransmission of the biblical Gospel and Christianity in Africa. Will Andrew Walls' pilgrim and indigenizing principles be useful for a genuine retransmission of the gospel in a post-colonial Congo?[6]

WESTERN INFLUENCE

In looking at the influence of the West, this research will scrutinize numerous aspects related to the subject. It will examine the following: Cross-cultural transmission of the gospel, prosperity theologies, missional impact and evangelism, social gospel, liberation theologies, enculturation of the gospel, contextualization of the gospel, and traditional evangelism.

Cross-Cultural Transmission of the Gospel

The cross-cultural process is the matrix sustaining Christianity and the survival of the Gospel when people from different places and cultures interact and become the body of Christ. The intercultural relationships among cultures make Christianity a universal religion and translatable. Tennent argues, "The cross-cultural transmission of Christian faith has always been integral to the survival of Christianity. Andrew Walls among others, has pointed out the peculiar nature of Christian expression through history, that it has been one of serial, not progressive growth."[7]

---

6. According to Walls, "The pilgrim principle is the universal force of the gospel that transcends all the particulars of our own cultural background and gives us what Walls calls a common adaptive past, whereby we are linked to the people of God in all generations. The pilgrim principle emphasizes our common or collective identity in Jesus Christ, quite apart from our particular language, culture, or background. In contrast, the indigenizing principle is the particular force of the gospel that reminds us that the gospel does penetrate and become rooted in the specific particularities of our cultural life. We live out our Christian lives within specific contexts, each of which has its own peculiar challenges and opportunities." See Tennent, *Theology in the Context of World Christianity*, 12.

7. Tennent, *Theology in the Context of World Christianity*, 12. Tennent argues, "The purpose of this brief snapshots is to underscore the fact that the lifeblood of Christianity is found in its ability to translate itself across new cultural and geographic barriers; and to recognize that areas that once were the mission field can, over time

Christianity has no single or unique geographical center; therefore, because of its cross-cultural geographical and theological frontiers for its retransmission and translation, Christ's message is accessible in multiple languages and cultures (Cf. Acts 2:7–8).

Robert suggests, "It can be argued, therefore that, the late twentieth-century was the greatest period of cross-cultural expression in the history of Christianity. It seems that in the twenty-first century, no one culture will be the dominant force."[8] She further sustains, "The story of Jesus is repeatedly translated anew. Because of its embodiment in human cultures–an idea that theologians refer to as incarnation–the Christian message has outlasted clans and tribes, nations and empires, monarchies, democracies and military dictatorships."[9]

The reason for this durability is, in part, because the Gospel is culturally and geographically translatable. So, as universal good news, the Gospel remains good news. It has the power to penetrate any culture, nationality, places, peoples, or continents and, at the same time, arrive at or settle in a new home. However, it is critical to understand that every culture possesses both positive and negative prototypes. Christ's gospel contains a supernatural power to overcome cultural trends and blind spots.

Walls posits, "Every culture in every age has blind spots and biases that we are often oblivious to, but which are evident to those outside of our culture or time."[10] Theological exchange across the spectrum of nations and cultures is critical for equipping the global church to face challenges resulting from social ills and human inadequacies. Hence, in the twenty-first century, the global church needs a theology that is translatable and reflects a cross-cultural expression of the Christian gospel.

Theological education is critical for the growing African Christian community to alter self-theologizing and spontaneity. Also, cross-cultural

---

become the very heart of Christian vitality. While those sectors or regions that were once at the heart can lose faith, they once espoused. Jerusalem, Antioch, North Africa, and Constantinople were all at one time the center of Christian vibrancy. All of these places have only a tiny remnant of Christianity remaining and, except for Jerusalem, are almost entirely Islamic. In contrast places like Lagos, Nigeria, and Soul, South Korea, where the presence of Christianity at one time seemed almost unimaginable, are today vibrant centers of the Christian faith." See Tennent, *Theology in the Context of World Christianity*, 6.

8. Robert, *Christian Mission*, 70.
9. Robert, *Christian Mission*, 8.
10. Tennent, *Theology in the Context of World Christianity*, 12.

theological education is needed for a truly global church that honors Christ's mandate and exemplifies the Great Commission. His mandate is a cross-cultural mission beginning at a grassroots level and proceeding to the global community. Therefore, even people who were once ignored and lived at the periphery of the geo-historic map are now recognized as part of the global church. As G. C. Oosthuizen says, "Attention should be seriously given to the development of an indigenous liturgy."[11] He further argues, "Theological education is perhaps the main focus in the development of young Churches in Africa. Theological education should not just be limited to the so-called ministry but should also reach the laity."[12]

However, theologies produced in the US are peculiar to Congolese worldviews, and they are not able to answer systemic questions arising within the recipient's context or cross-culture because they are not universal but "peculiar." The gospel as a force is a pervasive message when it crosses frontiers, transforms the recipients' cultural worldview, and recognizes them as part of God's family.

Prosperity Theologies

Prosperity theologies that encourage Christians to sow seeds in exchange for divine blessings are reshaping traditional African religion. As a result, prosperity theologies have been fashioned into local expressions while retaining a global outlook. While the nineteenth century exemplified a turning point for the gospel to cross frontiers into Africa, the dawn of the twentieth century marked the birth of prosperity theologies within the post-colonial Congo. These North American expressions of Christian worldviews of self-progress and capitalism have been well received within the Congolese religious worldviews. Due to its geographical and cross-cultural translatability, the gospel has been trans-nationalized and enabled to cross frontiers as well as survive in its new home.

This writer argues that during the post-colonial era, emerging generations have witnessed a significant move of geographic and cultural

---

11. Oosthuizen, *Post-Christianity in Africa*, 8. Oosthuizen observes the need to pay attention to indigenous development: "There are Churches which transplant what they have received in *toto*, with the result that no spontaneous or natural development can ever take place. Every form of indigenous expression has been discouraged, without ever being studied. The Church in Africa was forced to continue a parasitic mode of existence because no scope was given to its spontaneous development"(8).

12. Oosthuizen, *Post-Christianity in Africa*, 8.

transmissions of the biblical Gospel. The proliferation of these religious or theological expressions of prosperity teachings across the continent of Africa and beyond are proof of the shift in theological discourses.

Missional Impact and Evangelism

Missional impact arises from the desire to evangelize; the activity of one taking the gospel to a foreign culture and crossing socio-geographical frontiers. However, the activity of crossing frontiers with a mandate to share the gospel with people of different places was rooted in the process of trade, including trade ships and freight. From the 1400s to 1800s, missionaries sailed to the shores of the Congo through the merchant ship's trade routes. Elizabeth Isichei records, "The first Portuguese vessel anchored off the Zaire river in 1483. As in the West Africa, it was a tragedy that the European brought not only Christianity but slave trade."[13] Missionaries chose to use the trade or commerce routes to take the gospel to foreign nations because it seemed like one of the safest ways for them to travel abroad during a time marked by violence.

Even though missionary endeavors may have been linked to colonialism and imperial legacies, the missionary enterprise was a genuine response to the Great Commission (Matt 28:18–20). Evangelism was done primarily by educated or trained local evangelized indigenous people who were sent to share the gospel with their fellow villagers. Missionaries in this respect played a role as scholars, pastors, and instructors. Robert says, "Postcolonial perspectives vary widely, but in general both the missionary and the convert are treated as agents of hybridity, as cultural brokers in the border-crossing production of worldviews."[14] According to her, "The evangelization of the world . . . is not chiefly a European and American enterprise, but an Asiatic and African enterprise."[15]

13. Isichei, *From Antiquity to the Present*, 63.

14. Robert, *Christian Mission*, x. Robert asserts, "But, another challenge is that the historiography of Christian mission has been changing rapidly. Before the mid-twentieth century, a narrative of European expansion documented the field. By the mid-1960s, the subject of Christian mission—if noticed at all—was treated as a form of Western hegemonic discourse wedded to economic and cultural imperialism, or European colonialism. By the late twenty century historians emphasized the complexity of intercultural and interreligious encounters, including the need to put indigenous leaders at the center of the picture" (x).

15. Robert reports "During the 1960s, the voices of young nationalists grew louder in national and international churches councils, and they accused missionaries of

This writer recognizes that missional principles might have been influenced by business, commerce, or trade activities, but the primary concern of men and women in missionary work drove them to take risks to tell the story of Jesus Christ. On the other hand, Oosthuizen argues, "Livingston blazed the trail for Christianity and commerce. If Christianity can utilize politics in its service, why can't the peoples of Africa employ Christianity for their political ends?"[16] Oosthuizen's argument implies that missionaries were part of an imperial project and Christianity was an intentional force to civilize Africans.

Yet, the term "missions" must be analyzed critically to understand the impact of missions and evangelism in the post-colonial Congo. Robert defines the concept of missions from a missional and anthropological lens. She states, "The movement of Christianity from one culture to another can be explained by the concept mission. The word mission comes from the biblical Greek word for sending."[17] The history of Christian missions, as recorded in the transcripts or pages of the gospels, reflects an imperative mandate which traces its history 2,000 years ago. The mandate instructs Christ's disciples to traverse the globe and make disciples of Jesus Christ for the transformation of the world. In this respect, the Great Commission, as stated in Matthew 28:18–20 (Also Cf. Mark 16:15–16; Luke 24:46–47; John 20:21; Acts 1:8), is a sanctioning missionary strategy which brought about massive shifts regarding intercultural encounters and cross-cultural acceptance.

---

paternalism and failing to turn over church leadership structures to national control quickly enough. In the early 1970s, leaders of Christian councils in the South Pacific, Southeast Asia, Latin America, and Africa called for a moratorium on the sending of foreign missionaries so they could break long-term patterns of dependency that had been established during the colonial era. The paradox of the anti-missionary sentiment of mid-twentieth century was that mission education had created the opportunities and climate for indigenous leadership" (68).

16. Oosthuizen, *Post-Christianity in Africa*, 6.

17. Robert, *Christian Mission*, 1. Robert poses a critical question: "How did Christianity get to be diverse and widespread? Christianity like Islam is a sending religion. Within its philosophical structure is the idea of universality – that the message it proclaims about Jesus Christ should be shared with all peoples. Its sacred texts the Bible contains missionary documents that command Jesus' followers to go into the entire world. Within its 2000-years history is myriad examples of Christians deliberately being sent or else informally crossing geographic or cultural barriers and founding new groups of believers wherever they go. New groups in turn launch missions of their own" (1).

William C. Dyrness surmises that in order "to do theology in a global context [one] must begin by taking into account the realization that the Western ways are no longer unique, superior, or unsurprised."[18] Global Pentecostalism has proven itself to be successful when missionaries cross frontiers because it tends to find accessible resources available in primal belief systems within the receiving culture, or elements that resemble the missionaries' chosen expression of their faith. However, both the missionary and recipients are considered agents who engage in missional encounters and witnesses of the redemptive grace of the gospel and the cross of Christ. Thus, the meaning of Christian mission is integral to Christianity as a world religion that "exists across time, space, and cultures."[19]

Social Gospel

The North American social gospel prepared the terrain for the theologies of social lift and the prosperity gospel. Walter Rauschenbusch attempted to utilize Christianity and the gospel to reform or alter the socio-political and economic crises in the US. His pastoral approach reshaped Protestantism and brought in a new era of evangelical Christianity. In the wake of the revolutionary industrialization of North America, the rise of social crises, economic inequality, poverty, and social injustices, Rauschenbusch's personal experience was affected by the number of funerals he conducted for children in Hell's Kitchen, New York City, a place for immigrants. His experience was a turning moment in his theological shift that resulted in the application of the gospel for social change.[20]

---

18. Dyrness and Garcia-Johnson, eds., *Theology without Borders*, 20.

19. Dyrness and Garcia-Johnson, eds., *Theology without Borders*, xi.

20. Wendy J. Deichmann holds, "The social gospel movement in the United States began as a faith-based, grassroots movement of laity and clergy in the aftermath of Civil War. During this era, American society faced extreme levels of social instability resulting not only from wartime trauma and loss but also relocation of massive numbers of those emancipated from slavery, a rapidly accelerated pace of both industrialization and urbanization and unprecedented waves of immigration. In addition to the obvious, dire need for reconstruction, the post-millennial era was characterized by wage depression. High illiteracy and unemployment rates, extensive poverty, racial discrimination, inadequate sanitation, and plagues of human crises pressed hard upon large segments of the populace. Compelling the attention of many American Protestants who, along with the progressive view of history, had inherited from early

Nevertheless, these North American Christian expressions adopted philosophies of ethics, progress, social science, and holiness theologies in the quest for answers to human plights. In other words, the theologies aimed to maximize the gospel for addressing the failing economic systems and systemic social crises. These models were later exported to Africa. According to Rauschenbusch, God's kingdom is fulfilled when humanity's conditions are repaired. Nevertheless, one may surmise that the kingdom of God has not yet arrived because poverty continually confronts people. The application of the Christian Gospel to address the social crisis was a new millennial hope. In his article "Rauschenbusch's Christianity and the Social Crisis: Kingdom Coming," Gary Dorrien suggests, "For all its faults, the social gospel created a movement and perspective that reshaped modern Christianity."[21]

For Rauschenbusch, "Jesus proclaimed and launched a postmillennial reign of God, and the church was supposed to be a new kind of community that transformed the world by the power of Christ's kingdom-bringing Spirit."[22] As a result, social gospel "movement leaders maximized the persuasive power of the pulpit, platform and press . . . the broad mission of the social gospel to build the kingdom of God on earth, starting at home in the United States of America."[23] Yet this writer argues that the Congolese have needs for pursuing a theological reflection that recognizes biblical and social implications of the gospel rather than an eschatological social gospel. The reader of these materials may surmise there is a distinct relationship between the twentieth-century social gos-

---

evangelical and Puritan visionaries a vision of a godly nation." Deichmann, "The Social Gospel as a Grassroots Movement," 203–06.

21. Dorrien, "Rauschenbusch's Christianity and the Social Crisis: Kingdom Coming," 27.

22. Dorrien, "Rauschenbusch's Christianity and the Social Crisis: Kingdom Coming," 27.

23. Deichmann, "The Social Gospel as a Grassroots Movement," 203–06. Deichmann posits that the "Social gospel movement associated itself with concerns about unchecked capitalism and limited democracy by supporting fair, living wages for workers and by issuing scathing critiques about discriminatory labor and voting laws and practices. It provided programs for social betterment and reconstruction that addressed poverty and the myriad other problems facing society. The social gospel commitment was institutionalized in legalisms such as child labor and health and safety laws and denominational home mission societies and organizations such as the Methodist Federation for Social Service (1907). The Federal Council of Churches and Social Creed (1908) and the National Association for the Advancement of Colored People (1909)" (203).

pel movement and the twenty-first century prosperity theology because the gospel is used as a means for social change while giving a generic notion of salvation.

However, the social gospel is not a gospel of Christ but a socialistic and capitalistic gospel or doctrine. How, therefore, can theological discourse in the twenty-first century be useful to negotiate the areas of race, gender, transnational, classism, economic justice, social-political, nationality, immigration, and identity?

Liberation Theologies

Liberation theology is a Latin American theological fabric and a 1960s Roman Catholic phenomenon which became popular within mainline Protestant denominations. This theological and social belief is not suited to an African theological worldview. Greenman and Green illustrate the historical and theological background of the liberation theology in three different lines: "a pastoral line, an academic line, and a radical revolution."[24] Though these theologies have been massively embraced in many parts of the world, especially within the Neo-Pentecostal renewal and charismatic branches, they fail to be assets for genuine discipleship

---

24. Greenman and Green, *Global Theology in Evangelical Perspective*, 77. Greenman and others insist, "The challenge of liberation theology may be summarized in the three new perspectives it proposed. First, it offered a new and critical reading of the history of the Catholic Church in Latin America from the standpoint of a critical reading of the history of Spanish colonialism and American and European neocolonialism. Protestants had always been critical of the Catholic Church and agreed with this essential or critical reading. Second, liberation theology offered a new interpretation of Scripture, fresh reading from the perspective of the poor, a vision from the underside. Nevertheless, this was the most engaging aspect of liberation theology for evangelicals. It underscores the abundant biblical material about God's special preference for the poor and the prophetic criticism of the social injustice. Evangelicals had not paid enough attention to it. The third proposal of liberation theology was a new vision of what Christian practice of faith should be in Latin America. They were asking the hierarchies to take sides with the poor and not with the rich, as they used to do to keep their privileges and political power" (77–78).

The writers continue: "It is important to acknowledge that after World War II, a new generation of Catholic missionaries from Canada, the United States, Belgium, and France went to serve among the poorest of the poor in Latin America. They painfully discovered that the traditional alliance of the Catholic hierarchies with the landowners, the Army and the rich was one of the factors that preserved the unjust structures. From that practice of service to the poor came the theological quest for a preferential option for the poor" (78).

within Sub-Saharan Africa. Greenman and Green argue, "Since the publication of Gustavo Gutierrez's classic, *A Theology of Liberation*, in 1973, this new way of doing theology caught the attention of theologians and leaders in the English-speaking world."[25] Today, these theologies have penetrated the heart of Francophone and Asian worldviews.

It is a challenge for evangelicals, who stress the need for a literal translation of the gospel. This new way of doing theology proposes a use of Scripture and new hermeneutics as a response to human struggle. Whether consciously or unconsciously, the interpretation of Scripture from the vantage point of liberation theology deconstructs the orthodoxy of special revelation and transcends into a social-economic structure.

Liberation theology overlooks the cosmic dimensions of the struggle between the divine and evil demonic powers, spiritual forces within an African worldview. In other words, liberation theology ignores the presence of those worlds which are reflected in the Bible and within an African worldview.[26] As Greenman and Green opine, "It is the emerging church of the poor with its oral theology, narrative preaching, dreams and visions, signs and wonders, and transformative spiritual power, which at given points does far more for the poor than the elaborate social agendas of traditional denominations."[27]

The sympathetic tendency that suggests God sides with the poor and marginalized creates a different Christianity. Marxism and social sciences are not a final push for adequate solutions to the problems facing Africans. Brazilian Lutheran Valdir Steuernagel has said, "Missiological Reflection had to struggle with issues such as poverty and justice, working with the assumption that evangelization and quality of life are not strangers to each other. Both are branches of the Gospel tree and should

---

25. Gutierrez, *A Theology of Liberation*.

26. Roberts, *Liberation Thinking*, 5. Roberts asserts, "Liberation theologies end up very attractive to Latin Americans. They jive with Latin social theory and promise immediate, political solutions to their most excruciating problems. However, they offer a promise that is exclusive—one not rooted in fundamental cosmic reality. Because unless sin and salvation are understood regarding deliverance from Satan's power, they are not understood at all. Solutions that are developed within the restricting limits of Marxism thus are unable to get to the root of the human problem. Since they take for granted that every evil derives from class conflict, they cannot deal with the deeper issues of sin and guilt and demonic corruption. They are caught up in the shadows of dialectic materialism" (5).

27. Greenman and Green, *Global Theology in Evangelical Perspective*, 82.

not be separated from each other."[28] Several African nations besides South Africa have embraced liberation theologies because of their history of systemic racial division and Apartheid.

Another example is Zimbabwean theologians who have attempted to use liberation theology to alter or redress the social crisis and political miscarriage. These efforts have made little or no impact on the broader challenges facing the nation. Many other attempts by Angolans and Congolese have also proven to be ineffective. As Dyrness and Garcia-Johnson observe,

> What if we thought about the gospel as liberation as well as forgiveness? What if the evil addressed by the cross is social as well as personal? It was not the case that the gospel was suddenly less relevant; quite the contrary, the gospel took fresh meaning. The problem was with us-We did not understand the gospel. We missed critical dimensions of God's dynamic intervention in Christ.[29]

Liberation theology is not liberating for African cosmic spiritualized worldviews.

Enculturation and Inculturation of the Gospel

The twenty-first century human race lives in the heart of the missionary field as people interact with other cultures in everyday life experience. This interaction creates a systemic endless enculturation, inculturation, and acculturation within multi-cultural and ethnic societies. For instance, each time a person encounters another by crossing cultures they are encultured as they interact and accept each other with respect and dignity as humans. Walls' indigenizing principle stresses that God accepts humans despite their traditional primal beliefs, origins, and place.[30] This is the root of the enculturation of the gospel.

---

28. Greenman and Green, *Global Theology in Evangelical Perspective*, 76.

29. Dyrness and Garcia-Johnson, eds., *Theology without Borders*, 25–26.

30. Walls asserts, "Church History has always been a battleground for two opposing tendencies, and the reason is that each of the tendencies has its origin in the Gospel itself. On the one hand, it is of the essence of the gospel that God accepts us as we are, on the ground of Christ's work alone, not on the ground of what we have become or are trying to become. However, if He accepts us 'as we are' that implies He does not take us as isolated, self-governing units because we are not. We are conditioned by a particular time and place, by our family and group and society, by 'culture' in fact. In

The recipients of this gospel feel at home and accepted as they transition from Gentile status into Christian family based on Christ's work. The indigenizing process creates a welcoming space for the incarnation of the gospel whenever it crosses a frontier. The culture and its people are often affected and shaped as a result of the encounter. This paradox of belonging exemplifies a genuine enculturation of the Gospel because locals are invited and given an opportunity to experience God's redemptive grace, not as isolated entities but as God's own people.

Enculturation is, therefore, an endless process of divine revelation. The gospel is central when it penetrates a culture or frontier; in this, there is often a cost to pay. On the one hand, there is a cultural shift in the loss of traditional heritages and new discoveries. On the other hand, the gospel transforms both the receiver and the missionary. As a revelation, the gospel purifies pre-existing belief systems, while, at the same time, it embodies a new culture. As Carolyn Osiek posits, "The essential task of enculturation of the gospel is not one of inserting an abstract entity called the gospel into a culture. Rather the gospel is and always has been radically acculturated, from the first preaching of Jesus through contemporary biblical interpretation. Enculturation means creating something new, and with a price to pay."[31]

Christianity's attempt to change the ritual laws of marriage, the role of women in the church, and tribalism was a result of an ongoing effort to acculturate the Gospel. However, Congolese resisted forgoing their traditional or ancestral belief systems at the expense of faith. For instance, after a religious wedding is administrated in the church, the married couple and family return to their traditional rites and dances. The equivalent is true for healing the sick through the hospital. If medicine does not

---

Christ, God accepts us together with our group relations; with that cultural conditioning that makes us feel at home in one part of human society and less at home in another. However, if He takes us with our group relations, then surely it follows that He takes us with our 'dis-relations' also; those predispositions, prejudices, suspicions, and hostilities, whether justified or not, which mark the group to which we belong. He does not wait to tidy up our ideas any more than He wants to tidy up our behavior before He accepts us sinners into His family. The impossibility of separating an individual from his social relationships and thus from his society leads to one unvarying feature in Christian history. The desire to 'indigenize', to live as a Christian and yet as a member of one's own society, to make the Church (to use the memorable title of a book written in 1967 by F. B. Welbourn and B. A. Ogot about Independent churches in Africa) A Place to Feel at Home." See Walls, *The Missionary Movement in Christian History*, 7–8.

31. Osiek, "Forum Gospel and Enculturation," 83.

work, they seek traditional healers. People attend worship services within the mission-established churches, though if their needs are not met, they often turn to AICs and ATR prayer meetings for deliverance.

For many, Christ was a foreign savior. As Osiek discusses, "There are gospel elements that must inform and challenge culture, and there are cultural elements that must inform and challenge the current interpretation of the gospel."[32] Christ had to be acculturated as an ancestor for Him to be understood within the Congolese worldview.

Christ presented as a Congolese ancestor meant that He became one of them. In places like the US or Europe, the issues of racism and poverty are critical to their worldview, and they influence the ways they encounter the Christian message. The pre-existing contexts of recipients, or the evangelized cultural traditions, affect the ways the gospel is received and assimilated into the new culture. Moreover, inculturation determines the impact of Christendom within the receiving nation. This writer argues that a right re-enculturation of the gospel is achieved when new forces arise that did not exist before within the evangelized worldview or community.

The essential method of re-enculturation is keeping what is good in the elements of the receiving culture while rejecting elements incompatible with Christianity. Osiek describes that Paul related this view to the community at Thessalonica: "Paul tells us how to be enculturated in 1 Thessalonians 5:20—21: Do not quench the Spirit, do not despise prophecy, but test everything and keep what is good. What is perceived to be good, and thus kept, is what will be enculturated or contextualized."[33] However, African communities seek a hermeneutic approach that enculturates the gospel.[34] The cultural broker's, or the missionary's, task is to trade in the new culture the gospel as he would currency.

P. A. Oguntoye opines:

> An enculturation hermeneutics approach integrates social issues such as poverty, political oppression, etc. . . . it is based on the holistic concept of culture and seeks to develop its tools from African sources—it operates at the interface of academic and ordinary readings of the Bible. . . . it aims to make average

32. Osiek, "Forum Gospel and Enculturation," 90.

33. Osiek, "Forum Gospel and Enculturation," 90.

34. Oguntoye, "African Culture and Its Implications for Effective Presentation of the Gospel," 185. See Njoroge, "The Orthodox Church in Africa and the Quest for Enculturation," 405–38.

Africans and their context and worldview the subject of [biblical] interpretation. African socio-cultural perspectives inform the conceptual framework of analysis. Thus, while all of the other approaches consist of reading the Bible with a Western grid and applying the result to the African grid, thus making the African context the subject of the interpretation (preaching and reading).[35]

On the contrary, according to J. David Bosch, "Enculturation is not used in missiological circles as a term but more as a concept. It is a concept that denotes the procedural patterns in which the character of contemporary Christian faith manifests itself in a given cultural context, in a given time and space."[36] Moreover, John N. Njoroge sustains, "This procedural manifestation of Christianity means the planting of the gospel, the seeds of Christian faith, in the soil of a new cultural context. . . . enculturation is a missiological process that through the guidance of the Holy Spirit allows the gospel, the faith in Jesus Christ, to develop roots and mature at its own pace."[37] These factors of enculturation, which relate to an adaptation of Christian worldviews and liturgies to the non-Christian experience, derive from a literal translation of a culturally contextualized hermeneutical framework within the Congolese socio-religious milieu. The Congolese milieu is shaped by spontaneity, self-theologizing, demonic forces, symbols, and dreams.

CONTEXTUALIZATION OF THE GOSPEL

Paul G. Hiebert advocates a critical contextualization while posing a decisive question: "How far can the gospel be adapted to fit into a culture without losing its essential message?"[38] Missionaries' rejection of traditional African customs seen as pagan has created contextual and missiological setbacks. Hiebert articulates that missionaries' approaches relating to an uncritical rejection of old ways and an uncritical acceptance of African traditions tend to undermine the task of mission. He proposes

---

35. Oguntoye, "African Culture and Its Implications for Effective Presentation of the Gospel," 185.

36. Bosch, *Transforming Mission*, 447.

37. Njoroge, "The Orthodox Church in Africa and the Quest for Enculturation," 405–38.

38. Hiebert, *Anthropological Insights for Missionaries*, 183.

a third approach called critical contextualization in which old beliefs and customs are neither rejected nor accepted without examination.

However, missionaries' approaches in engaging Congolese cultural expressions through rites such as death, birth, and marriage were depicted as incompatible with the Christian faith. The encounter, in effect, left a vacuum in the translation of the Gospel, vis-à-vis the recipient's culture. There was no clear line of demarcation between secular and sacred or religious and nonreligious practices at the time the Gospel was presented to the Congolese. Rather, there was rejection and uncritical examination. As Hiebert puts it, "Sometimes this rejection was rooted in the ethnocentrism of the missionaries, who tended to equate the Gospel with their own culture and consequently judged other cultural ways as bad."[39]

Hiebert goes on to state: "First, it left a cultural vacuum that required to be lifted, and too often this was done by importing the customs of the missionary."[40] The lack of a contextualization of the Christian message to fit the Congolese spiritualized worldviews not only created a vacuum and incomplete holism, but it also led to syncretism as locals became engaged in a search for alternative ways to satisfy their void of spiritism. Therefore, due to uncritical contextualization Africans misunderstood and misinterpreted Christianity

For example, the translation of songs or hymnals into vernacular cultures, such as Swahili, was often mistranslated. The Swahili lyrics to a traditional Gospel are translated, "*Bwana Uniwoshe Niwe Mweupe, Kama Thelugi.*"[41] That means, "Lord, wash my sins to be white as snow." Instead,

---

39. Hiebert, *Anthropological Insights for Missionaries*, 183.

40. Hiebert, *Anthropological Insights for Missionaries*, 184. "Cymbals and other traditional instruments were replaced with organs and pianos. Instead of creating new lyrics that fit the native music, Western hymns and melodies were translated into the local idiom. Pews replaced mats on floors, and British–and American-style churches we built, although they appeared incongruous alongside wickiups and mud huts. Western suits were often required of pastors preaching in hundred-degree temperatures to scantily dressed audiences. It was no surprise, then that Christianity often viewed as a foreign religion and Christian converts as aliens in their own land" (184).

41. The expression "*Uniwasheniwemweupesawathelugi*" originates from the translated song of the Baptist minister Robert Lowry in 1876. The text reflects the Psalmist's plea for pardon in Psalm 51:7. After the fall he pled and appealed to the mercy of God for forgiveness and purification. He says, "Cleanse me with hyssop, and I will be clean; wash me, and I will be whiter than snow" (Ps 51:7). Lowry contextualizes two biblical texts Hebrews 9:22, "Without the shedding of blood there is no remission of sin" and Psalm 51:7. The themes of pardon, cleansing, atonement, and righteousness permeate the remaining stanzas. The United Methodist Hymnal changes one word in the refrain.

the missionaries may have translated this psalmist's cleansing plea in Psalm 51 as follows: "*unisafishe niwe mweupe sawa mpemba*," meaning, "Wash me, Lord, to be white like limestone or *calcaire*." The term snow is foreign within Congolese traditions. Rather, the term "*Mpemba*," translated from French "chaux" or blanche, means "white," similar to the white material extracted from *calcaire*, known as limestone used in traditional invocations of ancestors, often applied by elders to decorate their faces and bodies as before the invocation of ancestors' spirits.

Contextualization means communicating the message from the known to the unknown, from inductive to deductive. The recipients must be accepted first as they feel invited or part of the body of Christ; therefore, a contextualization of the Gospel is needed. It is the power of the Holy Spirit and Gospel transformation that leads one to change his life. It is critical to recognize the value of others and a deep respect for humans for missions to take place. Olubayo O. Obijole reasons, "Contextualization is a dynamic process of the church's reflection, in obedience to Christ and his mission in the world, on the interaction of the text as the word of God and the context as a specific human situation. It is essentially a missiological concept."[42]

Therefore, inculturation, acculturation, enculturation, and contextualization are mediums through which God speaks to people. Pentecostalism in Acts 2 made the Gospel understood in everyone's language that God speaks through cultures. The vernacular is a vehicle of contextualization of the Gospel that the church in Africa needs to take seriously.

The original text is "white as snow," an allusion to Isaiah 1:18, "though your sins be as scarlet, they shall be as white as snow." The hymnal committee changed this to "bright as snow." See Hawn, "History of Hymns,'" accessed September 15, 2016, http://www.umc discipleship.org/resources/history-of-hymns-nothing-but-the-blood. The translated lyric was misread when it crossed frontiers and was attempted to be contextualized within a Congolese worldview. Also, see The *United Methodist Hymnal*, 362.

42. Obijole, "The Church and the Gospel Message in the African Cultural Context," 105. Obijole argues, "In fact, Sanneh shows how the vernacular power in the translation of the confession idea of the pygmies of the Congo left a very lasting impact on them. Sanneh also shows how the translation of the name God in Yoruba and the Massai of East Africa created great impact. He concluded that such evidence is assurance, too, that indigenous and enculturation of the gospel stand to benefit the wider church" (105).

Traditional Evangelism

Traditional evangelism rooted in classical Pentecostalism originated from North American Christianity and planted lasting seeds and new theologies not limited to the holiness movement and reborn-Christianity. However, the evangelical wing was the most powerful ingredient within the emerging Congolese worldviews and missions, which exported a dimension of the prosperity theology. As a result of traditional evangelism that stressed both the salvation of the soul and physical needs, the Gospel of Jesus Christ was retransmitted over and over within local Congolese expressions.

Traditional evangelism began with the arrival of the first Baptist missionary in 1885, and a second attempt at evangelism in the Congo took place in the Bakongo kingdom and penetrated the culture. During this period, several missional attempts were made both by Europeans and North American evangelists through evangelistic crusades throughout the twentieth century. Missionaries came armed with classical Pentecostal and evangelical expressions of Christianity to the Congo; this included the holiness movement and prosperity gospel.

Among other missionaries, Jimmy Swaggart, a North American televangelist and charismatic preacher (1980s), arrived in the Congo. David Van Reybrouck argues, "In Kinshasa in the early nineties he had seen the arrival of the first generation of American evangelists a new kind of missionary who brought a charismatic variation of Christianity; Pentecostalism."[43] Swaggart and Bonnke's ministries influenced converts who took missions to a new level. For instance, Fernando Kutino, shaped by North American evangelists, became the founder of Congolese *Eglise du Réveil*, or "church of awakening," based on the prosperity gospel and charismatic expressions.[44] In addition, Bonnke's prosperity messages

---

43. Van Reybrouck, *Congo*, 489.

44. Van Reybrouck explains, "Fernando Kutino, still, an unremarkable boy at the time, heard about Jimmy Swaggart, the American TV evangelist who had achieved world fame in the West with his weepy confession of sexual infidelity. In Kinshasa, Swaggart became known for his rousing services that brought many thousands into a state of ecstasy. But the German evangelist Reinhard Bonnke came to town as well, as did the Dutchman John Maasbach, married men in neat suits who bore witness to their faith with lively shows and impeccable coiffures. These reborn Christians booked up with the local prayer groups that gathered weekly to lift up their hearts unto the Lord outside the regular Sunday services. It did not take long before native men of the cloth arose as well, and Fernando Kutino was a key figure among them. Kutino put on a tie, called himself Reverend and delivered a message that ran quite counter

that emphasized healing and deliverance left a vacuum and incomplete holism. Fernando Kutino is now the self-proclaimed Archbishop of the Neo-Pentecostal *Eglise du Reveille* that perpetuates the theologies of the prosperity gospel, which tend to exploit and impoverish the adherents.

Van Reybrouck states:

> Pentecostalism was a variation of Christianity that closely matched the spiritual cosmos of African ancestor worship. Praying aloud, casting out demons, speaking in tongues: it reminded one of Simon Kimbangu's rise in 1992. Then too, fervent faith had been a remedy against witchcraft. Then too, people had begged for instant healing. However, Kutino added another layer, that of la prospérité. Redemption was not only spiritual but also material by nature. During the bitter crisis years of the 1990s, this was the message people wanted to hear. What good did it do to the poor, in spirit or otherwise, to be blessed when their children were dying of starvation?[45]

John Mbiti emphasizes there must be a dialogue between Christianity and African traditions. He asserts, "African Christological has put Jesus at both the center and peripherals. It has embraced classical and traditional Christology, but has added its own understanding of who Jesus Christ is."[46] Is this African understanding of Christ being exported to the West through reverse missions and immigration?

THE DIASPORATIC HISTORY

This section will scrutinize the diasporic phenomenon, the hermeneutics of Psalm 137, exile, identity, nationalism and transnationalism, and the Diaspora.

Diasporatic Phenomenon: A Reverse Mission

This section explores William Edward Burghardt Du Bois' double-consciousness philosophical concept along with the exilic experience and the

---

to the traditional churches and rituals. It was a starting shot for the Congolese église du réveil, the churches of the Awakening, the revival, the new beginning. The curious were drawn in by the emphasis placed on charismatic worship, in which healing and salvation could be obtained during moments of an intense religious rapture of the Holy Spirit." Van Reybrouck, *Congo*, 489.

45. Van Reybrouck, *Congo*, 490.

46. Van Reybrouck, *Congo*, 490.

struggle to construct an identity in a foreign land.⁴⁷ This will be achieved by examining the postcolonial theory and definitions of Diaspora, home, exile, transnational, and the notion of home against the essentialism ideology in postmodernism. It will re-examine historical evidence on exile and critically re-read Psalm 137 by scrutinizing voices from the text. Therefore, through critical analysis, this writer will investigate how those who are exiled can create an identity and freedom in a foreign land. Besides, the study re-examines the role of songs as a model to colonize or, perhaps, decolonize one's mind set.

In *The Next Christendom*, Philip Jenkins discusses the rising numerical growth of the church outside the West. The numerical growth serves as the basis for a reverse mission seen as the force for Christian distribution since people from the Global South are moving to the West. In other words, immigrants are making foreign lands their new home. There are several underlying issues related to this global phenomenon: socio-political, economic, theological, and missiological. Diaspora is a phenomenon that has shaped twenty-first century Christianity as people move from their homelands to dwell in foreign cultures.

These seekers move with their own expressions of Christianity and spiritual experience; they have shaped a global Christendom or awakening within the host nation. Yet to some extent, they suffer a double consciousness as they attempt to fit into the host land. Even though the church is declining in the West, there is hope for North American Christianity to grow. On the other hand, European Christianity faces a crisis because a number of those who immigrate to Europe are either Muslim, or they quickly convert to atheism.⁴⁸ Craig Keener and M. Daniel Carroll R. assert, "Jenkins Chronicles the numerical growth of Christian faith

---

47. Du Bois, *The Souls of Black Folk*, 7. The term "double – consciousness" originated from Du Bois and described the state of an individual's feeling to reflect his own identity. This idea is divided into several parts and implies the loss of one's identity and representation. Nevertheless, Du Bois is an American scholar and civil rights supporter who was involved in Pan-Africanism. He asserts, "After the Egyptian and Indian, the Greek and Roman, the Teuton and Mongolian, the Nigro is a sort of seventh Son, born with a veil; and gifted with second-sight in this American world. The World which yields him no true self-consciousness, but only left him see himself through the revelation of the other world. It is a peculiar sensation this double-consciousness, this sense of always looking at one's self through the eyes of others" (7).

48. Ott and Netland surmise, "Whereas in 1900 the majority of Christians were in Europe and North America, and Christianity was identified as a Western religion, today most of Christians reside in the non-Western world, and Christianity is declining in much of Europe." See Ott and Netland, *Globalizing Theology*, 7.

outside the West as well as the migration of believers from those areas to the West. These immigrants, refugees, and asylum seekers leave their homelands looking for safety, jobs and a fresh start for their families; some come with the express purpose to do mission in the West."[49] As immigrants move to North America and Europe, they plant churches and faith-based ministries which reflect their origins and cultures with an indigenous character. In other words, they conserve their style of worship, music, and spirituality. While they are physically in a foreign land, their models and memories reclaim the authenticity of their original worldviews.

Hermeneutics of Psalm 137

The cry of the psalmist pierces one's contemporary struggle for identity. Music can lead people to remember their origin, land, and identity. The Psalmist asks, "How can we sing the Lord's Song in a strange land? (Ps 137:3–4). Psalm 137 speaks to those in exile, in a strange land, who are oppressed by others, consumed by rage, and filled with fear and uncertainty. As Roger E. Van Harn states in his book *Psalms for Preaching and Worship*, "Babylonian tormentors who mock the Judeans sing us a song of Zion they scoff. However, the psychic trauma is too deep."[50] The people of Israel lose their identity because they are forced to sing a song of joy while their heart weeps.

The experience of being abroad in a non-native land can lead to mixed feelings. Reading the text through the eyes of an exile can reveal a sense of a double consciousness. This writer observes that there is a struggle within this Diaspora community to construct an identity and fit into a foreign land. It seems challenging for exiles to create a space and social identity in a land that is not their own.

For instance, this writer has observed a dramatic shift in his biological children's behavior as they become more Americanized. They are losing their heritage because of the effects of immigration. One can only wonder, as they grow up in the US, whether they will behave more as Americans or Africans. Nevertheless, this writer envisions or foresees a significant change, cultural shift, and implication that may happen to his offspring a few generations ahead. Are they going to behave as Congolese

49. Keener and Carroll R., eds., *Global Voices*, 7.
50. Van Harn, *Psalms for Preaching and Worship*, 347.

or Americans? What will happen if they return home? Will they be perceived as foreigners in their own land?

To some extent, offspring may not be embraced fully in the Congo. Rather, they will be viewed as Americans and a threat to take over. While in the host land, they struggle to fit in because of their speech and language deficiencies. Therefore, once people cross into another culture, they automatically lose their identity and place. How do people think of national identity considering a Diaspora experience, and how do they view their relationship to their homeland while thousands of miles away?

The ideas of nationalism, space, gender, patriarchy, and transnationalism are important as one asks, "Where is home?" Is home a geographical place on the visual map, or is it a location? Children brought up in the US struggle to see their homeland as a distant place. The concept of home is a constructed ideology and not realistic. It is a location in which one settles. As Caryl Phillips suggests, "For people of the African Diaspora, home is a word that is often burned with a complicated historical and geographical weight."[51] Moreover, home is not a physical place on the map or landscape, but it is a fixation or social construct of one's imagination. In addition to the umbilical tie, this writer argues that home might be any space where a generation settles and connects with a new culture because culture is not a static but dynamic experience. Memories are the core of human existence because of a double-consciousness.

Thus, a diaspora is essential or central to constructing a sense of identity and belonging. For some scholars, even when a person remains at home, he is forced to travel because of his surroundings. One's cultural identity does not necessarily come from home, but it is located wherever an individual is rooted. A birthplace cannot be identified as a homeland, so one cannot view his homeland as a distant place.

Furthermore, what are the relationships between people from different locales—especially if one's locale is another global entity? Where is home for those living in this Diaspora? How can ministers translate the gospel to meet the needs of a multi-cultural community while speaking prophetically as a voice in this millennium?

The Psalmist states, "We were by the river of Babylon, and we wept for we remembered Zion" (Ps 137:1). A double-consciousness articulated by Dubois' creates a real struggle of constructing a communal identity that seems lost in history. A person's memories are shaped by their origin

---

51. Justin D. Edwards, *Postcolonial Literature: A Reader's Guide to Essential Criticism* (New York: Palgrave Macmillan, 2008), 151.

and rooted in the cultural worldview of his or her birthplace. As Grauray Desai surmises, "Associational identification with the cultures of origin remains strong, even into the second and third generation, though the places of origin are no longer the only source of identification."[52]

Immigrant church members have domesticated and, at the same time, kept their original forms of worship, songs, and cultural patterns. Though they are presently in a foreign land, their songs and melodies are still traditional melodies that tell the stories of their homelands. During worship, their memories tend to travel to their original respective nations. Admittedly, songs have been used as tools to colonize people. For example, during the liberation war in the DRC, the opposition convinced the population to sing songs of liberation to symbolize the end of the despotic Mobutu's regime, but in truth, the effort was an internal effort to re-colonize the marginalized.

A song can be used as political propaganda within an imperial setting to abuse and oppress minorities as well as enforce a colonial strategy. For example, certain songs sung during worship on Sunday seem to carry stories and memories behind them. For instance, "Amazing Grace" reminds worshipers about the struggle of racial differences and efforts for unity in US history. Moreover, those who sing songs of sorrow are often denied their rights to exercise freedom and assert or reclaim personal identity.

Exile

The Babylonian exile has often been seen by contemporary scholars as a period of suffering and distress for the people of Judah. Being away from home can create mental or psychological depression and emotional distress because the memory often suffers double consciousness. As Bob Becking posits, "Exile is construed as referring to a life away from home, in a foreign country where people have to survive in miserable circumstances."[53] The Babylonian Exile was a terrible period, often mirroring the misery of the day. Becking holds that he never truly lived but only existed in a foreign land. Non-immigrant visa recipients tend to feel the weight of this foreignness.

It seems that the singer of Psalm 137 experienced fractures, turmoil, and emotional, spiritual, and physical trauma. How could one pray to

52. Desai et al, *Post-Colonialism*, 544.
53. Becking et al., *Exile and Suffering*, 183.

God while his or her enemies surrounded him or her? Can pastors help to heal the brokenness of self, family, and faith? Only then do people become vulnerable to hear and learn from the desperate needs of those who have been abused, violated, rejected, abandoned, or sinned against.

Identity

Gregory Castle says, "If the nation is an imagined community, as Anderson maintains, the maintenance of coherent identity relies on a historical narrative that posits and secures continuance."[54] Therefore, national identity can be conserved, maintained, or lost throughout people's history dislocation. When does a settler become a native? Is there a possibility to return to an originally lost identity?

Frantz Fanon argues, "It is the notion of resistance that lies at the heart of the postcolonial debate. However, the centrality of resistance does not entail a return to a past essentialized identity. For there is no possibility of such return; rather it is the continual reconstitution of identity under different circumstances which becomes important."[55] This dual personality gives birth to a character shift or changes wherein the individual becomes a new person. This writer refers to this experience or theory as a triple consciousness because he is an African, alien, and African-American. It is hard to live a double life or double consciousness as such individuals tend to live at a crossroads.

For instance, Anthony Johae, a French-born Lebanese, was asked if he felt more French or Lebanese? He replied, *"L'unou l' autre,"* meaning both. Hafid Gafaiti explains, "What makes me myself rather than anyone else is the very fact that I am poised between two countries, two or three languages and several cultural traditions. It is precisely this that defines my identity. Would I exist more authentically if I cut off a part of myself?"[56]

Nationalism and Transnationalism

Paul Gilroy, in his book *The Black Atlantic*, asserts that modernity and double consciousness have played a major role in this shift. Gilroy foregrounds the movement of "Black Atlantic's to avoid the ethnic

---

54. Castle, *Postcolonial Discourses*, 369.
55. Castle, *Postcolonial Discourses*, 509.
56. Gafaiti, *Transnational Spaces and Identities in the Francophone World*, 289.

essentialism that often characterizes cultural nationalism."⁵⁷ *The Black Atlantic* then is a transnational space of traversal, cultural exchange, and belonging that spans several continents and connects people through its history of diasporic paths. In other words, for Gilroy, the Atlantic was the contact zone where European settlers, traders, and the exploited met. As he puts it, "Modernity is characterized by colonialist expansion, slavery, genocide, and indenture, then the connections between cultures present in the Black Atlantic offer a counterculture to modernity."⁵⁸

Immigration and Diaspora play key roles in shaping the social structure as a transforming social phenomenon and globalization of Christianity. The ideas of transnational spaces and identities are rooted in the history of humanity. Immigrants bear cultural traditions within themselves which have the capacity to transform host communities and are, in turn, transformed.

Diaspora

Scholars tend to define the term "'Diaspora" from the Greek word *diasporein*, meaning to sow or scatter."⁵⁹ In this sense, Edwards argues that "Diaspora can be referred as people who have been dispersed, displaced or dislocated from their homeland due to exile, forced migration, immigration or settlement."⁶⁰ However, other origins of the word Diaspora can be traced back to the Old Testament (OT) (Deut 28:25). The Hebrew Bible calls attention to the dispersion of Israel. Therefore, the word Diaspora can refer to anyone living outside of their homeland.

Gilroy asserts the term Diaspora is rooted in social change and cultural theory. As several scholars have pointed out: "Within postcolonial studies and critical cultural theory Diaspora has become an emblem of multilocality, post-nationality and the non-linearity of both movement and time."⁶¹ Fortier declares, "Diaspora constitutes a rich heuristic device to think about questions of belonging, continuity, and community in the context of dispersal and transnational networks of connection."⁶²

57. Edwards, *Postcolonial Literature*, 151.
58. Edwards, *Postcolonial Literature*, 151.
59. Edwards, *Postcolonial Literature*, 150.
60. Edwards, *Postcolonial Literature*, 150.
61. Atkinson et al. *Cultural Geography*, 182.
62. Atkinson et al. *Cultural Geography*, 182.

In sum, Diaspora signifies a place where new geographies of identity are negotiated across multiple terrains of belonging. Diaspora is essential to the effective construction and maintenance of one's sense of identity and belonging. Hence, a birthplace cannot be identified as one's homeland, but the new place is still home.

CONCLUSION

Western theological worldviews rooted in the philosophies of the holiness, social, and prosperity gospels continue to influence the Congolese religious terrain. Swaggart, Osborne, and Bonnke's ministries in the twentieth century exported Western theologies of the social gospel in the Republic of Zaire. The foreign translation explains the current rapid growth of Neo-Pentecostalism and prosperity theologies. However, these Christian expressions test the evangelical mandate for a faithful translation and transplantation of the biblical Gospel and Christian mission in Africa.

Walls' pilgrim and indigenizing principles are critical for the gospel as they transcend human culture as a force with its adaptive quality. These principles, emphasizing a common identity in Christ, exemplify the universality of the gospel. The indigenizing principle helps the reader discern the power of the gospel as a transformative force that can penetrate every culture and become rooted in the recipients' lives. The latter shows how the gospel, as a transforming message, acculturates the host's cultural worldview.

Walls' philosophy of indigenizing and pilgrim principles is useful for a genuine communication of the gospel because his methods allow negotiating the context, while, at the same time, recognizing the gospel message does not change its tenet of sacred character while penetrating the host culture. Each culture and context has its own challenges, pitfalls, and opportunities.

The concept of gospel contextualization is critical because if the primacy of genuine discipleship and its translation are not reached, the mission to evangelize becomes syncretized. Contextualization is neither accommodation nor syncretism in the cross-cultural translation or retransmission of the gospel.[63] It is also not a naïve acceptance of elements

---

63. Yamamori and Taber, *Christopaganism or Indigenous Christianity?*, 17. Yamamori and Taber surmise, "With critical consideration, however, we observed that

from the host culture which are incompatible with an orthodox interpretation of Christian teachings.

The prosperity gospel within Neo-Pentecostalism syncretizes the gospel into a new belief system. Yamamori and Taber question the concept of Christopaganism: "How [does one] avoid syncretism and achieve an indigenous Christianity?"[64] Nonetheless, achieving this object that promotes indigenous Christianity is critical for the changing face of the global church. As these authors put it, "Thus, on the one hand, we try to preserve a pure faith and essential gospel, and on the other hand, we seek to give it an indigenous garment. For example, the moment we translate a portion of Scripture into a language which has hitherto built its vocabulary only for a pagan worldview and belief, we are confronted with the problem not only of translation but with reception."[65]

Indeed, translation allows the Gospel to be universal, yet the Gospel has been indigenized and domesticated. It has undergone a diffusion to successfully achieve its mission. Yamamori and others argue that, "Mission means translation."[66] The missional dimension of the gospel is to call God's people to discover a divine desire to change and repent of sins. Hiebert argues, "The gospel calls not only individuals but societies and cultures to change. Contextualization must mean the communication of the gospel in ways the people understand, but that also challenge them individually and corporately to turn from their evil ways."[67]

There is a continuity of Christian cultural patterns as members of the body of Christ sometimes feel alienated and lost in their new land. Lamin Sanneh states, "The worldwide Christian resurgence is a proof of the religion transcending ethnic, national and cultural barriers."[68] For example, Koreans often attempt to preserve their homeland culture, so the

---

either of two kinds of mixtures might be defined as syncretism: on the one hand, a distortion of Christian theology by mixing it with pagan myth to form a new kind of teaching; on the other hand, the singing of, say, a Western Calvinist theology in an unfamiliar chant to a drumbeat previously used only for pagan dances." Moreover, the authors state, "Syncretism may be defined as the union of two opposite forces, beliefs, systems or tenets so that the United form is a new thing, neither one nor the other" (17).

64. Yamamori and Taber, *Christopaganism or Indigenous Christianity?*, 13.
65. Yamamori and Taber, *Christopaganism or Indigenous Christianity?*, 14.
66. Yamamori and Taber, *Christopaganism or Indigenous Christianity?*, 89.
67. Hiebert, *Anthropological Insights for Missionaries*, 184.
68. Sanneh, *Whose Religion Is Christianity?*, 7.

church becomes an educational center where they spend time with their families, sing songs in their native language, and share meals together.

The phenomenon of the continuity of primal belief systems regarding Christian consciousness is an essential paradigm that is foreign to the recipients of the gospel at a particular time and place.[69] These continuities stress "the desire to indigenize, to leave as a Christian yet as a member of one's own society, to make the church a place to feel at home."[70] The concept of home is an essential piece of understanding cross-cultural missions. Foreigners seek to fit into the existing system while living apart from their host cultures. They promote and preserve their cultural trends and reality to educate their children on their own values and cultural heritages.

---

69. Walls, *The Missionary Movement in Christian History*, 7.
70. Walls, *The Missionary Movement in Christian History*, 7.

7

An Analysis of Selected Passages
The Prosperity Gospel Hermeneutic

INTRODUCTION

THE SEVENTH CHAPTER OF this research explores the hermeneutics of selected biblical texts perceived as the basis for the increase of prosperity teachings within post-colonial Congo.[1] Hermeneutical practices of selected passages by leading Neo-Pentecostal Congolese believers are a step toward a new Christendom. The study critically interacts with the meth-

---

1. The biblical hermeneutic theory is a theological discourse used in a broader sense to examine principles of interpreting biblical literature from Congolese worldviews. As Justo L. Gonzalez argues, "The main concerns of hermeneutical theory in which the main debate was whether and how a text from the past and a form of different culture, can be understood by readers in the twenty-first century." See Gonzalez, *Essential Theological Terms*, 74–75. Also, Cephas N. Omenyo and Wonderful Adjei Arthur surmise, "Hermeneutics is the art of interpreting a biblical text to understand its original meaning and then delineate its significance for the contemporary audience. It is, therefore, the science of discerning how a thought or event in one cultural context may be understood in a different cultural context." See Omenyo and Arthur, "The Bible Says!," 52. The communication of the gospel has faced alterations that have been rooted in a traditional and symbolic interpretation of Scripture. Neo-Pentecostal exegesis is drawn from primal belief systems. Furthermore, biblical texts have been translated and retransmitted concerning the reading methodologies which tend to fit the socio-political, economic, and environmental needs of recipients. As Justo L. Gonzalez posits, "Hermeneutics is the discipline that studies the rules of interpretation of a text—in theological discourse, this usually refers to biblical interpretation." See Gonzalez, *Essential Theological Terms*, 74.

odologies of Neo-Pentecostals' uncritical readings and holistic interpretation of biblical literature. The self-theologizing implications resulting from uninformed interpretations of the biblical texts present challenges in translating Christianity in the twenty-first century. Uncritical theological reflection enables neither an effective and efficient evangelism nor a contextual understanding of the gospel in African contexts.

Nevertheless, contextual hermeneutics rooted in a prophetic voice and holistic engagement of sharing the Gospel might be a transformative force within the Congolese milieu. In other words, a prophetic engagement of missional initiatives carried out by locals might alter or reconstruct westernized sanctioned neoliberalism and neoclassical economics. These sanctioned or authorized systems are outside forces influenced by the cultural, economic, and political systems of Europe and North America. The Congolese hermeneutical methodologies have been revolutionized due to a misreading, mistranslation, and uncritical contextualization of the Gospel. Because of the Westernized forces, the Congolese matrices of reading Scripture have presented a hermeneutical miscarriage at the heart of its translation.

In his book, *Habits of the Mind: Intellectual Life as a Christian Calling*, James W. Sire asserts, "Our sacred reading is not merely for the movement. We read for with the purpose of evangelizing our lives—just we eat not only to enjoy the taste of food but to nourish our whole body and generate sufficient energy to implement our ambitions."[2] Daniel Sanchez states, "Understanding worldview is essential to communicate the gospel."[3] However, uncritical interpretation of the biblical literatures

---

2. Sire, *Habits of the Mind*, 156.

3. Sanchez, *Worldview*, 13. Sanchez offers several factors that contribute both to syncretism and *Christopaganism*. Nevertheless, his model and methodology for reading worldviews from the perspective of an indigenous voice are crucial to discern a comprehensive analysis of Congolese worldviews. He notes the dynamics of "partial conversion, untransformed discipleship that is not contextualized, or inadequate contextualization in training leaders and the importation of faith expressions in spiritual and human factors" (47). Sanchez elaborates on these conceptual terms to show that if primal belief practices rooted in animistic and syncretic worldviews are not addressed, there will be no genuine and adequate discipleship. First, "With the term partial conversion, we mean that because the gospel has not been explained in a clear and substantial manner, some people make a decision to receive Christ without understanding the implications of that decision. Second, this failure to deal with the previous Animistic realities often results in people identifying themselves as Christians yet secretly going to healers or diviners to seek solutions to their problems. Third, inadequate, when a Mission (a group of missionaries) fails to produce an indigenous

causes Christopaganism. Moreover, it caused the rapid expansion of Americanized prosperity doctrines. The explosion of Neo-Pentecostalism and the rise of charismatic churches are a radical response to the socio-economic and political empowerment. In *Under the Radar: Pentecostalism in South Africa and Its Potential Social and Economic Role*, Peter Berger and James Hunter relate to the ethical and rational aspects of social activity and family life culminating into consumerism. These trends, according to Berger and Hunter, "promoted savings, capital accumulation, and economic advancement, all in the context of a worldview free of magic and superstition."[4] Hunter's assessment implies the exported models of reading Scripture have been a foreign influence upon the land of Africa, free of magic and superstition and not the direct result of an indigenous voice.

Nonetheless, scholars across the spectrum of interests who conducted research in a post-Apartheid South African emerging context recognized critical data and findings based on Pentecostalism and religious faith. They asserted that religious faith rooted in new Pentecostal expressions of entrepreneurship influenced not only the policies, but also the rise of new denominations and social lift in South Africa. Religion is critical and alters the socio-economic and political environment underlying African issues as it implores adherents to excel socially and financially. Neo-Pentecostalism and charismatic trends have empowered women, children, education, and the eradication of elitism within the global South.

Paul G. Hiebert's theological framework suggests an anthropological reading of the recipient's cultural patterns that might alter the hermeneutical challenges. Ronald J. Allen echoes missionaries' voices: "We are willing to give up who we are for the greater good of the gospel."[5] Missionaries within the context of colonialism often attempt to transmit their own cultural ideas in place of the gospel. Classical Pentecostalism has been therefore seen as a tool to colonize Africans.

Church the result is going to be syncretistic movement. He explains that when there is a significant deficiency in the indigenous instruction of the pastors, the movement tends to be syncretic. Finally, imported expressions of faith, he says that there are two paths to syncretism. One is by introducing or importing foreign expressions of the faith and allowing the receiving people to attach their own worldview suppositions to these practices with little or no guidance from the missionaries" (48–51). Sanchez argues, "Understanding worldview is essential to communicating the gospel" (13).

4. Berger and Hunter, "Under the Rader," 66.
5. Allen, *Patterns of Preaching*, 52.

THE ROLE AND IMPACT OF THE NEO-PENTECOSTAL GOSPEL IN AFRICA

The role of Neo-Pentecostalism in the life of ordinary people and faith in Jesus of Nazareth is a real transformative force and means of liberation. The prosperity gospel in the post-colonial Congo is a tool for personal economic engagement and radical change, and its distribution correlates with a high marketplace. National economies play a fundamental role in the shape of the prosperity gospel because poverty is both a religious and societal problem. Wariboko opines, "The influence of the logic of finance on religious believers as faith in God coincides with faith in return on investment. How actors on Wall Street dealt with practical issues of moral hazards. How men and women of religion deal with practical matters of expectation of economic returns from faith."[6]

Wariboko's scholarship of mathematical equation rooted in the scientific theory of economics offers a framework to assess the prosperity gospel movement in postcolonial Africa structurally. Nevertheless, the Wall Street culture of capital investment, neoliberalism, and trans-Atlantic policies translates the reality of the prosperity gospel as recipients expect returns from God when they give to further the cause of the gospel. Read through the lens of economic reconstruction and progress, the prosperity gospel translates into a global phenomenon.

Wariboko translates the Pentecostal prosperity gospel into a simple economic equation: as architecture of thought the equation helps readers uncover the hidden *pneumatological* concepts of prosperity.[7] Wariboko's ability to bridge economic discourses of reasoning to Pentecostalism shapes an understanding of the theology of the prosperity gospel from an African perspective. He connects finance theory and examines its inner logic from the standpoint of mathematics and statistics. These innovative discourses of reading the Bible are critical for a dialogue between theology and economics.

Thus, the Neo-Pentecostal prosperity gospel becomes an art rather than a subject of study. Wariboko suggests, "Prosperity gospel depends upon a delicate composition of relations of faith and investment return; which enables a calculated and calculating mentality of self-governance

---

6. Wariboko, *Economics in Spirit*, 87.
7. Wariboko, *Economics in Spirit*, 86–87.

AN ANALYSIS OF SELECTED PASSAGES 155

to be harnessed by economic agents."[8] Readers of the biblical literature within the Sub-Saharan African contexts need a holistic understanding of socio-economic and political realities of the contexts into which the gospel is translated.

Wariboko argues, "The focus of the prosperity message on economic issues, on bread and butter, to the exclusion of *action*, the politics of social transformation, is a reflection, albeit an unfortunate one, of its larger socioeconomic milieu."[9] He further says, "The prosperity model is based on agricultural mindset; sowing and reaping. Sowing tithes and offerings into the church and reap a bumper harvest of wealth."[10]

The mathematical formula for prosperity in Hebrew's translation 7959 שַׁלֵּו(*sheh'-lev*) can be abridged to zero if the source is cut off the equation. God is the source of prosperity.

$=\beta\,((1)$
(2)[11]

and is in equations.

Wariboko explains, "Like the universe, giving to God expands one's wealth by creating the space it goes into. That is considered infinite

---

8. Wariboko opines, "I argue that the focus of the prosperity message on economic issues on bread and butter, to the exclusion of action the politics of social transformation, albeit on unfortunate one, of its larger economic milieu. Both neoclassical economics and the prosperity preachers regard the process of growing wealth as a natural process that must inevitably follow its own (spiritual or market) laws." See Wariboko, *Economics in Spirit*, 88. Furthermore, Wariboko asserts, "Prosperity gospel depends upon a delicate composition of relations of faith and investment return, which enables a calculated and calculating mentality of self-governance to be harnessed by economic agents. Collective veneration and obedience (or faith in God, which Pentecostal preachers say is indifferent to contrary or falsifying material evidence) are held together and reinforced by a belief in a socio-scientific or technical truth of investment return" (88). Wariboko, Economics in Spirit, 88.

9. Wariboko, *Economics in Spirit*, 89.

10. Wariboko, *Economics in Spirit*, 90.

11. Wariboko argues, "Equation (1) states that the expected return to a believer who invests in giving to God as prescribed by the prosperity message is the normal or standard rate of return. Any investor receives for investing in the economy plus a special bonus, which is a function of believers' sensitivity to the Holy Spirit. Fr (r) is the expected rate of return on faith or a portfolio of faithful investment. Nr stands for the natural rate of prosperity which may be zero. Pr stands for the special rate that one gets as a Pentecostal believer in the prosperity message. The expected premium a person gets from investing with God is dependent on the difference between A and B, Write B = (Beta) = 0–1 add A represents the risk in stocks and investments." See Wariboko, *Economics in Spirit*, 95–96. Success depends on the relationship with the Holy Spirit and divine risk level of faith. So the value of B is zero.

because, at least, it is believed there is an unlimited potential that all who invests in God's stock can become millionaires or controllers of the wealth of their nations."[12] The value of β is zero because faith is a leap one might faithfully invest into stock, but the returns are probable. This is to argue that both the prosperity preacher and the recipient are taking a risk; there is no guarantee that the return might be received soon after sowing seeds. Some people die without realizing such prophetic promises.

In his article, "Writing African Christianity Perspectives from the History of the Historiography of African Christianity," an African scholar of religion, Elias Kifon Bongmba posits,

> Bénézét Bujo from the Democratic Republic of Congo in a work that calls for dialogue between Africa and other parts of the world has grounded an African approach on theocentric, anthropocentric foundations which allow the scholar to interrogate and appropriate the common model of ethics. Bujo then deploys the collective approach to study justice, marriage and monogamy, feminist theology, human rights, state and development, health, growing old in Africa, ecology and Christian responsibility.[13]

Bongmba's argument relates to the ability of Christian worldviews to challenge human behavior. In this instance, the theocentric and anthropocentric approaches allow emerging scholars to interrogate and appropriate the common model of ethics. This is a roadmap to construct a systematic structure and ethos or culture of social and spiritual transformation.

The role of Christian mission has shifted from colonial legacy to address basic, ethical, theological-spiritual, and physical needs. Jesus and the gospel become the means for social, spiritual, and moral liberation. Bongmba opines, "While the story that should be told must be an African story, the nature of the dialogue between Africa and the rest of the world needs to be mapped out carefully."[14]

There is no longer a concern to tell the stories of missionaries' engagement in Africa. Instead, there is a need to document what has been transferred to the converts, after the gospel has been received, and what Western Christianity has become. The statistics and terminologies have

---

12. Wariboko, *Economics in Spirit*, 96.

13. Bongmba, "Writing African Christianity Perspectives from the History of the Historiography of African Christianity," 275–312.

14. Bongmba, "Writing African Christianity Perspectives from the History of the Historiography of African Christianity," 275–312.

shifted, and the church is rapidly growing in the global South. Christians can no longer suggest which are the sending and receiving churches, since every locality becomes a receiving and, at the same time, a sending agent. There are no more languages of mission fields and mission stations as was articulated in nineteenth and twentieth centuries.

Bongmba communicates,

> The landmark 1910 Edinburgh Missionary Conference was largely a Western festival which ignored the so-called mission fields, even though it was called to take stock and put in place an aggressive plan to reach the whole world or the entire planet with the Christian gospel; a project which contributed to the myth of the Christian century. Ignoring Africa which was already a vast field of Christian activity also ignored some of the important questions that had already been raised by Christian intellectuals of African descent such as Edward Wilmont Blyden, and the Pan African Movement that held its own inaugural meeting at Manchester.[15]

Hence, it is the crucial role and place of Africa to map the history of global missions and Christianity. Neither the Edinburgh Missionary Conference in 1910 nor Azusa Street in 1906 were the pinnacles of African Christianity.

THE GOSPEL AND CULTURE

The gospel, since its original translation, has been rooted in culture. These two forces are intertwined and inseparable. The Gospel itself emerges through a distinct culture. As Craig Ott and Harold A. Netland explain, "From the human point of view, there is no way we can engage with the gospel independent of culture. Our interaction with the gospel relies on human language, worldview, and cultural context."[16] Religion's survival depends on traditional norms related to the shared sets of moral codes and practices which govern social structures. The gospel can alter belief systems which seem irrelevant to the Christian faith. In other words, sustained through Congolese culture, the gospel has survived. From its original translation, the Gospel embodies unique values rooted

---

15. Bongmba, "Writing African Christianity Perspectives from the History of the Historiography of African Christianity," 275–312.

16. Ott and Netland, *Globalizing Theology*, 9.

in a Judeo-Christian worldview. The missionary carries his or her own cultural baggage. Missions are increasingly secularized. Is the Gospel a culture of its own? Is one single culture superior to others?

Uncritical contextualization left a vacuum or gap within the host culture. Western attitude toward the indigenous cultures and voices, in addition to missionaries' misreading of Congolese cultures, have contributed to the rise of new expressions of Christianity of the third world.

Allan Anderson argues:

> The beginning of the twentieth century was the heyday of colonialism when western nations governed and exploited the majority people on earth. This rampant colonization was often transferred into the ecclesiastical realm and was reflected in the attitudes of missionaries, who so often moved in the shadows of colonizers. In the late nineteenth century, there was an almost universal belief in the superiority of western culture and civilization, bolstered by social Darwinism that suggested that the world of the West was the pinnacle of human evolution.[17]

This writer recognizes that there is no exceptional culture; however, higher than another, each culture presents a negative and positive side. As Ott and others assert, "All cultures are seen as relative. None can stand in judgment of another."[18] Missionaries' superior attitudes towards African cultures and mores has not allowed an opportunity for the locals to appreciate Christ and the gospel as their stories. However, Anderson documents, "Western culture was Christian culture and all other cultures were dark problems to be solved by the light of the gospel, replacing the old paganism with the new Christianity."[19]

According to Ott and Netland, "The Western insertion into other cultures–first in the form of geographical exploration and the creation of systems of trade, followed by conquest and colonization–set in motion aggressive attempts to modernize and westernize the rest of the world. Frequently, the West did not read the cultural signals correctly."[20] The recipients or host culture must come to appreciate the gospel within

---

17. Anderson, "Writing the Pentecostal History of Africa, Asia, and Latin America," 141.

18. Anderson, "Writing the Pentecostal History of Africa, Asia, and Latin America," 293.

19. Anderson, "Writing the Pentecostal History of Africa, Asia, and Latin America," 147.

20. Ott and Netland, *Globalizing Theology*, 10.

its own cultural contexts. Ott and Netland further assert, "The modern missionary movement played an active role as a midwife in introducing modernity—along with the Christian message to other people of the world."[21]

Interpreted through contextual hermeneutics, Neo-Pentecostalism can be a resourceful and transformative force to overshadow the traditional paradigms of missional engagement rooted in colonial expressions. However, the current Pentecostal patterns of local initiative outside mainline missional-established churches, including the AICs, might respond to the social-economic and political crises within the Congolese systems. For instance, *La mission civilizatrice* as an imperial effort has authorized an imbalance of economic, geographic, and political resources by mighty powers. Peter Eichstaedt, an American scholar, writes,

> Every time you use a cell phone or log on to a computer, you could be contributing to the death toll in the bloodiest, most violent region in the world: the eastern Congo. Rich in "conflict minerals"—valuable resources mined in the midst of armed conflict and egregious human rights abuses--this remote and lawless land is home to deposits of gold and diamonds as well as coltan, tin, and tungsten, all critical to cell phones, computers, and other popular electronics.[22]

Eichstaedt explores the violence suffered by the Congolese and examines ways in which the global community has participated in the birth of the underlying issues or problems in Eastern Congo but might also become part of the solution.

June Gonzalez illustrates the effects and mechanism of dominant cultures in Latin America. He engages in a practical case study within the context of the banana republic, surmising, "Many immigrants–a harvest of empire are coming to the United States . . . on the very tracks built by the Anglo-American politico-economic machinery."[23] The dominant culture has the power to influence its worldviews.

---

21. Greenman and Green, *Global Theology in Evangelical Perspective*, 11.

22. Eichstaedt, *Consuming the Congo*, 5. Eichstaedt argues, "Eastern Congo defies comparison. The loss of life far exceeds deaths in Iraq and Afghanistan combined. This is not some distant tragedy, not just another African horror story. The lives and deaths of these millions are linked to us all. Each time we use a mobile phone, use a video game console or open a tin can, we hold the lives and deaths of the eastern Congolese in our hands" (5).

23. Dyrness and Garcia-Johnson, *Theology without Borders*, 4.

The Gospel's integral assimilation to cultures in crossing frontiers traces its roots from the first century. From the eighteenth to nineteenth centuries, the Great Awakening in the US became a final push and force for sending missionaries to Africa, Asia, and the rest of the globe. However, African Pentecostalism is an African response rather than an imported expression from the West to the South; the locals received the same general and special revelations from God that the rest of the continents on planet earth had experienced.

Hiebert states, "Marginal people have a significant contribution to make to any group. In a sense, they are prophets who speak from outside."[24] The African religious voices are prophets who speak relevant oracles to their own cultural contexts. This writer is a voice of an insider who examines the prosperity gospel phenomenon from an outside perspective. At any given time, when the Gospel encounters a culture, or a cross-cultural paradigm takes place, both the receiving and the host culture experience change. However, American anthropological engagements and scientific methodologies which attempt to explore Africans as objects of the study reinforce the same culture of colonizing.

Greenman and Green opine, "The current global engagement of Scripture and theology with culture are parallel to the way the early church took the message of Jesus rooted in the land of Judea and the Aramaic language and translated it both culturally and linguistically as it ran throughout the Roman world."[25] Greenman and Green's assertion justifies the universality and translatability of the gospel.

There must be a bridge or dialogue between the host and sending cultures to evangelize in a foreign context. The authors point out, "There have to be bicultural bridge builders yet, culture brokers."[26] This

24. Hiebert, *Anthropological Insights for Missionaries*, 230.

25. Greenman and Green, *Global Theology in Evangelical Perspective*, 10. Also, Tennent suggests, "Christianity began as a Jewish movement fulfilling Jewish hopes, promises, and expectations. Indeed, the continuity between Judaism and Christianity seemed so seamless to the earliest believers that they would have never thought of themselves as changing their religion from Judaism to something else. They understood Christianity as the extension and fulfillment of their Jewish faith. Right in the pages of the New Testament, we read the story of those unnamed Jewish believers in Antioch who took the risky—and controversial move—to cross major cultural and religious barriers and share the gospel with pagan, uncircumcised Gentiles." See Tennent, *Theology in the Context of World Christianity*, 3.

26. Hiebert avers, "The bicultural community is where the two worlds meet. It is made up of people who retain ties to their original cultures, but who meet and exchange ideas. Such people are culture brokers. Like money changers who trade

discourse means establishing a dialogue between cross-cultural elements from the perspective of both the evangelizer and the evangelized or the missionary and the locals.

In this case, a missionary as a culture broker becomes a link for theological reflection within the new hybrid faith community emerging out of a cross-cultural experience. There is a risk for the missionary to bring his culture instead of engaging the gospel holistically. Even so, missionaries encounter two different cultures which must be appreciated and negotiated for a new culture to emerge. The success of transmitting and translating the gospel depends on how this relationship is interacted with and sustained.

Hiebert posits, "Building bridges between cultures is, however, the central task of missions."[27] Locals have the potential to grow to participate in the story. So, in learning the new culture and primal belief systems, the behavior as well as values of those who participate in missions helps missionaries acculturate into the bicultural paradigm. For Hiebert, enculturation adds a new culture to a primary cultural pattern or expression. How can a twenty-first century missionary successfully engage in crossing frontiers by giving up their mores, adopting other cultural lenses, while remaining a prophetic voice in this millennium? Anderson asserts, "We need to correct the historiographical imperialism and ethnocentrism of the past. The revising of the history of Pentecostalism in the twenty-first century must be undertaken, not by emphasizing the missionary heroes of the powerful and wealthy nations of the world. However, it is by giving a voice to the world, most marginalized past."[28]

ORIGINS OF THE PROSPERITY GOSPEL

Traditional Western scholarship argues that the prosperity gospel movement started in the US in the 1950s. Kate Bowler "traces the roots of the prosperity gospel movement in the late nineteenth century to its flowering in the Pentecostal revivals of the World War II years and maturity in

---

dollars for yen or rupees, they are essential to the communication between two cultural worlds. Missionaries are such brokers. Although they do not trade in money or political power, they do bring the gospel from one culture to another." See Hiebert, *Anthropological Insights for Missionaries*, 229.

27. Hiebert, *Anthropological Insights for Missionaries*, 229.

28. Anderson, "Writing the Pentecostal History of Africa, Asia, and Latin America," 149.

the ripe individualism of post-1960's America."²⁹ In other words, Bowler traces its roots to "mesmerists, metaphysical sages, Pentecostal healers, business oracles, and princely prophets of the early twentieth century, through mid-century positive thinkers."³⁰ Nevertheless, Bowler argues, "Millions of American Christians came to see money, health and good fortune as divine."³¹

Since that time, its theology has been exported to Africa, Asia, Latin America, and Eastern Europe. However, the twenty-first century Sub-Saharan African prosperity expression is an African fabric. Western missionaries met Neo-Pentecostalism and the prosperity gospel in Africa. Therefore, these Western trends of consumerism and progress are neither imported nor exported patterns to Africa. However, a general census of scholars believes that classical Pentecostal trends of consumerism and progress were imported to Africa. David W. Jones and others argue that, "In its modern form, the prosperity gospel can be traced to the thought of E. W. Kenyon (1867–1948), an evangelist, pastor, and founder of Bethel Bible Institute in Spenser, Massachusetts."³² Kenyon is the founder of the health and wealth charismatic movement that influenced the prosperity gospel. Oral Roberts of Tulsa, Oklahoma, is one of the fathers of the prosperity gospel movement in the US.

However, there is no one single prosperity gospel but rather prosperity gospels. The attempt to delineate the American prosperity gospel and an African Congolese expression of prosperity is critical to this scholarship. Has the reality of a Wall Street economics that is shaped by the idea of progress and capital influencing the American prosperity gospel? African philosophical expressions of prosperity have proven the opposite notion. Congolese relate to the culture of prosperity and abundance for humanitarian survival. The prosperity gospel plays a significant role in the Congolese context because people seek God's providence knowing that the Lord can supply their pressing and basic needs, such as food, affordable medical care, housing, a vehicle, deliverance, and their children's education.

Walter Brueggemann, speaking from the consciousness of prophetic imagination, insists, "The contemporary American church is

29. Bowler, *Blessed*, 7.
30. Bowler, *Blessed*, 7.
31. Bowler, *Blessed*, 7.
32. Jones and Woodbridge, *Health, Wealth, and Happiness*, 51.

largely acculturated to the American ethos of consumerism that it has little power to believe or to act."[33] Western prosperity trends capitalize on the gospel to meet their luxurious lifestyles within a demanding economic system. The seekers aspire to mansions and private airplanes, while banking millions through gifts requested from their followers as acts of obedience and faithfulness to sow seeds.

In his book, *Economics in Spirit: A Moral Philosophy of Finance*, Nimi Wariboko recognizes "the diversities of prosperity message as it crosses into different cultural, economic contexts."[34] This writer argues that the Wall Street paradigm of financial concern and the America prosperity gospel are influencing the African cosmological worldviews. Prosperity preachers reproduce the American prosperity model. However, the American expressions do no justice to the African contexts. The financial demands contribute to the economic bankruptcy of the most vulnerable poor members of the Global South Church. However, practiced holistically, the prosperity gospel can be transformative as schools, micro-businesses, and clinics are built by renewalists and Neo-Pentecostal-charismatic missional engagements.

A BIBLICAL ANALYSIS

The increase concerning prosperity theology across the globe underscores the systemic use of religion to justify materialism and capitalistic strategies. Congolese self-proclaimed prophets read Solomon's story of accumulating possessions, wealth, and royal consciousness found in 1 Kings 8. Here, the text states that Solomon functioned as a priest and a king. To some extent, the pulpit is often misused or abused as a throne on the expense to reclaim personal financial power and to engage in political propaganda.

Dennis Tongoi advocates prosperity teachings using biblical literature and historical figures such as Solomon. He points out that in Proverbs, Solomon mentions wealth and poverty as major themes to give prudence to the naïve. Tongoi believes that naïve Christians often ignore money because they think it is worldly. Moreover, he suggests, "We must mix God with money which we are going to live out fully God's purposes

---

33. Brueggemann, *The Prophetic Imagination*, 1.
34. Wariboko, *Economics in Spirit*, 102.

for our lives here in the world."³⁵ Tongoi's counter-voice is significant to this research to understand the phenomenon from an African perspective informed by social-economic crisis, poverty, and exploitation.

The royal consciousness in Solomon's lifestyle and biblical stories appeals to Congolese leaders and translates into a status quo of man force. Traditional kings, within the context of the Congo, are offered tributes, wherein they capitalize on these resources. The traditional models of kingship and cultural patterns have been imported into Christianity, whereas the prophet monopolizes resources and assets. Sometimes, in the Congo, prophets and pastors use their power and positions to colonize believers. A Congolese missiologist scholar asserts, "The Congolese church and its people are not yet liberated but are still colonized. This is because the prophets distort the scriptures to exploit and manipulate resources and their adherents."³⁶ Makuta equates the current phenomenon of the proliferation of the prosperity gospel, sowing seeds, and prophecies in post-colonial Congo to the practices of trade indulgences over the past five hundred years ago when Martin Luther saw corruption in the church.

Solomon used religion and power to colonize people, exploit human resources, and gain prosperity. During the rebuilding of the Jerusalem Temple, a systemic capitalistic exploitation of human resources undermined the prophetic quality of the religion at the expense of a consumeristic culture of the monarch. In 1 Kings 5:13–18, Solomon recruited laborers in Lebanon and assigned Adomiran to lead the forced labor to build the Temple. Solomon's regime presented social injustices and the exploitation of human resources. Houses were built in which people did not live. Others planted vineyards and did not drink wine. Such models of an exploitative regime resemble capitalistic consciousness machinery. Brueggemann concludes, "The entire program of Solomon now appears to have been a self-serving achievement with its sole purpose the

---

35. Tongoi, *Mixing God with Money*, iv-ix.

36. Bijoux, Interviewed May 15, 2017. Makuta argues, "Some Pastors and prophets exploit and enslave their members, the reason being that most people who join their movements are either jobless or experience extreme poverty therefore persons in this category have less or no options. As a result, they massively join these prophetic movements because they are appealing to them." Makuta further suggests that if the body of Christ can work from the grassroots, and if the Congolese government would be responsible, these prosperity renewal movements will end their exploitative character. In other words, people have limited or no choices.

self-securing of the king and dynasty."³⁷ Prosperity preachers in the postcolonial Congo seem to be self-serving.

As Brueggemann puts it, "Fundamental to his social policy was the practice of forced labor that benefited the state or the political economy."³⁸ In 1 Kings 4:13–18, Solomon uses tens of thousands of men for forced labor. This is an example of capitalistic exploitation. Such policies seem to be exploitative. The African's adherence to Solomon's methods seems compelling for the church to be a prophetic voice because the same exploitative policies of abuse are reinforced.

The Abrahamic covenant is another metaphor used by Congolese Neo-Pentecostal and charismatic preachers as a warrant to justify the practices of the prosperity gospel. Since Abraham is recognized as the equivalent to a modern multi-millionaire, Congolese equate themselves as adopted sons and daughters or the seed to inherit Abrahamic prosperity. Genesis 13:6 interprets Abram's material wealth as a mass substantially greater than anything the land could support. The agricultural implication in the reading of Old Testament texts appeals to Congolese religious and cosmic spiritualized worldviews. Zulu Xakalashe states, "Prophets read the O.T. texts especially in Leviticus to argue that, 'The rest of the grain offering belongs to Aaron and his Sons (Lev 2:3a).'"³⁹

---

37. Bijoux, Interviewed May 15, 2017.

38. Brueggemann asserts, "The establishment of a controlled, static religion in which God and his Temple have become part of the royal landscape, in which sovereignty of God is fully subordinated to the purpose of the king. This static religion for me implies that the imperial system benefitted in the name of God by exploiting its subjects. This explains the current struggle of separation between religions and states. Sometimes, religion is used to support political propaganda. It is disheartening when people use God's name to enslave others economically, politically, and socially. Moses' ruling system was based on covenant tolerated divine promises. Moreover, his main programs necessarily and systematically subordinated the question of justice and freedom." See Brueggemann, *The Prophetic Imagination*, 28. For the task of prophetic leadership, unlike Solomon's reign, God was not available or accessible to all people, for Moses tended to stress the freedom of God at the expense of His accessibility" (27–28).

39. Prophets use and read this Scripture as a justification to collect wealth but leave their clients bankrupted. Xakalashe, Interviewed April 22, 2017, Potchefstroom, South Africa. Xakalashe is the senior pastor of a new branch of the orphan church of Zion which has been transformed from being a traditional African Independent into a charismatic renewal church. Xakalashe has broken the institutional policy of the sect. Originally, according to him, Zionism was a spectacle of Western trends of Christianity. Even though they use the Bible, they have nothing to do with the Western model of church or worship. Second, their priests do not attend theological training.

THE ROLE OF THE BIBLE

The Bible has been misused and misinterpreted for various purposes. Biblical literature, in some contexts, has sanctioned the effects of colonialism, imperialism, patriarchy, and justification of violence within oppressive or exploitative settings. Brenner Van Henten states, "In a world soaked in global capitalism, the Bible has become another commodity, a material-cultural object in a capitalist period of Western civilization. Especially, in relation to the commodity culture of the consumerist society in which we in the West all live now."[40]

Likewise, within academia or academic settings in the global marketplace, volumes are written and reproduced to raise money and sanction greed and prosperity. Can theological education be offered free of charge? Kenyan leader Jomo Kenyatta complained, "When the missionaries came to Africa they had the Bible, and we had the land. They said let us pray. We closed our eyes, and when we opened them, we had the Bible, and they had the land."[41] Was the Bible's role to colonize its recipients while its translation into vernacular cultures gave it an indigenous voice? This writer argues that Africans had access to both the Bible and land while the imperialistic agenda related to social economic exploitation of human resources attempted to overcome the sacred character of the biblical Gospel.

Fashole-Luke argues, "Following the availability of the Bible translation in the vernaculars, the vast majority of Africans have an uncritical approach to Scripture."[42] Biblical hermeneutics has become an ongoing process and necessity within locally founded churches. Van Henten posits, "On the other end of the spectrum of translating and appropriating the Bible, it becomes a fetish. A major factor for the adequate use of the Bible is the practice of venerating it, leading to either magical or idola-

---

Xakalashe is the first to cross that line of traditional policy as he attended Timothy Bible Institute and is a trained theologian. This implies that when prophets demand believers or clients to slaughter an animal such as a cow or goat or perform a cleansing deliverance, the prophet takes all the meat in addition to the money based on his misreading of OT texts.

40. Van Henten, *Bible Translation on the Threshold of the Twenty-First Century*, 116.

41. Jenkins, *The Next Christendom*, 52. "The remark has been quoted by Archbishop Desmond Tutu, and plenty of observers share this view."

42. Van Henten, *Bible Translation of the Threshold of the Twenty-First Century*, 110.

trous practice."⁴³ The problem, however, is what has happened to current Christendom as the Bible is now in the hands of indigenous people.

The theological discourse shows the book that contains sacred writings has been used as a magical nuclear code. The Bible has been misunderstood and misinterpreted. The Bible has been used for centuries as a tool, to colonize, exploit, and silence the margins. The Scriptures have been used as a tool to justify polygamy, child sacrifice, and systemic oppressive regimes.

The Bible is becoming an African book as it has been appropriated and owned by the locals. Van Henten states, "This is already true of the Greek translation of the Hebrew Bible which was produced in the second and third centuries BCE in North Africa, and which became the Bible of the early Christian church."⁴⁴ Bediako asserts, "It is also a metaphor for the *enculturation* of the gospel characterized by the incarnational quality of Christianity that reached its zenith in the human form ascribed to Jesus Christ since the process of translating the Bible submitted the Christian faith to the terms of local culture."⁴⁵ The Bible and the Gospel are not alien in Africa; the Bible was made in Africa, and the gospel is an African story.

Missionaries brought their Western version of the Bible, but they found the Bible and God in Africa under different names and categories. Missionaries' efforts and evangelism clarified the pre-existing revelation. Bediako argues, "Once this essential, universal relevance of Jesus Christ

---

43. Van Henten, *Bible Translation of the Threshold of the Twenty-First Century*, 117.

44. Van Henten, *Bible Translation of the Threshold of the Twenty-First Century*, 95.

45. Van Henten, *Bible Translation of the Threshold of the Twenty-First Century*, 99. Van Henten argues, "This is conspicuous in the influence of translated Bibles in contributing to the formation of local or indigenous churches, theologies, as well as to social and cultural development in Africa. The process of vernacular translation regularly initiated the first detailed inventory of local language and culture and had far reached consequences and—in subversive contradiction to an often-dominant Western paradigm of the missionary translators—providing the root for nationalism. Vernacular Bibles, although the real engine of the mission, have led to the transmission of authority in both the mainline and independent churches in Africa. Whereas in the past before translations were available, authority was often related to the historical centers of missions and churches, access to vernacular Bibles relocated such authority to Africa"(99–100). Vernacular cultures and Bible translations gave power to the recipients to domesticate Christ and the Gospel and reclaim their belonging to the body of Christ.

is granted, it is no longer a question of trying to accommodate the gospel in our culture, and the gospel becomes our story."[46]

Furthermore, Van Henten asserts, "It is often claimed that vernacular Bibles were primarily responsible for the spread of Christianity in Southern Africa, enabling Christian groups and churches to develop and grow independently from established, mainline church formations."[47] The translation of the Bible was a critical achievement and force for the development of the indigenous church and the emergence of the new face of Christendom. As a result, the Hebrew Bible has increasingly become an African book, since the conceptual context of the Hebrew language is closely aligned with the connotation of African languages as people still living in a worldview adjacent to an OT and NT biblical context. There is a close connection between the stories in the Hebrew Bible relating to demonic forces, poverty, lack of resources, and African worldviews. For instance, occult sacrifices, divination, prophetic activities, poverty starvation, demonic forces, and the high place of oral traditions are trends within African Christianities.

BIBLICAL HERMENEUTICS

Biblical hermeneutics are critical for a comprehensive understanding of verbal and non-verbal communiqué of the gospel within a prehistoric dominant oral tradition culture. The gospel is communicated through the vehicle of individuals' mouths to ears and is translated from the French, *De la bouche à l'Oreille*, referring to self-theologizing in the streets without paying attention to the theological implication of the texts. As a result, people have become victims of alteration. Instead of the gospel being a transformative force, it is altered into a new expression.

The biblical and theological distortion of the Gospel translates into a "new gospel." Indeed, the theology of this new gospel seems far more to fit the American dream than it does the teaching of Him who had nowhere to lay His head."[48] Gordon D. Fee surmises, American Christianity is rapidly being infected by an insidious disease, the so-called wealth and health Gospel-although it has very little of character of the Gospel in it. The message goes like this: It is in the Bible God says it. So think

---

46. Bediako, *Jesus and the Gospel in Africa*, 25.
47. Van Henten, *Bible Translation on the Threshold of the Twenty-First Century*, 94.
48. Fee, *The Disease of the Health and Wealth Gospels*, 7.

God's thoughts. Claim it, and it is yours."[49] According to Fee, "The basic problems here are hermeneutical; i.e., they involve questions as to how one interprets Scripture."[50] The prosperity gospel is attractive to many believers in Africa because it contains elements of biblical facts.

New Testament Texts

Neo-Pentecostal preachers often read 3 John 2 to legitimize prosperity and health as a warrant for Christians to prosper. The text does not suggest an accumulation of health and wealth for Christians. According to Fee, the "Greek word translated prosper," means a wish or a formula of greetings.[51] In short, John uses a metaphor.

Moreover, the interpretation of "abundant life" in John 10:10 does not warrant materialism or owning private airplanes. In John 3:16, the gospel's translation of eternal life means life after this present life. It "literally means the life of the age to come. The Greek word used *with*, translated more abundantly in the King James Version means simply that believers are to enjoy the gift of life to the full NIV."[52] John records the anticipated fulfillment of the age to come as an eschatological paradigm referring to God's kingdom.

Matthew 11:28 is another biblical text used by charismatic preachers in the Congo to justify social, economic relief instead of spiritual deliverance from the yoke and weariness of human sin. First, the phrase "come to me" is a gracious invitation that Jesus offers to the universal church. Read through the lens of Matthew 23:4, as it relates to Acts 15:10 and 13:39, these texts talk about freedom, being delivered from the yoke of slavery and self-accountability. Also, the texts speak against the systemic abuse of imposing heavy burdens on another.

---

49. Fee, *The Disease of the Health and Wealth Gospels*, 7

50. Fee, *The Disease of the Health and Wealth Gospels*, 9.

51. Fee, *The Disease of the Health and Wealth Gospels*, 10. 3 John 2 states, "I pray that you may prosper in all things and be in health, just as your soul prospers." Fee discusses that, "Just as a friend in a letter, say I wish this letter finds you well. This combination of wishing for things to go well and for the recipient's good health was the standard form of greetings in a personal letter in antiquity. To extend John's wish for Gaius to refer to financial and material prosperity for all Christians of all times is entirely foreign." Fee, *The Disease of the Health and Wealth Gospels*, 10.

52. Fee, *The Disease of the Health and Wealth Gospels*, 11.

These texts in Matthew 23:4 and Acts 15:10 and 13:39, read parallel with John 14:27, 16:33, and Romans 5:1, explain the same message from Christ on peace. As a result, all these texts interpret Christ's point in Matthew 11:28. Matthew 11:29 tells how this peace can be imparted to believers as the peace that transcends human understanding. Philippians 4:7 affirms the essence of this anticipated peace distinct from material prosperity.

Mark 10:30 is also misread and mistranslated to suggest that if faithful believers sow seeds, they will receive a hundredfold of the following: houses, airplanes, beautiful children, husbands/wives, and so forth. Matthew's theology of "the poor in spirit" strongly conflicts with the ideology of storing treasures in Matthew 6:19–20. It also contradicts the woe that Jesus declares against the rich in Luke 6:20, 24.

2 Corinthians 8:9 points out, "Christ became poor so that you through his poverty might become rich." The text is often removed from its original context or literary and historical contexts. The Congolese reading materializes the biblical message to raise money. Bijoux Makuta asserts, "Some Congolese prophets and pastors distort the scriptures to exploit their members. Members give money to the prophet or the preacher this mechanism of giving enriches one person the prophet but impoverishes the givers. I think people can sow seeds of love and social change by making a difference to improve the condition of life."[53]

Old Testament Texts

Biblical metaphors in the pages of sacred writings are filled with words of prosperity from Genesis to Revelation. God is the author of prosperity, but He is not a God of consumerism equivalent to modern banking systems. As Hermen Kroesbergen argues, "Prosperity in the Old Testament is provided by God. It is God that makes one prosper, and it is a gift from God (Deut. 8:18)."[54] Kroesbergen argues "We are therefore in agreement with C. E Green (2010:128) who summarizes that God is certainly a God of prosperity, but definitively not a God of consumerist values and materialism."[55] The OT presents both the ethical and spiritual dimensions of prosperity as its texts are linked to the covenant.

---

53. Makuta, Interviewed May 15, 2017.
54. Kroesbergen, *In Search of Health and Wealth*, 22.
55. Kroesbergen, *In Search of Health and Wealth*, 22.

Jones and Woodbridge argue:

> For example, at one end of the economic spectrum, Scripture appears to present poverty as both a blessing and a curse. Compare Proverbs 23:21, which warns, the drunkard and the glutton will come to poverty, with Jesus' teaching in Luke 6:20 which reads: Blessed are you who are poor, for yours is the kingdom of God. Likewise, at the other end of the economic spectrum, a number of passages describe wealth as both a blessing and a curse.[56]

The OT Mosaic laws of economic policies and theocratic regulations were ethical codes of conduct for labor meant to protect the minority communities. The policies were also meant to defend the oppressed poor against the wealthy and promote a just system of social, economic equality. These policies were instrumental to the understanding of God concerning wealth and poverty. They were not limited to civil laws, cancellation of debts in the Sabbath year (Deut 15:1–3), and reversion of property in the year of Jubilee (Lev 25:34).

Deuteronomy 28:2 is often interpreted as a hallmark of prosperity teaching that God blesses the obedient through material prosperity. The OT instituted the giving of a "tenth of one's material increase, including agricultural products, livestock, grain, wine, oil and other material goods" to support the priest for worship, organizational structure, foreigners, orphans, widows (Cf. Lev 27:30–34; Deut 12–14).[57] The tithe system in the Congo benefits the prophets and excludes recipients of the Gospel.

Malachi 3:8–10 is used to legitimate giving a tenth of a percent of resources gained. God says, "Bring the whole tithe into the storehouse, that there may be food in my house. Test me in this, says the LORD Almighty, and see if I will not throw open the floodgates of heaven and pour out so much blessing that there will not be room enough to store it" (Mal 3:10). Malachi was "calling people back to God by giving their hearts in surrender to the Lord."[58]

---

56. Jones and Woodbridge, *Health, Wealth and Happiness*, 125.
57. Jones and Woodbridge, *Health, Wealth and Happiness*, 143.
58. Jones and Woodbridge, *Health, Wealth and Happiness*, 152. The writers aver, "Malachi 3:8–10 is a call to repentance from the sin of wandering from God. As Andrew Hill notes, By calling for full tithe the prophet invites genuine repentance, a return to God with the whole heart. Jones and Woodbridge, *Health, Wealth and Happiness*, 152. In other words, "the failure to give was an external symbol of Israel's internal spiritual bankruptcy. A valid principle from this text is that one is giving can be used to

The original word "test" translated from the Hebrew means to examine or prove one's faithfulness and generosity. The test is a call to repentance of sins and to honor the Mosaic laws. This is because the Temple was regarded as the center of Jewish life. Travelers, or believers, from distant lands would come to Jerusalem for Passover celebration or to attend worship in the Temple. Malachi calls people to bring food into the Temple to sustain strangers and foreign worshipers upon their arrival.

The Westernized prosperity gospel's trend has often become an appropriation of African Christianity. The biblical canon is constantly being rewritten and reclaimed to fit into Congolese socio-political, cultural, economic, and spiritual paradigms. Kroesbergen declares, "One reason for the prosperity gospel's success in Africa is that Christians receive a steady diet of the gospel from the television and the radio and few people have the tools and preparation to evaluate the message, as to whether or not it is biblical."[59] It is critical to understand that there is a lack of solid theological tools to interpret the Scripture in Africa.

CONTEXTUAL HERMENEUTICS

The contextual hermeneutical interpretation is a literal translation of the biblical literature. There is a need for radical biblical discernment for the development of a culturally contextualized and biblically based hermeneutical framework. It is critical to reclaim and re-establish a hermeneutic of mixed methodologies, both qualitative and quantitative approaches, for an actual interpretative process. For instance, the qualitative approach is to assess what has happened to the recipients of the gospel, the Congolese. Since they received the good news, has there been a holistic transformation? The contextual hermeneutical approach interrogates the post-realities, and asks, "What has happened in the life and mind of the receiving side, the natives"? Have they discarded or discontinued the pre-historic belief system? On the other hand, the quantitative approach is to analyze the rapid growth of the new Christendom and its implications for the global church. In other words, the interpreter must

---

measure one's love and devotion to God. If a person is generous in giving toward God's work, it reflects positively on that person's spiritual maturity. If one neglects to give sacrificial seed, it demonstrates a lack of love or worship toward God. This application reflects God's desire for worship and is a timeless principle that is repeated in the New Testament" (152).

59. Kroesbergen, *In Search of Health and Wealth*, 36.

seek solutions by using combined methods to construct a contextual and critical interpretation of the Bible in the Congo.

The literal, contextual translation is a tool in the hands of Congolese interpreters to recognize the historical context of the Bible and its humanitarian aspects. This is to argue that the Bible records God's revelation to humanity and, at the same time, analyzes specific human situations. Therefore, the contextual process is to evaluate the historical and textual aspects of the biblical passages. To avoid the African pre-assumption of cultural baggage, which affects how the Congolese interpret the Bible, the interpreter has to be neutral so that the text might speak to humanity's conscience and experience the voice of Christ in the text instead of the voice of Congolese culture. The Bible is not another book in the hand of the librarian and on the shelf of the humanity's library. Instead, it is God's story and His interaction with the human race.

To evaluate the historical and contextual realities, the Congolese interpreter must consider the context of a worldview rooted in extreme poverty, demonic forces, spirit-power, dreams and symbols, and people confronted by humanitarian concerns, such as displacement and starvation. These worldviews inform the ways Congolese interpreters read and exegete the Scripture but tend to ignore reconstructing the original intent of the biblical canon. Thus, a literal translation or literary framework means an ability to exegete without cultural pre-assumption, to re-establish the religious, social-historical, and political contexts from which the text emerges to reconstruct the authentic meaning of the story. For instance, the interpreter should consider the scientific methodologies and evaluate the text in light of Congolese multi-culturalism, with its diverse languages and dialects. There are underlying issues in play related to grammar, syntax, contemporary meaning of the text, and historical and literary contexts. However, the interpreter must rediscover a plain meaning of the text for a critical-contextual framework to inform the translation of the prosperity theology in Sub-Sahara Africa.

DIVINE HEALING

Sub-Saharan Africa is one of the regions of the continent experiencing the highest human afflictions caused by tropical epidemics and endemic diseases. The lack of adequate medical and sanitation resources, along with affordable health care systems, are reasons for the rapid growth of the health and wealth gospel. As a result, traditional medicine and occult systems remain practical or favorable options for those who suffer. Praying and neo-prophetic churches maximize the opportunity to offer prayer healing as an alternative solution to humanity's plight. Healing prayer is the center of the whole doctrine of the prosperity gospel and the rise of a different gospel within the Congolese religious terrain. Missionaries were not prepared to deal with African worldviews of demonic forces, disease, and affliction, which sometimes required exorcism and cosmological experiences.

Medical discourse is often the last option as believers tend to consult traditional healers and Ngangas while still affiliating with their churches. Prayer has been replaced by the invocation of spirit-filled and occult powers. Congolese believe in divine intervention and God's power to heal their physical and spiritual ills through faith and fervent prayers. James 5:14 asks, "Is anyone among you sick? Let them call the elders of the church to pray over them and anoint them with oil in the name of the Lord."

Praying churches and overnight prayers of deliverance are standard practices within charismatic renewal churches. The Congo is a post-war community experiencing a dehumanizing state of socio-economic and political crises and ecological turmoil. In this context, divine healing is viewed as an answer and liberation against both physical and spiritual misfortune.

Traditional healers' roles and application of traditional medicine become integral to the phenomenon of the search for wellness within the renewal movement. To that end, North American theologies of the health and wealth gospel attract multitudes because the theology finds a fertile soil across the spectrum of the Congolese religious terrain. The theory of healing transcends physical healing to engage in speaking in tongues as a radical response to misfortunes caused by spiritualized demonic forces.

"GLOSSOLALIA" TONGUES

The charismatic practice of tongues and its interpretative politics present sociological, theological, and spiritual implications vis-à-vis the integrity of the gospel. Glossolalia, the gift of speaking in tongues, has been translated as a legitimate force for spiritual elite, classism, and religious oppression.⁶⁰ These trends reinforce the philosophical tradition of man force in post-colonial Congo. For instance, there are class privileges caused by the systemic accumulation of wealth among self-made millionaires. Neo-Pentecostals claim a supernatural authority and ability to receive or verbally hear a direct instruction of the Holy Spirit.

This writer argues that to speak in innovative tongues is an evidence of the Holy Spirit incarnated in one's life, which symbolizes the new birth. However, Glossolalia has become the machinery of Pentecostals' consciousness sanctioning either spiritual or social change, or renewal. Wariboko asserts, "New birth, born again, born of water and spirit, new creation—all these terminologies that emphasize new beginnings, the renewing of mind for a new phase in life, and then initiation of something new."⁶¹ Besides the ethical ethos upside of tongues, there is a political downside which makes up Pentecostal characteristics.

These worshipers imagine themselves as having access to the supernatural presence of the divine nature by placing God in a box. Here, God only listens to certain people. Self-proclaimed bishops, apostles, evangelists, and pastors use glossolalia to legitimize a new culture of neo-colonial systemic ethos. Tongues attract massive Congolese believers as

60. The term "glossolalia" refers to heavenly evangelic languages or artifacts of trance considered as signs of one being filled with the power of Holy Spirit and as a gift for self-edification as illustrated in Pauline writings. 1 Corinthians 14 is better used than Acts 2 where Luke writes about tongues as a power received by people to communicate in other languages so that the recipients of the gospel would hear the gospel in their own mother tongues. However, Paul preferred glossolalia as a speech or prophecy translation of the gospel. Justo L. Gonzalez defines the term glossolalia as a name originated: "Since [the] nineteen[th] Century to speaking in tongues. It appears in the New Testament in what are apparently two different forms. In the account of Pentecost in Acts, the disciples speak in tongues of others who are present. In the Pauline epistles: speaking in tongues is certainly a gift of the Spirit, but here it seems to occur within the community of believers. This is even when no one can understand what is being said, and serves for the edification of the person speaking in tongues rather than of others or the community (1 Cor 14:4)." See Gonzalez, *Essential Theological Terms*, 66.

61. Wariboko, *The Pentecostal Principle*, 134. Wariboko insists that both language and the new birth coincide with natality independent from pre-existing human languages. He says, "The new language he or she speaks may be conditioned, but it is not entirely determined by preexisting human languages; its grammar, rules, and contents are not an imitation of preexisting languages. By this innovation, the new believer is an actor in the (Arentian) [sic] sense of the word" (135). He further argues, "The political natality is the actualization of gifts (spiritual and non-spiritual), which makes space for individuals in shared common existence as distinguished carriers of the Holy Spirit and creative transformers of culture in the name of Christ" (135).

they subscribe to the movement. Nonetheless, the mystical ramification of glossolalia is a distinctive feature and indicator of the socio-economic and spiritual state. Their implication is seen during the translation of the gospel.

Paul says in 1 Corinthians 14:4, that if no one can understand or translate tongues, it serves for the edification of the person and does not benefit the church. Gonzalez explains, "In such cases, Paul refers to prophecy—preaching –and suggests that any speech in tongues should be translated so that the church may be edified."[62] The problem of the rise of glossolalia is that speaking in tongues has been reduced to a mystical encounter between the human-divine and normalized as an essential means to fit the material needs of the prophets rather than the evangelized. Thus, prioritizing a prophetic voice that is focused on evangelism or the kerygma of the gospel, rather than apocalyptic prediction, is critical for a genuine translation of Christianity in the twenty-first century.

Members of the body of Christ who claim to have the ability to predict the future control their followers and spiritually colonize them. Moreover, tongue speakers often use their spiritual gifts and experience to manipulate or twist the Gospel and control the mind of believers. As a result, the recipients become easy targets to contribute their money and assets to the ministries of the self-proclaimed prophets and prophetesses. Charles D. Isbell shares, "Thus, when Paul enjoined the Corinthians to seek the *pneumatika*, especially the ability to prophecy. It was not because Paul believed that it was possible for every member or participant of the congregation to predict the future. But, it is believed that because he thought that everyone could proclaim the gospel and so produce learning and comfort or exhort (14:30)."[63] Therefore, Paul prioritizes the kerygma of the Gospel or prophecy over glossolalia.

THE ROLE OF PROPHETS IN THE HEBREW BIBLE

Succession narrative scholars claim that a "court of David" in 1 Kings 1–2 sanctions the mechanism of systematic corruption, monopolization, and the abuse of power, and structures of injustice and inequalities.[64] 2 Samuel 11 records David's violence of rape condemned by the

---

62. Wariboko, *The Pentecostal Principle*, 135.
63. Isbell, "Glossolalia and *Propheteialalia*," 15.
64. Coogan, *The Old Testament*, 250–51.

prophet Nathan. Nathan plays a key role as a prophetic voice and God's messenger. Neo-prophetic voices in the Congo are used by government officials and politicians to perpetuate abusive policies. Still, in 1 Kings 1–2, Nathan used his role to manipulate his audience. For instance, in 1 Kings 1, Nathan manipulates David's plan for political propaganda to convince Bathsheba to appeal to the king on behalf of his son to be given the throne.

Prophetic cycles are equated to capitalistic, centralized, self-serving systems available to only the elite, and those in power are served rather than the marginalized poor. Solomon's achievements were made possible by oppressive social-political policies. There were established alliances with surrounding states, especially through marriage, extensive building projects, foreign human resource exploitation, forced labor trade, and prosperity. There was political centralization, social stratification, shifts in land tenure, and domestic repressions of trade, diplomacy, and war.[65]

---

65. Brueggemann explains that God did something new during the Exodus by using Moses. He used Moses in freeing Israel. He worked against Pharaoh's oppressive rule. Moses' birth initiated the formation of a new community which was God-centered and focused upon freedom, justice, and compassion. Contrary to the autocratic oppression of Pharaoh and his exploitative leadership, Moses' movement assured Israel's liberation. This liberating system developed a new social order as prophetic leadership. Micah 2:1–5 reveals typical structures of prophecy like in Isaiah and Jeremiah. Here, the key issue is the narrative which discusses the rich oppressive classes, or the elites of society, who continue to get richer at the expense of the poor because these elites control the power structures of society. Also, the landowners appropriated the resources. The economic system or practice that Micah criticizes is the established authority of the king. Micah is criticizing a broken and corrupt system and the economic practices of social injustice. Hence, the prophecy or prediction of disaster becomes a strategy to persuade the audience. This formula plays a critical role in bringing about a revolution and transformation. The phrase "says the Lord" can be traced back to the OT. Prophets placed God in the middle of the drama and said He commanded them to bring forth the message of economic production and social inequality. Thus, the voiceless had to suffer because the wealth and prosperity were shared among the elites. In this way, the priests played a vital role in supporting the systematic abuse of the poor to reinforce the policies and productivity of the agricultural products and sometimes high taxes through collections and tithes. Today, people deal with issues of the struggle of separation between the state and church. The church has become corrupt and is sometimes used to promote political propaganda and sanction the mechanism of impoverishment.

THE ROLE OF PROPHECIES IN THE POST-COLONIAL CONGO

Neo-prophetic leaders view themselves as "porte-paroles or spokespersons," anointed with a supernatural unction to foretell God's consciousness and people's matters.[66] Prophecies play a critical role in reconstructing new religious systems that attract millions. On the one hand, prophetic enterprise grants freedom and opportunities, empowering individuals to fulfill their potential regardless of their gender, race, and social relations and classes. Wariboko states, "If one was free before the Reformation, and some became free under Pentecostalism. This is the moral interpretation of Pentecostal core belief that all can prophesy, all can lead, all can initiate the new, and all can equally be carriers of the Spirit."[67] Wariboko talks about the Pentecostal spirit that captures the Christian expression of self-consciousness.

On the other hand, the *prophethood* of all believers must interrogate whether prophecy democratizes Christianity and, at the same time, perpetuates or enhances the neo-liberal culture practice of progress and baptized capitalism. Neo-Pentecostalism's spirit resists the spirit of capitalism at the same time it furthers or enhances the same ethos.[68] Pentecostalism enables capitalism to flourish. Wariboko surmises, "Protesting or hard work is one of the ways of answering to the system."[69] Neo-Pentecostal drives for social lift motivate them to hard work to improve their social-economic living condition. Wariboko avers, "Work is also a spiritual fact of human freedom, a means, to transcend the limitations of both nature and history, to affirm the divine matrix from which humans stand in and stand out. Work stands at the juncture of immanence and transcendence.

---

66. Coogan defines a Prophet as a "spokesperson. The prophets were believed to be the recipients of direct communication from God's sayings." Coogan, *The Old Testament*, 551.

67. Wariboko, *The Pentecostal Principle*, 132.

68. Wariboko, *The Pentecostal Principle*, 147. The belief is that all believers can directly hear from the Holy Spirit, all can speak forth the Word of God (prophecy), and all are endowed and empowered (Spirit-baptized) to form new groups to serve the Lord to do good works on earth. "The more interesting and productive question to ask is how the twentieth-and twenty-first-century Pentecostal spirit comes about in capitalism and further enhances the progress of capitalism" (147).

69. Wariboko, *The Pentecostal Principle*, 147.

Its depth is both its destiny and *telos*. Its destiny is both its depth and *telos*."[70]

Prophetic miscarriage emerged from the prophetic lines in the Hebrew Bible context. Prophetic voices fail to alter abusive policies which sanction socio-economic exploitations. In some cases, bishops and prophetic leaders engage to perpetuate the same corrupt systems when they are hired in a high range of governmental offices. As insiders of the same autocratic, oppressive system, they remain silent in the face of socio-political and economic crisis. Moreover, false prophecies divide families and create a pattern of conflict within household systems; they promote corruption and social inequality similar to the prophetic line and succession in the Hebrew Bible theories within the prosperity gospel movement.

THE ROLE OF THE HOLY SPIRIT IN POST-COLONIAL CONGO

The Holy Spirit plays a significant role in constructing a cosmological paradigm as Congolese are empowered to respond to Christian missions. For instance, within the paradigm of third world countries of Sub-Saharan Africa exclusively in the post-colonial Congo, the Holy Spirit has played a critical role in altering social, political, moral, and humanitarian struggles. First, the Holy Spirit anointed Jesus to preach the good news to the poor and the oppressed and give hope to those who are brokenhearted, to proclaim freedom and liberty or release the prisoners living in the shadow of captivity and to announce the year of God's favor (Isa 61:1–2).

Second, the Pentecost experience of the Acts 2 community in the first century was a turning point for global revival, and since that time, Christianity has become a world-wide religion. The dispossession of the Holy Spirit at Pentecost was a transformative force which generated not only the birth of the global church, but also the disciples were empowered to carry on the mission of discipleship. Nonetheless, the universal nature of Christianity occurred after the global dispensation of the gifts of the Holy Spirit. As a result, ordinary people became missionaries and had a heart to follow Jesus' commands by taking the Gospel to the ends of the earth. Gregg R. Allison states, "The chief event of the Holy Spirit

---

70. Wariboko, *The Depth and Destiny of Work*, 4–5.

is after the ascension of Christ to heaven, rather than before his coming into the world. For, before that, it was upon the prophets alone, and upon a few individuals. However, after the advent of the Savior, the Spirit is poured out on all Christians."[71] The Spirit poured out upon the Congolese is reforming the religious landscape to suggest social lift, empowerment, and development.

The Holy Spirit inspires the Congolese to initiate a revolutionary movement as a new form of awakening that breaks through and reforms their social fabric. For instance, Simon Kimbangu's movement during 1921 was regarded as a Congolese holiness movement. In the dawn of the British Baptists' missionary evangelization, Kimbangu inspired a movement that has generated a big number of followers globally. His healing ministry and miraculous operations in the name of Jesus contributed to the liberation of the Congolese from cosmological trends to political liberation that included resistance against colonialism. However, Dieudonné Sita Luemba, a Congolese missiologist scholar argues that, "Kimbangu never converted to Christianity, but that he and his followers use Christian concepts as they practice syncretism."[72] This writer argues that the Kimbangu movement was a Congolese Pentecostal experience.

Congolese Christians receive the same general revelation as Western Christians. Missionaries did not bring the Holy Spirit to Africa; some encountered Him while on the mission field. Also, the locals' engagement in spiritual and social lift exemplifies the mission and role of the Holy Spirit in the life of Congolese. The *parakletos* is identified as a helper, power, comforter; and yet, Jesus is the one who causes Him to be bestowed on humankind. Allison opines, "A chief role of the Holy Spirit was

71. Allison, *Historical Theology*, 332.

72. Luemba, Interviewed May 19, 2017. Luemba, who is the current Dean of Centre de Missiologie au Congo and an eye witness of the phenomenon, asserts, "Missionaries brought a non-contextualized gospel in the Congo, instead of a Westernized Christianity and culture. Congolese were baptized without experiencing actual conversion. Once individuals were evangelized, Missionaries wanted them to wear clothes in the same manner like Westerners civilized do. In other words, Luemba says that Missionaries brought a gospel in the marmite or mask of Europeans. This had left a vacuum especially at the dawn of political shift in 1971 with Mobutu's proclamation of 'Retour à l'authenticité' a number of Congolese rejected Christianity as a Western culture or religion of the colonizer. Even though in 1875 Baptist Missionaries evangelized persons like Simon Kimbangu, people started mixing Christian worldviews with traditional belief systems, or they practiced syncretism. Kimbanguism is one such example which has operated over the decades as a syncretic movement, in this sect persons were baptized not converted." Luemba, Interviewed May 19, 2017

to bring comfort to Christians, as the term *Paraclete* (the Apostle John's preferred word for him) emphasized."[73] The Holy Spirit plays a significant role in the life of believers.

CASE STUDIES

It is worth to document that throughout the post-colonial era, new prophetic leadership visions were birthed among those who inspired a revolution within the Congolese Christianity. One of the Congolese Pentecostal prophets whose ministry and methods of re-transmitting the gospel have significantly impacted Christians is the prophet Mechac of Kaboto near Lenge village in Kabongo, Katanga's Province. His prophetic ministries are based on spirit-filled prosperity gospel practices that have proven to be effective tools and healthy or authentic models for evangelism and complete holism. Nevertheless, his prophetic teachings provide healing where patients or adherents are kept for a period of time. The integrity of his prophetic ministry is built on the foundation that he does not require followers to sow seeds in order to sponsor his ministry, but instead, he prays, minister and feeds them freely. Mechac ministers to them with the Word and offers a high quality of pastoral care and counseling therapy. Also, he trains adherents to work with their hands for self-sustaining and liability. As a result, once these patients are healed, they are able to return to their respective homes well-equipped as responsible citizens. At the same time, he prays for them and performs deliverance without using traditional occult practices such as anointing oil, ritual bathing, and drinking of blessed water. In addition, these patients are fed with healthy food, and they receive spiritual, physical and emotional treatments. People come from all over the country and overseas to seek and experience true deliverance, renewal, and real prosperity for the body, mind, and spirit. For instance, during liberation war (1997) in the wake of oppression and violence by Rwandan forces' invasion in the Congo his ministry contributed the peacebuilding resolution and reconciliation between the malicious rebels the "*May May*" and the Congolese government.

Therefore, the rationale of this thesis is to provide a systematic examination of the neo-Pentecostal movement in order to understand the prosperity gospel. Growing generations and readers in the 21st century

---

73. Allison, *Historical Theology*, 331.

and years to come in the Global South and North will be able to appreciate the effects of neo-Pentecostalism's revolutions and its missional impacts. It is also imperative to alter the hermeneutic that seems manipulative and exploitative and instead, develop an authentic, comprehensive model for evangelism and discipleship for the Congolese.

Prophet Ngoy Kisula's Pentecostal holiness movement in the city of Lubumbashi in Katanga's Province provides social development, spiritual deliverance, and a complete holism. His megachurch and use of the prosperity gospel attracts many. His version of the prosperity gospel has proven to be life-giving rather than exploitive of his adherent's resources. He has responded to the felt needs of the Congolese society. Through his healing ministries, Kisula has built vocational schools, orphanages, and offers spiritual and material support for the marginalized suspected witches, including street children who are often stigmatized and rejected by their families and society. He is involved in the efforts to eradicate poverty by offering assistance in the rebuilding of broken lives and relationships through his rehabilitation center. His prosperity ministry in multi-generational as he addresses spiritual, emotional and physical needs is crucial to the Congolese society. He donates clothes, food, and agricultural equipment. Kisula's case study is an example of neo-Pentecostalism's surging appropriation of the gospel. Prophets Mechac and Kisula's evangelistic approaches prove to be a reliable resource for evangelism. Their evangelistic and missional methods sanction broad analysis of neo-Pentecostal forms which systematically feeding the spirit of prosperity gospels. On the other hand, Reinhard Bonnke and L'Abbé Kasongo's methods of evangelism and prosperity gospel reproduce forms of incomplete holisms.

CONCLUSION

The Congolese version of the prosperity gospel is neither an imported expression of the Azusa Street revival in the US, nor is it Neo-Pentecostalism cut from a Western fabric. The emerging resurgence of the prosperity gospel and the fast growth of Neo-Pentecostal Christianity exemplifies post-colonial responses to the gospel of Jesus Christ. The rise of these trends symbolizes an active engagement of locals in missions and evangelism.

The natives' engagement in mission enterprises is the basis for the changing face of Christianity. In his article "Writing the Pentecostal History of Africa, Asia, and Latin America," Anderson "refutes the idea of American *Jerusalem* and urges a rewriting of this history from the perspective of those who received the Pentecostal missionaries from the West."[74] Native heroes' engagement in missions and evangelism prove there were many centers or Jerusalem's that contributed to the shape of Christianity as it was transformed into a world religion

Moreover, seeing Neo-Pentecostalism and full gospel phenomena as emerging from the US or Europe ignores the extent to which slaves and immigrants brought their cultural religiosity, charisma, and spiritualities to the new world. No one center can be regarded as the birthplace of Pentecostalism. Nor should Neo-Pentecostalism be considered a refuge for the poor and marginalized. The pre-millennial, eschatological spiritual conquest of the world is a Western paradigm of Pentecostalism. This paradigm or trend has been a problem to the shape of global Christianity. The pre-millennial conquest theology saw Western Christianity as liberating to non-Western worlds. The imminent return of Christ, a philosophy that stresses that Christianity must be spread across the planet before humanity's destruction, re-enforced the same cultural imperialisms.

The gospel is a transformative force aimed at altering cultural idioms that produce new and different gospels. The Western model of evangelizing and its application to the gospel of prosperity have constructed new cultural paradigms in African worldviews because the beneficiaries are the prophets, while recipients are often bankrupt. However, a holistic reading of the biblical hermeneutics of the Gospel might yield a systemic spiritual and social transformation.

Lamin Sanneh sustains, "Christianity did not come into a religious vacuum in Africa. Christianity came into a rich religious atmosphere as Africans practiced local religions which have been called either religions or indigenous religions."[75] African traditional cultures offer some positive aspects for the enculturation of Christianity, such as respect for human life, family, ancestors, elders, and communal solidarities. These are all things to appreciate.

---

74. Anderson, "Writing the Pentecostal History of Africa, Asia, and Latin America," 139.

75. Anderson, "Writing the Pentecostal History of Africa, Asia, and Latin America," 139.

There is no one single prosperity gospel, but there are prosperity gospels. However, the gospel of Christ takes root in contexts influenced by social, economic, political, and religious realities. The North American prosperity gospel, for example, is shaped by the history of Pentecostalism and holiness movements rooted in the ethics of progress and neoliberalism. The social, economic, and political realities of the Western worldviews justify preachers' accumulation of assets equivalent to millions and billions of U.S. dollars, living luxurious lifestyles with airplanes and multi-million-dollar mansions.

The Western paradigm is a pattern prompting some African Neo-Pentecostal and charismatic preachers to collect assets from poor members. This North American model of the prosperity gospel seems ineffective to empower and influence the transformation of life in the post-colonial Congo. Hence, the Western pattern of prosperity rooted in classical neoliberalism encourages uncritical hermeneutics.

The African prosperity gospel is meant for survival as people seek God to meet their basic needs, such as a vehicle, home, job, decent life, and healthcare. African churches need to be equipped with notions on finance, critical readings, and interpretations of the Bible for holistic and transformative ministries and discipleship. Hence, church members and religious leaders, as well as the public populace, need expertise in global marketing, Wall Street, the World Bank systems, and transnational and trans-Atlantic trade as they aspire not only for spiritual growth, but also social alteration.

8

Prophetic Voices in the Twenty-First Century

A Congolese Context

INTRODUCTION

THIS CHAPTER DISCUSSES PROPHETIC voices in a twenty-first century Congolese context. Traditionally, the church has operated as a voice for the voiceless and amended structures and policies of systemic repression. For decades, religious organizations in post-colonial Congo have sustained and promoted systems of disempowerment. Neo-Pentecostalism's role and mission are to engage and improve decades of authorized social crisis.

Paradigms of social justice and liberation theologies are reshaping and reinventing African Christendom. For instance, research based on a post-Apartheid residue or remnant of South Africa and other parts of Sub-Saharan Africa has proven social justice's ability to contribute to social change. The church in South Africa has long stood alongside the ignored and oppressed. Donna M. Mertens asserts, "The transformative paradigm offers a philosophical framework to researchers who desire to be part of the change process that is needed to address violations of human rights. Based on ethical assumptions that reflect a commitment to the furtherance of human rights and social justice."[1] To address the

1. Mertens," Advancing Social Change in South Africa Through Transformative Research," 5–17. Mertens sustains, "Examples from South Africa and elsewhere

prophetic voices in the Congolese context, this chapter scrutinizes five areas: (1) The need for prophetic voices, (2) holistic ministries and social justice, (3) spirit-filled power, (4) pre-Christian patterns, and (5) Christianity reshaped and domesticated.

THE NEED FOR PROPHETIC VOICES

Post-colonial Congo, a country torn by civil war, corruption, and socio-political and economic instabilities, needs prophetic and holistic ministries. Mvwala Katshinga insists, "The role of prophetic voices is to proclaim an authentic gospel that will free nations and citizens. Nevertheless, prophetic initiatives consist of caring for the underprivileged, powerless, giving a voice to the voiceless, empowering the weak, and restoring systemic broken structures."[2] James Limburg captures the consciousness of the prophetic task of the OT and draws parallels to contemporary life. He avers that OT prophets were concerned with the treatment of widows, orphans, and the poor, and thus, they were advocates for the powerless.[3] However, some missionaries in the Congo have remained silent in addressing issues of social, economic, moral, and political corruption. In other words, the church in the Congo has often remained silent. Moreover, for decades, religious organizations have either been silent or resisted the structures for the exploitation of minorities. The silence in the face of atrocities and oppression dehumanize humanity and the moral quality of the prophetic character of the gospel. John M. Perkins argues, "There are already signs that the evangelical community, which has been faithful in preaching a bold message of salvation but long silent on social issues like poverty and race is beginning to make its presence felt."[4]

---

illustrate the application of the transformative paradigm." This transformative paradigm relates to social justice which redistributes the social change and transformation of societies in Sub-Sahara Africa. Social justice theologies have influenced the African milieu in different ways when citizens want to emancipate their lives. Mertens documents that "Social inequity, and thus injustice, includes several types of inequalities, namely, economic resources, power structures, and areas of recreation, degradation of living conditions, the environment social structures, and relationships, and direct or indirect exploitation of groups on the basis of gender, race, ethnicity, nationality, disability or sexuality" (16).

2. Katshinga, Interviewed May 19, 2017.
3. Limburg, *The Prophets and the Powerless*, vi.
4. Perkins, *Restoring At-Risk Communities*, 10. See footnote 8 on page 188.

Coretta Scott King argues, "In a world gone mad with arms buildups, chauvinistic passions, and imperialistic exploitation, the church has either endorsed these activities or remained appallingly silent."[5] In the Congo, to an extent, the voices of those living in the margins have been either silenced or ignored for decades. Nonetheless, Bijoux Makuta observes, "Here in Kinshasa, Democratic Republic of Congo churches are not free to voice and advocate for the weak because prophetic religious leaders who attempt to advocate against injustice and abuse are often arrested."[6] The global church's mission is not solely an activist enterprise; instead, its role is integral to God's salvific plan, which bears witness to the eternal gospel of hope. The gospel has the power to transform systemic social systems of political structures and endorse equal opportunities. The gospel has a force to liberate the victims. Katshinga posits, "If the gospel is well received and understood it liberates and transforms the Evangelized."[7]

The gospel is essential; it penetrates the hearts of believers by altering and underlying social-political, economic, and spiritual problems facing the human race. Prophetic leaders must advocate for fundamental human rights, social justice, religious reforms, and political and economic alterations. These men and women are symbols and rainbows of hope, freedom, liberty, and justice to the heart of the consciousness of a broken humanity. The following section will undertake an analysis and history of prophetic voices. Who are prophetic voices, and what is their role?

PROPHETIC VOICES

Prophetic voices are networks of prophetic leaders who risk their lives to initiate a grassroots capacity-building process in the original activist drive. Jesus says, "Greater love has no one than this: to lay down one's life

---

5. King, *A Gift of Love*, 63. Moreover, King avers, "And those who have gone to church to seek the bread and economic justice have been left in the frustration midnight of economic privation. In many instances, the church has aligned itself with the privileged classes and so defended the status quo that it has been unwilling to answer the knock at midnight. If the church does not recapture its prophetic zeal, it will become an irrelevant social club without moral or spiritual authority. If the church does not participate actively in the struggle for peace and economic and racial justice, it will forfeit the loyalty of millions and cause men everywhere to say that it has atrophied its will" (63–64).

6. Bijoux, Interviewed May 15, 2017.

7. Katshinga, Interviewed May 17, 2017.

for one's friends" (John 15:13). These prophetic leaders are voices who arise from and on behalf of the margins to resist structures of oppression and exploitation. Writing from the perspective of at-risk communities in the US inner-cities' social fabric, Perkins argues, "The desperate conditions that face the poor call for a revolution in our attempts at a solution. Desperate problems cannot be solved without strong commitment and risky actions on the part of ordinary Christians with heroic faith."[8]

Prophetic voices respond to the critical needs and challenges confronting their fellow humans. The critical basic human needs and rights are ultimate realities not limited to social-economic, political, and moral reforms that enable the transformation of systemic structures of oppression and exploitation. Prophetic leadership paradigms must be delineated from political activists. Prophets are voices of the voiceless who advocate that spiritual and moral reforms are essential for social change, a just structure of justice, peace, and reconciliation. Prophetic voices' efforts and their blood became the martyr's seed for the ultimate sacrifice and freedom.

The Congolese are, themselves, agents of their freedom; however, it cost the Congolese bloodshed and loss of innocent life. One of the prominent prophetic voices that emerged in the twentieth century was Emery Patrice Lumumba. His voice in quest of democracy caught the world's attention. Adam Hochschild sustains, "Lumumba believed that political independence was not enough to free Africa from its colonial past; the continent must also cease to be an economic colony of Europe."[9] In 1960, the Congo achieved geopolitical independence but missed economic freedom.

Edward Tshibangu states, "Social crisis created a political crisis; the United States and Europe were part of the problem because they wanted to return in Africa [sic], after segregation, end of slavery [sic], Americans wanted to continue exploiting the Congo. As a result, thirty percent of revenue, raw materials, such as uranium, benefited the modern nations."[10]

---

8. Perkins, *Restoring At-Risk Communities*, 17. "It is the time that we demand more of ourselves as Christians. We are the hands and feet of Jesus, if we want people to feel and touch him, it has to be through us. We need more troops who are willing to give up their personal ambitions and maybe even risk their lives by going into our inner-cities—the frontlines" (12).

9. Perkins, *Restoring At-Risk Communities*, 301

10. Tshibangu, Interviewed May 25, 2017.

Lumumba's assassination, in January 1961 in Elizabethville, was a turning point for the geopolitical independence of the Congolese state. Hochschild describes, "After being arrested and repeatedly beaten, the prime minister was secretly shot in Elizabethville in January 1961. A Belgian pilot flew the plane that took him there, and a Belgian officer commanded the firing squad. Two Belgians then cut his body and dissolved it in acid; to leave no martyr's grave."[11]

Christian religion and its prophets have to be agents of transformation of societies. A prophet is a voice for the ignored and advocates for the weak, liberating the oppressed and spreading the life-giving message of the gospel of hope, reconciliation, and equality. However, for centuries, the Congolese church has participated in enforcing policies of abuse and exploitation. The church's mission is to change structures of exploitation and political constituencies, yet evangelicalism and Pentecostalism are often used by politicians to endorse their theories. Hochschild documents those decades after Leopold's death: "Catholic Bishop Jean-Felix de Hemptinne, an arrogant nobleman, was a Leopold reincarnated. He wielded great political influence on the Congo; he ordered to the police to fire on striking mineworkers."[12] In times of political, social, and religious crisis, the church is critical to the conceptual process of peace talk, recompilation, and reconciliation. Catholic bishops in the Congo have participated in the process of reconciliation by negotiating peace talks. In the wake of social-political uprisings, violence, and fighting between civilians and armed forces, Christians can present the gospel.

Historically, the church has stood along the oppressed through the proclamation of the gospel of freedom and reconciliation. David Nelson Persons writes of the prophetic voices around the time of Lumumba in Katanga: "Moïse Tshombé and Jason Sendwe were Methodists and led

---

11. Hochschild, *King Leopold's Ghost*, 302. Hochschild records: "Less than two months after being named the Congo's first democratically chosen prime minister, a U.S. National Security Council subcommittee on covert operations, which included the CIA director Allen Dulles, authorized his assassination. Richard Bissell, CIA operations chief at the time, later said, the President (Dwight D. Eisenhower) . . . regarded Lumumba as I did and many other people did, like a mad dog. . . . Eisenhower clearly told the CIA chief Dulles that Lumumba should be eliminated. Alternatives for dealing with the problem were considered among them poison . . . a high-powered rifle, and free-lance hit men. But it proved hard to get close enough to Lumumba to use these, so instead, the CIA and Belgians still working in the Congo's Army and police supported anti-Lumumba factions in the Congo government" (302).

12. Hochschild, *King Leopold's Ghost*, 300–01.

the movement for freedom. The Catholics who were tied in with the Belgian government seemed quite quiet at the time, and it was the Methodists that stood out in Katanga."[13] On the contrary, Tshibangu argued, "In 1971 the Catholic Church was part of neocolonial efforts; they supported Mobutu's autocratic political leadership in the second Republic of Zaire."[14] Moreover, in the 1970s, Protestants were at the frontline, reclaiming freedom and liberation of the Congo. However, today, most Protestant leaders remain silent. There has been an attempt to maintain Liberation theology and social justice within the post-colonial Congo. The global church might strategically apply these metrics of social change, but these are not suited to African worldviews.

PROPHETIC LEADERSHIP: MATTHEW AND THE EMPIRE

Matthew 5:3, "Blessed are the poor in spirit, for theirs is the kingdom of heaven," as well as other biblical texts, served the colonizers as a tool to support a colonial theology rooted in social, economic, and political exploitation. In particular, this verse was used to shape, affect, and maintain economic policies, systems of governance, as well as the state and other microstructural decisions that systematically weakened the people. R. S. Sugirtharajah, an Indian post-colonial and biblical scholar, mentions, "The Sermon on the Mount became an important narrative in the hands of the colonized in silencing any critique of native behavior."[15] Thus, he notes, "Rome had complete power over its subjects, including the power

---

13. Persons, e-mail correspondence, June 30, 2017. Persons is a former Dean of Universite Methodiste au Katanga, Mulungwishi Theological Seminary in the Congo.

14. Tshibangu, Interview. Tshibangu argues, "Although Protestants are the first missionaries to evangelize the Congo, Belgium signed a treaty at Berlin following that contract the Catholics became involved in government. Catholics were in charge of hospitals, education, the priests represented the state. As a result, Catholic Church was Africanized with the Cardinal Joseph-Albert Malula. Mubutu proclaimed le Retour a l'authenticite in 1971. Mobutu's political move was de-Christianization of Africans by removing their first name and refusal to celebrate Noel Privatization of Catholic Schools, the church, and its doctrines became the properties of the government. Since Malula opposed to the autocratic leadership, then Mobutu created a structure to control the Eglise du Christ au Congo a Unitarian body of all Protestant denominations in the Congo ECC." Tshibangu's documentation demonstrates that the Congolese government has, over the past century, used the church, both Catholic and Protestant, to enforce neo-colonialism and exploitation of human resources.

15. Patte et.al., *Global Bible Commentary*, 361.

to force people to pay high taxes and hard labor." Matthew's Gospel is an imperial product because it emerged from the Empire.

Matthew 5:3 empowers elites but leaves minorities vulnerable. The text is also an instrument of the empire, a hierarchal power, dominated by elites. Therefore, the poor in spirit must comply with the rules and regulations of the elites who make policies to fit their own needs and interests. The poor are forced to negotiate with the Empire for their survival. However, those who do not agree, or who resist the regime's policies, are viewed with suspicion as enemies of the Empire.

Warren Carter states, "The key part of what Matthew's gospel is doing is providing ways for followers of Jesus, crushed by the empire, to negotiate with Roman power."[16] The Matthean community, as an oppressed group, had to negotiate to assure its survival. Neo-Pentecostal streams of Christianity empower women and give them a voice in a patriarchal social fabric.

NEO-PENTECOSTALISM AND WOMEN OF AFRICA

Unlike classical Pentecostalism, which supported the effects of oppression and exploitation, Neo-Pentecostalism has been liberating to women. In *Pentecostalism in Africa: Christianity in Postcolonial Societies*, Martin Lindhardt opines, "During the first half of the twentieth-century foreign Pentecostal missionaries in Africa were small in number and relatively unsuccessful in their soul winning efforts. As a study by Anderson (2005) of early Pentecostal missionary journals indicates that possible reasons for their limited success include cultural insensitivity and patronizing and racist attitudes toward Africans."[17] Yet classical Pentecostalism has survived the threats. Concerning Pentecostalism, Garrard argues, "To arrive at this place Pentecostalism has had to survive severe opposition from a number of sources: from the adherents of traditional forms of religion which soon saw it as a threat to its continued existence."[18] However, Neo-Pentecostalism has given them a voice and freedom, which provides

---

16. Carter, Hauerwas, and Campbell, *Preaching the Sermon on the Mount*, 15.

17. Lindhardtt, *Pentecostalism in Africa*, 4.

18. Garrard in Lindhardtt, *Pentecostalism in Africa*, 4 argues "The outright efforts of the Belgian regime and Roman Catholicism to oust it from the Colony. The threats and martyrdom which followed by independence in the nation after 1960 with the Jeunesse (Youth Movement) and civil war, the restrictions and internal divisions and politicking of the Mobutu years" (95–96).

a sense of security. Congolese women now have a voice, and they participate in leadership positions within churches and other organizations such as social economic and political networks. Neo-Pentecostal expressions of Christianity have liberated and freed them from patriarchal systems.

Katrien Pype observes,

> The post-Mobutu teleserials in Kinshasa, DRC, and the Mobutu's authenticity campaigned against women emancipation, and other African countries, a kind of reality and development that does not reflect secular views. The leaders of born-again Christians believe that their work will change the world, will help society, the political system to improve in various ways. Hence, Pentecostalism has lots of trouble as the teleserials focused on one's spiritual development. The representation of the witchcraft related to Pentecostalism diagnosis of crisis, the prosperity gospel, and holding women from doing anything.[19]

Pype's opinion demonstrates that the Pentecostal expression of Christianity had little or less impact on the emancipation of the Congolese society. On the contrary, Linda van Kamp documents how Pentecostal teachings are liberating to women and give them a voice by allowing them to erase the history of hierarchies within patriarchal societies. For instance, "The Afro-Brazilian Pentecostalism helps young and older women reshape their relationships with kin, (ancestral) spirits and men age plays a vital role in their lives, seeking to erase a generation of hierarchies and differences when they are turned into spiritual issues that affect all women of every age."[20]

Like van Kamp's argument, Dena Freeman opines, "In most African family systems, the Pentecostals were encouraged to accord women significant space and status to develop their skills and aspirations. So that they might also, like their male counterparts, achieve positions of responsibility within the church as well as within broader organizational networks."[21] Both Freeman and van Kamp concur that Pentecostal expressions of Christianity offer space, voice, and empower women.

---

19. Pype, "We need to open up the country's development and the Christian key scenario in the social space of Kinshasa's teleserials," 101–16.

20. Van Kamp, "Afro-Brazilian Pentecostal Re-formations of the Relationships Across Two Generations of Mozambican Women," 433–52.

21. Freeman, *Non-Governmental Public Action Series*, viii. "From the early 1980s, a new wave of Pentecostal movements swept across the African continent, promoting new conceptions of belief, personhood, salvation, emotion, and ambition that

The messianic enterprise was sustained by Jewish women disciples, including Mary Magdalene, Joanna, Herod's household manager Chuza, and Susanna, as they accompanied Jesus during His ministry and supported Him out of their private means (Luke 8:2b–3). Paul's apostolic movement survived through the material support of wealthy women and widows. Elizabeth Schüssler Fiorenza argues, "Women's actual social-religious status must be determined by the degree of their economic autonomy and social roles rather than by ideological or prescriptive statements."[22] Lydia, Phoebe, Chloe, and Rufus' mother were among women missionaries. Fiorenza reconstructs a hermeneutic theology of liberation by describing how women's private domestic homes were turned into spaces for public religious leadership that opened opportunities for Pauline missional enterprises. However, Paul neither recognized nor honored his patrons.[23]

NEO-PENTECOSTALISM: CONGOLESE WOMEN IN MINISTRY

Women's participation in holistic ministries in the post-colonial Congo has played a critical role and made an essential impact as they advocate for social change. In the twenty-first century Post-colonial Congo, Neo-Pentecostalism and the gospel have been liberating and empowering women to become prophetic voices. In other words, Neo-Pentecostalism in paradigm has enabled or commissioned them to develop grassroots organizations by launching micro-businesses. Women's involvement and roles have not only advanced African Christendom, but also have helped them make safe or protect their marriage and reduce domestic violence and divorce. This phenomenon of women's engagement to advance God's kingdom is not a new trend.

---

contrasted markedly with existing mainline Protestant churches and Catholic orders. The arrival of this new Pentecostalism brought with it a strong evangelical style associated with the need to be born again into Christian faith and immersed in its spiritual and codified morality" (viii).

22. Fiorenza, *In Memory of Her*, 102.

23. Fiorenza, *In Memory of Her*, 102. Pype says, "Pentecostal Christianity has lots of trouble as the teleserials focused on one's spiritual development. The representation of the witchcraft related to Pentecostalism diagnosis of crisis, the prosperity gospel, and holding women from doing anything."

Jesus gave a voice to a voiceless Samaritan woman and empowered her to be an evangelist to her people and village. Jesus raised the morality and value of women and broke the wall of the cycle of systemic gender inequality and social injustices. Jesus freed the woman caught in adultery in John 8:11 by saying, "Then neither do I condemn you, Go sin no more." Mary Magdalene, who became one of Jesus' followers, was liberated from demonic forces. In Luke 8:2, women ministered to Jesus and his disciples with their means, or they were the engine of providing the resource.

The Congolese might become agents of their liberation as they are enabled to create a theology adapted to their contexts. In some cases, women are activists capable of redeeming themselves from oppressive systemic structures of patriarchy and misogyny. Congolese women are evangelists who engage their husbands with the gospel. Many of these men end up converting and become Christ's disciples. Thus, women have been active disciple-makers and missionaries from the inside. Freeman argues, "Women are encouraged to rise above stigmatization and victimhood. Conversion to Pentecostalism is widely considered to bring about a sense of liberation and opening up a new moral order in which people can redeem themselves and their situation."[24] Moreover, Neo-Pentecostalism has occurred successfully in the contexts of the Global South due in part to women's engagement in Pentecostal Christianity.

Freeman insists, "Thus, as well as stressing the healing process and deliverance from destructive forces, many of these Pentecostal churches provide innovative ways of responding to prevailing economic conditions and, in some cases, they resort to certain modes of political activism."[25] Sub-Saharan African prophets must engage in holistic and transformative missions relevant to their worldviews.

HOLISTIC MINISTRIES AND SOCIAL JUSTICE

Integral ministry engagements do not exonerate the priority of eternal destiny. Presenting Christ and the gospel to the recipients or consumers must take priority in the vast marketplace of God's economy of salvation in the mission to save souls. Heidi Rolland Unruh and others insist, "We all talk about exercise good for the body, but God and his kingdom are for eternity. So I think we're doing part of the job, if we don't introduce

---

24. Fiorenza, *In Memory of Her*, 219.
25. Fiorenza, *In Memory of Her*, ix.

people to Christ."[26] Sider uses the term wholeness to describe the integral relationship between the spiritual and social engagement in Christian evangelism: "The church mission is to minister to the whole person and bring people to saving faith in Jesus Christ."[27]

The philosophy of the wholeness of life is ingrained into African worldviews. Neo-Pentecostalism and prosperity theologies enforce this knowledge of wholeness. As Ronald Sider and others opine, "We're not only taking care of the spiritual side of people but the whole man."[28] The author's argument relates to the liberal progressive philosophy of evangelism rooted in an American consumeristic worldview. Sider and others define evangelism as a means to meet the physical needs of the evangelized: "Evangelism meets the needs of the whole man, just as Christ did . . . You cannot just tell a person that God loves them when they're hungry. You've got to feed them."[29]

However, a different voice emerges from the text: "I want to reach the whole person . . . Human beings don't live by bread alone, but by the word and ministry of God."[30] This writer believes it is imperative to engage in a holistic mission for social change, spiritual endeavor, and the transformation of broken systems. However, social justice should never be intended to replace the gospel; rather, it includes a significant component of the same mission to save one's soul, heart, mind, and spirit. As David E. Garland puts it, "The individual whole being, value system, and behavior are changed through conversion."[31]

Furthermore, Richard Foster avers, "The greatest risks of social justice streams are caring for social needs without reference to the condition of the heart."[32] Heitzenrater discusses: "One common thread in that lineage is a holistic concern for the well-being of God's creatures—mind, body, and soul. The Methodist program of medical clinics and interest-

---

26. Unruh and Sider, *Saving Society*, 175.

27. Unruh and Sider, *Saving Society*, 175.

28. Unruh and Sider, *Saving Society*, 175.

29. Unruh and Sider, *Saving Society*, 175.

30. Unruh and Sider, *Saving Society*, 175. Sider and others argue "The transformative power of the gospel ought to be evident, not by looking at people on their way into the church, but, on their way out of the church. They should be allowed to come in as broken as society has caused them to be but leave as whole as God desires them to be." Unruh and Sider, *Saving Society*, 175

31. Cannon, *Just Spirituality*, 287.

32. Cannon, *Just Spirituality*, 10.

free loans, orphanages, and schools, housing for widows and meals for the poor, were of a piece with Wesley's understanding of the love of neighbor."[33]

Methodism initially emerged as a holistic parachurch movement. The holiness doctrine was rooted in John Wesley's beliefs and practices to emancipate the poor and oppressed. This holistic paradigm involved an intentional unwavering life of holiness. John Wesley, in his Sermon on Works of Mercy, said, "All works of mercy relate to the bodies or souls of men; such as feeding the hungry, clothing the naked, entertaining the stranger, visiting those that are in prison, or sick, or variously afflicted."[34] Wesleyan theology dignifies the prophetic vision of holistic evangelism and missions. Two aspects of the social implications of the gospel require further investigation: Christian mission and social change and the re-reading of the story through Congolese eyes.

CHRISTIAN MISSIONS AND SOCIAL CHANGE

Christian mission encompasses evangelism and humanitarian efforts to emancipate the poor and underprivileged groups. Since the 1800s, Missionaries in the Congo have aimed to improve economic development, health care systems, social-economic and political development, and education, as well as provide shelters for orphans, while altering literacy. The third-wave of the Neo-Pentecostal gospel engages new missiological paradigms in the 21st-century Congolese society. These streams of Pentecostal phenomena operate as Para-ecclesia apparatus due to their commitment to social, political, and spiritual–and quest for economic–reform. Freeman is of the opinion, "Many scholars have interpreted Pentecostal doctrines as a means of enabling adherents to make the best of rapid social change."[35] The rise of NGOs and the Neo-Pentecostal gospel has opened a new era of global Christendom.

In the post-colonial Congo, spiritualism is seen as a sign of wealth to counter or overcome material deficiencies. Thus, the prosperity gospel becomes a prescription for social development. This way of materializing the gospel becomes a predicament in Christian missions in Africa. Freeman says, "Both the spread of Pentecostalism and the resurgence of

---

33. Heitzenrater, *The Poor and the People Called Methodists*, 358.
34. Wesley, "Sermon on Mercy," 48.
35. Freeman, *Non-Governmental Public Action Series*, 70.

occult beliefs and practices have been related to economic transformations of the neoliberal economy."[36] These dual discourses offer spiritual support to counter the spirit of capitalism and construct links to personal and social-economic development and network systems. Freeman discusses, "In Tanzania despite micro-level economic growth, the economic reforms and the liberalization of the economy have resulted in increased unemployment and a reduction in social services at the grassroots, as well as increased differences in access to product, accumulation, and consumption."[37]

The imported streams of neo-liberal policies in Sub-Sahara Africa have little distribution of capacity-building leadership advancement and no impact on the desired transformation of economic development. Capacity-building leadership is a process involving theologizing and contextualizing. Freeman states, "The structural reforms evoked strong hopes of improvements in social and economic living conditions, but it soon turned out that the blessings of neoliberalism were distributed extremely unevenly and that only a few benefited."[38] Neoliberal policies have done little to alleviate poverty and sanction social and economic changes or development within the African continent. These Western systems or policies contributed instead to the rise of impoverishment.

Freeman states, "Some of the most important transformations relate to the economic ethos of third-wave Pentecostal and charismatic Christianity are the legitimization of unlimited access to miracles, or the accumulation of wealth offers a sense of escapism from social-political and economic engagement."[39] In other words, Freeman discusses the Neo-Pentecostal gospel's spiritual discourses and infers that their implications for personal empowerment, social responsibilities, and development are unique in Africa. The emphasis is placed on how multiple forms of these third-waves of Pentecostal Christianity transform individuals and produce new paradigms adapted to the changing social and economic circumstances in the wake of modernity and globalization. These churches preach both the prosperity gospel and a gospel based on deliverance against demonic or spiritual forces.

---

36. Freeman, *Non-Governmental Public Action Series*, 67.
37. Freeman, *Non-Governmental Public Action Series*, 67.
38. Freeman, *Non-Governmental Public Action Series*, 67.
39. Freeman, *Non-Governmental Public Action Series*, 67.

SOCIAL JUSTICE AND GOSPEL

For social justice and gospel professionals, it is critical to draw a line between the third-wave, independent, Neo-Pentecostal churches in Africa and the first-wave, which is rooted in classical western Pentecostalism. The holiness movement, which inspired the social gospel movement within mainline Protestant circles, was more a precursor of the prosperity gospel than the third-wave movements that have developed over the centuries. For example, in the late nineteenth and early twentieth centuries, Rauschenbusch applied the gospel of Christ to respond to the social-economic crisis among immigrant communities in New York City. Rauschenbusch argued that the kingdom of God could be fulfilled only when human conditions are fixed. In *Christianity and the Social Crisis* (1907), Rauschenbusch argued, "Whoever uncouples the religious and the social life has not understood Jesus. Whoever set any bounds for the reconstructive power of the spiritual life over the social relations and institutions of men, to that extent denies the faith of the Master. The significance of this work is that it spoke of the individual's responsibility toward society."[40]

The *remonstrative power* signifies the noble role that faith-based religion must play to do justice and liberate the ignored. These are the remnants of Congolese and survivors whose past stories lie heavily on atrocity, oppression, colonialism, and several years of Atlantic and Arab continental slave trade that has often been ignored or misread.

RE-READING THE STORY FROM CONGOLESE EYES

The recorded Congolese story must be re-read from the perspective of postcolonial eyes. The documented sources represent voices that echo foreign missionaries and their missional impacts on Congolese soil. However, African voices and their participation in oral traditions are to be recognized. Anderson asserts, "History cannot be understood from written sources alone, especially when these sources are the only written documents from this period and almost exclusively reflect the official positions of power and privilege of their authors. We have to read between

---

40. Rauschenbusch, *Christianity, and the Social Crisis*, 7.

the lines of the documents, minutes, and newsletters to discover the hints of a wider world than they described."[41]

There is little, or no space left for formerly colonized people to tell and read their stories. The written literature as it is read in Congolese missional history tells the evangelist's side, or Western observer's voice, while ignoring the very heroes, laity, and natives who accomplished the actual mission. European observers are not limited to journalists who write Congolese history in a way that misrepresents the real context or reality of the people. However, this writer suggests that emerging Congolese scholars and theologians need to document the stories from the perspectives of African voices objectively or academically. For instance, most of the modern Western scholars misread African stories. They tend to not pay attention to the social-political, economic, cultural, historical, and religious discourses and categories of the peoples. As Anderson says:

> One of the reasons for the distorted picture we have of Pentecostal history is the problem of the documentary. Our writing of Pentecostal history outside the Western world almost entirely depends on letters, reports, and periodicals of western Pentecostals and their missionaries. These documents were usually loaded for western consumption to bolster financial and prayer support in the North America and Europe, and so the reports talked about the activities of missionaries themselves and not their so-called native workers.[42]

The readings were by far for the elite class, not the proletariat or people from the grassroots, because missionaries had full control of the printing press. Also, they had control over the vernacular and grammar. As such, they injected their dominant voices within an oral tradition. The colonial reading provided no justice for the natives but emerged as the dominant voice. In other words, the reading of the country's past through neo-colonial voices systemically perpetuated the same colonial legacy.

To that end, the emerging generation in the twenty-first century will read its story as free and liberated citizens. Edward Glaeser asserts, "Kinshasa was built by a brutal colonial regime . . . ruled by an evil despot . . . . Everyone of the world's older cities once fought epidemics of disease and violence. The ultimate success of those hard-fought battles should bring

---

41. Anderson, *An Introduction to Pentecostalism*, 12.
42. Anderson, *An Introduction to Pentecostalism*, 12.

hope even to Kinshasa."⁴³ They will appreciate and discover the narrative of how the Congo became a failed state through war, massacres, civil wars, and ethnic conflicts: "Kinshasa was founded and named Leopoldville by the adventure of Henry Morton Stanley in 1881 to provide a trading post for King Leopold of Belguim whose name became synonymous with a barbarous colonialism that forced African labor to extract resources from the earth and use mass killings as a management tool."⁴⁴

To recapture the African tradition, one ought to re-read the Congolese story of the history of the mission with fresh eyes. From 1881, marking the year of Henry Morton Staley's arrival in Léopoldville, the Congo experienced a long history. Re-reading the story through an objective lens is critical. Nonetheless, it has to be done within the paradigm of African worldviews and cultural expressions of symbolism and cognitive streams of oral traditions. Kwame Bediako asserts, "In the African setting, it is through an African reading of the Scriptures, particularly in African languages, and by paying attention to the resources of the biblical categories into the African primal worldview that the desacralizing impact of the gospel is experienced afresh."⁴⁵

The challenge of oral tradition is preserving a verbal story without losing its originality and integrity. Nevertheless, Congolese storytellers' memories or libraries rooted in traditional wisdom are long gone. Thus, the individuals and eyewitnesses who experienced the history have already died. Oral storytellers' voices and skills narrated their histories from lived experiences. Therefore, as Anderson states, "Reading between the lines critically might rediscover. The lost stories and memories of those who have died. Missionaries' stories, mission bulletins, and reports read in the West were Western missionaries' rather than the reflection of locals whom they served."⁴⁶

---

43. Glaeser, *Triumph of the City*, 97.

44. Glaeser, *Triumph of the City*, 96. Moreover, Glaeser argues, "For thirty-two years, Mobutu Seseseko ruled with a rampantly corrupt regime that impoverished Zaire (as he renamed the country) by nationalizing industries, engaging in foreign military escapades, and failing to invest in either human or physical capital. The years after Mobutu's ouster have hardly been better for the country (now called Congo again) as hundreds of thousands died in the war, and corruption continued unabated" (96).

45. Bediako, *Jesus and the Gospel in Africa*, 104.

46. Anderson, *An Introduction to Pentecostalism*, 12. Anderson states, "This is certainly a hazardous exercise; the possibilities of misinterpretation become greater with incomplete information, especially in the case of those who have already died and whose voices have been lost. The importance of retrieving oral traditions is underlined

Anderson argues, "Early Pentecostal missionaries frequently referred in their newsletters to then objects of their mission as the heathen, and were slow to recognize national leadership when it arose with creative alternatives to western forms of Pentecostalism."[47] However, not all missionaries patronized and exploited their converts.[48] Anderson states that missionaries were catalysts but not central to the story of the mission: "Asia, Africa, Latin America had their own Christian heroes and not only missionaries who went there. He believes that the voices of these national pioneers should be heard in the writing of our histories."[49] Furthermore, "A serious and extensive writing of global Pentecostal history needs to be done in which the enormous contributions of these pioneers is correctly recognized so that classical Pentecostals, in particular, shed their often heard assumption that Pentecostalism is a 'made-in-the-USA' product that has been reported to the world."[50]

Contrary to the traditional view of Pentecostalism being an import from the US and Europe, this writer argues that Pentecostalism and the Holy Spirit's power had been experienced by the Congolese on their native land like the movement that transpired on the day of Pentecost in Jerusalem in the Acts 2 community. Lindhardt records, "Burton estimated that during the two weeks of meetings at Mwanza 'about the same number were baptized in the Holy Spirit as on the day of Pentecost in Jerusalem.'"[51]

Neo-Pentecostalism must consider the contributions of the majority world so that Christianity might be radically reformed.[52] The

---

here, for we must record for posterity the stories of those still living who remember the past. Where the early histories of Pentecostalism are still within living memories, these must be recounted before it is too late."

47. Anderson, *An Introduction to Pentecostalism*, 12–13.
48. Anderson, *An Introduction to Pentecostalism*, 13.
49. Anderson, *An Introduction to Pentecostalism*, 14.
50. Anderson, *An Introduction to Pentecostalism*, 14.
51. Lindhardt, *Pentecostalism in Africa*, 95. Because of this Luban Pentecost, many converted to Christianity. Restitution was made for wrongs that had been done, stolen goods were returned, and many not committed to their faith expressed a desire to become involved in evangelism. The result was that many began to volunteer to go to Kisale, one of the most undesirable places because of the swarms of mosquitoes, and the lack of manioc/casava, the staple diet of all inland dwellers (74).
52. Lindhardt, *Pentecostalism in Africa*, 14. Anderson states, "We must rectify the historiographical imperialism and ethnocentrism of the past. The revising of the history of Pentecostalism in the twenty-first century must be undertaken, not emphasizing

native's voice is critical for an adequate understanding of the African experience. Anderson deduces, "The experiences of ordinary people who were inspired to establish Spirit-empowered movements, is important. Pentecostal growth and expansion have very often been a lay endeavor involving Christians from the margins of church life."[53] The history of missions on the Congolese land and their wealth of spiritual encounters have to be re-read from the vantage point of Congolese eyes or experiences of spirit-filled power and power.

SPIRIT-FILLED AND POWER: A CONGOLESE RESPONSE TO THE GOSPEL

Spirit-filled and power are related activities in African spiritualized cosmological worldviews in the twenty-first century. This cosmological reality is an eschatological paradigm in which devotees claim to be in communion with the spirits of dead bodies. The souls or spirits of deceased humans survive the death of the physical embodiment of the body and communicate with the living through a medium. Is spirit-filled power a global condition that transcends geographical or cultural worldviews? Unlike the post-colonial Congo, in the US, or Western world, Spiritualism is a phenomenon where many believers claim to be spiritual but deny either the Master Jesus Christ or being religious. In this respect, yoga and other spiritual disciplines (gods) have replaced God. This precondition reinforces the decline of churches and the paganism in the Western hemisphere.

In the post-colonial Congo, Spirit power shape how believers respond to the biblical Gospel of Jesus Christ. The message and presence of Pentecostals appeared to build a bridge between the past and unknown future. The form of Christianity which embraced the concept of power, the supernatural, and the use of indigenous forms was attractive and

---

the missionary heroes of the powerful and wealthy nations of the world, but by giving a voice to the people living in the world's most marginalized parts. We must listen to the margins by allowing the hitherto voiceless and often nameless ones to speak, and by recognizing the contribution of those unsung Pentecostal laborers of the past who have been overlooked in our histories and hagiographies. Then together we will come to an honest appraisal of our histories and be better able to suggest solutions to the problems of division, parochialism, racism, and ethnocentrism that still plague Pentecostalism today" (14).

53. Lindhardt, *Pentecostalism in Africa*, xxvii.

comprehensible by the people. The teaching appeared to help the adherents of the introduced faith make sense of some of what was happening around them.[54] The magical practices and invocation of ancestral spirits have reshaped the Pentecostal movement. While Christians must engage in the ministry of the gospel, many have remained attached to the traditional belief systems and practices which lead to syncretism. The Apostle Paul challenged syncretic traditions as he admonished the Galatian community to refrain from partaking in the animistic and syncretic behaviors of mixing holiness and flesh activities (Gal 5:20). In Revelation 21:8, the Apostle John warns his listeners to avoid associating with Spiritism and pursue God's kingdom.

Nevertheless, the indigenous practice of venerating ancestral spirits mirrors the needs for a theological reflection and contextual critical reading of the Bible in the Congo. Western scholars believe that the popularity of Pentecostalism in Africa relates to the spiritual worldviews it encounters, a context of ancestors' spirits and demonic forces. Anderson asserts, "This world of ancestors, evil spirits, hobgoblins, and demonic forces is believed to be responsible for all manner of events—including misfortune, illness, poverty, and host of social problems. In its encounter with this spirit world, Pentecostalism offers solutions to these problems through the emphasis on the power of the Spirit and the exercise of spiritual gifts."[55]

In this context, African spirituality infuses the whole person's experience or encounter with the supernatural force and makes Jesus more real or relevant to daily life. However, new converts in the Congo are often not receptive to the gospel partly because they fear losing power, spiritual forces, and a connection with the world of ancestral spirits. The evangelized expect to be guaranteed lasting security and deliverance against evil forces. Jesus is sometimes presented as an incarnated ancestor mediator who connects the devotee to the realms of ancestral spiritual powers. This cosmological world of spirits offers reassurance that Jesus' disciples have the transcendent force and ability to free them from demonic forces and malevolent spirits.

Bediako says, "Christian conversion and Christian conviction need to find concrete expression about elemental forces—ethnicity, race, social class, culture, and customs—that shaped individual and social identity

---

54. Lindhardt, *Pentecostalism in Africa*, 95–96.
55. Lindhardt, "The Spirit and the African Spiritual World," 305.

and destiny in the old order."⁵⁶ Spirit-filled power as natural essentials are the basis of the rise of a new expression of African Neo-Pentecostal or prophet-healing churches, resulting in Christian awakenings across the African continent. The search for power against demonic forces and malevolent spirits is the force of the Neo-Pentecostal gospel of prosperity.

Bediako further avers, "African tradition, authority and political power, neither resides with human beings nor even with a sacral ruler, for he is merely the man who sits on the stool of the ancestors. From the Christian perspective, ancestors had to become desacralized. The authority belongs only to God."⁵⁷ Also, he argues, "Historically Christianity has been a desacralizing force."⁵⁸ Anderson echoes the same voice as he surmises, "When Christianity is entangled in this materialistic and rationalistic web; it becomes less meaningful for most people."⁵⁹

However, Anderson's argument that Pentecostalism offers solutions to the current spiritual world can be deconstructed as a general assessment. Disease and poverty are not only physical issues; they are also spiritual. Anderson asserts, "A religion that does not promote deliverance from evil or promote health and prosperity is a dysfunctional religion. This is why the so-called prosperity gospel has flooded this [sic] the economically poorest continent."⁶⁰ In a sense, this writer argues that the prosperity gospel is prevalent in Africa not because of poverty alone but due to the underlying issues of Spiritism and power rooted in pre-Christian patterns.

THE PRE-CHRISTIAN PATTERNS

The pre-Christian categories of African Christianity and their integrity have to be taken seriously for a global theological reflection. The encounter between Christian faith and African pre-Christian heritages is a continuous event. Appiah-Kubi argues, "Not what Western missionaries did or said (or failed to do or say). However, what African Christians would do with their Christian faith and commitments were now the

---

56. Bediako, *Jesus and the Gospel in Africa*, 106.
57. Bediako, *Jesus and the Gospel in Africa*, 103.
58. Bediako, *Jesus and the Gospel in Africa*, 102.
59. Anderson, "The Spirit and the African Spiritual World," 314.
60. Anderson, "The Spirit and the African Spiritual World," 305.

determining factors in the development of Christian faith in Africa."[61] The question no longer concerns what Western missionaries organized or failed to accomplish. Instead, how can emerging African scholars and churches develop a theology that is African and suited to Africa?

Bediako states, "The Christian faith is capable of translation in African terms without injury to its essential content."[62] The African primal religions and their experience in the encounter with the Christian Gospel validated the religion as a global phenomenon. The validation of traditional belief systems does not equal the acceptance of all indigenous practices, although elements which are compatible with Christianity are adopted and desacralized.

African primal belief systems are fertile soil for Pentecostal trends of the prosperity gospel. The task of African theology is to shape Christian expressions, so there is no longer a concern about indigenizing its religious traditions. Instead, the gospel is conceptualized whenever it encounters the Christian Gospel, and it shapes African patterns of tradition or culture. Christianity is not foreign to Africa; it has deep roots in the long histories, memories, and heritages of people. Bediako asserts, "The eternal gospel has already found a local home within the African response to it, showing that Christ has become the integrating reality and power linking old and new in the African experience."[63]

Pre-Christian religious discourses influence the spread of the prosperity gospel. The pre-Christian heritages or primal elements are the matrices of the rapid growth of Christianity in Africa. This writer argues that the pre-Christian categories are characteristics of the emerging African Christianity rooted in African theological discourses.

The Congolese scholar and theologian Mulago, at the *Centre d' Etudes des religions Africaine* in Kinshasa in 1957, argued in favor of the relevance of the Christian message for Africa. "The process of forging the new integration cannot be solid and viable except as it remains faithful to ancestral traditions and as it manages to be judicious in its contact with

---

61. Bediako, *Jesus and the Gospel in Africa*, 56. Appiah-Kubi in his papers, African Theology en Route: Papers from the Pan African Conference of Third World Theologians, December 17–23, 1977, at Accra, Ghana, stated that Africans are now new forces of the Christendom.

62. Bediako, *Jesus and the Gospel in Africa*, 55.

63. Bediako, *Jesus and the Gospel in Africa*, 55.

the civilizations of other peoples and revealed religion."[64] Mulago's argument is a radical and rational discourse to rediscover or recognize the integrity of African traditions, elements, and religious expressions as fundamentally relevant on their right to an African contextual Christianity.

For Mulago, the Christian Gospel brought few new contributions to the worldviews of African religious groups. However, Byang Kato, a Nigerian theologian, stresses the contributions of evangelism and rejects the positive assessment of pre-Christian religious traditions which focus on the centrality of the Bible as a unique contribution to African Christianity.

African pagan traditions must be taken seriously for forging a rational African theological reflection adapted to Africans. Synan and others state, "Also pre-Christian beliefs and practices have been transformed in many Pentecostal churches so that Christianity is presented as an attractive and spiritual alternative."[65] These writers believe "Pentecostalism has been more relevant because it has continued some pre-Christian religious expressions and ritual symbols and invested them with new meanings."[66] The indigenous theology has been a justification for the continuity or continuation of pre-Christian religions.

CHRISTIANITY RESHAPED AND DOMESTICATED

Jesus and the Gospel are central to daily life experience within a Congolese worldview. The Christian Gospel has been reshaped and domesticated. Christianity's diffusion authenticates Lesslie Newbigin's argument about the need for dialogue and connection between the Christian story and the stories of the people of the world. Newbigin articulates the need for a "dialogue between the Christian story and other stories. The congregation as the hermeneutic of the Gospel; the central role of congregations in mission and urgent need to equip ministers whose primary task will be the enabling of grass-roots participation."[67] Grassroots participation

---

64. Bediako, *Jesus and the Gospel in Africa*, 55. Bediako submits, "A widespread consensus that there exists an African pre-Christian religious heritage to be taken seriously. There has also been the realization that it is important to recognize the integrity of African Christian experience as a religious reality on its own right, and that Christianity as a religious faith is not intrinsically foreign to Africa."

65. Synana, Yong, and Asamoah-Gyadu, *Global Renewal Christianity*, 318.

66. Synana, Yong, and Asamoah-Gyadu, *Global Renewal Christianity*, 317.

67. Newbigin, *The Gospel in a Pluralist Society*, viii.

initiated by and for the Africans seems beneficial for the emergence of African Christianity.

The attempts to domesticate Christianity and the gospel help to universalize the religion. John Mbiti deduces, "What the southward shift of the church has done is to cause to emerge new centers of Christianity's universality."[68] The emergence of African Christianity and its domestication of Western theological and cultural trends support Bediako's assessment, which suggested, "Wherever the faith has been transmitted and assimilated are equally centers of Christianity's universality."[69] This writer, however, asserts that the host cultural worldviews shape the gospel of Christ as they are developed or formed by the same gospel of Jesus Christ. The cross-cultural influence makes the Gospel at home within a new or foreign environment. Nevertheless, the gospel's power to transform the culture is critical to its missional engagement. Evangelization is taking place or being accomplished because Christianity has been domesticated.

CONCLUSION

The biblical Gospel may be released from its neo-colonial patterns to enhance God's mission for the proclamation of the gospel when a theological reflection suited to Africans takes place. Africans have to engage in prophetic leadership and create a dialogue and theological reflection. Therefore, it is essential to participate in an active mission for social justice and equity to advance God's kingdom. There are socio-economic, political, cultural, and religious aspects, but the past emphasis has been on the importance of the economy of materialism rather than the economy of salvation. An authentic Congolese voice must emerge from the margins and exploited, these are people whose voices have not been heard.

A Congolese response to the gospel would emerge from strength rather than weakness, as new faith communities are rebuilt–social, economic, spiritual, and entrepreneurial restoration. The restoration implies that new souls and disciples are gained, and their lives are holistically transformed. God's Spirit offers the freedom to participate in the mission and confront the effects of the theology of a biblically sanctioned mechanism of manipulation and impoverishment. Moreover, it is imperative to alter the systemic authorized corrupt structures that hinder

---

68. Bediako, *Christianity in Africa*, 163.
69. Bediako, *Christianity in Africa*, 163.

the proclamation of an authentic and contextual translation of the gospel as well as a sustainable social justice.

Holistic ministry is a key to Christianity because the gospel has a critical role to play in human life while providing relief that is both spiritual and physical. The Spirit of God is to respond to the vocation of social justice, spiritual development, moral reconstruction, equality, and inclusiveness while inspiring prophetic voices across the world. Liberation is in the hands of the oppressed minority group who must take a stand to speak up against social injustice and exploitation. Today, "Free people will set the course of history." Free Congolese are now able to redress centuries of a biblically sanctioned theology of the poor when they resist patterns of colonialism, which implies the necessity of resisting neo-colonialism and of the struggle to liberate those who are incarcerated by it.

9

Conclusion

THE FINDINGS FROM THE research will be divided into four sections. The first section deals with the problems created by Neo-Pentecostalism. The second focuses on the commercialization of spiritual gifts in the Neo-Pentecostal movement. The third section will provide the solutions to the problems brought on by the Neo-Pentecostal movement. The last section will deal with the globalization of the gospel.

THE PROBLEMS CREATED BY THE NEO-PENTECOSTAL MOVEMENT

The prosperity gospel and its theologies have reached a zenith in the twenty-first century post-colonial Congo where it has been translated into a different and deceiving gospel. Practiced without literal translation and hermeneutics, the prosperity gospel translates into a misleading and deceiving neocolonial progressive and materialistic endeavor that bankrupts its adherents. It has increasingly become a religious machinery that aims to incarcerate the body of Christ without the possibility of parole. Frederick Kakwata argues:

> Salvation is understood as being spiritual only; the physical aspect is misapprehended. Besides, there is a heretical prosperity gospel in the denomination which teaches that poverty is the result of personal sin and unfaithfulness to tithing. They believe that giving large amounts of money will release blessings and prosperity. This view has skewed the denomination's approach towards the eradication of poverty. As a result, the 30ème

CPCO's involvement in poverty eradication is described as rudimentary; it is limited to sporadic assistance to the poor.[1]

Mvwala Katshinga, a Congolese scholar and missiologist observes: "Prosperity gospel in Kinshasa is a business which promotes the prophets but leaves the body of Christ in deep poverty becoming dependents or beggars."[2]

Practiced through syncretism and social lift, the gospel of prosperity is a deceiving gospel that perpetuates humanity's malady of social ills. In this context, charismatic renewal streams of Christianity have developed into an engine for social-economic exploitation, elitism, classism, and religious manipulation.

Katshinga observes that in Kinshasa, "A Prophet says your vehicle is possessed by demons or your house is haunted by demonic forces. God spoke to me. Give the car or house to me, and I will deliver it. The reason childlessness is because you have been bewitched by your neighbor or family members. I urge you to sleep with me you will be liberated or delivered and conceive."[3]

---

1. Kakwata, "The Pentecostal Church in the Congo/ 30ème Communauté," iii. Anderson argues that Burton and Salter officially launched the Congo Evangelistic Mission in 1919. Burton remained in the Congo until 1960, when he retired to South Africa. He recruited many European missionaries from Britain. During the civil war (1960), two CEM missionaries were killed, and most missionaries left the Congo. The church that has resulted from this mission is now called Communaute Pentecoste du Congo, CPCO (Pentecostal Community of the Congo). It is found in the south of the country where it has more than half a million members. Johnathan Ilunga became the leader of this church in 1960. Anderson, *An Introduction to Pentecostalism*, 122.

2. Katshinga, Interviewed May 17, 2017. Katshinga argues that in Kinshasa, "Prosperity preachers preach that because God is rich. His children have to become productive. However, the Bible defines prosperity as shalom or wellbeing not only materialism. Pastors own beautiful and expensive cars, and they wear expensive suits, golden jewelry, big houses, to impress their adherents to give more. The prosperity gospel works in favor of the pastor, not the poor disciples." Katshinga asserts, "No one ever said that I had one hundred disadvantaged or underprivileged individuals in my church they have all become rich, but most of these preachers have their kids and wives abroad in France, Belgium, South Africa because they are wealthy. Some divorce their legitimate wives but abuse women in their respective churches." For instance, says Katshinga, "These prophets when they meet someone with a nice suit or expensive jewelry will begin to prophesy in public. The prophet claims that God says to me that give me this suite or Jewelry and they expect people to obey and respond positively to God's voice and force the exploited individual to respond by saying Amen. When the people resist, they will receive a curse from God according to the prophet." Katshinga, Interviewed May 17, 2017.

3. Katshinga, Interviewed May 17, 2017.

Katshinga's remark relating to the underlying issues of abuse and oppressive acts against women and children reflects the struggle of people in the Congo. For instance, some children are beaten and abused because prophets of practicing witchcraft have accused them. In the aftermath of multiple civil wars, the diseases HIV and AIDS have left many children as orphans who live in streets. However, a myriad of children are homeless due to divorces, many of which are caused by prophecies. Some are compelled to work in mining or become professional beggars without an education.

At the same time, emerging renewal theologies are reshaping African Christendom. These religious expressions have left lasting effects. A gap and vacuum have created a mass of poor in many African towns, as well as a socio-spiritual dependency syndrome in the African social fabric. Emerging African scholars have to rethink the relationship between the gospel and culture. The prosperity gospel is the product of bicultural patterns of both local and foreign elements incorporated into Christianity.

The challenge facing the new heartland of Africa is that it is hard for one to be an African while at the same time a Christian. The African culture of invoking the spirits of the ancestors has to be understood in an African context. Marius Nel says that, "Africa is a foreign world of ancestral spirits."[4] Andrew F. Walls surmises, "The gospel in its relationship with the culture; it is both a prisoner and liberator of the culture."[5] Walls' argument suggests that the gospel has the transformative power to liberate Congolese culture and free it from its belief systems. However,

---

4. Nel, Interviewed April 22, 2017. Nel argues, "We cannot separate African Christian worldviews from their culture and values. Westerns do neither respect themselves nor their values or history. There is a lot of knowledge, practices, and values Westerners can learn from Africans. For example, the Ubuntu an African value might help Western audiences. The invocation of the ancestor's spiritual worldviews is part of African history and values. Among these are respect and solidarity with our values and family members. Americans should learn from what is happening in Africa." Marius Nel, Interviewed April 22, 2017. The term *Ubuntu* is an African expression referring to the value of human's existence, and it means "humanity" (I am because you are, I need you, and you need me). Moreover, the term echoes the African value of solidarity and common good of the respect for the other or human integrity. The spirit of togetherness, of being humane to others, symbolizes Ubuntu. Africans share everything they have in the society, which is the opposite of the Western individualism. For example, locals share food, ideas, heritages, advice, counseling under a tree as an established system of pastoral care, enculturation, and reconciliation.

5. Walls, *The Missionary Movement in Christian History*, 1–15.

a culture of prosperity rooted in capitalism and economics attempts to alter the gospel.

Park Hyung Jin suggests, "The gospel not only has the transformative power to make its message understandable in across cultures (the "indigenizing" principle), it also has the power to change cultures (the "pilgrim" principle). According to Walls, the gospel thus has both particularizing and universalizing factors."[6]

First, the thesis asked whether Congolese primal religions or belief systems reflected neo-Pentecostal trends and were translated into a syncretized superstructure that has been transposed into an underlying worldview not radically transformed by the biblical Gospel. Second, the thesis interrogated whether the neo-Pentecostal gospel has been a contextualized transformative force to influence an adequate discipleship for effective evangelism and missions. Third, the research argued that the American-exported expression of the prosperity gospel is a different gospel and a misleading neocolonial progressive worldview that bankrupts its adherents.

Moreover, the selling and trading business of miracles, prophecies, holy water, apples, and olive oil, have made prophets in Sub-Saharan Africa multi-millionaires. The Christian Gospel has been exploited as a for-profit investment of capital. Preachers and elites benefit from the revenue, while the victims and poor adherents, who have no access to returns, are gradually impoverished and exploited. Traditional magical practices and belief systems have been exported to African Christianity. Prophets claim the root causes of illness, misfortune, and one's loss of a job exists because of the demonic spirits of in-laws or parents bewitching that person. The US expressions of prosperity theologies are domesticated in post-colonial Congo. These religious expressions have not been contextualized transformative forces for discipleship models because of uncritical readings of the Bible. There are countless emerging cases of abuse and manipulation of the poor.

COMMERCIALIZATION OF SPIRITUAL GIFTS

The spiritual gifts are being commercialized and treated as a means of revenue and income. *Glossolalia*, speaking in tongues, prophecy, and deliverance phenomena have systemically colonized African cosmological

---

6. Jin, "Journey of the Gospel," 340.

worldviews. The proliferation of charismatic prophets in Congolese religious streams has created a hierarchy within the African social fabric. The prosperity gospel does not do justice to its recipients because the Bible and spiritual power have been used to reinforce social and economic exploitation, classism, elitism, hierarchy, and economic disempowerment. As a result, a few people who claim to be anointed use their charisma as opportunities to enslave others.

Henry I. Lederle states: "He (Frank Macchia) sees glossolalia as a symbol of empowered ministry that bridges linguistic and cultural boundaries. He maintains that tongues were characteristic in the New Testament and can be for us, but Tongues cannot be turned into the law that governs how spirit baptism must be received without exception within the actions of a sovereign God."[7]

SOLUTIONS TO THE PROBLEMS

Solutions to the problems presented by the Neo-Pentecostal movement begin with a need for the re-education of Congolese Christians within both the Church and academia to read the Bible and engage the biblical texts objectively. There is an urgent need for Africa to train and equip the body of Christ to avoid uncritical hermeneutics without ignoring the indigenous voice. As Luemba articulates in the context of the Congo, "We have to attract people to get the theological education."[8] Hence, it is necessary to train and equip leaders who will respond to the challenges to alter uncritical hermeneutics or interpretation that exploits the weak.

To this end, a literal translation of the Scripture would alter the Congolese self-theologizing and redress the underlying issues of a social-economic, systemic, religious, political gap and syncretism. There must be a theological reflection suited to Africans. There is a need to reinforce the theological education in Africa by African scholars.

Theological education is critical and urgent for the growing African Christian community to alter self-theologizing and spontaneity. Also, a cross-cultural scholastic or theological training is needed for a truly global church that honors Christ's mandate and exemplifies the Great Commission. Luemba defines the twenty-first century's paradigm of

---

7. Lederle, *Theology with Spirit*, 170.
8. Lederle, *Theology with Spirit*, 170.

mission as "transcultural."⁹ The Christian mandate, therefore, is a cross-cultural mission beginning at a grassroots level and proceeding to the global community.

G. C. Oosthuizen says, "Attention should be seriously given to the development of an indigenous liturgy."¹⁰ Nevertheless, "Theological education is perhaps the main focus in the development of young Churches in Africa. Theological education should not just be limited to the so-called ministry but should also reach the laity."¹¹ This writer suggests a holistic theological implementation in Africa by Africans and for Africans.

GLOBALIZATION

The fundamental question is why the massive populace has been attracted to the neo-Pentecostal gospel of posterity? The neo-Pentecostal gospel of prosperity is well received despite the exploitative adverse effects of manipulation, potential, and false hope it offers. On the one hand, Pentecostalism establishes a reliable network of healing industries and the ability to provide pastoral care. This expression speaks to the socio-spiritual consciousness and economic needs of many Africans. The social lift and hope paradigms the theology of prosperity offers renders neo-Pentecostalism relevant and appealing to Africans affected by poverty and crushed by the social, economic, and political crisis. On the other hand, its manipulative and exploitative dimensions can make the prosperity gospel, in the wrong hands, an instrument of oppression and corruption.

Dieudonné Sita Luemba says, "The dramatic shift in the center of gravity is to be celebrated. When I was the lead pastor of the Evangelical Church in Kinshasa my parish sent and supported missionaries to

---

9. Lederle, *Theology with Spirit*, 170. Luemba states, "Mission paradigm has been understood from a Western perspective because it is defined as equal to Evangelization. However, the concept or term mission is transcultural when we take the gospel to people who are closer to us, at the same time we the Congolese cross-frontiers and take the same gospel overseas."

10. Oosthuizen, *Post-Christianity in Africa*, 8.

11. Oosthuizen, *Post-Christianity in Africa*, 8. Oosthuizen argues, "There are Churches which transplant what they have received in to, with the result that no spontaneous development can ever take place. Every form of indigenous expression has been discouraged, without ever being studied. The Church in Africa was forced to continue a parasitic mode of existence because no scope was given to its spontaneous development" (8).

Brazzaville, Chad, Niger, and Sweden."[12] Luemba sees these prosperity preachers as vehicles to take the gospel of Jesus Christ and cross frontiers and engage in mission. He posits, "It is a good thing as the Apostle Paul says that at least the gospel of Christ is proclaimed. On the other hand, Prosperity Preachers distort the Scriptures because of a lack of adequate theological education."[13]

Christian engagement in missional activities is a significant task. The same cultural analysis formerly applied by missionaries in distant places is now valued in local contexts. The global church is located next door. Christian missions have broadened to include a variety of social concerns, with the "whole gospel for the whole person" becoming central. Therefore, the concern is no longer focused exclusively on church growth but everything from at-risk children to human trafficking, racial reconciliation, institutional brokenness or poverty alleviation without the loss of evangelistic zeal.

A critical contextualized theology and holistic reading of the biblical text might be a transformative force for discipleship and evangelism in the post-colonial Congo. In this way, a genuine cross-cultural expression of Christianity and efficient enculturation will be achieved.

Translating the Scripture literally would alter the underlying Congolese issues of social economic and socio-political injustices. Missionaries face challenges to translate the gospel because, in the past, they were unprepared to deal with the African cosmological realities.

OBSERVATION

The Deuteronomist narratives, along with Job, establish a framework for anti-prosperity theology. Job's friends (Eliphaz, Bildad, and Zophar) accused him of doing evil (Job 4–23). Job's narrative is a strategic approach

---

12. Luemba, Interviewed May 19, 2017. Luemba asserts. "Locally we reach people of other cultures who take the gospel in turn to their own people. The Church Growth in Africa is critical for the changing face of Global Christianity." Luemba surmises, "Qualitative and quantitative Church Growth has to be realized. (1) The growth is more numerical quantitative rather than spiritual or qualitative. In most cases, many Congolese believers do not acquire qualitative growth which leads to syncretism (2) Miracles and Prophecies are possible the Bible is a prophetic book. However, we have now a lot of false prophets in DRC; many whom practice magic and divination to get more wealth."

13. Luemba, Interviewed May 19, 2017.

to justify misery based on causality. Job's account is one such example of the gravity of the symptoms of an anti-prosperity gospel.

In the twenty-first century, prosperity advocates use the same strategies of causality, the root causes of human's suffering, and poverty to justify suffering. For example, the prophet says the reason one suffers is that he or she has sinned, done something wrong, or does not have enough faith. Also, these people insist that difficulties such as cancer, a stock market crash, and poverty are caused by personal liabilities or outside forces. The assumption behind these endemic practices is that God's will is for everyone to be wealthy, healthy, and fruitful.

Nel argues that the prosperity gospel is rooted in the Deuteronomist laws or principle related to the Hebrew Bible. The Deuteronomist principle states that the root cause of your misfortune or you are sick, and suffer because you have sinned against God."[14] Job is rooted in causality and the quest for a Deuteronomist identity. Questioning how and why events happened is the core of prosperity theology. This theology originates from the exilic experience of Judah as Israel had to re-write and reconstruct a new identity as a colonized people.

This writer observes that the qualitative and quantitative metrics and findings have proven that prosperity theology is the most rapidly growing stream of Christianity in Africa. However, the qualitative assessment of African worldviews determines that the theology deviates and bankrupt believers. Also, its methods and theories have less impact on the mission of making disciples of Jesus Christ. On the contrary, quantitatively Christianity is proliferating in Africa with less impact in authentic disciple-making and nurturing.

Moreover, there is surging phenomenon of new churches and ministries emerging within these contexts, characterized by demonic forces, hunger, political crisis, and poverty. There are, on average, fifteen to twenty planted churches on every street, avenue, and block in Congo. As a result, the Congo has become one of the most Christianized societies in Sub-Saharan Africa.

The number of "prophets" is on the rise as individuals increasingly search for answers and deliverance. Prophetic endeavors seem to be the most desired gifts Congolese seek. As Luemba argues, "In Kinshasa, there are many false prophets, people are deceived. Prophets and individuals

---

14. Nel, Interviewed April 22, 2017.

go for three months to the mountains to pray."[15] Praying churches, or prophetic renewal streams of Christianity, tend to attract a massive following. This is because they promise solutions to people's problems.

Africans must retrieve essential biblical paradigms and avoid the past mistakes of Westerners' missional enterprises. The West might be able to learn from an African experience as it is the developing section and new heartland of Global Christianity. Moreover, the West has to collaborate with the growing global South for a truly contextual global church. The new Christendom is at a crossroads in African theology as it must address mixing traditional belief systems and the Christian Gospel. Westerners came to "civilize" Africans. As a result, Africans have little to teach and a small voice.

The subject matter of prosperity gospel in Africa requires a comprehensive and *holistic investigation* to interpret missiological matrices and *scientific methodologies* adapted to Africans.[16] An indigenous hermeneutic of the biblical Gospel must be encouraged in Africa.

The prosperity phenomenon must be understood within the context of African culture. The central emphasis for many Africans is to have many wives, cars, and homes, and, furthermore, being physically fat is a sign of success and greatness. Africans react to prosperity theology within the framework of their cultural paradigm. The U.S. models of capitalistic televangelism have been exported to Africa. This writer believes that the problem of Neo-Pentecostal Christianity is economic rather than spiritual. Charismatic preachers in the Congo are making money and driving

15. Nel, Interviewed April 22, 2017.

16. The holistic investigation is a theory which focuses on the wholeness rather than one single aspect of the discipline. The theology of prosperity has often been investigated from the vantages of religion, social economics, and history, but it has not been examined culturally, politically, and morally (holistically). The problem is more economical than religious. The holistic investigation is a systematic approach to answer the questions and problems in relation to the interpretation of the biblical Gospel. These methodological and integral investigations will dictate the metrics of reading the Bible and objective research related to the ability to transmit the gospel of Jesus Christ.

Scientific methodologies are a series of steps toward a resolution process. The prosperity gospel in Africa requires scientific methodologies to experiment and explore why massive populations are attracted to this theology of giving and sowing seeds. In other words, a reading method that recognizes and rediscovers the root causes of the proliferation of the theology of prosperity across the board. Since scientific method is a process for experimentation that is used to explore observations and answer questions, this writer believes that without a transparent or genuine scientific methodology it would be difficult to address the problems of misinterpretation.

expensive vehicles while their members become poorer and poorer. The prosperity gospel promises people that by giving financially, they will escape poverty.

The prosperity gospel is a vital betrayal of the next Christendom. As Nel says, "The prosperity gospel is influenced by U.S. models of here and now capitalistic expressions."[17] The phenomenon oppresses the poor who are taught and promised to expect returns but receive zero percent after investing. An entrepreneurial package of prosperity gospel adapted to the Congolese worldviews might change their circumstances. Nonetheless, it is critical to train, equip, empower, and re-educate Africans. As Nel suggests, "It is crucial to teach people entrepreneurship, provide them with the knowledge to improve their lives and transform the world."[18] Nevertheless, building a reliable network of innovative of entrepreneurial ecosystems designed to assist recipients in transforming ideas into solutions is critical for the twenty-first century global church.

GENERAL REMARKS

This writer treated the subject of the prosperity gospel from theological and missiological perspectives. The conclusions are based on the data or findings analyzed, on theories, and a test of the phenomenological paradigm. However, the movement is a complex subject engaging twenty-first century readers, pastors, and scholars. The hypothesis relates to real life people who are being exploited, deceived, oppressed, and destroyed. An extensive investigation or study of neo-Pentecostalism and prosperity gospel movements is critical for both African and Western audiences in the twenty-first century global church.

There is a greater need for future research to broaden the subject from historical, political, psychological, sociological, and economic vantages in Sub-Saharan Africa. Holistic engagement of missional purpose allows for making prophetic, transformative, empowered disciples of Jesus Christ. There is also a need for biblical discernment on the topic of spirits phenomenon to sort out what is from God, what is from humans, and what is from the demonic world. The re-education of Congolese Christians is critical in order for the Congolese Church and academia to read the Bible literally and engage objectively.

17. Nel, Interviewed April 22, 2017.
18. Nel, Interviewed April 22, 2017.

Moreover, future researchers ought to focus on twenty-first century mission, prophecy, and evangelism in Africa. The demographic paradigm shift in twenty-first century missional enterprise is an indicator of the need to recapture and reconstruct the concept of the transformation in the center of gravity within the new heartland African worldviews. For example, former government public buildings such as shops and movie theaters are being transformed into churches in Africa. On the contrary, in the US, in the wake of the dramatic decline of religion, church buildings are sold and replaced with shops and businesses or marketplaces.

Psychologically, one might ponder whether the attraction to the prosperity movement in the post-colonial Congo represents a mechanism of emotional survival for temporary pain relief. The recipients receive and experience hope at the moment, yet their lives remain miserable. The prosperity gospel operates like the prescription of a symptom or pathology of the social fabric which offers false hope.

In 1971, Mobutu's *Le Retour à l'authenticité* was a systemic way to re-colonize the population. However, fundamental human rights, a freedom of speech, and freedom of the press were deprived; yet, there was liberty in entertainment industries, not limited to music, soccer, and wine industries, instead of education, agri-business, and social development.

In a twenty-first century metric to engage post-Christendom, an African theology that is holistic to train pastors in a multi-disciplinary culture promotes workforce science and economics to improve the lives of believers. The gospel must be contextualized to answer to the needs of Congolese. Ignatius Ferrera concludes, "Africa needs to learn adequate biblical theologies within the paradigm of the early church; disciples transformed the world without depending on economics and capitalism."[19] He believes that the Western model of the church depending on money, economics, materialism, and progress has less impact on spiritual life.

The purpose or question of the present thesis is to rediscover an authentic translation, or holistic, orthodox hermeneutic of the biblical Gospel. Its objectives have been a roadmap to test the effects of abusive

19. Ferrera, Interviewed April 22, 2017. Ferrera argues, "Crossing point of the history Westerners have to understand the changes God has allowed and changed the process of globalization they have not all the answers. Re-contextualization and African theology have to be recommissioned because Western theology is a prosperity gospel in itself. I think the culture captured the gospel and dictates what we ought to do. The essential of African Christianity, the new Christendom, needs to be African not inspired by Western models."

and oppressive readings of the biblical Gospel rooted in primal belief systems. The emerging global church can be prophetic if the concept of prosperity is defined and translated from a biblical paradigm rather than as systems of capitalism and economics. Translation means a holistic embodiment of life change, changing eighty-five million Congolese living in dire poverty. It is not merely a literal interpretation of printed words on manuscripts.

The prosperity gospel is a recipe to continue the cycle of poverty and the oppressive systems of neo-colonial imperialism. The gospel of Christ has to be re-contextualized and recommissioned through the lens of critical readings of the Bible; as such, these interpretations might be prophetic and transformative for Congolese worldviews. However, if the funds are used to self-serve, buy themselves big houses, private jets, and vehicles, the theology then is worthless. Reclaiming and reconstructing an authentic hermeneutic for Congolese theological education is crucial for the growing global church. Well-versed readings alter systemic corruption and economic exploitation. To be lasting, meaningful, prophetic, and biblical, emerging new heartlands have to connect the church in mission and take the gospel to the unreached and proclaim Christ's redemptive message of hope to this broken and lost world.

The original thesis argument has been the Pentecostal gospel has not been a transformative force to alter the cosmological spiritualized Congolese social-religious fabric. Therefore, a prophetic translation of the biblical Gospel is a genuine literal translation that allows the evangelized to discontinue prehistoric belief systems rooted in animism and syncretism. Furthermore, the thesis tested the readings, retransmission, and retranslation of the gospel within the paradigms of Congolese worldviews. Then, the thesis suggested a contextual and critical interpretation hermeneutic of the gospel that is transformative and liberating, stating that an authentic translation of prophetic translation of the biblical Gospel is vital for holistic missions

The broad body of this thesis navigated the findings and data collected in this manner. First, the hypothesis asked a critical question: whether Neo-Pentecostalism is a syncretized super-structure that has not been radically transformed by the biblical Gospel. Second, it analyzed the historical overview of the Congo and how it became a failed state. Third, the thesis explored the metrics of translation of the Bible into vernacular culture and how it empowered the recipients. Fourth, the research assessed the proliferation of Neo-Pentecostal and charismatic churches how they had reshaped the African Christendom. The fifth section critiques the imported American expressions of prosperity gospel in the post-colonial Congo, reinforcing the systemic exploitation of the poor.

The sixth section explored the rise of televangelism, which has reinvented and revolutionized the Christian terrain. The seventh section articulated how the Western foreign theologies rooted in the social gospel of progress and capitalism has influenced African Christianity. The eighth section has explored the case studies of selected Congolese leaders who use prosperity theologies to bankrupt the adherents. Their methods of reading and their hermeneutics sanction spiritual and financial exploitation of the most vulnerable poor, while rendering the preachers rich. The ninth section has examined the role of prophetic voices and argued that the church can become a voice for the voiceless. The tenth section discussed the possibilities of change and resolutions to the underlying issues of prosperity gospel. Also, it suggests recommendations as well as further research, suggesting that a prophetic hermeneutic and re-education of the recipients might help to balance uncritical translation of the biblical Gospel.

To sum up, based on the findings, this writer suggests that the prosperity gospel is a humanitarian condition that needs advanced investigation through a global perspective. The expression assimilates into social, religious, economic, political-cultural, and theological problems adopted into human structures of nations. Thus, to address and alter the difficulties of uncritical and misreadings of the biblical Gospel, the subject of the theology of prosperity must be approached not from cognitive but rational metrics.

Appendix 1

Interview Questions

APPENDIX 1A: PRELIMINARY INTERVIEWS

Neo-Pentecostals and Charismatic Church Adherents

DEAR SIR/MADAM X, WILL you tell me a little more about your early life? What brought you here to this church/town? What caused you to change or leave mainline denominations and create your own house of worship?

What does theological education mean to you? You say that you do not have seminary training. Could you indicate how you believe theological training can equip a pastor to preach the Gospel and become an effective leader in the twenty-first century?

Initiated Churches

How do you define the role of neo-Pentecostal and charismatic renewal trends and prosperity theology's impact in post-apartheid South Africa?

Mainline Denominations

What attracted you to attend spirit churches and revival praying churches? Can you tell me more the reason being which motivated you to decide to leave the mainline Mission Established Church (e.g., Methodist,

Catholic, Presbyterian, etc.) and what happened in your life which led you to make such a decision to leave?

APPENDIX 1B: PROSPERITY GOSPEL

The prosperity gospel is influential among neo-Pentecostal churches in the Republic of the Congo and Sub-Sahara Africa. Why has their preaching and message been so well received? Is it a betrayal of the Gospel or a retrieval of one of its vital and overlooked dimensions?

Nevertheless, what is the prosperity gospel? Is it biblically sound? Where did it originate? Is it an imported phenomenon or an appropriation of Western concepts, values, and views regarding progress and a culture of prosperity?

Is the prosperity gospel movement an imported phenomenon made in the United States or an African expression and response to the Gospel of Christ? Are its appropriation and domestication a response to the Gospel of Christ or continuity of African belief systems?

Why has the prosperity gospel movement been successful in Africa as millions have adhered to its teachings? What are the neo-Pentecostal and Renewalist preachers teaching that attracts so many adherents? Is it a good theology or bad philosophy--why and how?

Is the attraction to the prosperity theology and the rise of neo-Pentecostalism an indication of the failure of enculturation and contextualized Christianity?

Televangelism

How have televangelism stations and electronic media technologies such as FM and AM radios within a consumeristic culture influenced neo-Pentecostalism and a theology of prosperity?

How has a digital culture of RTMV Radio, Amen TV, "Message de Vie," and Sangu Malamu shaped African Christianity?

How would you assess the proliferation of sects and the birth of televangelism?

This gospel teaches that God wants to fulfill humanity's desire for health, wealth, and happiness. All it takes is to have faith. Adherents are asked to sow seeds. Is the prosperity gospel a for-profit business? Does it represent an incorrect way of looking at health and wealth, or can we learn something positive from it?

APPENDIX 1C: THEOLOGICAL CROSS-EXAMINATION

Short term missional enterprises often create a dependency syndrome in third-world countries as long as Westerners continue to provide economic resources, funds, and financial aid to African churches. Will Africa remain a missionary field for decades to come despite its rapid growth and role in the global church? What is the distinct timeframe when partners exit?

Self-theologizing and translating the Gospel into the vernacular are significant. How can the biblical Gospel be released from its colonial disposition or pattern and used to empower local people?

Why do massive numbers of individuals of Christianity adhere to renewal churches, charismatic, and neo-Pentecostal preaching, and house churches?

Can you explain why there are churches on seemingly every street corner?

Today, the majority of Christians live in the Global South. Will the new heartlands of emerging growing theologies of minority voices be accepted as normative forces and given a voice in the conversation by Western scholars?

Will the theological schools in the Global North change to fit the needs of the global church and non-Western societies?

APPENDIX 1D: PHILOSOPHICAL CROSS-EXAMINATION

To what extent did Mobutu's rhetorical ideology of 1971, *Retour à l' authenticité*, shape Zaire's social-political and religious landscape?

APPENDIX 1E: HISTORICAL CROSS-EXAMINATION

Who is a Congolese, and what is his or her origin?

What was the role and function of oral tradition prior to the arrival of electronic communication technology and phones in traditional Congolese society?

What was the impact of the 1992 *La Conference Nationale Souveraine* (literally "the sovereign Conference") in Kinshasa concerning sociopolitical and religious realities?

APPENDIX 1F: MISSIOLOGICAL CROSS-EXAMINATION

Who were the first missionaries to come to the Congo, and what were their roles and impact on Congolese soil?

How did Reinhard Bonnke's spiritual healing ministries of deliverance and the evangelicalism of the twentieth-century crusades shape neo-Pentecostalism ,charismatic theologies, and Christianity in Zaire?

L'Abbé Kasongon holds revival services of healing prayer exorcisms, anointing oil, and blessed water in Lubumbashi. In your opinion, as an eyewitness, survivor, and recipient of L'Abbé's ministry, how would you assess the outcome of his prophetic movement?

[To Mr. L'Abbé Kasongo] How would you describe the origin of the healing ministries you initiated in the 1980s?How is your movement separate from local traditional healers (Ngangas) or conventional spiritual mediators who use the same substances, such as anointing oil and blessed water, to cure the sick and overcome demonic forces?

How is a Nganga different from Christian prophets? How would you delineate Ngangas, who once practiced their healing services and divinations in their houses and asked their clients to pay fees as they claimed to be Christian apostles, prophets, and healers?

What is the role of African pre-Christian retransmission and the indigenous assimilation to Christian worldviews? Are Ngangas' practices the basis for the spread of neo-Pentecostalism and the prosperity gospel?

APPENDIX 1K: CRITERIA FOR SELECTION

The selection of interviewees was based on qualitative and quantitative methods. Most of the interviewees were experienced in the field, and the objective was to obtain a balanced view on the subject. Therefore, the interviewees emerged from theological and missiological fields. Some are theologians and missiologists who are active teachers, while others are pastors, prophets, apostles, and evangelists in active ministries. The investigation solicits diverse voices and values individual opinions from both those who advocate prosperity theology and those who oppose it.

Rationale and Material Selection Criteria

This research used several sources of contextual hermeneutics, personally focused oral histories, and a biblical-theological hermeneutic. There was also a group-focused research-based approach, including asking permission to access libraries in various theological institutions: Northwest University in Potchefstroom, South Africa; Stellenbosch University in South Africa; and Université Protestant au Congo. Nevertheless, as is indicated in the research schedule, the researcher traveled to the African continent in the Democratic Republic of the Congo and Republic of South Africa to test first-hand the phenomenon. The international travel and use of governmental and local sources of information helped to broaden his knowledge of the prosperity gospel phenomenon. The data collected benefited the understanding of authentic evangelism and prophetic voices within both Congolese churches and the West.

The research analyzed various sources of information used for authenticity and contribution to the mission field. This writer has translated the data received into useful information to enhance future research. The interviews were done professionally with consideration of the integrity and originality of the collected data to enable future researchers to achieve a high level of scientific and scholarly work that will contribute to the field of world Christian studies, missiology, and evangelism.

APPENDIX 1L: CHALLENGES

Most of the scheduled interviews had to be re-scheduled because interviewees were afraid to open up due to security problems. The interviewees, especially those who are involved or approve of the prosperity gospel as a normative approach to Christianity, were either unwilling to meet and do an interview or entirely refused to cooperate or tell their stories. Some pastors had military guards in their offices for security purposes. These "ministers" operate like kings or political dignitaries, and it was difficult to access them. As a result, the interviewer had to go through security checks and sign paperwork to meet the prophet or the minister.

The subject of the prosperity gospel is a divisive topic most believers felt challenged to discuss the movement because most of them believe in this theology of prosperity. This writer interviewed various groups within the sections of Sub-Saharan social fabric. The overall reaction and result among Renewal churches of charismatic roots and Pentecostal churches were afraid to engage in the conversation. Hence, the primary challenge this prosperity theology has penetrated the heart of African consciousness and its domestication is trying to undo.

Appendix 2

Oral Interviews

APPENDIX 2A: DIEDONNE SITA LUEMBA INTERVIEW TRANSCRIPTION

THE DEAN OF THE School of Missiology in the Kinshasa Democratic Republic of the Congo. This writer interviewed him May 19, 2017, in Mongafula, Kinshasa, DRC. The following is this writer's own translation of the responses, from French to English, organized by topic through sub-headings.

> Paradigm missions has been understood from a Western worldview because it is defined as equal to evangelism. However, the conception of the mission is transcultural when we bring the Gospel to people who are within our vicinity. There is also the idea of crossing cultural frontiers through overseas missions. Nevertheless, "We Congolese are now sending missionaries in several African countries not limited to Chad, Congo Brazzaville, Niger, and Swede. When I was appointed as the Senior Pastor of the Evangelical Church of Congo, during my two years tenure, we sent missionaries to other African countries, even to Europe."
>
> Despite our limited financial assets, we engage in missions and reach people of different cultures with the Gospel, persons who in turn take the Gospel to their people. This development is the very essence of the dramatic shift in the center of gravity.
>
> The proliferation of pastors and prophets is an African phenomenon because Africans proclaim or self-ordain themselves as pastors and prophets, apostles, or doctors. On the one hand,

these uneducated apostles are proclaiming the Gospel, and this is a good thing; it signals what Paul said--that at least the name of Jesus is proclaimed. On the other hand, the self-proclaimed apostles distort and misinterpret the Bible because of their lack of theological education. We have to attract people to receive theological education.

Growth of the Church: Qualitative and Quantitative

There is a quantitative and quantitative paradigm aspect of spiritual growth among Congolese believers. The extension is more numerical as many do not have a transformative encounter with Christ, thus leading to syncretism.

Prophecy

God is powerful to communicate prophecies and miracles because the Bible is a prophetic book. However, false preachers often use magic and divination done under the name of prophecy to get more money. In Kinshasa, there are many false prophets; there, a number of people have been deceived. For example, you may meet a prophet on a bus who informs you of various life issues. The prophet says, "If you want to receive a solution to these problems, I can pray for you." The recipient responds, "Yes, I have financial issues." The very prophet who presented himself or herself as a Messiah to liberate the destitute then asks the client to sow seeds.

Moreover, many go to the mountains for three months to pray. The prophets hide to listen to the petitions and prayer concerns of people, and they secretly record some believers' voices who pray out loud. The false prophets return to their station of operation to provide "solutions" to their victims. The majority of victims tend to be women searching for answers to their problems: "God has spoken to me. I see in my spirit that you have no child, and as a result, your in-laws are troubling you. Your marriage is in trouble." These false prophets speak mostly about what is in people's hearts. "I will fight for you. Give me $100.00."

There are prophets and those who use TV network to deceive their clients. "God sent me to pray for you at your home." These prophets move from home to home delivering their messages about deliverance and prosperity. Divinators are true-false prophets. They are true because they speak to the real problems facing their clients, yet they are false because they are diviners using spiritual forces which are not from God.

Miracles

Most of the operated miracles are fake and pre-arranged as these pre-paid people fake sickness to impress other clients. In one scenario, the false prophet failed to keep the promise in paying money to persons involved in the operation of faking illness. Since their transactions went wrong--they were not paid--they decided to reveal the secret on national television. Thus, organizing miracles to gain money and resources from vulnerable individuals is a crime.

Seed-Sowing, Prosperity Gospel

Many of these expressions come from the US and are being reproduced and repeated in the Democratic Republic of the Congo. God is a God of prosperity, but the problem: false promises. If you give me money or sow seed into my ministry, God will bless you. I recognize that we can use people to promote or advance God's work. For instance, we built a church with our local resources, including the pastor's parsonage.

Many churches become shopping centers for miracles, sowing and reaping phenomenon. The prosperity gospel in the Congo manipulates adherents by creating various names of giving offerings. Leviticus 1–7 speaks of different kinds of offerings. However, I wonder if this was Christ's goal of the cross. "Give Me money for the remissions of your sins. Give and you will be blessed!"

Deliverance

Deliverance is biblical, but there is an exaggeration in the prophet use of magic to chase demons. For example, some prophets demand their adherents to stay outside all day to be delivered from demons. At the same time, others whip their clients while exposing them to intense suffering. The prophet convinces the victim to believe that the felt pain represents the demons are feeling the same way.

While there are countless reasons for deliverance--not limited to maladies, sickness, lack of traveling, poverty, misery, finance, visas, or promotions--all these problems tend to be transformed into demons. If the state becomes responsible for creating jobs, some of these practices will end. Genuine translation of the Gospel has affected people's lives to emancipate them both spiritually and physically, such as the creation of micro-companies.

The Word of God is transforming people's lives in the DRC. All glory belongs to God because the government has failed, but the church is succeeding in making a difference. Our hope is in God, His word, and the Church, which is an instrument of God for the transformation of the nations.

Dependency

Churches in DRC have potential to auto-finance with local resources. However, when a church depends on external aid, it will not grow. Mission-established churches need "the umbilical cord" cut off so they can grow. I started my micro-project agricultural activities. When I was supported by West Europe, I had no courage to do my project and grow, but the separation has helped me.

Missionaries brought the Gospel to Africa, but they did not teach us how to produce locally. Local development came later. In other words, missionaries spread the Gospel but ignored the social circumstances of the people. I understand that in this period, people were against the social gospel. Furthermore, they did not preach social development, even though they built good roads and evangelized while building hospitals to ease the problems. However, the greatest impact was the investment in primary school education. Individuals were trained to cultivate and count money. Consequently, Protestants formed businessmen while Catholics sent people to secondary school at Catholic University of Louvain (The Université catholique de Louvain) and produced politicians. Evangelical churches were limited to proclaiming the Gospel. Missions redefines both social and spiritual aspects to people. Missionaries were supported by their sending agencies. There was a need to preach the Full Gospel.

Full Gospel Holistic Evangelism

The Western paradigm of mission churches taught an aspect of the soul. The spiritual aspect was well done, but the physical aspect of the transmission of the Gospel was incomplete. Missionaries brought a non-contextualized, a Westernized, civilization. This meant that when people received Christian missionaries, they wanted them to wear clothes like Westerners. I believe missionaries brought the Gospel in an accidental garment. This is why when independence was achieved in 1960, by 1971 some of the converts rejected the Gospel as Western culture. Others started to mix Christian worldviews with traditional cultures or belief systems. As a result, syncretism was dominant in places where the Gospel did not penetrate the culture.

Syncretism

People were baptized but not converted. For instance, Simon Kimbangu never converted to Christianity. He and his followers used Christian vocabularies but with a syncretic character. I pray that theological training or education be considered as a priority so that the true Gospel will change the paradigm.

APPENDIX 2C:
MISSIOLOGIST INTERVIEW TRANSCRIPTION

A missiologist is a Professor of Missiology in the Kinshasa Democratic Republic of the Congo. I interviewed him on May 17, 2017, in Ngaliema, Kinshasa, DRC. The following is this writer's own translation of the responses, from French to English, organized by topic through sub-headings.

Dependency Syndrome

A dependency emerged due to missionaries' weakness who failed to teach locals. Missionaries planted churches rooted in paternalism. People were taught as consumers. Nevertheless, paternalism does not equip people to develop. In other words, dependency created laziness. God never created Africans to live a life of poverty. The same God who blessed Americans or Westerners can help us too. We must start sending help to America because we have many resources.

Paternalism

A systemic system of control was introduced by some missionaries who taught our parents only the Gospel. If the Gospel is well received and understood, it both liberates and transforms the evangelized. Western missionaries are surprised when they come to the DRC with its emerging new expressions of African Christianity. Missionaries were too spiritual; they taught only the Bible without a solid sense of leadership development or managerial tools. As a result, missionaries were uninformed; this became an obstacle to meet the challenges.

Translation Impact

The Gospel without translation is worthless. As Africans, we are rich with a diversity of languages. In the nineteenth century, the new trend of translation of the Bible into vernacular cultures was a success in missionary enterprise. However, the challenges we encounter today are the effects of misreading the Bible, in part because of the failure of translation. In fact, some terms were mistranslated and misinterpreted. The problem is that the task of translation is done outside the church by a secular organization. Yet I believe it is the role of the church to engage in translation. I suggest that each local church must be involved in the work of translating the Bible.

For example, instead of translating the Bible into the Pygmies' language, the Bible is to be translated into Bantu's language for the Pygmies, who are taught in the Bantu languages. Every church has to transmit the Gospel into the evangelized language. We should not depend on American resources because the same God who provides for Americans can do it for us too. This is one of the reasons there are many mistranslations--because of the lack of critical translation and presentation of the Gospel in the receiving people's language. Translation is a vehicle to communicate God's revelation. However, people in Africa tend to convert to Christianity by emotions rather than true conversion.

Missions and Evangelism

The mission starts by people leaving their home country to go to other nations with an intent to evangelize. Evangelizing the unreached is a prerogative because missions is also a term used to raise money in some contexts. Missions is often going overseas to reach only people who look and speak like them. That is not mission, but somewhat of a tribal phenomenon. On the contrary, missions is to leave your culture and go unto others with the Gospel of Christ. The term missions is often misused to raise money from the US. Missions takes the Gospel to other cultures. Every culture is an instrument God uses to spread the Gospel.

Culture and Gospel

Missionaries did their job, but we should develop. There is a problem of cultural translation. For instance, in some Congolese tribes (like the Pygmies cultural traditions) pastors sleep with people's wives and engage in drunkenness. Some cultural values are not abandoned even after conversion to Christianity, so the Gospel has not provided a permanent solution to the Congolese problems.

Social Media

Social media must be used to reach people. We need various channels so that the Gospel can reach many people, not simply those in the pews on Sunday morning. Renewal churches started or initiated the usage of social media to reach people with the Gospel, but the problem is that there is a distortion of the Gospel caused by false prophecies and prophets.

In Kinshasa, genuine pastors who preach the true Gospel have to use the same media to reach many people with their true Gospel. Unfortunately, good and genuine pastors, along with well-trained theologians, have no means to access the needed resources to spread the good message and overcome false preaching because of their limited resources. Mainline denominations have never sought to use these metrics and trends of media or social networks, such as TV, to reach many souls with the Gospel of Christ.

People have believed in the false gospel because this is what consumes their lives. For instance, renewal preachers publish and use media because they can afford them. However, mission-established churches or mainline denominations have not developed the habit to use these mediums as vehicles to share the good news. Thirty years from now, if mainline denominations do not attempt to solve this matter, they might disappear on the religious landscape. We need to use media in global missions in the twenty-first century to be successful in spreading the Gospel. The impact and power of media is a new trend for the church of Africa.

Holy Spirit Gifts, Miracles, and Deliverance

Due to social-economic situations, everyone has become a self-proclaimed pastor with a purpose to attract people who have needs of miracles. If you are honest and wish to pray for persons in need without promising deliverance, people leave your ministry or your church, but people go where the prophet promises healing and deliverance.

Bus Preachers

Congolese intellectuals who have no jobs but know French have the freedom to take the Bible and read one verse on the bus then start asking for money. It is crucial to recognize that many of these bus preachers have no theological training.

The lack of theological education is in part due to corruption. Even though the State requires pastors and church planters to hold at least a Master of Divinity diploma in theology, many have created fake theological institutions which offer an M.Div. degree in three months. Others buy their M.Div. diplomas.

Sowing Seeds

The underlying issue of sowing seed is a problem of misreading Galatians 6:6 in renewal churches.

Prosperity Gospel

The problem of uncritical interpretation is that because God is rich, we children have to be rich. This is the motto of prosperity gospel preachers in the DRC. The Bible defines prosperity as *shalom* in terms of well-being and not simply material possessions. However, here in Kinshasa, pastors own Mercedes, BMW, golden jewelry, expensive suits, and private jets to impress people and show them that the prosperity gospel is real.

The prophet pre-organizes networks to give them one hundred dollars each. When he or she calls people to sow seeds, his or her people come out to sow seeds. This strategic model attracts and traps many into the web of financial exploitation as they give and give more to the ministry. The prosperity gospel is fed by poverty because everyone wants to become rich or escape poverty.

The prosperity gospel is a business that promotes the pastor because no one ever said that he or she has one hundred poor persons in their church who have become rich. On the contrary, the members remain poor beggars because they depend on the pastor. These prosperity pastors have relocated their immediate families to France, South Africa, or abroad while the church and the body of Jesus Christ remains poor or in poverty.

The pastor may demand costly jewelry or a nice suit to persons seeking to speak with them. In the name of God, they deceive innocents. If the pastor says, "God says to me that give me your suit, give me your house," the victim is obligated to respond with, "Amen" or "yes." Otherwise, they are cursed and have no faith. The prophet often asserts that the victim suffers from demonic possession. "Give me money, and I will deliver you from this demonic spirit." To women who have no children or who are barren, the prophet deceitfully states, "Come and sleep with me, you will bear children."

APPENDIX 2E: A CONGOLESE SCHOLAR INTERVIEW TRANSCRIPTION

Professor Emeritus of Political Science and History at the University of Kinshasa, was interviewed in Binza-Ozone, Kinshasa, DRC, May 18, 2017. The following is this writer's own translation of the responses, from French to English, organized by topic through sub-headings.

Appendix 2

Ideology

Retour à l'authenticité was an ideology which emerged in the second Republic by Mobutu. The Catholic Church in 1971 was an autocratic system that emerged since Mobutu controlled the Army and political leaders. Moreover, Catholicism was part of the colonial effort initiated by Belgium. However, Protestants were the first missionaries who evangelized the Congo.

Belgium signed a contract at the Berlin conference. In the aftermath of the signed treaty, the Catholics became involved in governmental affairs. Catholics built hospitals, engaged in education, and other responsibilities while Protestants disapproved of such involvement because they were English, Americans, and Scandinavians. The Catholics were in charge of evangelism.

Catholic priests were also government representatives who played a critical role in shaping the second Republic of Zaire. As a result, the Catholic Church was Africanized during the tenure of Archbishop of Kinshasa cardinal Joseph-Albert Malula in 1971. In 1971, Mobutu took control and initiated the *Retour à l'authenticité* philosophy, which was a political strategy to boycott Western values and rule, but at the same time, *Retour à l'authenticité* was meant to control and recolonize the Zairians and served as the basis for neo-colonialism.

The concept of Africanism or negritude, a philosophy championed by Sedar Singor, was a turning point in the history of Congo and reinforced or legitimated the idea of *Retour à l'authenticité* as a normative move. However, the practice was dangerous because it changed the religious landscape and was an effort to de-Christianize Africans. This political move culminated in removing European names. Mobutu also opposed celebrating Noel or Christmas when it fell on a day other than a Sunday. He prohibited believers from praying for the president.

Cardinal Malula opposed Mobutu's autocratic regime because Mobutu imposed his doctrines which led to privatization of schools, yet Catholic schools became government's property. The Catholic Church was a door of entry into the civilization of Africa. Mobutu created structures to control the Protestant Church ECC (Eglise du Christ au Congo), formerly known as the ECZ (Eglise du Christ au Zaire). The ECC reunited all denominations under one umbrella, and Bokeleale became the representative of the ECC. This group included Simon Kibangu's sect.

Simon Kimbangu

Kimbanguism was a movement born out of the colonial umbrella and was a mixture between Christianity and traditional belief systems of syncretism. Kimbangu was arrested in 1951 in Lubumbashi after his opposition to Belgian rule. Mobutu supported his children as a strategy to oppose the Catholics and Muslims.

Conference National Souveraine du Zaire

In the aftermath of political miscarriage and economic crisis, as Mobutu controlled every sector, a *Conference Nationale Souveraine du Zaire* (CNS. French: translated in English: Sovereign National Conference) was convened to discuss the process or possibilities of a democratization of the nation. The social crisis created political crisis, and the US and Europe were part of the problem because they wanted to return to Africa after the abolition of slavery and segregation.

The role of the conference was to restructure the system. In 1990, Mobutu democratized the nation, and in 1992, the Conference National Souveraine was launched. This was a retrospective moment of reviewing and restructuring the state of national development holistically: economic, social, and politically, as well as internally. Nothing was achieved in this conference.

Independence

Even though the Congo received geo-political independence, it never received economic independence, thirty percent of revenue and raw materials, such as uranium, were returned to the country, while seventy percent belonged to the metropolitan nations. The US strategically wanted to control Congo because of its wealth regarding raw materials.

Economic independence was never achieved. As a result, Belgium transferred all the companies to Belgium. This move violated the Berlin treaty. The army and administration were left in the hands of the Belgians. Mobutu nationalized and privatized all the companies. As a result, forty percent of the revenue returned to the foreign government while sixty percent was given to the Congo. The Congo's economic power depended on foreign currencies.

The Berlin Conference

The Berlin Conference was another turning point because whoever was interested in the Congo ended up killed. This is one of the reasons Lumumba was killed by the US. Nevertheless, in the process, Mobutu restored freedom of the press and freedom of religion for democratization. This provided an opportunity for the beginning of renewal churches in Zaire.

Patrice Lumumba

Lumumba was a patriot who sought to unite the nation and independence; he believed that the liberation of the Congo was a vehicle for the freedom of Central Africa. He wanted total independence, political and economic, but Belgians wanted only political independence.

Renewal Churches

During Mobutu's era or reign, renewal churches emerged due in part to the liberalized freedom of the press and religion. The renewal trends brought a religious reform, yet false pastors took advantage of poverty to manipulate people. Pastors demanded money. These pastors owned private jets, expensive cars, and jeeps, while their church members remained poor. Their declaration of the Gospel is rooted in social-economic and religious exploitation. The Gospel was distorted and failed to address the problems of the people. These churches offered a wrong gospel by invoking false spirits and occult practices.

Prosperity Gospel

A pastor in Kinshasa was arrested by the police and brought to justice because a young man accused him of breach of contract. The minister's failure to respect a signed agreement shed light on the abusive side of the prosperity gospel movement. In reality, the pastor hired these young men to fake. They were instructed to fall while the pastor prayed, claiming that they were healed and delivered.

Deliverance is biblical since Jesus healed the sick, lame, blind, but the abusive acts are not acceptable. However, what is taking place in Kinshasa is occult practices. The Congo is becoming a missionary nation, but we must understand the roots of the problem as economical. Also, it is essential to understand the social-political, economic, and history of dynamics and factors that have contributed to the rise of the new face of Christianity.

APPENDIX 2G: A CONGOLESE FEMINIST AND MISSIOLOGIST INTERVIEW TRANSCRIPTION

A Congolese feminist and missiologist, Professor of Missiology and Ecumenism, Universite Protestante de Kinshasa, was interviewed May 15, 2017, at Commune de Kinshasa, Kinshasa,DRC. The following is this writer's own translation of the responses, from French to English, organized by topic through sub-headings.

Dependency Syndrome

The churches of the DRC must be self-sufficient in order to develop micro-projects, such as agricultural activities, to overcome the underlying issues of poverty. In other words, the church as a faith institution can utilize traditional and available tools, cultivate the soil, and harvest. However, some pastors make their church members slaves and exploit them in the name of Jesus and the Gospel. In the twenty-first century, the Congo continues to sell indulgences as was practiced in the medieval era. Martin Luther fought against this systemic abuse within the body of Christ.

Mission of the Church

The church's mission is to be a prophetic voice. Nonetheless, the issue of sowing seeds, which I view as similar to the practice of indulgences, continues to operate in the church of the Congo. Grace must be free. In other words, the Gospel must be free, and persons must freely contribute financially, with their free will, to advance the cause of God's kingdom.

The church reinforces social and spiritual injustices. For instance, a person who gives more money, such as one thousand dollars, receives long prayers and pastoral care. Those who give one hundred dollars for prayer are not prioritized, and if a person gives ten dollars, the pastor will only state, "May God bless you!"

Prosperity Gospel

Church members give money to enrich one person, the self-proclaimed prophet. While pastors exploit and adherents distort the Scriptures, the pastors get rich. That is why there are too many churches in Kinshasa. The problem facing the church in DRC is irregularity, the state of the state, corruption, and poverty. Many churches across the board are underground and not registered with the government.

Most of these self-claimed, self-made prophets and pastors have no theological training. If these individuals received good theological education, they might be able to respond to the spiritual needs of the Congolese and engage in a biblical mission. The prosperity gospel's phenomenon has divided families and created a dependency. For instance, many children have been abandoned in the streets because the prophets accuse them of being sorcerers. As a result, many are subjected to abuse and intense suffering.

Praying Churches

For instance, hospitals have no resources. They lack medicine and adequate medical care, so people tend to run out of options. As a result, they go to the church and seek prayer. People go to church be prayed for, seek visas and air tickets through prayer. I think if one wishes to travel they should work and pay for the ticket themselves. I have never seen a church miraculously produce passports and visas. This is how people are exploited and manipulated in the church of the Congo.

The lack of resources leaves people with limited options so that many are attracted to false prophets' house churches and occult movements. Some people are deceived to the point they give money and spend more time at the church; some prophets take their members to cemeteries or mountains to pray. The gift of prayer is commercialized like a business.

Many people do not have time to work due to these renewal movements; the church is ethically destroying lives as some pastors encourage their members not to go to hospitals. When people are challenged with sickness, the prophets claim that sin is the reason for Satan's torment. When they are cured, the prophet takes the credit. The church in the Congo is not free because most church leaders are corrupt.

Dependency Syndrome

Poverty is a problem for the proliferation of churches in the DRC. Missionaries created this dependency syndrome because they did not teach locals self-sustenance or independence but to expect financial aid from Europe and the US.

Televangelism

Tele-evangelists fake miracles; they pay people to claim on television that they have received healing from their physical disabilities. For instance, persons claim that they were crippled before, but now they can walk. Others claim to have been blind, but now they have received sight. These miracle operations are preplanned deceptions many believers are trapped in. On the contrary, tele-evangelists exploit, manipulate, and bankrupt the body of Christ as they collect money from poor people. Tele-evangelists sell anointed water, anointed oil, apples, and other ritualistic elements in the name of Jesus and miracles. Yet, in reality, buyers are deceived while the prophets are enriched.

Appendix 3

Systematic Analysis of Materials

THIS SECTION CRITICALLY ANALYZES the materials translated from oral interviews. Nevertheless, based on the data and resources received, this writer argues that the problem facing Sub-Saharan Africa is economic. Moreover, most of the interviewees concluded that the prosperity gospel is a betrayal of Christian standards and Christ's redemptive action on the cross for humanity. However, its development is due to poverty and prehistoric patterns. There is a connection between African traditional culture, the philosophical trends of man force, and the theology of prosperity. In Africa, one must be physically fat, a tall man, drive a big car, and have money and many wives to show people he has prosperity.

The prosperity gospel does not liberate the poor, women, and children, but rather, this expression of Christianity oppresses minorities. The prosperity gospel is an expression of capitalism wherein the poor get poorer while the rich become richer because vulnerable people are taught to expect unrealistic returns. Most of the interviewees believe that the theology of prosperity is an imported expression of Christianity from the West, especially the US. Most of the interviewees believe that there is a connection between false prophets and magicians who deceive the body of Christ. The main question for future research to address is how to engage in biblical theology in post-Pentecostalism and Christendom in Sub-Sahara Africa while remaining prophetic in this millennium.

Bibliography

Books

Kabanda, André Kana K. *L'interminable crise du Congo-Kinshasa. Origines et conséquences*. L'Harmattan, 2005.

Maier, Karl. *This House Has Fallen: Nigeria in Crisis*. London: Penguin, 2000.

Perriman, Andrew. *Faith Health and Prosperity: A Report on Word of Faith and Positive Confession Theologies by the Evangelical Alliance (UK) Commission on Unity and Truth Evangelicals*. Waynesboro, GA: Paternoster Press, 2003.

Allen, Ronald J. *Patterns of Preaching: A Sermon Sampler*. St. Louis: Chalice Press, 1998.

Allison, Gregg R. *Historical Theology: An Introduction to Christian Doctrine*. Grand Rapids: Zondervan, 2011.

Anderson, Allan. *African Reformation: African Initiated Christianity in the 20th Century*. Asmara, ERI: Africa World Press, 2001.

———. *An Introduction to Pentecostalism: Global Charismatic Christianity*. 2nd ed. New York: Cambridge University Press, 2014

Attanasi, Katherine, and Amos Yong. *Pentecostalism and Prosperity: The Social - Economics of the Global Charismatic Movement*. New York: Palgrave MacMillan, 2012.

Becking, Bob. *Exile and Suffering: A Selection of Papers Read at the 50th Anniversary Meeting of the Old Testament Society of South Africa*. Boston: Brill, 2009.

Bediako, Kwame. *Christianity in Africa: The Renewal of a Non-Western Reformation Religion*. Maryknoll, NY: Orbis Books, 1995.

———. *Jesus and the Gospel in Africa: History and Experience*. Maryknoll, NY: Orbis Books, 2004.

Berger, Peter, and James Hunter. "Under the Radar: Pentecostalism in South Africa and Its Potential Social and Economic Role." In Katherine Attanasi and Amos Yong, *Pentecostalism and Prosperity: The Social-Economics of the Global Charismatic Movement*. New York: Palgrave Macmillan, 2012.

Bonhoeffer, Dietrich. *Creation and Fall, A Theological Exposition of Genesis, 1–3*, vol. 3. Minneapolis: Fortress Press, 2004.

Bonnke, Reinhard. *Evangelism by Fire: Keys for Effectively Reaching Others with the Gospel*. Lake Mary FL: Charisma House, 2011.

Bosch, J. David. *Transforming Mission: Paradigm Shifts in Theology of Mission.* New York: Orbis Books, 1991.

Bowler, Kate. *Blessed: A History of the American Prosperity Gospel.* New York: Oxford University Press, 2013

Bowman, Jr., Robert M. *The Word-Faith Controversy: Understanding the Health and Wealth Gospel.* Grand Rapids, MI: Baker Books, 2001.

Brown, Candy Gunther. *Global Pentecostal and Charismatic Healing.* New York: Oxford University Press, 2011.

Brueggemann, Walter. *The Prophetic Imagination*, 2nd ed. Minneapolis: Fortress Press, 2011.

Burrows, William R., Mark R. Gomik, and Janice A. Mclean. *Understanding World Christianity: The Vision and Work of Andrew F. Walls.* Maryknoll, NY: Orbis Books, 2011.

Burton, Keith A. *The Bible and African Christianity: The Blessing of Africa.* Downers Grove, IL: Intervarsity, 2007.

Caldwell, Kirbyjon H. *Be in It to Win It: A Road Map to Spiritual, Emotional, and Financial Wholeness.* New York: Simon & Schuster, 2007.

_____. *The Gospel of Good Success: A Road Map to Spiritual, Emotional, and Financial Wholeness.* New York: Simon & Schuster, 1999.

_____. *Entrepreneurial Faith: Launching Bold Initiatives to Expand God's Kingdom.* Colorado Springs, CO: WaterBrook Press, 2004.

Cannon, Mae Elise. *Just Spirituality: How Faith Practices Fuel Social Action.* Downers Grove, IL: Intervarsity Press, 2013.

Carter, Warren, Stanley Hauerwas, and Charles Campbell. *Preaching the Sermon on the Mount: The World It Imagines with Essays and Sermons.* St. Louis: Chalice Press, 2007.

Castle, Gregory. *Postcolonial Discourses: An Anthology.* Maden, MA: Blackwell Publishers, 2001.

Césaire, Aimé. *Discourse on Colonialism.* Translated by Joan Pinkham. New York: Monthly Review, 2000.

Clarke, Clifton R., and Kwabena Asamoah-Gyadu. *Pentecostal Theology in Africa.* Eugene, OR: Pickwick Publications, 2014.

Coleman, Robert E. *The Heart of the Gospel: The Theology Behind the Master Plan of Evangelism.* Grand Rapids: Baker Books, 2011.

Coogan, Michael. *The Old Testament: A Historical and Literary Introduction to the Hebrew Scriptures.* New York: Oxford University Press, 2006.

Desai, Grauray, and Supriya Nair.*Postcolonialism: An Anthology of Cultural Theory and Criticism.* New Brunswick, NJ: Rutgers University Press, 2005.

Dharmaraj, Jacob S. *Colonialism and Christian Mission: Postcolonial Reflections.* Delhi: Indian Society for Protecting Christian Knowledge, 1993.

Dube, W. Musa. *Postcolonial Feminist Interpretation of the Bible.* St. Louis: Chalice Place, 2000.

Du Bois, William Edward Burghardt. *The Souls of Black Folk.* New York: Simon & Schuster Inc., 2005.

Dyrness, William A., and Oscar Garcia-Johnson. *Theology without Borders: An Introduction to Global Conversations.* Grand Rapids, MI: Baker Academic, 2015.

Edgerton, Robert B. *The Troubled Heart of Africa: A History of the Congo.* New York: St. Martin's Press, 2002.

Edwards, Justin D. *Postcolonial Literature: A Reader's Guide to Essential Criticism.* New York: Palgrave Macmillan, 2008.
Eichstaedt, Peter. *Consuming the Congo: War and Conflict Minerals in the World's Deadliest Place.* Chicago: Lawrence Hill Books, 2011.
Escobar, Samuel. *The New Global Mission: The Gospel from Everywhere to Everyone.* Downers Grove, IL: InterVarsity Press, 2003.
_____. *Jesus and the Gospel in Africa: History and Experience.* New York: Orbis Books, 2004.
Estock, Beth Ann, and Paul Nixon. *Weird Church: Welcome to the Twenty-First Century.* Cleveland, OH: The Pilgrim Press, 2016.
Ewin, James. *Prosperity or Greed: Exploring the Errors and Dangers of the Prosperity Gospel.* Denver: Outskirts Press, 2009.
Falk, Peter. *The Growth of the Church in Africa.* Grand Rapids: Zondervan, 1979.
Fee, Gordon D. *The Disease of the Health and Wealth Gospels.* Vancouver, BC: Regent College Publishing, 2006.
Fiorenza, Elisabeth Schüssler. *In Memory of Her: A Feminist Theological Reconstruction of Christian Origins.* New York: The Crossroad Publishing, 1983.
Freeman, Dena. *Non-Governmental Public Action Series: Pentecostalism and Development Churches, NGOs and Social Change in Africa.* New York: Palgrave Macmillan, 2012.
Gafaiti, Hafid. *Transnational Spaces and Identities in the Francophone World.* Lincoln, NE: University of Nebraska Press, 2009.
Gilford, Paul. *Christianity and Politics in Doe's Liberia.* Cambridge: Cambridge University Press, 1993.
Glaeser, Edward. *Triumph of the City: How our Greatest Invention Makes Us Richer, Smarter, Greener, Healthier, and Happier.* New York: Penguin Books, 2011.
Gonzalez, Justo L. *Essential Theological Terms.* Louisville: John Knox Press, 2005.
Granberg-Michaelson, Wesley, and James H. Billington. *From Times Square to Timbuktu: The Post-Christian West Meets the Non-Western Church.* Grand Rapids: William B. Eerdmans Publishing Company, 2013.
Greenman, Jeffrey P., and Gene L. Green. *Global Theology in Evangelical Perspective: Exploring the Contextual Nature of Theology and Mission.* Downers Grove, IL: Intervarsity Press, 2012.
Gutierrez, Gustavo. *A Theology of Liberation: History, Politics, and Salvation,* rev. ed. Maryknoll, NY: Orbis, 1988.
Hadeyemo, Tokunboh, et al. *Africa Bible Commentary: A One-Volume Commentary Written by 70 African Scholars.* KEN: WordAlive Publisher, 2010.
Hanciles, Jehu J. *Beyond Christendom: Globalization, African Migration, and the Transformation of the West.* Maryknoll, NY: Orbis Books, 2008.
Heath, Elaine A. *The Mystic Way of Evangelism: A Contemplative Vision for Christian Outreach.* Grand Rapids, MI: Baker Academic 2008.
Heitzenrater, Richard P. *The Poor and the People Called Methodists.* Nashville: Abingdon Press, 2002.
Hiebert, Paul G. *Anthropological Insights for Missionaries.* Grand Rapids: Baker Academic, 1985.
Hochschild, Adam. *King Leopold's Ghost: A Story of Greed, Terror, and Heroism in Colonial Africa.* New York: Houghton Mifflin Company, 1999.
Horton, Michael. *The Agony of Deceit.* Chicago: Moody Press, 1990.

Hutchinson, Mark, and John Wolffe. *A Short History of Global Evangelicalism*. New York: Cambridge University Press, 2012.
Isichei, Elizabeth. *From Antiquity to the Present: A History of Christianity in Africa*. Lawrenceville, NJ: William B. Eerdmans Publishing Company, 1995.
Jenkins, Philip. *The New Face of Christianity: Believing in the Bible in the Global South*. New York: Oxford University Press, Inc., 2006.
_____ . *The Next Christendom: The Coming of Global Christianity*, rev. ed. New York: Oxford University Press, 2011.
Jones, David W., and Russell S. Woodbridge. *Health, Wealth, and Happiness: Has the Prosperity Gospel Overshadowed the Gospel of Christ?* Grand Rapids: Kregel Publishing, 2011.
Kalu, Ogbu U. *African Pentecostalism: An Introduction*. New York: Oxford University Press, 2008.
_____. *African Christianity: An African Story*. Trenton, NJ: Africa World Press, 2007.
_____. *Interpreting Contemporary Christianity: Global Process and Local Identities*. Grand Rapids, MI: William B. Eerdmans Publishing, 2008.
Kalu, Ogbu U., and Alaine Low. *Interpreting Contemporary Christianity: Global Processes and Local Identities*. Grand Rapids: William B. Eerdmans Publishing Company, 2008.
Kato, Byang H. *Theological Pitfalls in Africa*. Nairobi, KEN: Evangel Publishing House, 1987.
Kay, William K. *Pentecostalism: A Very Short Introduction*. New York: Oxford University Press, 2011.
Keener, Craig, and M. Daniel Carroll R., eds. *Global Voices: Reading the Bible in the Majority World*. Peabody, MA: Hendrickson Publishers, 2013.
Kiboko, Kabamba J. *Divination in 1 Samuel 28 and Beyond: An African Study of the Politics of Translation*. Denver: University of Denver, 2010.
King, Coretta Scott. *A Gift of Love: Sermons from Strength to Love and Other Preachings*. Boston: Beacon Press, 2012.
Kroesbergen, Hermen. *In the Search of Health and Wealth: The Prosperity Gospel in Africa, Reformed Perspective*. Eugene, OR: Wipf & Stock, 2014.
Lederle, Henry I. *Theology with Spirit: The Future of the Pentecostal and Charismatic Movement in the 21st Century*. Tulsa, OK: Word and Spirit Press, 2010.
Limburg, James. *The Prophets and the Powerless*. Atlanta, GA: John Knox Press, 1977.
Lindhardt, Martin. *Pentecostalism in Africa: Christianity in Postcolonial Societies*. Danvers, AM: Brill, 2015.
Long, Meredith W. *Health, Healing and God's Kingdom: New Pathways to Christian Health Ministry in Africa*. Waynesboro, GA: Regnum Books International, 2000.
Mbiti, John. *Introduction to African Religion*, 2nd ed. Nairobi, KEN: East Africa Educational Publisher, 1995.
McConnell, R. Dan. *A Different Gospel: Updated Edition*. Peabody, MA: Hendrickson Publishers, 1988.
McLaren, Brian D. *A New Kind of Christianity: Ten Questions that Are Transforming Faith*. New York: HarperOne, 2010.
Miller, Donald E., and Tetsunao Yamamori. *Global Pentecostalism: The New Face of Christian Social Engagement*. Berkeley, CA: University of California Press, 2007.
Mitchem, Stephanie Y. *Name It and Claim It: Prosperity Preaching in the Black Church*. Cleveland, OH: The Pilgrim Press, 2007.

Mulimbe, V. Y. *The Idea of Africa: African System of Thoughts*. Indianapolis, IN: University Press, 1994.

Newbigin, Lesley. *The Gospel in a Pluralist Society*. Grand Rapids: William B. Eerdmans Publishing Company, 1989.

———. *The Open Secret: An Introduction to the Theology of Mission*. Grand Rapids: William B. Eerdmans Publishing Company, 1995.

Ngong, David Tonghou. *The Holy Spirit and Salvation in Africa: Imagining a More Hopeful Future for Africa*. New York: Peter Lang Publishing, 2010.

Nolan, Albert. *Hope in an Age of Despair: and Other Talk and Writings*. Maryknoll, NY: Orbis Books, 2009.

Noll, Mark A. *Turning Points: Decisive Movements in the History of Christianity*, 3rd ed. Grand Rapids: Baker Academic, 2012.

Noll, Mark A., and Carolyn Nystrom. *Clouds of Witness: Christian Voices from Africa and Asia*. Downers Grove, IL: Intervarsity, 2011.

Nussbaum, Stan. *A Reader's Guide to Transforming Mission: A Concise, Accessible Companion to David Bosch's Classic Book*. Maryknoll, NY: Orbis Books, 2005.

Oden, Thomas C. *How Africa Shaped the Christian Mind: Rediscovering the African Seedbed of Western Christianity*. Downers Grove, IL: Intervarsity Press, 2007.

Oosthuizen, G. C. *Post-Christianity in Africa: A Theological and Anthropological Study*. London: Hurst and Co, 1968.

Ott, Craig and Harold A. Netland. *Globalizing Theology: Belief and Practice in an Era of World Christianity*. Grand Rapids: Backer Academic, 2016.

Patte, Daniel, et al. *Global Bible Commentary*. Nashville: Abingdon Press, 2004.

Perkins, John M. *Restoring At-Risk Communities: Doing It Together and Doing It Right*. Grand Rapids: Baker Books, 1995.

Perriman, Andrew. *Faith Health and Prosperity: A Report on Word of Faith and Positive Confession Theologies by the Evangelical Alliance UK Commission on unity and truth among Evangelicals*. Waynesboro, GA: Paternoster Press, 2003.

Quebedeaux, Richard. *The New Charismatics: The Origins, Development, and Significance of Neo-Pentecostalism*. Garden City, NY: Doubleday and Company, INC., 1976.

Rainer, Thom. *Effective Evangelistic Churches: Successful Churches Reveal what Works and what Doesn't*. Nashville: Broadman & Holman Publishers, 1996.

Rauschenbusch, Walter. *Christianity and the Social Crisis*. New York: Macmillan, 1907.

Reese, Robert. *Roots of Remedies of Dependency Syndrome in World Mission*. Pasadena, CA: William Carey Library, 2010.

Reid, Alvin, and Thomas S. Rainer. *Evangelism Handbook: Biblical, Spiritual, International, Missional*. Nashville: Holman Publishers, 2003.

Robert, Dana L. *Christian Mission: How Christianity Became a World Religion*. Malden, MA: Wiley-Blackwell, 2009.

Roberts, W. Dayton. *Liberation Thinking: An Evangelical Assessment*. Vol. 4. Monrovia, CA: Marc Publications, 1987.

Rolland, Heidi Unruh, and Ronald Sider. *Saving Society: Understanding the Faith Factor in Church-Based Social Ministry*. New York: Oxford University Press, 2005.

Rommen, Edward. *Spiritual Power and Missions Raising the Issues*. Evangelical Missiological Society Series 3. Pasadena, CA: William Carey Library, 1995.

Rynkiewich, Michael. *Soul Self, and Society: A Postmodern Anthropology for Mission in a Postcolonial World*. Eugene, OR: Cascade Books, 2011.

Saldivar, Jose David. *Border Matters: Remapping American Cultural Studies.* Berkeley, CA: University of California Press, 1997.

Sanneh, Lamin. *Disciples of All Nations: Pillars of World Christianity.* New York: Oxford University Press, 2008.

_____. *Translating the Message: The Missionary Impact on Culture.* 2nd rev. ed. New York: Orbis Books, 2009.

_____. *Whose Religion is Christianity?: The Gospel beyond the West.* Grand Rapids: Eerdmans Publishing Company, 2003.

Sanneh, Lamin and Joel A. Carpenter. *The Changing Face of Christianity: Africa, the West, and the World,* New York: Oxford University Press, 2005.

Shank, David A. *Mission: What Western Christianity Can Learn from African-Initiated Churches.* Edited by James R. Krabill. Elkhart: IN Mennonite Board of Mission, 2000.

Shaw, Mark. *Global Awakening: How 20th Century Revivals Trigged a Christian Revolution.* Downers Grove, IL: Intervarsity Press, 2010.

Shenk, Wilbert R. *Enlarging the Story: Perspective on Writing World Christianity.* Rev. ed. Eugene, OR: Orbis Books, 2002.

Sider, Ronald J., Philip N. Olson, and Heidi Rolland Unruh. *Churches That Make A Difference: Reaching Community with Good News and Good Works.* Grand Rapids: Baker Books, 2002.

Sire, James W. *Habits of the Mind: Intellectual Life as a Christian Calling.* Downers Grove, IL: Intervarsity Press, 2000.

Stinton, Diane B. *Jesus of Africa, Voices of Contemporary African Christology.* Maryknoll, NY: Orbis Books, 2004.

Stone, Bryan. *Evangelism After Christendom: The Theology and Practice of Christian Witness.* Grand Rapids: Brazos Press Division and Baker Publishing Group, 2007.

Stott, John. *Understanding the Bible.* Grand Rapids: Baker Books, 1984.

Streett, Alan R. The Effective Invitation: *A Practical Guide for the Pastor.* Grand Rapids: Kregel Publications, 2004.

Sugirtharajah, R. S. *Exploring Postcolonialism: Biblical Criticism: History, Method, Practice.* West Sussex, UK: Blackwell Publishing, 2012.

Synan, Vinson, Amos Yong, and J. Kwabena Asamoah-Gyadu. *Global Renewal Christianity: Spirit-Empowered Movement Past, Present and Future,* vol. 3. Lake Mar, FL: Charisma House, 2016.

Tempels, Placide. *Bantu Philosophy.* Lexington, KY: HBC Publishing, 2014.

Tennent, Timothy C. *Theology in the Context of World Christianity: How the Global Church is Influencing the Way We Think About and Discuss Theology.* Grand Rapids: Zondervan, 2007.

Tonghou Ngong, David. *The Holy Spirit and Salvation in African Christian Theology: Imagining a More Hopeful Future for Africa.* New York: Peter Lang, 2010.

Tongoi, Dennis O. *Mixing God with Money: Strategies for Living In An Uncertain Economy.* Nairobi: Bezalel Investments Ltd., 2001.

The United Methodist Hymnal: Book of United Methodist Worship. NP: The United Methodist Printing House, 1989.

Van Harn, Roger E. *Psalms for Preaching and Worship: A Lectionary Commentary.* Grand Rapids, MI: William B. Eerdmans Publishing Company, 2009.

Van Henten, Brenner. *Bible Translation on the Threshold of the Twenty-First Century: Authority, Reception, Culture, and Religion.* New York: Sheffield Academic Press, 2002.

Van Reybrouck, David. *Congo: The Epic History of a People.* New York: HarperCollins Publisher, 2014.

Walker, J. K. *The Concise Guide to Today's Religion and Spirituality.* Eugene, OR: Harvest House, 2007.

Walls, Andrew. *The Cross-Cultural Process in Christian History: Studies in the Transmission and Appropriation of Faith.* Maryknoll, NY: Orbis Books, 2002.

———. *The Missionary Movement in Christian History: Studies in the Transmission of Faith.* Maryknoll, NY: Orbis Books, 1996.

———. *Mission in the 21st Century: Exploring the Five Marks of Global Mission.* Maryknoll, NY: Orbis Books, 2008.

Wariboko, Nimi. *The Depth and Destiny of Work: An African Theological Interpretation.* Asmara, ERI: Africa World Press, 2008.

———. *Economics in Spirit: A Moral Philosophy of Finance.* New York: Palgrave MacMillan, 2014.

———. *The Pentecostal Principle: Ethical Methodology in New Spirit.* Grand Rapids: William B. Eerdmans Publishing Company, 2012.

West, Gerald O., and Musa W. Dube. *The Bible in Africa: Transactions, Trajectories and Trends.* Leiden: Brill, 2000.

Wright, Christopher J. H. *Biblical Theology for Life, The Mission of God's People: A Biblical Theology of the Church's Mission.* Grand Rapids: Zondervan, 2010.

Yamamori, Tetsunao, and Charles R. Taber, *Christopaganism or Indigenous Christianity?* Pasadena, CA: William Carey Library, 1975.

Articles

Aduro, Thomas. "African Theology: The Contribution of African Initiated Churches." *Ogbomoso Journal of Theology* 13 (2008) 58–73

Anderson, Allan. "African Independent Churches and Pentecostalism: Historical Connections and Common Identities." *Ogmoso Journal of Theology* 13 (2008) 22–41

———. "Writing the Pentecostal History of Africa, Asia, and Latin America." *Journal of Beliefs and Values* 25, no.2 (2014) 139–153.

Aronson, Torbjorn. "Community in Charismata: Swedish Mission and the Growth of Neo-Pentecostal Churches in Russia." *Religion in Eastern Europe* XXX (2011): 33–40.

Asamoah-Gyadu, J. Kwabena. "'Born of Water and Spirit': Pentecostal/Charismatic Christianity in African." In Ogbu U. Kalu, *African Christianity: An African Story.* Asmara, ERI: Africa World Press, 2007.

Barrett, David B. "The Worldwide Holy Spirit Renewal." In Vision Synan, *The Century of the Holy Spirit: 100 Years of Pentecostal and Charismatic Renewal, 1901-2001.* Nashville: Thomas Nelson, 2001.

Bledsoe, David Allen. "Prosperity Theology, Mere Symptom of Graver problems in Neo-Pentecostalism." *Revista Batista Pioneira* 3 (2014) 301–07.

Bongmba, Elias Kifo. "Writing African Christianity Perspectives from the History of the Historiography of African Christianity." *Religion and Theology* 23 (2016) 275–312.

Clarke, Clifton R. "Pan-African and Pentecostalism in Africa: Strange Bedfellows or Perfect Partners?: A Pentecostal Assist Towards A Pan-African Political Theology." *Black Theology Regent University School of Divinity* 11, no. 2 (2013) 152–84.

Dada, A. O. "Prosperity Gospel in Nigerian Context: A Medium of Social Transformation or an Impetus for Delusion?" *Ibadan Journal of Religions Studies* 36½ (2004) 95–105.

Deacon, Gregory, and Gabrielle Lynch. "Allowing Satan In?: Moving toward a Political-Economic of Neo-Pentecostalism in Kenya." *Journal of Religion in Africa* 43 (2013) 108–130.

Deichmann, Wendy J. "The Social Gospel as a Grassroots Movement." *Church History* 84, no. 1 (2015) 203–06.

Dilger, Hanjorg. "Healing the Wounds of Modernity: Salvation, Community, and Care in the Neo-Pentecostal Church in Dar-Es-Salaam Tanzania." *Journal of Religion in Africa* 37 (2007) 59–83.

Dorrien, Gary. "Rauschenbush's Christianity and the Social Crisis: Kingdom Coming." *Christian Century* 27 (2007) 27–29.

Gbote, Eric Z. M. "Prosperity Gospel: A Missiological Assessment." *Department of Science of Religion and Missiology* (2014) 1–10

Gilliland, Dean S. "How Christian Are African Independent Churches." *Missiology* 14 (1986) 259–72.

GoloKwalu, Ben-Willie. "Africa's Poverty and Its Neo-Pentecostal Liberators: An Ecotheological Assessment of Africa's Prosperity Gospellers." *Brill Pneuma* 35 (2003) 366–84.

Haynes, Naomi. "Pentecostalism and the Morality of Money: Prosperity, Inequality, and Religious Sociality on Zambian Copperbelt." *Journal of the Royal Anthropological Institute* (2012) 123–39.

Isbell, Charles D. "Glossolalia and Propheteialalia: A Study of 1 Corinthians 14." *Wesleyan Theological Seminary* (2008) 15–22.

Jenkins, Philip. "The Next Christianity." *Atlantic Monthly* (2002): 53–68.

Johnson, Todd M. "Symposium: Global Perspectives on Pentecostalism: The Global Demographics of the Pentecostal and Charismatic Renewal." *Springer Science Business Media, LLC* (2009) 483.

Kay, William K. "Martyn Lloyd-Jones' Influence on Pentecostalism and Neo-Pentecostalism in the UK." *Journal of Pentecostal Theology* 22 (2013) 275–94.

Kwalu, Ben-Willie Golo. "Africa's Poverty and Its Neo-Pentecostal Liberators: An Ecotheological Assessment of Africa's Prosperity Gospellers." *Brill Pneuma* 35 (2003) 366–84.

Mukeni Beya, Marie Rose. "Socio-Economic Collapse in the Congo: Causes and Solutions." *Georgist Journal News &Views from the International Georgist Movement*, no. 23 (2012) 1–2.

Myers, Bryant L. "Progressive Pentecostalism, Development, and Christian Development NGOs: A Challenge and an Opportunity." (2005) 115–20.

Muyingi, Mbangu Anicet. "African Traditional Religion: A New Struggle for African Identity." *Asia Journal of Theology* 29 (2015) 88–98.

Njeri Mwaura, Philomena. "Gendered Appropriation of Mass Media in Kenyan Christianities: A Comparison of Two Women-Led African Instituted Churches in Kenya." In Ogbu U. Kalu et al. *Interpreting Contemporary Christianity: Global*

Process and Local Identities. Grand Rapids: William B. Eerdmans Publishing Co, 2008. 274–295

Njoroge, John N. "The Orthodox Church in Africa and the Quest for Enculturation: A Challenging Mission Paradigm in Today's Orthodoxy." *St. Vladimir's Theological Quarterly* 554 (2011) 405–38.

Obijole, Olubayo O. "The Church and the Gospel Message in the African Cultural Context." *Ogbomoso Journal of Theology* 17 (2012) 99–116.

Oguntoye, P. A. "African Culture and Its Implications for Effective Presentation of the Gospel." *Journal of Religion* 17 (2012) 173–88.

Ojo, A. Mathews. "Transnational Religions Networks and Indigenous Pentecostal Missionary Enterprises in the West African Coastal Region." In *Christianity in Africa and African Diaspora: The Appropriation of a Scattered Heritage*. Edited by Afe Adogame, Roswith Gerloff, and Klaus Hock. London: Continuum International Publishing, 2008.

Omenyo, Cephas N., and Wonderful Adjei Arthur. "The Bible Says! Neo-Prophetic Hermeneutics in Africa." *Studies in World Christianity* 19, no. 1 (2013) 50–70.

Osiek, Carolyn. "Forum Gospel and Enculturation: The Long Road." *Religion and Theology* 6 (1999) 83–92

Pearson, Robert L. "Gatsby: False Prophet of the American Dream." *The English Journal of Teachers of English* (2015) 638–45

Penttila, Maija. "Saint Peter's New Churches: The Indigenization of Neo-Charismatic Christianity in ST Petersburg." *Nordic Journal of Religion and Society* (2014) 19–39.

Peterson, Cheryl M. "Pneumatology and the Cross: The Challenge of Neo-Pentecostalism to Lutheran Theology." *Wiley Periodicals and Dialog* (2011) 400–402.

Phiri, Isaac. "Saving Witches in Kolwezi: Accused of Witchcraft by Parents and Churches, Children in the Democratic Republic of Congo Are Being Rescued by Christian Activists." *Christianity Today* (2009) 65.

Pype, Katrien. "'We Need To Open Up the Country': Development and the Christian Key Scenario in the Social Space of Kinshasa's Teleserials." *Journal of African Media Studies* 1, no. 1 (2009) 101–16.

Ribeiro Caldas, Carlos. "The Role of Brazilian Universal Church of the Kingdom of God in Globalization of Neo-Pentecostalism Today." *Society for the Scientific Study of Religion* (2010) 108–121.

Rich, Jeremy. "Zaire for Jesus: Ford Philpot's Evangelical Crusades in the Democratic Republic of Congo, 1966–1978." *Journal of Religion in Africa* 43 (2013) 4–28.

Ringvee, Ringo. "Charismatic Christianity and Pentecostal Churches in Estonia from a Historical Perspective." *Approaching Religion* 5 (2015) 57–65

Robert, Dana L. "Shifting Southward: Global Christianity Since 1945." *International Bulletin of Missionary Research* (2000). 50–58

Sanneh, Lamin. "The Horizontal and the Vertical in Mission: An African Perspective." *International Bulletin of Missionary Research* 7 (1983). 165–171

Schieman, Scott, and Jong-Hyun Jung. "Practical Divine Influence: Socioeconomic Status and Belief in the Prosperity Gospel." *Journal for Scientific Study of Religion* (2012) 738–56.

Togarasei, Lovemore. "Cursed be the past: Tradition and Modernity among Modern Pentecostals." *BOLESWA, Journal of Theology, Religion, and Philosophy* (2006) 109–118.

_____. "Modern Pentecostalism as an Urban Phenomenon: The Care of the Family of God in Zimbabwe." *Exchange* 34 (2005) 349–75.

_____. "The Pentecostal Gospel of Prosperity in African Context of Poverty: An Appraisal." *University of Botswana* 40 (2011) 336–350.

Vail, Mark. "The Integrative Rhetoric of Martin Luther King Jr.'s 'I Have a Dream' Speech." *The University of Memphis* 9, no.1 (2006) 51–78.

Van Kamp, Linda. "Afro-Brazilian Pentecostal Re-formations of the Relationships Across Two Generations of Mozambican Women." *Journal of Religion in Africa* 42 (2012) 433–52.

Walls, Andrew F. "The Gospel as Prisoner and Liberator of Culture: Is There a Historic Christian Faith?" In Robert L. Gallagher, *Landmark Essays in Mission and World Christianity*. Maryknoll, NY: Orbis Books, 2011.

_____. "The Mission of the Church Today: In the Light of Global History." *Word and World* 20 (2000) 17–20.

Wesley, John. "Sermon on Mercy." In *The Works of the Rev. John Wesley. A. M. Sometime Fellow of Lincoln College, Oxford*, vol. 4. 4th ed. London: James Nichols, 1940.

Wild-Wood, Emma. "'Free from Shackles' or 'Dirtied'?: The Contested Pentecostalisation of Anglican Congregations in the Democratic Republic of Congo." *Milton Keynes* 3 (2008) 103–115.

Wright, Chris et al. "Lausanne Theology Working Group Statement on the Prosperity Gospel: From the Africa Chapter of the Lausanne Theology Working Group in Akripong, Ghana, October 8–9, 2008 and September 1–4, 2009." 99–102.

Yung, Hwa. "Endued with Power: The Pentecostal-Charismatic Renewal and the Asian Church in Twenty-First Century." *AJPS* 6 (2003) 63–82.

Zink, Jesse. Anglocostalism in Nigeria: Neo-Pentecostalism and Obstacles to Anglican Unity. *Journal of Anglican Studies* 10 (2012) 231–50.

Interviews

BBC WorldNews. January 17, 2013.

Belz, Mindy. Interview by author February 7, 2024. Lubumbashi Democratic Republic of the Congo.

Ferrera, Ignatius. Interview by author April 22, 2017. North West University, Potchefstroom, South Africa.

Hoover, Jeff. Interview by author February 10, 2015. Lubumbashi, The Democratic Republic of the Congo.

Katshinga, Mvwala. Interview by authro May 17, 2017. Kinshasa, The Democratic Republic of the Congo.

Luemba, Dieudonné Sita. Interview by author May 19, 2017. Kinshasa, The Democratic Republic of the Congo.

Makuta, Bijoux. Interview by author May 15, 2017. Kinshasa, The Democratic Republic of the Congo.

Mwanza, Jascques Kalabo. ÉvangéliqueViens-et –Vois. Interview by author May 11, 2017. Lubumbashi, The Democratic Republic of the Congo.

Nel, Marius. Interview by author April 22, 2017.North West University, Potchefstroom, South Africa.

Persons, David Nelson. Interview by author December 25, 2014. Mulungwishi Seminary Democratic Republic of the Congo.
Tshibangu, Edward. Interview by author May 25, 2017. Kinshasa, DRC.
WaMushidi, Mutwale. «United Methodist Church.» Interview by author July 15, 2015. Dar-Es-Salaam, Tanzania.

Dissertations

Arnett, Randy Ray. "Pentecostalization: The Changing Face of Baptists in West Africa." Ph.D. diss., Southwestern Baptist Theological Seminary, 2012.
Jin Park, Hyung. "Journey of the Gospel: A Study in the Emergence of World Christianity and the Shift of Christian Historiography in the Last Half of the Twentieth Century." Ph.D. diss., Princeton University, 2009.
Kawata, Frederick. "The Pentecostal Church in the Congo/30ème Communauté: Engaging in Poverty Eradication." Ph.D. Dissertation, Stellenbosch University, 2014.
Monroe, Lonn S. "Corroboration and Contention Congo Consecrations: An Anthropological Analysis of Cuban Reglas Congas." Ph.D. diss., University of Florida, 2007.

Internet Sources

Hawn, C. Michael, "History of Hymns: 'Nothing but the Blood.'" Discipleship Ministries. http://www.umcdiscipleship.org/ resources/history-of-hymns-nothing-but-the-blood.
Kabongo, K. M. "The United Reformed Church in Congo." www.urccongo.org/2101.html.

Other Sources

Africana Studies Course. Africa University Mutare Zimbabwe, course taken during 2007-08 academic year. Mutare, Zimbabwe.
Anderson, Allan. "The Pentecostal Gospel and Culture in Africa: Charismatics of the Pentecostal Full Gospel." *Graduate Institute of Theology and Religion*. Selly Oak, UK: University of Birmingham, 2000. Paper read at the History of Religion Seminar, University of Oxford, May 29, 2000.
Augustin, "Les vendeurs de Foi. Un reportage sur les églises dites de réveil à Kinshasa." An Internet video watched April 1, Published on Sep 13, 2015 Kinshasa Democratic Republic of the Congo. https://www.youtube.com/watch?v=OFgJAOLOFOY.
TsambuBulu, Léon. *Refonder l'idéal panafricaniste à l'aune de l'intellectualité symbolique de la musique* [archive]. Conférence commémorative du trentième anniversaire de CODESRIA (2003).

Index

Abraham, 165
"abundant life," 169
acculturation, 139
Adamo, David, 87
Adeboye, A., 8
Adomiran, 164
advertising, the gospel of Jesus, 108
Africa
    ceasing to be an economic colony of Europe, 188
    mapping the history of global missions and Christianity, 157
    as now one of the Christian heartlands, 2, 14, 66, 123
    as one of the leading voices within the Judeo-Christian religion, 5
    supplying missionaries to the Western world, 5
    waves of revival, 36n30
African(s)
    accessing both the Bible and land, 166
    avoiding past mistakes of missional enterprises, 217
    Christian experience, 206n64
    de-Christianization of by Mobutu, 190n14, 238
    empowering and re-educating, 218
    engaging in prophetic leadership, 207
    going to the church and seeking prayer, 242
    growth in the number of Christian, 5n12
    as new forces of Christendom, 205n61
    practiced local religions, 183
    proclaiming or self-ordaining themselves, 229–30
    reading emerging North American key philosophical and Christian theologies, 124
    sharing everything, 211n4
    tending to convert to Christianity by emotions, 234
    uncritical contextualization by, 138
African Christendom, theologies reshaping, 211
African Christianity
    double marginalization in the West, 92
    integrating pre-Christian traditions, 47
    needing to be African, 219n19
    Neo-Pentecostals as the new face of, 8
    new expressions of, 234
    reshaping Christianity in the twenty-first century, 2
    as a syncretized religious worldview, 49
African communities, enculturating the gospel, 136
African cosmological realities, dealing with in translations, 215
African council of churches, 48
African evangelical belief systems, 42

INDEX

African Independent Churches. *See* African Initiated Churches (AICs)
African Initiated Churches (AICs)
  different from the newer, independent Neo-Pentecostal churches, 11
  distinctive characteristics of, 68
  emergence of, 19n61, 28
  independent of denominations planted by Western missions, 28n2
  proliferation of, 4
  promoted a gospel of socio-economic exploitation, 39
  rise of, 109
  understanding the felt needs of the larger population, 49
African Instituted Churches. *See* African Initiated Churches (AICs)
African necrology, 46
African pagan traditions, 206
African social fabric, socio-spiritual dependency syndrome in, 211
"African Traditional Religion" (ATR), 10, 11n34
African Traditional Religion (Muyingi), 11n34
Africanism or negritude, 238
Africanization, 47
Afro-Brazilian Pentecostalism, 192
agricultural mindset, prosperity model based on, 155
AIDS, children orphaned by, 211
Allen, Ronald J., 153
Allison, Gregg R., 179–81
Alphonso the Congolese king, baptism of, 33
"Amazing Grace" (hymn), 145
"Amen TV," 110
America, sending help to, 234
American Christians, seeking money, health and good fortune, 162
"American Dream," 36–37, 72
American prosperity gospel
  adopted within Congolese cultural expressions, 1, 2
  compared to Congolese expression of prosperity, 162
  influencing African cosmological worldviews, 163
  overshadowing the evangelical vocation, 79
American-imported gospel, 83
Americans, exploiting the Congo, 188
Ancestor, Jesus as, 120n43
ancestors
  African culture of invoking the spirits of, 211
  incarnation essential to Congolese religious life and experience, 46
  invocation of spiritual worldviews of, 211n4
  as mediators, 64
  venerating for occult practices, 40
ancestral spirits, 22, 203
Anderson, Allan H., 3, 14–15, 37–38, 65, 158, 161, 198–99, 200, 200n46–201n46, 201n52–2n52, 202, 203, 204, 210n1
animism, 34n25, 43, 152n3
animistic worldviews, 6
"Anointing Through the Screen: Neo-Pentecostalism and Televised Christianity in Ghana" (Asamoah-Gyandu), 103, 111n17
Anthropological Insights for Missionaries (Hiebert), 138n40
anti-missionary sentiment, 129n15
anti-prosperity theology, 215–16
Apostolic Church, 12
Appiah-Kubi, 204–5
Arnett, Randy Ray, 8, 8n22, 11
Aronson, Torbjorn, 7
Arthur, Wonderful Adjei, 151n1
Asamoah-Gyandu, Kwabena, 38, 103, 110
"Assemble Chretien de Kinshasa," 110
Assemblies of Gods, 12
assimilation, literature advocating, 20
association international Africaine, 31n12
ATR (African Traditional Religion), 10, 11n34

INDEX

259

authentic evangelism, as critical for holistic discipleship and change, 6
authentic meaning, reconstructing, 173
Azusa Street Revival, in the United States, 12

Babalola, Joseph, 36n30
Babylonian exile, 145
Bakker, Jim and Tammy, 37n31
Bakongo kingdom, 41n42
the Bantu, describing God, 30
Bantu Philosophy (Tempels), 2
Bantus, migrations of, 29
Baptist Missionary Society (BMS), 32–33
Bathsheba, 177
Becking, Bob, 145
Bediako, Kwame, 47, 56, 57, 59, 65, 66, 73, 167, 167–68, 200, 203–4, 205, 206n64, 207
Belgian Congo, 4n9, 19n61, 41
Belgians
    efforts to oust Pentecostalism, 191n18
    introduced literacy, 31
    leadership attempted to control the missionary effort, 52
    transferred all companies to Belgium, 239
    wanting only political independence for the Congo, 240
Berger, Peter, 153
Berlin Conference, 240
Beya, Marie Rose Mukeni, 17, 29, 45
Bible
    becoming an African book, 167
    defining prosperity, 210n2, 237
    effects of misreading, 234
    as God's story, 173
    in the hands of indigenous people, 167
    lending support to traditional African customs, 65–66
    misinterpreted, 166, 167
    multiethnic global readings of, 85
    as not a Qur'an, 58n22
    as a prophetic book, 230
    recording God's revelation to humanity, 173
    reinforcing social and economic exploitation, 213
    rereading with fresh eyes, 97
    role of, 166–68
    supporting colonizers efforts to exercise control, 54
    taken out of context, 67
    translation, effect and impact on the vernacular cultures, 51–76
    translation, enabled the spread of the gospel, 55
    translation, into Bantu's language for the Pygmies, 234
    translation into the vernacular gave authority to local religious expressions, 33, 167
    translation of as the vehicle of indigenous cultural development, 58n22, 168
"The Bible Says!" (Omenyo and Arthur), 151n1
biblical analysis, of prosperity theology, 163–65
biblical faith, should not be for sale or gain, 79
biblical Gospel
    addressing and altering misreadings of, 221
    interpretation of, 24
    mistranslation and misreading of, 80
    proponents of prosperity theology misuse, 23
    rediscovering an authentic translation, 219
    releasing from its neo-colonial patterns, 207
biblical hermeneutic, 24
biblical hermeneutic theory, 151n1
biblical hermeneutics, 166, 168–72
biblical integrity and justice, standing on equity, 23
biblical interpretation, suffering without non-Western voices, 88

biblical literature
  literal translation of, 172
  read through a liberating approach, 96
  uncritical interpretation of, 152–53
biblical message, materializing to raise money, 170
biblical texts, 55, 151–84
bicultural community, 161n26
Bildad, 215
Billington, James H., 15
Binti, John, 47
Bissell, Richard, 189n11
The Black Atlantic (Gilroy), 146
Bledsoe, 78–79
"blessings," obtaining, 47
blog, also known as a weblog, 114n25
Blyden, Edward Wilmont, 157
body of Christ
  having no frontiers or nationality, 112
  lack of authentic discipleship within, 84
  needing a factual, original, and orthodox gospel of Jesus Christ, 91
  people of different places and cultures gathering and forming, 61
  urgent need for Africa to train and equip to avoid uncritical hermeneutics, 213
Bokeleale, as representative of the ECC, 238
Bongmba, Elias Kifo, 156, 157
Bonnke, Reinhard, 39, 106, 123–24, 140–41, 140n44, 148, 182
born-again Christians, 14n46
Bosch, David J., 137
Bowler, Kate, 161–62
brokenness, rebuilding of the forms of, 13
Brown, Candy Gunther, 8
Brueggemann, Walter, 163, 164, 165, 177n65
Bujo, Bénézet, 156
Burton, 210n1
bus preachers, 236

Caldwell, Kirbyjon H., 23–24
"Canal de Vie," in Lubumbashi, 110
capitalism, 101, 178n68, 244
capitalistic exploitation, by Solomon, 165
Carpenter, Joel A., 67–68
Carroll R., M. Daniel, 121, 142
Carter, Warren, 96, 191
case studies
  of ministries of complete holism, 181–82
  of Neo-Pentecostal thoughts, practices, belief systems, and influences, 6
  of the socio-economic implications of the prosperity gospel, 12
Castle, Gregory, 146
Catholic bishops, participated in reconciliation, 189
Catholic Church
  as an autocratic system, 238
  involved in governmental affairs, 190n14, 238
  part of neocolonial efforts supporting Mobutu, 190
  produced politicians, 232
Catholic missionaries, death rate from tropical diseases, 33
Catholic priests, shaping the second Republic of Zaire, 238
Catholic schools, became government's property, 238
center of gravity, dramatic shift in, 1, 5, 86, 214–15, 229
Césaire, Aimé, 95–96
charisma, meaning gift, 8
charismatic churches, 153, 223
Charismatic movement, 36
charismatic preachers
  making money and driving expensive vehicles, 217–18
  preaching to the most desperate and vulnerable, 70
  on sowing of seed, 43
charismatic prophets, creating a hierarchy within the African social fabric, 213

INDEX 261

charismatic renewal churches, practices within, 174
charismatic renewal streams of Christianity, 210
charismatic revival, from the 1960s and onwards, 7
charismatic worship, 141n44
charismatic/spiritual churches, as more gender-friendly, 71n58
Bishop Charles, 110
children, 143–44, 211, 242
China, rapid expansion of the church in, 119
Chloe, 193
Christ. *See* Jesus Christ
"Christ for all Nations," Neo-Pentecostal renewal branch, 124
Christian ethics, 22, 82, 83
Christian faith. *See also* faith
    in African terms, 205
    changing, 90, 121, 126n7
    entering into the vernacular culture, 21
    global conversation about, 85
    numerical growth of, 142
Christian message
    accessible in multiple languages and cultures, 126
    business of advertising, 106
    ignored while greater emphasis and attention are drawn toward humanitarian concerns and social lifts, 81
    translated into local trends and cultural expression, 68
Christian Mission (Robert), 128n14
Christianity
    blending traditional practices with Euro-American styles of worship, 109
    changing face of, 90
    in decline in much of Europe, 89n20
    developed as a vernacular faith, 59
    development in Congolese society, 27
    effort to indigenize, 61
    emergence within a Congolese context, 3
    encounter with African primal religious traditions, 66
    enculturated and domesticated by locals, 117
    expansion of, 21
    as the extension and fulfillment of Jewish faith, 160n25
    failed as a transformative force in the Congo, 83
    as a force to civilize Africans, 129
    as a foreign religion, 138n40
    indigenized, 33, 56
    less influence on true discipleship development, 69
    local expressions of, 28
    mixed with traditional practices, 40
    as the most culturally translatable, 59
    most rapid growth outside the West, 121
    no single or unique geographic center, 126
    not foreign to Africa, 205, 206n64
    offering new dimensions or expressions of, 109–10
    proliferating in Africa, 216
    providing space for non-Western theologies, 120
    reborn into a non-Western religious character, 66
    as a refuge against paganism and demonic oppression, 42
    reshaped and domesticated, 206–7
    shift from the Atlantic North to the South, 114
    shifting center of, 1, 60n29
    syncretistic character of, 11
    transformed into a world religion, 183
    translated itself into local cultures, 63
    as a universal idiom from a global church and missions, 112
    universality of, 129n17
    as a world religion, 111, 130, 179
Christianity and the Social Crisis (Rauschenbusch), 198

INDEX

Christians
  combining African traditions, 34n25
  coming from places other than Europe and North America, 90
  needing re-education, 91
  as pioneers of linguistic development, 58
  taking the Bible seriously, 48
Christopaganism, 149
Christopaganism or Indigenous Christianity? (Yamamori and Taber), 148n63
Christ's mandate, of a cross-cultural mission, 127
church
  aligning itself with the privileged classes, 187n5
  as critical to peace talk, recompilation, and reconciliation, 189
  growth of, 215n12, 230
  literature review of growth, 14–15
  mission of, 241–42
  as a missional and connectional institute, 114
  parasitic mode of existence in Africa, 127n11, 214n11
  as a place to feel at home as a challenge in the Congo, 21
  promoting political propaganda and sanctioning the mechanism of impoverishment, 177n65
  reinforcing social and spiritual injustices, 242
  remaining silent on social issues in the Congo, 186
  succeeding in making a difference, 232
  "The Church and the Gospel Message in the African Cultural Context" (Obijole), 139n42
church beyond the four walls, as an evangelistic approach, 113–14
Church of God, 12
Church of Pentecost, 12
Church of the Foursquare Gospel, 12
churches
  advertising activities and mission statements, 107
  established by the missionaries no longer addressing daily realities, 4n9
  members giving money to enrich one person, 242
  needing to be equipped for holistic and transformative ministries and discipleship, 184
  not being free to voice and advocate for the weak, 187
  practicing both evangelism and social ministry, 7n17
  underground and not registered with the government, 242
Chuza, accompanied Jesus, 193
Ciongio, Dianna L., on the iPhone, 107
class privileges, 175
classical Pentecostalism
  compared to Neo-Pentecostalism, 3–4
  described, 7n18
  imported foreign patterns and practices from, 36
  paradigms failed to engage the gospel as a transformative force, 75
  referring to the holiness movement originating from the Azusa Street Revival, 12
  supported the effects of oppression and exploitation, 191
  trends of consumerism and progress imported to Africa, 162
classical Pentecostals, 12, 201
clothes, practices of anointing, 85
colonial theology, Matthew 5:3 supporting, 190
colonized countries, writers attempting to reclaim cultural identities, 94
colonized people, telling and reading their stories, 199
commodity culture, of the West, 166
Communaute Pentecoste du Congo, CPCO (Pentecostal Community of the Congo), 210n1

INDEX

communication, between two cultural worlds, 161n26
"Community in Charismata" (Aronson), 7n18
complete holism, ministries producing, 181–82
Conference Nationale Souveraine du Zaire (CNS), 239
confidence, in divine wealth, 16
"conflict minerals," 159
Congo
    acceptance of prosperity theologies, 15, 29, 124
    economy still controlled by the West, 100–101
    as a failed state, 38, 200
    as a fragile post-conflict country, 17
    history of, 19n61
    as one of the most Christianized nations in the world, 67
    as one of the most Christianized societies in Sub-Saharan Africa, 216
    pressing issues confronting, 82
    rewriting and reconstructing the past of the people of, 97
    stable and prosperous prior to the arrival of Western civilization and missionaries, 30
"Congo Free State," 41
Congolese
    accessing God's revelation, 59
    as adopted sons and daughters or the seed to inherit Abrahamic prosperity, 165
    as agents of their freedom, 188
    appropriated the gospel and domesticated it, 4–5
    attracted to prosperity messages as a means of survival, 20
    baptized without experiencing actual conversion, 180n72
    developing an authentic, comprehensive model for, 25
    hearing the gospel in their own languages, 57
    imitating North American and European lifestyles, 110
    lacking contextualized discipleship of Christian faith, 22
    lives and deaths of eastern, 159n22
    longing to have a limitless life, 47
    misrepresented in both academic and public arenas, 97
    mistranslations and misinterpretations of the biblical texts, 26
    received the gospel and translated it into their cultural approaches, 56
    reclaimed ancestral traditional patterns and beliefs systems in 1971, 20
    relating to the culture of prosperity and abundance for humanitarian survival, 162
    resisted forgoing traditional or ancestral belief systems at the expense of faith, 135
    retransmitting the gospel, 66–67, 83
    self-theologizing character of, 87
    spiritual growth among believers, 230
    taking the gospel to other nations, 23, 111, 229
    using the Scriptures as a shield against evil and demonic forces, 87
    witnessing God's saving grace and sharing it with others, 75
Congolese Christians
    believing in utopia of the future or tomorrow, 69
    receiving the same general revelation as Western Christians, 180
    re-education of, 213
    televangelism and social media globalized by, 106
Congolese church, 14, 164, 189
Congolese cultural patterns, 67, 68, 97–98
Congolese feminist and missiologist, interview transcription, 241–43
Congolese kingdom, as peaceful and sustainable, 30

Congolese multi-culturalism, evaluating the text in light of, 173
Congolese scholar, interview transcription, 237–43
Congolese story, re-reading with postcolonial eyes, 198–202
Congo-Vrijstaat, 19n61
connectivity, relating to holistic evangelism, 107
consumers, people taught as, 233
Consuming the Congo (Eichstaedt), 159n22
contextual hermeneutics, 81, 152, 172–73, 227
contextualization
   challenging people to turn from evil ways, 149
   of the Christian expressions, 117
   of the gospel, 60, 137–41
   as neither accommodation nor syncretism, 148–49
   of the Neo-Pentecostal movement, 38–41
   uncritical, 158
continuity, 72, 76
conversion, 21
converts in the Congo, often not receptive to the gospel, 203
Copeland, Kenneth, 37
Corbett, Steve, 100
corrupt structures, altering systemic authorized, 207–8
corrupt systems, bishops and prophetic leaders perpetuating, 179
cosmic realities, connected to spirit encounter, 38
cosmological world of spirits, 203
cosmological worldviews, 202
"court of David," 176
critical contextualization, as an approach, 138
cross-cultural elements, dialogue between, 161
cross-cultural influence, making the Gospel at home, 207
The Cross-Cultural Process in Christian History (Walls), 122n1

cross-cultural theological framework, 119
cross-cultural transmission, of the gospel, 125–27
cultural baggage, avoiding, 173
cultural frontiers, crossing through overseas missions, 229
cultural identity, 144
cultural mores, 68
cultural translation, problem of, 235
cultural vacuum, 138
culture(s)
   in the Black Atlantic offering a counterculture, 147
   gospel and, 235
   negative and positive sides, 158
   possessing positive and negative prototypes, 126
   prosperity phenomenon in the context of African, 217
   relativizing every, 112
culture brokers, 161n26
culture change, as always difficult, 91
cyber culture, 113

Dalit, Jesus as, 120n43
David Oyedepo's Winner's Chapel, 8
David's violence of rape, 176–77
Day of Pentecost, 57
De George, Susan G., 114
de Hemptinne, Jean-Felix, 189
De la bouche à l'Oreille, referring to self-theologizing, 168
de Witte, Marleen, 104, 105
Deacon and Lynch, as Neo-Pentecostal narratives, 38
the dead, dwelling among the realms of the living, 46
debts, cancellation of, 171
Deichmann, Wendy J., 130n20–31n20, 131n23
deliverance, 231–32, 241
Democratic Republic of the Congo, 4n9, 41
demographic shifts, changing the face of global Christianity, 89
demons, 204, 231

dependency, 15, 100, 232
dependency syndrome, 100, 233–34, 241, 243
Desai, Graurary, 145
Detweiler, Craig, 107, 108
Deuternonomist narrative, framework for anti-prosperity theology, 215
Deuteronomist principle, 216
Deuteronomy 28:2, as a hallmark of prosperity, 171
Diaspora
   central to constructing a sense of identity and belonging, 144
   community constructing an identity and fitting into a foreign land, 143
   described, 147–48
   as a phenomenon shaping twenty-first century Christianity, 142
   signifying a place where new geographies of identity are negotiated, 148
diasporatic history, 141–48
different gospel, developed by Neo-Pentecostals in post-colonial Congo, 2n3, 90–91
Dilger, Hanjorg, 50
disease and poverty, as spiritual issues, 204
diseases, afflictions caused by, 173
'dis-relations,' 135n30
Divination in 1 Samuel 28 and Beyond (Kiboko), 54n10
divinators, as true-false prophets, 230–31
divine healing, 173–74
divine healing and restoration, promises of, 39
diviners, using spiritual forces not from God, 231
divorces, children homeless due to, 211
Dollar, Creflo A., 124
domestication, of the prosperity gospel, 75
Dorrien, Gary, 131
double consciousness, 142–45
drums, 30–31, 109

Du Bois, William Edward Burghardt, 141–42
Dube, Musa W., 96
Dulles, Allen, 189n11
Duncan-Williams, Nicholas, 110
durability, of the story of Jesus, 126
Dyrness, William A., 88, 89–90, 121, 130, 134

economic collapse, literature review of, 17
economic ethos, of third-wave Pentecostal and charismatic Christianity, 197
economic factors, contributing to the expansion of Neo-Pentecostalism, 44–45
economic independence, never received by the Congo, 239
economic inflation, causing the church to engage in missional and social actions, 45
economic power, of the Congo depending on foreign currencies, 239
economic privation, frustration midnight of, 187n5
Economics in Spirit: A Moral Philosophy of Finance (Wariboko), 163
ecumenical declaration, in 1971, 48
ECZ (Eglise du Christ au Zaire), 238
Edgerton, Robert B., 53
Edinburgh Missionary Conference (1910), 122, 122n1, 157
education, 45, 54–55, 61
Edwards, Justin D., 147
Eglise de reveilles (revival churches), 79
Eglise du Christ au Congo, 190n14
Eglise du Réveil (church of awakening), 80, 140, 141n44
Eichstaedt, Peter, 159, 159n22
Eisenhower, Dwight D., 189n11
electronic churches, evangelism and, 117
electronic media technologies, 120
Eliphaz, 215
employment opportunities, lack of, 45

enculturation
  adding a new culture to a primary cultural pattern or expression, 161
  eliminating stereotypes, 101
  as an endless process of divine revelation, 135
  of the gospel, 134
  as a medium through which God speaks to people, 139
  as a missiological process, 137
entrepreneurial ecosystems, critical for the twenty-first century global church, 218
entrepreneurial gospel, 24
equation, specifying the expected return to a believer investing in giving to God, 155n11
Escobar, Samuel, 112, 112n18
Etat Independent du Congo, translated as the Congo Free State, 19n61
eternal life, 46–47, 169
Ethiopian churches, 28n2
Europe, wanting to return to Africa, 239
European Christianity, facing a crisis, 142
Europeans, brought Christianity and slave trade, 128
Europeans and Westerners, having the monopoly in decision making, 100
Evangelical Church of Congo, missionaries to other African countries and to Europe, 229
evangelical churches, limited to proclaiming the Gospel, 232
evangelical missions, emphasizing spiritual prosperity, 79
evangelicalism, 22, 189
evangelicals, 133
evangelism
  in the Congo, 34n22
  as the core of missions, 112
  defined, 195
  described, 9–10
  educated or trained local evangelized indigenous people, 128
  from a profound and personal relationship with Jesus Christ, 107
  rooted in an American consumeristic worlview, 195
  traditional, 4n9, 34, 140–41
  without frontiers, 111–16
evangelization, 128, 235
evangelized Congolese, adapted the gospel to their cultural patterns, 35
evangelized language, transmitting the Gospel into, 234
evil, deriving from class conflict, 133n26
exile, as a period of suffering and distress, 145–46
the exiled, creating an identity and freedom in a foreign land, 142
expected rate of return, on faith or a portfolio of faithful investment, 155n11
exploitation of human resources, by Solomon's regime, 164

face of Christianity, reinvention of, 67–69
Facebook, 107
faith. *See also* Christian faith
  as a leap one might faithfully invest into stock, 156
  massive resurgence of, 1
  rooted in new Pentecostal expressions of entrepreneurship, 153
  sowing seeds today for tomorrow's decent life, 70
faith force, humans having before the Fall, 18n60
"Faith Movement," prosperity gospel emerged from, 37n31
faith-gospel, 68n52
Falk, Peter, 4n9, 32–35
false preachers, 230, 235, 240
false promises, 15
false prophets, 215n12, 230
Fanon, Frantz, 57, 62, 96–97, 146
Fashole-Luke, on Africans having an uncritical approach to Scripture, 166

Federal Council of Churches and Social Creed, 131n23
Fee, Gordon D., 168, 169, 169n51
fees, to receive prayers and be seen by pastors and prophets, 79
Ferrera, Ignatius, 219, 219n19
Fiorenza, Elizabeth Schüssler, 96, 193
forced labor, Solomon's use of, 165
foreign context, evangelizing in, 160
foreign prosperity influence, literature review, 18
foreign TV channels, importing, 106
foreigners, living apart from host cultures, 150
Fortier, on Diaspora, 147
Foster, Richard, 195
free Congolese, resisting patterns of colonialism and neo-colonialism, 208
free market economy, Congo not participating in, 100
Free State, 41, 41n42
freedom, 169
freedom of the press, 59
"Freedom shall come tomorrow," 69
Freeman, Dena, 192, 194, 196–97
"Full Gospel" churches, cross-cultural aspects of, 119
Full Gospel Fellowship Church, 49, 50, 50n58
full gospel holistic evangelism, 233

Gafaiti, Hafid, 146
Garcia-Johnson, 89–90, 134
Garland, David E., 195
Gbote, Eric Z. M., 77n2, 81–82
gender dynamic, in the AIC's, 71n58–72n58
generosity, in giving toward God's work, 172n58
Ghana, spiritual churches of, 28n2
Gifford, Paul, 17, 37–38
A Gift of Love (King), 187n5
Gilroy, Paul, 146–47
giving to receive, as a problem, 77–79
Glaeser, Edward, 199–200

global and multicultural church, strategy for, 86
The Global Awakening: How 20th Century Revivals Triggered a Christian Revolution (Shaw), 32
global church
  cannot avoid or ignore globalization, 114
  cross-cultural scholastic or theological training needed for, 213
  location of, 123, 215
  mission of, 187
  needing a translatable theology, 126
  overcoming the global nature of denominational character, 86
  rooted in local expression, 120
  shaped by diverse theologies, 115
  theological education needed for, 127
The Global Mission (Escobar), 112n18
Global North, church of in great decline, 89
global Pentecostal history, needing to be written about, 201
global Pentecostalism, successful when missionaries cross frontiers, 130
Global South
  anti-poverty prescription for, 44
  church rapidly growing in, 157
  ecclesiastic challenges facing the churches of, 85
  emergence of Christianity and the socio-structural development within, 3n9
  most Christians living in today, 62
  people from moving to the West, 142
  poorest nations of, 73
  works of emerging scholars from as critical, 115
global theology, 86, 89
Global Theology in Evangelical Perspective (Greenman and Green), 120n43
globalization, at the heart of the Christian awakening, 33

268   INDEX

globalized church, massive mutation over the centuries, 91
Globalizing Theology: Belief and Practice in an Era of World Christianity (Netland), 89
Globalizing Theology: Belief in an Era of World Christianity (Ott), 121
Glocalization, implying hybrid and transnational dynamic, 78
glossolalia
    exploitation of, 212, 213
    forms of, 175n60
    the gift of speaking in tongues, 174–76
God
    accepting people as they are, 61
    accepting us together with our group relations, 135n30
    blessings as limitless, 47
    as a God of prosperity, 155, 170, 231
    mixing with money, 164
    only listening to certain people, 165n38, 175
    power as an effective force, 42
    providing the faithful with physical healing, 20
    regarded by the Bantu as the causative agent and sustainer of forces, 30
    rendering a cosmic transaction analogous to banking systems, 77
    speaking to people, 115–16
    speaking Twi, Swahili, and Setswana, 56
    spreading the gospel all over the world, 98
    translated into a specific segment of social reality, 21
    translated into humanity, 57
    viewed as the creator of all forces, 32
    will for every believer to be materially successful and wealthy, 77
    work using people to promote or advance, 231
God of ancestors, assimilated into the Yahweh of ancient Israel, 51n1
Gonzalez, June, 159
Gonzalez, Justo L., 151n1, 175n60, 176
gospel
    affecting the receiver's lifestyle, 6n16
    as an African story, 167
    altered into a new expression, 168
    being shaped or transformed by culture, 80
    biblical and theological distortion of, 168
    Congolese response to, 202–4
    contextualization of, 90, 137–41, 148, 219
    cross-cultural transmission of, 125–27
    dignifying every culture for God's revelation, 112
    enculturation and inculturation of, 134–37
    entering an interaction with the local expression and accent, 115
    exploited as a for-profit investment of capital, 212
    failing to address the problems of the people, 240
    as good news, 10, 60, 101, 126
    as holistic and directed at the whole person, 73–74
    impact on the worldviews of African religious groups, 206
    must be free of fees, 241
    penetrating the hearts of believers, 187
    penetrating the host cultural expressions, 20–21
    power to liberate Congolese culture, 211
    promoting a prophetic proclamation of, 101
    radical transformation by, 91–92
    re-contextualizing and recommissioning, 220
    rejected by some converts as Western culture, 233
    retranslated by locals, 34
    retransmitted over and over, 140
    role to play in human life, 208
    rooted in culture, 157

separating from progress and
capitalism, 82
as a shield against demonic forces,
42
social justice and, 198
social lift and, 98–99
survival of, 158
taking upon itself Congolese
characteristics, 114
as a transformative force altering
cultural idioms, 183
transforming both the receiver and
the missionary, 135
transforming culture, 21
translatable as a universal medium,
5
translation and retransmission of,
66–67
universality and translatability of,
160
without translation as worthless, 234
"The Gospel as Prisoner and Liberator
of Culture" (Walls), 61n32
government
enforcing neo-colonialism and
exploitation of human resources,
190n14
failure of, 44–45, 232
Granberg-Michaelson, Wesley, 15
grassroots participation, initiated by and
for the Africans, 206–7
Great Awakening in the US, 160
Great Britain, associated with the
expansion of the Christian faith,
61n32
Great Commission, 9, 128, 129
Green, C. E., 170
Green, Gene L., 114–15, 132, 133, 160
Greenman, Jeffrey P., 104, 114–15, 120,
120n43, 123, 132, 133, 160
Gutierrez, Gustavo, 133

*Habits of the Mind: Intellectual Life as a
Christian Calling* (Sire), 152
Hadeyemo, Okunboh, 69
Hagin, Kenneth, 124
Harris, William Wade, 36n30

Haynes, Naomi, 16, 98, 99
healing, emphasis on in Congolese
worldviews, 71
healing and deliverance, literature
review on, 16–17
healing prayer, as the center of the
prosperity gospel, 174
healing the sick through the hospital,
traditional healers sought after,
135–36
Health and Wealth. *See* Word-Faith
movement
health and wealth gospel, attracting
multitudes of Congolese, 174
health care systems, lack of, 43, 173–74
Heath, Elaine, 55
Hebrew Bible, 147, 168, 176–77
Hebrew language, 168
Heitzenrater, Richard P., 195
hermeneutic, developing an authentic,
comprehensive model for, 182
hermeneutic and mixed methodologies,
172
hermeneutical methodologies,
Congolese revolutionized, 152
hermeneutics, 143–45, 151n1
Hiebert, Paul G.
advocating a critical
contextualization, 137
on the bicultural community,
161n26
on building bridges between
cultures, 161
on the gospel calling societies and
cultures to change, 149
on marginal people having a
significant contribution to make,
160
on missionaries' approaches, 137–38
theological framework of, 153
hierarchical and patriarchal society,
Africa historically known as,
72n58
historic mission churches, failed to
integrate the charismatic
renewal phenomenon, 108–9
historical background, of the Congo,
29–35

historical cross-examination, interview
        questions about, 225–26
historical factors, contributing
        to the expansion of Neo-
        Pentecostalism, 41–42
history, rewriting, 96–97
"History of Hymns" (Hawn), 139n41
HIV, left many children as orphans, 211
Hochschild, Adam, 188, 189
holiness doctrine, 196
holiness movement, 42, 198
holistic African theology, 219
holistic church, ministry vision of,
        74n63
"holistic development," 6n16
holistic engagement, of missional
        purpose, 218
holistic investigation, focusing on
        wholeness, 217n16
holistic ministries
    healthy churches and ministries
        participating in, 74
    as a key to Christianity, 208
    social justice and, 194–96
    women's participation in in the post-
        colonial Congo, 193
holistic missional engagement, 73
holistic translation of the gospel, lacking
        in the Congo, 22
holistic vision, integrating into the
        internal life of the church, 7n17
Holy Spirit
    critical for the growth of renewal or
        new generation churches, 43
    descent of upon the followers of
        Jesus-Christ, 8
    enabling rational development
        of science and technology in
        Africa, 14
    experienced by the Congolese on
        their native land, 201
    experiencing the power of God
        through, 61
    role of in post-colonial Congo,
        179–81
The Holy Spirit and Salvation in Africa
        (Ngong), 42n43
home, concept of, 144, 150

hope, 48, 69, 70
hospitals, having no resources, 242
host cultural worldviews, shaping the
        gospel of Christ, 207
human consequences, of controlling a
        country, 93
human cultures, tending to transform
        the gospel, 91
Hunter, James, 153

Idahosa, Benson, 37
identity, 146
ideology, 238
Ilunga, Johnathan, 210n1
immigrant church members, keeping
        original forms of worship, songs,
        and cultural patterns, 145
immigrants
    brought cultural religiosity,
        charisma, and spiritualities to
        the world, 183
    coming to the United States, 159–60
    planting churches and faith-based
        ministries, 143
imperial product, Matthew's Gospel as,
        191
imperial project, missionaries as part
        of, 129
imperialism, terms sanctioning, 118
incarnation, of the story of Jesus in
        human cultures, 126
incomplete holism
    caused by mistranslation, 55
    fueled a Neo-Pentecostal re-
        transmission of the prosperity
        gospel in Africa, 15
    pointing to materialism, 16
    reproducing forms of, 182
    sanctioned by the syncretized
        gospel, 84–85
    within Neo-Pentecostalism, 40
    within the Congolese religious
        worldview, 39
inculturation, 136, 139
independence, 239
indigenization, 123, 135
indigenizing principle, 125n6, 134, 148

indigenous churches, as translating churches, 66n48
indigenous languages, missionaries relying on, 51n1
indigenous liturgy, development of, 127, 214
indigenous practice, of venerating ancestral spirits, 203
indigenous traditional belief systems, Congolese proliferated, 20
indigenous voice, as crucial for a productive Christian mission, 97
individual self-awareness, development of, 60
indulgences, sold in the Congo currently, 241
influence, of the West, 125–37
initiated churches, interview questions for, 223
integrity, of the poor, 99–101
intercultural relationships, making Christianity a universal religion, 125
International Central Gospel, Mensa Otabil's, 8
International Church of God, 12
International Mission Council of Madras, India (1938), 63
internationalization, of religious movements, 103
interview questions, 223–28
interviewees, 226–27, 244
An Introduction to Pentecostalism (Anderson), 200n46, 210n1
investment return, belief in a socio-scientific or technical truth of, 155n8
iPhone, effects of, 107
Isbell, Charles D., 176
Isichei, Elizabeth, 53–54, 93n28, 128

James 5:14, on calling the elders of the church to pray and anoint with oil in the name of the Lord, 174
Jenkins, Philip, 5, 5n12, 14, 86, 87, 89, 142
Jerusalem Temple, rebuilding of, 164

Jesuits, 33
Jesus and the gospel
    as central to daily life experience within a Congolese worldview, 206
    as means for social, spiritual, and moral libeation, 156
Jesus and the Gospel in Africa (Bediako), 206n64
Jesus Christ
    acculturated as an ancestor, 136
    African understanding of, being exported to the West, 141
    available and accessible to any culture, village, and people, 5
    being the hands and feet of, 188n8
    domesticated within neo-traditional cultures, 112
    as a foreign savior, 136
    freed the women caught in adultery, 194
    gave a voice to a voiceless Samaritan woman, 194
    hearing from the text, 82
    Holy Spirit anointed, 179
    as an incarnated ancestor mediator, 203
    on laying down one's life for one's friends, 187–88
    as the mediator, 64
    message of, 69, 112
    ministry as holistic, 74
    "movies" of popular in Zaire through missionary efforts, 113
    as "Nganga Mukata," 43, 43n47
    personal relationship with, 14n46
    from the perspective of Congolese cultural patterns, 97–98
    sent the Holy Spirit, 18n60
    survival of the biblically defined gospel of, 78
    welcomed in the Congo as a Congolese priest, 115
    as a white man, 113
Jeunesse (Youth Movement), 191n18
Jin, Park Hyung, 212
Joanna, Mary Magdalene, accompanied Jesus, 193

Job, narrative of, 215–16
Jobs, Steve, 107
Johae, Anthony, 146
John, warning listeners to avoid associating with Spiritism, 203
Jones, David W., 162, 171
Joshua (Nigerian prophet), selling an aggressive prosperity gospel, 18
Judaism and Christianity, continuity between, 160n25

Kabila, Laurent-Désiré, 19n61
Kakwata, Frederick, 209–10
Kalu, Ogbu U., 13, 14, 17, 68, 71
Kalunga Nyembo, deceased going to, 46
Kasongo, L'Abbé, 40, 182, 226
Kato, Byang H., 206
Katshinga, Mvwala, 186, 187, 210, 210n2
Keener, Craig, 85, 86, 87, 121, 142
Kenyatta, Jomo, 166
Kenyon, E. W., 37, 162
Kenyon, William, 37
kerygma, 75
key terms, definition of, 7–12
Kiboko, J. Kabamba, 54
Kimbangu, Simon, 36n30, 141, 180, 180n72, 233
Kimbanguism, 11, 68, 180, 180n72, 239
King, Coretta Scott, 187
King Leopold's Ghost (Hochschild), 189n11
kingdom of God on earth, 131
kings, offered tributes, 164
Kinshasa, founded and named Leopoldville by Henry Morton Stanley, 200
Kisula, Ngoy, 182
"Kongo," meaning river or literally translated "by the river of the bakongo," 41n42
Kongo Kingdom, 27–50
Koran, translation of technically forbidden, 58n22, 75n64
Koreans, preserving their homeland culture, 149–50

Kroesbergen, Hermen, 12, 13, 38, 170, 172
Kutino, Fernando, 140, 140n44–41n44, 141

La mission civilizatrice, as an imperial effort, 159
laity, theological education for, 127, 214
language barrier, with Belgians, 31
languages
  diversity of African, 234
  translation of local into the vernacular, 45
Lausanne Forum for World Evangelization (2004), 118
Lausanne Theology working group, Statement on the Prosperity Gospel, 49–50
laziness, dependency created, 233
Lederle, Henry I., 213
King Leopold II of Belgium, 41–42, 41n42, 52–53, 200
"*Les vendeurs de la foi*," "sellers of faith," 79–80
Levy, Pierre, 113
liberating system, of Moses, 177n65
liberation theologies, 132–34
Liberation Thinking (Roberts), 133n26
Liberator, Jesus as, 120n43
life force, 2, 30
lifestyles, systematic collapse of, 45
Limburg, James, 186
Lindhardt, Martin, 191, 201
literacy, 31, 55, 58
literal translation, 173, 213
Liu, Eric, 108
Livingstone, David, 32n15, 34–35, 53, 129
local evangelism and missions efforts, effective on Congolese soil, 35
local expressions of the gospel, as an aspect of evangelism, 114–16
local religions, providing the idiom for Christian apprehension, 65
Lola, meaning "eternity," 46
longing, for a better tomorrow, 69

Lord's Song, singing in a strange land, 143
Low, Alaine, 68, 71
Lowry, Robert, song of, 138n41–39n41
Luban Pentecost, results of, 201n51
Luemba, Dieudonné Sita, 180, 180n72, 213–15, 215n12, 216–17, 229–33
Lumumba, Emery Patrice, 188, 189, 189n11, 240
Luther, Martin, 164, 241
Lydia, 193

Maasbach, John, 140n44
Macchia, Frank, 213
magic, using to chase demons, 231
magical force, overcoming demonic spirits, 80
mainline denominations, 223–24, 235
"Majority World," 118
Makuta, Bijoux, 164, 164n36, 170, 187
Malachi, 171, 172
malevolent spirits, search for power against, 204
Malula, Joseph-Albert, 190n14, 238
man, as a living force, 30
man force, 164, 175
mandate to share the gospel, 128, 129
Manuel, King of Portugal, 33
Mark 10:30, misread and mistranslated, 170
married couple and family, returning to traditional rites and dances after a religious wedding, 135
Marxism, 133n26
Mary Magdalene, 194
mass media ministries, transnationalizing Neo-Pentecostalism, 104
mass-mediated trends, mediating contextualizing theology, 103
material wealth, of Abram, 165
materialism, 92, 207
materials, systematic analysis of, 244
mathematical formula, for prosperity in Hebrew's translation, 155

Matthew 5:3, empowering elites but leaving minorities vulnerable, 191
Matthew 11:28, justifying social, economic relief, 169
Matthew 23:4, as it relates to Acts 15:10 and 13:39, 169
Maxwell, David, 104
Maxwell, Joe, 16
the "*May May*," 181
Mbiti, John, 10, 42, 42n43, 141, 207
Mechac of Kaboto, positive ministry of, 181
media, "showing" God's miracles to an audience outside the churches, 108
medical discourse, as often the last option, 174
meditation, trends in, 64
members
    giving money to the prophet or the preacher, 170
    remaining poor beggars, 237
memories, rooted in a cultural worldview, 144–45
Mensa Otabil's International Central Gospel, 8
Mertens, Donna M., 185, 185n1–86n1
Merveille, death of a ten-year-old girl named, 79–80
"Message de Vie" television program, 110
messianic enterprise of Jesus, sustained by Jewish women disciples, 193
Methodism, 196
Methodist Federation for Social Service, 131n23
Methodists, 190, 195–96
Meyer, Joyce, 18
Micah, 177n65
micro-projects, 241
military guards, in offices of pastors, 227
Miller, Donald E., 4
ministry
    of annointing cloth for healing, 84
    Congolese women in, 193–94
minorities, oppressed by the prosperity gospel, 244

Minsamu Miayenge, first periodical of Zaire, 4n9
"Miracle Hour," 110
miracles, 197, 231, 236, 243
Missio-Dei, 65, 66, 75
missiological cross-examination, interview questions about, 226
missiologist interview transcription, 233–37
mission(s)
  agencies casting durable and sustainable visions, 99
  center of gravity shift in, 86
  Christian engagement in, 215
  concept of, 129
  connecting the church through, 117–20
  evangelism and, 235
  expressing God's purpose and saving plan, 9
  fueled an incomplete holism, 4n9
  going unto other cultures, 112, 235
  history of, rewriting, 96–97
  impact of in post-colonial Congo, 129
  as increasingly secularized, 158
  near monopoly of education, 93n28
  re-transmission and translation through Neo-Pentecostalism, 23
  social change and, 196–97
  as transcultural, 214n9
  understood from a Western perspective, 214n9
  without evangelism as meaningless, 58
mission churches
  failure to forgo traditional religious expressions, 108
  members breaking away, 116–17
  needing "the umbilical cord" cut off, 232
  remaining recipients of aid, 100n41
mission civilizatrice, as a secularized activity, 41
mission education, creating new inequalities, 54
mission field, sources of information, 227
mission of the church, to be a prophetic voice, 241–42
The Mission of the Church Today in the Light of Global History (Walls), 5
missional church, defined, 9
missional dimension, of the gospel, 149
missional impact, 4n9, 128–30
missional initiative, involving connecting ministries, 9
missional model, change to, 51
missionaries
  African converts losing their identities, 11n34
  birthed the church in the Congo, 4n9
  as catalysts, 201
  classical Pentecostal and evangelical, 140
  on Congolese cultural expressions as incompatible with the Christian faith, 138
  connecting the church, 119
  control of the printing press and vernacular and grammar, 199
  as culture brokers, 161, 161n26
  death rate from tropical diseases of Catholic, 33
  defined, 9
  early arrival of, 32–34
  encountering two different cultures, 161
  failure to address, redress, or alter spiritual cosmological issues, 84
  found the Bible and God in Africa under different names and categories, 167
  ignored the presence of spiritual forces and phenomenon, 34n25
  ignored the social circumstances of the people, 232
  impact in spreading the gospel positively, 61
  left the Congo in 1971, 38
  misreading of Congolese cultures, 158
  moratorium on the sending of, 129n15

non-contextualized gospel of, 180n72
non-contextualized Westernized civilization of, 233
not addressing critical problems facing the locals, 22
not all patronized and exploited converts, 201
not challenging colonial exploitation, 53
not prepared to deal with African worldviews, 174
not teaching how to produce locally, 232
not teaching locals independence, 243
ordinary people becoming, 179
paved the way for revivals, 35
planted churches rooted in paternalism, 233
Protestant, the first to come to the Congo, 32
rejection of traditional African customs, 137
roles of, 128
superior attitudes towards African cultures and mores, 158, 201
taking risks to tell the story of Jesus Christ, 129
taught only the Bible, 234
translated the gospel into an African context, 52
transmiting their own cultural ideas, 153–54
using trade or commerce routes to take the gospel to foreign nations, 128
women, 193
missionary efforts, 45, 52–56
missionary enterprise, 22, 128
missionary mindset, of the West, 118
The Missionary Movements in Christian History Studies in the Transmission of Faith (Walls), 62
missionary paternalism, repudiation of, 56
missionary presence, lasting impact of, 75
missionary schools, 61
mistranslations, 234
Mobutu, Sese Seko (Joseph Désiré)
controlled the Army and political leaders, 238
created structures to control the Protestant Church ECC (Eglise du Christ au Congo), 238
democratized the nation in 1990, 239
forced the citizens of Zaire to forgo their baptismal names, 19n61
nationalized and privatized all the companies, 239
opposed celebrating Noel or Christmas, 238
philosophical decree against foreign influences, 19
proclaimed le Retour à l'authenticité in 1971, 19n61, 180n72, 190n14, 219
restored freedom of the press and freedom of religion for democratization, 240
ruled with a rampantly corrupt regime, 200n44
supported Kimbangu's children, 239
modern imperialism, "postcolonial" describing, 3n9
modern missionary period, 34–35
modernity, characterized by colonialist expansion, slavery, genocide, and indenture, 147
Morrison, William, 53
Mosaic laws of economic policies and theocratic regulations, 171
Moses, 165n38, 177n65
"*Mpemba*," translated from French "chaux" or blanche, meaning "white," 139
Bishop Mukuna, 79, 110
Mulago, Vincent, 42n43, 205–6
Mulimbe, V. Y., 54
Mushidi, Mutwale Ntambo Wa., 29, 29n4
music, leading people to remember, 143
Muslims, media ministries of, 104
Muyingi, Mbangu Anicet, 10–11, 11n34

Mwaura, Philomena Njeri, 32
Myers, Bryant L., 44
Myspace, 107

naïve Christians, ignoring money as worldly, 163
"Name it and Claim it," 18. *See also* Word-Faith movement
Nathan, 177
nation of the Congo, name changes, 41
National Association for the Advancement of Colored People, 131n23
national economies, role in shaping the prosperity gospel, 154
national identity, 146
nationalism, 146–47, 167n45
native translators, not the main voices at the table, 97
native's voice, critical for understanding the African experience, 202
natural disasters, 44
necrology, at the center of Congolese culture, 46
Nel, Marius, 211, 211n4, 216, 218
neo-charismatic churches, 116–17
"Neo-charismatic" movement, described, 8
Neo-charismatic types, proliferation of, 4
neoclassical economics, on growing wealth, 155n8
neo-colonial internal oppressors, 94
neo-colonialism, 17, 94–95
neo-colonizers, 95
neo-liberal culture, 178
neo-liberal gospel, 96
neo-liberal policies, 197
Neo-Pentecostal charismatic networks, 48
Neo-Pentecostal Christianity
    as an economic problem, 217
    factors on the cause of the rapid growth of, 27
    fundamental basis of the spread of, 59
    growing and expanding within non-Western and previously non-Christian societies, 71
    liberating and freeing women from patriarchal systems, 192
Neo-Pentecostal churches, 71, 105, 109
Neo-Pentecostal gospel, 27, 154–57, 197, 214
Neo-Pentecostal movement, 6, 35–41, 209–12, 213
Neo-Pentecostal preachers, 70, 91, 169
Neo-Pentecostal prosperity gospel. *See* prosperity gospel
Neo-Pentecostal trends of Christianity, 64
Neo-Pentecostalism
    abused pre-Christian cultural expressions, 22
    altered the face of Christianity in the Congo, 1
    Congolese women in ministry, 193–94
    considering the contribution of the majority world, 201
    contributed to gender balance and equality, 72n58
    contributing factors to the expansion of, 41–48
    defined, 2n2, 7
    emphasizing success and prosperity, 92
    facilitating the rapid growth of Christianity in Africa, 76
    giving Pentecostalism a voice and freedom, 191–92
    globalized Christianity shaping the religious landscape, 104
    growth of, 4
    historical development of in the Kongo Kingdom, 27–50
    impacts of, 23
    improving decades of authorized social crisis, 185
    interpreted through contextual hermeneutics, 159
    liberating and empowering women, 193

INDEX

meeting the felt needs of its members, 49
missiological and theological weight of, 85–87
not just a refuge for the poor and marginalized, 183
produced a different theology, 90–91
as a product of new Pentecostal trends developed in Africa, 71
proponents of as devotees and "born again" adherents of new revival churches, 14
radical response to socio-economic and political empowerment, 153
recipients of exploited, 23
role in the life of ordinary people, 154
women of Africa and, 191–93
Neo-Pentecostals
claiming supernatural authority, 175
Congolese religious worldview of, 18
creating a dependency syndrome and a religious neo-colonialism, 102
giving as a prerequisite for prosperity, 77
interview questions for, 223
referring to Pentecostal groups, 8
uncritical readings and holistic interpretation of biblical literature, 152
underlying issues advocated by, 85
understanding needs of the larger population, 49
using Scriptures to colonize their adherents, 95
using the gospel as a means for social change, 98
using the gospel as a vehicle to holistic renewal, 16
Neo-prophetic leaders, viewing themselves as "porte-paroles or spokespersons" with supernatural unction, 178
Neo-prophetic voices in the Congo, perpetuating abusive policies, 177
Netland, Harold A., 89, 157, 158–59
new Christianity, 72
new churches and ministries, phenomenon of, 216
"New Generation Churches," 11
new gospel, 90, 168
new languages, speaking, 175n61
new Pentecostalism, arrival of, 193n21
New Testament, justifying the prosperity gospel, 169–70
New Testament (NT) agricultural society, Christians in the Global South connecting with, 14
Newbigin, Leslie, 71, 75, 206
The Next Christendom (Jenkins), 142
Nfmu Makitu, signing an agreement with Stanley, 31
"Nganga Mukata," 43, 43n47
"Ngangas" (prophetic healers)
believers tending to consult, 174
practices of, 40
referring to traditional spiritual mediators, 40n40
transformed their profession from diviner to rising religious star, or self-proclaimed prophet, 40, 80
Ngong, David Tonghou, 14, 42n43, 92
Nicodemus, 14n46–15n46
Njoroge, John N., 137
non-Africans, shunning African Christianity, 92
non-Westerners, trained within the Western culture, 88
North America, epitomizing aspirations of young Africans, 110–11
North American prosperity gospel, 184

Obijole, Olubayo O., 139
occult practices, taking place in Kinshasa, 241
offspring, of emigrants crossing culture, 144
Ogungbile, David, 78, 79
Oguntoye, P. A., 136–37

278 INDEX

Ojo, Matthews A., 4
Olangi, Maman, 80
Old Testament, 170–72, 186
Omenyo, Cephas N., 151n1
"*on ne sais jamais*" ("You never know"), 69
online service communication, lacking physical contact, 107
online social networks and connectivity, 114
Oosthuizen, G. C., 127, 127n11, 214
oppressed minority group, liberation in the hands of, 208
oppressed poor, defending against the wealthy, 171
oral communication, trusted and retrusted, 31
oral interviews, 229–43, 244
oral tradition, 30, 200
orthodox gospel, fundamental basic beliefs of, 91
Osborn, T. L., 110, 123–24
Osborne, 148
Osiek, Carolyn, 135, 136
Osteen, Joel, 18, 37
Ott, Craig, 121, 157, 158–59
overnight ceremonial prayer invoking spiritual powers and ancestors, replaced with Christian night prayers, 68
overnight prayers of deliverance, in charismatic renewal churches, 174

Padilla, Osvalla, 88
pagan practices, associating with biblical scriptures, 43
pain, demons and, 231
Pan African Movement, 157
Paraclete, John's preferred word for Holy Spirit, 181
parakletos, identified as a helper, power, comforter, 180
partial conversion, defined, 152n3
passports and visas, people praying for, 242
pastoral leaders, foreign expectations for training, 100n41
pastors. *See also* preachers
demanding costly jewelry or a nice suit from persons seeking to speak with them, 237
encouraging members not to go to hospitals, 243
owning Mercedes, BMW, golden jewelry, expensive suits, and private jets, 210n2, 237
preaching the true Gospel using media, 235
some making their church members slaves, 241
paternalism, 233, 234
Paul
on being enculturated, 136
challenged syncretic traditions, 203
on cross-cultural values, 98
encouraging the Galatians not to accept a different gospel, 90–91
on glossolalia, 175n60
on the gospel, 10
prioritizing prophecy over glossolalia, 176
on the renewing of minds, 22
support from wealthy women and widows, 193
teaching of as free of charge, 50
on understanding or translating tongues, 176
peace, distinct from material prosperity, 170
Pentecost, 7–8, 75n64, 179
Pentecostal churches, 4, 194
Pentecostal gospel, 22, 76, 220
Pentecostal history, from western Pentecostals and their missionaries, 199
Pentecostal laborers of the past, recognizing the contribution of, 202n52
Pentecostal movements, promoting new conceptions, 192n21–93n21
Pentecostal patterns, of local initiative, 159

Pentecostal phenomena, commitment to reforms, 196
Pentecostal religious landscape, Congo increasingly becoming, 8
Pentecostalism
  adapting the gospel to audiences, 33
  African, 160
  compared to Neo-Pentecostalism, 3–4
  defined, 7
  effects on the people of Africa, 1
  embedding believers in social relationships, 16
  empowering women, 192
  enabling capitalism to flourish, 178
  entrepreneurial and social characteristics, 38
  experienced by the Congolese on their native land, 201
  feeding the sanctioned mechanism of adverse outcomes, 17
  fitting the context of the Global South, 33
  focused on Biblicism and eschatology, 22
  growth of, 71
  meeting neoliberal enterprise, 16
  modern form of, 7
  as more relevant, 206
  network of healing industries and pastoral care, 214
  offering solutions to the spiritual world, 43, 203, 204
  outreach to a larger public, 33
  providing education, social-political development, and health services, 44
  surviving severe opposition from a number of sources, 191
  transcending the social-religious world, 113
  as an umbrella term, 7n18
  used by politicians to endorse their theories, 189
  waves of classified as "Renewal" movements, 36
  as a way of life, 16
  well received in post-Congo, 71

Pentecostalism in Africa: Christianity in Postcolonial Societies (Lindhardt), 191, 201n51
Pentecostalization, 104, 123
"Pentecostalization: The Changing Face of Baptists in West Africa" (Arnett), 8
Pentecostals
  cashing in on poverty, 78
  materialistic view of salvation, 20
  mistranslating the gospel, 75–76
  promising divine healing, deliverance, and miracles, 16–17
Penttila, Maija, 8–9
Perkins, John M., 186, 188
Perriman, Andrew, 18
Persons, David Nelson, 189
Peter, brought the gospel to Cornelius, 119
Peterson, Cheryl M., 92
Phillips, Caryl, 144
Phiri, Isaac, 16
Phoebe, 193
physically fatness, as a sign of success and greatness, 217
pilgrim principle, 125n6, 148, 212
"Planet Television," 110
"Pneumatology and the Cross: The Challenge of Neo-Pentecostalism to Lutheran Theology" (Peterson), 92
political propaganda, songs used as, 145
politics of translation, supporting imperial propaganda and colonialism, 54
the poor, abuse and manipulation of, 212
poor in spirit
  complying with the rules and regulations of the elites, 191
  Matthew's theology of, 170
pop culture, offering an alternative route to a Jesus, 107
Positive Confession. *See* Word-Faith movement
Post-Christianity in Africa (Oosthuizen), 127n11, 214n11
post-colonial, defined as a term, 2n2

post-colonial Congo, 178–79, 186
post-colonial discourse, 10
post-colonial effort, empowering the weak, 93
post-colonial era, in missions, 99
post-colonial holistic hermeneutic, 24
post-colonial method, empowering the marginalized, 94
"post-colonial" period, 3n9
post-colonial prophetic translation, 6
post-colonial theory, 93, 94
post-colonial voice, 62, 102
post-colonialism, 10, 93–94
post-missionary activities, resulting in self-theologizing, 116
poverty
　as both a religious and societal problem, 154
　causes of, 49
　causing the prosperity gospel, 244
　continually confronting people, 131
　as a created condition, 101
　as a critical problem in the Congo, 45
　curing by ethical commitment and hard work, 101
　finding biblical texts sanctioning, 53
　Kisula eradicating, 182
　perpetuated by a systemic culture of dependency, 99
　as the root of the prosperity gospel, 100
power of religion, in the hands of ordinary people, 59
powerlessness and spilled blood, African reading of the Bible emerging from, 87
prayer, 174, 242
prayer groups, Pentecostals creating, 45
prayer healing, as an alternative solution to humanity's plight, 174
The Prayer of Jabez (Wilkinson), 124
prayers and pastoral care, based on the amount of money given, 242
praying churches, 28n2, 217, 242–43
preachers, 37n31, 41, 75. *See also* pastors
pre-Christian belief systems, 80

prepared Africans to receive Christianity, 52
pre-Christian patterns, of African Christianity, 204–6
pre-Christian period, of the Congo, 29–31
pre-Christian religious discourses, influencing the spread of the prosperity gospel, 205
preliminary interviews, questions for, 223–24
pre-millennial conquest theology, 183
priests, supporting the systematic abuse of the poor, 177n65
primal belief systems
　continuity of, 21, 150
　as fertile soil for the prosperity gospel, 205
　needing to be addressed, 152n3
　people remaining engaged with, 84
　prepared locals to access God's revelation, 52
primal cultural tradition, 1
primal religions, 42n43, 64–66, 205
primary school education, 232
problems, facing the Congo, 82
progressive Pentecostalism, 15–16
property, reversion of in the year of Jubilee, 171
prophecies, 178–79, 230–31
prophet-healing churches, 109
prophethood of all believers, 178
prophetic enterprise, granting freedom and opportunities, 178
prophetic hermeneutic, 97
prophetic initiatives, described, 186
prophetic leadership, 6n15, 181, 187
prophetic ministry, integrity of, 181
prophetic post-colonial hermeneutic, 93
prophetic reading, of Scripture, 6, 94
prophetic renewal streams, attracting a massive following, 217
"prophetic translation of the gospel," 6n15, 220
prophetic voices
　analysis and history of, 187–90
　failing to alter abusive policies, 179
　need for, 186–87

INDEX 281

in a twenty-first century Congolese
  context, 185–208
prophets. *See also* prosperity preachers
  as agents of transformation of
    societies, 189
  asserting that the victim suffers
    from demonic possession, 237
  becoming multi-millionaires from
    selling and trading, 212
  claiming that sin is the reason for
    Satan's torment, 243
  defined as a spokeperson, 178n66
  distorting the scriptures to exploit
    and manipulate resources, 164
  forcing exploited individuals to
    respond or be cursed by God,
    210n2
  hiding to listen to the petitions and
    prayer concerns of people and
    then recording them, 230
  monopolizing resources and assets,
    164
  number of on the rise, 216
  pre-organizing networks giving
    them one hundred dollars each,
    237
  promises of in Kinshasa, 210
  promising healing and deliverance
    attracting people, 236
  role in the Hebrew Bible, 176–77
  speaking relevant oracles to their
    own cultural contexts, 160
  taking their members to cemeteries
    or mountains to pray, 242
prosperity
  Bible defining as *shalom*, 237
  as biblically and theologically sound,
    50
  from both a sociological and
    anthropological vantage point,
    26
  characteristics of in Africa, 244
  culture of rooted in capitalism, 212
  defining and translating from a
    biblical paradigm, 220
  going beyond material wealth, 13
  linking to spirituality, 15
  natural rate of, 155n11

  pneumatological concepts of, 154
  from a Sub-Saharan African
    viewpoint, 13
prosperity gospel
  abusive side of, 240–41, 242
  aimed at social lift and
    entrepreneurship, 19
  altered the face of Christianity in the
    Congo, 1
  as an appropriation of African
    Christianity, 172
  associated with the Word-Faith
    movement, 17
  attractive to many believers in
    Africa, 169
  as a betrayal of the next
    Christendom, 218
  bringing a Congolese voice to,
    81–83
  as a business promoting pastors, 237
  challenge to churches, 13
  changing the nature of religion, 98
  charismatic renewal progressive
    movements proliferating, 8
  as a complex subject, 218
  Congolese critique of, 77–102
  Congolese version of, 182
  contributing to the rapid growth
    of Christianity in Sub-Sahara
    Africa, 47
  creating various names of giving
    offerings, 231
  critiqued as a superstitious cargo
    cult, 14
  defined, 2n2
  depending upon faith and
    investment return, 155n8
  distinct from the gospel of Christ,
    2n3
  dividing families and creating
    dependency, 242
  as a dominant force of the Neo-
    Pentecostal/charismatic
    movement, 22
  enriching those preaching it, 49
  as an entrepreneurial engagement,
    99
  fed by poverty, 237

prosperity gospel (*continued*)
  fundamental basis of the spread of, 59
  as the heart of Maman Olangi's message, 80
  as an imported phenomenon to Africa, 37
  interview questions on, 224–25
  introduced by North American missionaries, 72
  Kisula's version of as life-giving, 182
  linked to materialism and spiritism, 82
  literature review focused on, 12–20
  as manipulative and selfish, 49
  needing advanced investigation, 221
  no one single, 184
  not liberating the poor, women, and children, 244
  not limited to material progress alone, 99
  offering false hope, 219
  origins of, 161–63
  of Osteen, 37
  pastors refusing to cooperate or tell their stories, 227
  post-colonial re-transmission of, 3
  as a prescription for social development, 196
  problems presented by, 77–81
  promising people escape from poverty, 218
  reasons behind the rise of in Africa, 48–49
  as a recipe to continue the cycle of poverty, 220
  requiring a comprehensive and holistic investigation, 217
  requiring scientific methodologies, 217n16
  roots in North America, 37, 37n31
  selling miracles in the marketplace, 106
  socio-economic implications of, 12
  spiritism fed by Neo-Pentecostalism's teachings, 38
  syncretizing the gospel into a new belief system, 149
  televangelism translation categories of, 104
  theology of, 48
  as a tool for personal economic engagement and radical change, 154
  as a tool for social interrelation, 98
  transformative aspects of, 163
  translated into a different and deceiving gospel, 209
  translating into a global phenomenon, 154
  transnational character of, 41
  underlying issues of Spiritism and power rooted in pre-Christian patterns, 204
  understanding the surge of, 14
  working in favor of the pastor, 210n2
"Prosperity Gospel" (Gbote), 77n2
prosperity gospel movement
  biblical, missional, and theological patterns encompassing, 24
  exploiting impoverished adherents, 2n3
  fitting the Congolese context, 39
  local outlook of, 99
  re-colonizing the post-colonial Congo, 95
  as a self-generating expression of Pentecostalism, 44
prosperity preachers. *See also* prophets
  causing inequalities and injustices, 95
  creating reality by speaking a word, 13
  distorting the Scriptures, 215
  exploiting the poor, distorting the Scriptures, and partaking in and promoting greed, 78
  not addressing the structural reasons for poverty, 92
  on power to create reality by speaking a word, 13
  preaching that God is rich, 210n2
  regarding growing of wealth as a natural process, 155n8

INDEX 283

relocating immediate families to France, South Africa, or abroad, 210n2, 237
reproducing the American prosperity model, 163
seeming to be self-serving, 165
taking the gospel of Jesus Christ across frontiers, 215
prosperity teachings, new shape within Congolese society, 3n9
prosperity theology. *See also* Word-Faith movement
    appropriation of, 72–74
    basis of an incomplete holism, 23
    encouraging Christians to sow seeds in exchange for divine blessings, 127–28
    exploiting poor adherents, 23
    failing to be an effective biblically prophetic voice, 50
    as an imported expression of Christianity, 244
    literature review, 12–13
    materialistic in content and context, 79
    as the most rapidly growing stream of Christianity in Africa, 216
    not examined culturally, politically, and morally, 217n6
    posing a challenge to Evangelicalism, 78
    questioning how and why events happen, 216
    sects preaching, 116
    US expressions of domesticated in post-colonial Congo, 212
Protestants, 190, 232, 238
Psalm 137, hermeneutics of, 141, 143–45
Psalms for Preaching and Worship (Van Harn), 143
"pure gospel," Congolese needing, 95
Pygmies, 29, 235
Pype, Katrien, 192

qualitative approach, to hermeneutics, 172
quantitative approach, to hermeneutics, 172–73
quid pro quo, 77, 77n1
Qur'an, the untranslatable scripture of Islam, 58n22, 75n64

radical charismatics, 109
radical transformation, implying that the gospel becomes a means for holistic change, 91
Rauschenbusch, Walter, 83, 122, 130, 131, 198
"Rauschenbusch's Christianity and the Social Crisis: Kingdom Coming" (Dorrien), 131
Red Star, church of our Lord Jesus Christ in the World, 3
Redeemed Christian Church of God, A. Adeboye's, 8
redemption, as not only spiritual but also material by nature, 141
re-education, of Congolese Christians, 213, 218
re-enculturation, essential method of, 136
Reese, Robert, 15, 99, 100, 100n41
"reforms," of Mobutu, 19n61
religion
    dramatic decline of in the US, 219
    inclusive rule of African, 51n1
    justifying materialism and capitalistic strategies, 163
    serving as a survival strategy, 111
    supporting political propaganda, 165n38
religious leaders, African ignoring theological training, 75
religious predisposition, of the Congolese, 32
religious revolution, in post-colonial Congo, 36
renewal churches, 235, 240
renewal movements, 43, 108
renewal preachers, publishing and using media, 236
renewalists, 12–13, 15, 16, 119
"Renewalists Renewal Churches," 10

INDEX

Republic of Congo, 19n61, 41
research, 23–24, 26, 218
Restoring At-Risk Communities (Perkins), 188n8
Retour à l'authenticité, 19–20, 19n61, 180n72, 190n14, 219, 225, 238
retransmission, of the gospel, 3n9, 111
Revelation 7:9, fulfillment of, 112
Robert, Dana L., 55, 56, 59, 60, 61, 62–63, 74n64–75n64, 126, 128, 128n14, 128n15–29n15, 129
Roberts, Oral, 37, 77n2, 124, 133n26, 162
Robertson, Pat, 37n31
Roman Catholicism, efforts to oust Pentecostalism, 191n18
Rome, having complete power over its subjects, 190–91
Rommen, Edward, 34n25, 42–43
RTMV Radio, 110
Rufus' mother, 193

sacrifices, elders of the village offering, 43
Samaritan woman, empowered by Jesus to be an evangelist, 194
Sanchez, 152, 152n3–53n3
"Sangu Malamu," meaning "good news," 110
Sanneh, Lamin, 20, 21, 51–52, 51n1, 56–57, 58, 58n22, 60, 63, 64, 65, 66, 66n48, 67–68, 70, 76, 106, 139n42, 149, 183
King Saul, woman of Endor assisting, 54n10
Saving Society (Unruh and Sider), 195n30
"says the Lord," phrase traced back to the OT, 177n65
Schwartz, Glenn, 99
scientific methodologies, 217, 217n16
Scripture
  in African languages, 65
  interpretation by liberation theology, 133
  justifying polygamy, child sacrifice, and systemic oppressive regimes, 167
  misinterpretations of by the Congolese prosperity gospel movement, 23
  translating literally, 215
  translation transposing Christianity into local equivalents, 65
2 Corinthians 8:9, on Christ becoming poor, 170
sects, proliferation of, 116
seed faith (money), sending to a spiritual leader or pastor, 77n2
self-claimed, self-made prophets and pastors, having no theological training, 242
selfish intentions, social lift authorizing, 19
self-proclaimed apostles, prophets, and other titles, 79, 119, 163, 175
self-theologizing, 87, 115, 121, 152
"self-theorizing," African theological categories of, 104
sellers of the faith, as a problem, 79–80
seminaries, needing to reflect African realities, 86
Sendwe, Jason, 189–90
Shank, David A., 28, 64–65
Shaw, Mark, 28, 32, 33, 36, 43, 58, 59n29–60n29
Sheppard, William, 53
Sider, Ronald J., 7, 74, 195
signed agreements, against the will of most chieftains, 31
silence, in the face of atrocities and oppression, 186
Singor, Sedar, 238
Sire, James W., 152
slave traders, counteracting devastating activities of, 4n9
slaves, brought cultural religiosity, charisma, and spiritualities to the world, 183
snow, foreign from Congolese traditions, 139
social action, addressing sources of human problems, 74n63

INDEX 285

social aspect, of the prosperity gospel, 81
social Darwinism, 158
social development, not preached by missionaries, 232
social economic exploitation, of human resources, 166
social gospel, 15–16, 122, 130–32
"The Social Gospel as a Grassroots Movement" (Deichmann), 131n23
social gospel movement, 83, 130n20–31n20, 131
social inequalities, types of, 186n1
social injustices, of Solomon's regime, 164
social instability, after the US Civil War, 130n20–31n20
social justice, 185, 186n1, 195, 198
social lift
    gospel of prosperity practiced through, 210
    literature review, 18–20
    motivating hard work, 178
    Neo-Pentecostals and prosperity preachers using the gospel as a means for, 98
    televangelism translation categories of, 104
social media, 106, 107, 113, 235–36
social networks, theology of, 106–7
social-economic differences, theologies of, 39
socio-economic and spiritual state, glossolalia as a distinctive feature and indicator of, 176
sociological shift, in views and practices of the prosperity gospel, 16
solidarity and common good, African value of, 211n4
Solomon, 163, 164, 177
songs, as tools to colonize people, 145
songs or hymnals, mistranslation into vernacular cultures, 138
souls or spirits, of deceased humans, 202
South Africa, church stood alongside the ignored and oppressed, 185

South Africans, hope during the apartheid era, 69
sowing seeds
    asking clients to, 230
    continuing to operate in the church of the Congo, 241
    into a ministry, 231
    misreading Galatians 6:6 in renewal churches, 236
    strategic model attracting and trapping many into financial exploitation, 237
speaking in tongues, 175, 176
"The Specular and the Spirits: Charismatics and Neo-Traditionalists on Ghanaian Television" (de Witte), 104
spirit encounter, igniting revivals, 43
spirit of togetherness, symbolizing Ubuntu, 211n4
Spirit power, 202, 204
spiritism, done in secret, 105
spirits phenomenon, need for biblical discernment on, 218
spiritual factors, contributing to the expansion of Neo-Pentecostalism, 42–44
spiritual forces, 42, 44
spiritual gifting, within Congolese society, 71
spiritual gifts, 8, 212–13
spiritual mediator, traditional, 40n40
spiritual power, reinforcing social and economic exploitation, 213
spiritual support, countering the spirit of capitalism, 197
spiritual transformation and growth, realizing authentic, 73
spiritual trends, paradigm shift of, 63
spiritualism, 196, 202
spirituality, 15, 42, 203
spontaneity, of most Congolese preachers, 75
Stanley, Henry Morton, 32n15, 200
static religion, 165n38
Steuernagel, Valdir, 133–34
Stinton, Diane B., 30
Studd, C. T., 39

Sugirtharajah, R. S., 10, 93, 94–95, 190
supernatural healing, promised to the Congolese, 40
supreme force, 30
Susanna, accompanied Jesus, 193
Swaggart, Jimmy, 37n31, 123–24, 140, 140n44, 148
Swahili lyrics, to a traditional Gospel song, 138–39
Sweet, Leonard, 107, 113–14, 114n26
Synan, Vinson, 206
syncretism
    created by the relationship between the primal religion and Christian worldview, 34n25, 63
    curing the sick and giving hope to the vulnerable, 45
    defined, 149n63
    dominating in places where the Gospel did not penetrate the culture, 233
    failure to abandon traditional belief systems suggesting, 22
    as a global religious problem, 83–84
    gospel of prosperity practiced through, 210
    locals searching for alternative ways to satisfy their void of spiritism, 138
    paths to, 153n3
    practiced by Congolese believers, 40
    as a reason for a spiritualized society, 44
    reinforcement of, 42
    when a Mission fails to produce an indigenous Church, 153n3
syncretized Christianity, from mixing Christian worldviews and traditional belief systems, 80
syncretized gospel, within the Congolese religious worldviews, 83–84
syncretized religious worldview, African Christianity as, 49

T. D. Jakes Ministries, 18
Taber, on syncretism, 148n63–49n63
Taylor, Barry, 107, 108
TBN, Christian channel, 108
tech digital culture approach, 106
teleserials, campaigned against women emancipation, 192
televangelism
    changes initiated by, 111n17
    domesticated on the African continent, 108
    interview questions on, 224–25
    miracles faked, 243
    Muslims engaging in, 104
    rise of, 103–21
    transformed Christianity, 120
    U.S. models of capitalistic exported to Africa, 217
televangelists
    growing influence of American and European, 37n31
    selling ritualistic elements, 243
televised Charismatic Christianity, 111
televised Christianity, 105, 109
television broadcasting systems and entrepreneurship, promoted by Congolese pastors and evangelists, 38–39
television programs and broadcasts, American influencing the Congolese religious worldview, 18
television stations, "promoting Christian radio broadcast," 106
Tempels, Placide, 2, 29–30, 29n6–30n6, 40, 42n43
Temple, regarded as the center of Jewish life, 172
Tennent, Timothy C., 116, 118, 119, 123, 125, 125n7–26n7, 160n25
theologians, needing to recognize cross-contextual realities, 88
theological cross-examination, interview questions about, 225
theological discourses, 86, 89, 124, 128
theological education
    in Africa by African scholars, 213
    critical for the growing African Christian community, 126–27

focusing on Western realities in the US, 88
internationalization of, 120
lack of, in part due to corruption, 236
as a necessity, 88
need for, 230
need for change in, 87–90
as a priority, 233
reaching the laity, 214
reclaiming and reconstructing an authentic hermeneutic for, 220
theological exchange, across the spectrum of nations and cultures, 126
theological factors, contributing to the expansion of Neo-Pentecostalism, 47–48
theological institutions, offering an M.Div. degree in three months, 236
theological issues, facing the church in Africa, 85
theological renewal, listening to the majority of the world, 116
theological tools, lack of solid for interpreting the Scripture in Africa, 172
theology
   as about choices, 122n1
   addressing the failing economic systems and systemic crises, 131
   African shaping Christian expressions, 205
   globalization of, 120
   produced in the US as peculiar to Congolese worldviews, 127
   teaching of in most Western settings, 121
Theology in the Context of World Christianity: How the Global Church is Influencing the Way we Think About and Discuss Theology (Tennent), 123, 125n7
A Theology of Liberation (Gutierrez), 133
third-wave, independent, Neo-Pentecostal churches, distinguishing from the first-wave, 198
Tienou, Tite, 116
tithes, 78, 171, 171n58
Toco, Simao, 3
Tocoists, Portuguese practice of exiling, 3
Togarasei, Lovemore, 37, 47
Tongoi, Dennis, 163–64
tongue speakers, manipulating or twisting the Gospel, 176
Traditional African Christian theology, on lifestyles reflecting divine blessings, 111
traditional belief systems
   connecting with the American Dream philosophy, 72
   exported to African Christianity, 212
   local religious enterprises of, 64
   locals still practicing, 73
   paving the way for the Congolese quest for spiritual powers, 28
   validation of, 205
traditional cultures, 105, 183
traditional evangelism, 4n9, 140–41
traditional healers, 40, 174
traditional medicine and occult systems, 174
traditional religion, syncretistic character of, 10
traditional values, returning to, 19n61
traditional worldviews, 2
transformative paradigm, relating to social justice, 186n1
transformative power, of the gospel, 195n30
translated gospel, 6, 22, 83
Translating the Message: The Missionary Impact on Culture (Sanneh), 20
translation
   allowing the Gospel to be universal, 149
   as a change of life, 57
   done outside the church by a secular organization, 234
   effect and impact of Bible, 51–76
   effort of, 56–62

translation (*continued*)
    guaranteeing that each culture infuses its own meaning into the Bible, 75n64
    at the heart of Christian missions, 112
    impact of, 234
    meaning a holistic embodiment of life change, 220
    of the name God creating great impact, 139n42
    requiring that one institute the recipient culture, 20
    as a step towards liberation, 57
    transformed traditional religions and belief systems, 60
    of vernacular languages, 60
transnational spaces and identities, rooted in the history of humanity, 147
triple consciousness, as an African, alien, and African-American, 146
Triumph of the City (Glaeser), 200n44
Tshibangu, Edward, 188, 190n14
Tshombé, Moïse, 189–90
Turner, Harold, 64
Tutu, Desmond, 166n41
TV networks, using to deceive clients, 230
TV5, Christian channel, 108
twenty-first century missional enterprise, demographic paradigm shift in, 219
Twitter, people interacting with each other on, 107
Two-Thirds World, 73

Ubuntu, meaning "humanity," 211n4
unbiblical hermeneutics, of biblical literature, 70
uncritical theological reflection, 152
Under the Radar: Pentecostalism in South Africa and Its Potential Social and Economic Role (Berger and Hunter), 153
uneducated apostles, distorting and misinterpreting the Bible, 230
United Methodist Church, 118
United Methodist General Conference (2016), 86
United Methodist Hymnal, 138n41–39n41
Unruh, Heidi Rolland, 194–95
US
    cultural worldview, 82
    wanted to control Congo because of its wealth of raw materials, 239
U.S. National Security Council subcommittee, on covert operations, 189n11

Van Harn, Roger E., 143
Van Henten, Brenner, 166–67, 167n45, 168
van Kamp, Linda, 192
Van Reybrouck, David, 31, 140, 141
verbal story, preserving, 200
vernacular, 51n1, 139
vernacular cultures
    Bible translations and, 167n45
    imperial translation of, 54
    significance of translation, 59
    translation of the Bible into, 234
vernacular linguistic phenomena, ignited religious revivals, 55
vernacular literacy, for new Christians, 21
vernacular Scriptures, ushered in a fundamental religious revolution, 51n1
vernacular translation, process of, having far reaching consequences, 167n45
video cassettes, 107
viens-et-vois, literally meaning "come and see," 50, 50n58
violence, suffered by the Congolese, 159
visa recipients, tending to feel the weight of foreignness, 145
visual mediation, open to the public arena, 105

vital force, shaping the religious landscape within the Congolese tribes, 29
vocabularies, Christian with a syncretic character, 233
voice, giving to marginalized people, 202n52
"Voice of Inspiration," 109–10
voices of the voiceless, prophets as, 188
vulnerable people, taught to expect unrealistic returns, 244

Wall Street culture, 154
Walls, Andrew F., 2, 5, 21, 57, 61, 62, 67, 89, 109, 115, 116, 117, 119, 120, 122n1, 125, 125n6, 126, 134n30–35n30, 148, 211, 212
Wariboko, Nimi, 81, 154–55, 155n8, 156, 163, 175, 175n61, 178–79, 178n68
Washington Consensus, impact of, 44
Watchtower Society, 36n30
wealth
    accumulation of, 197
    as both a blessing and a curse, 171
    ways of gaining, 47–48
wealth and health Gospel, 168
"Wealth and Health Gospel of Success," 18
Wesley, John, 196
Wesleyan theology, 196
West
    influence of, 125–37
    needing to collaborate with the growing global South, 217
    not reading cultural signals correctly, 159
Western Christianity, changed into a new brand of religion in the Congo, 32
Western church, 89, 118
Western culture, belief in the superiority of, 158
Western imported trends, 27–28
Western influence, enculturation of, 122–50

Western missionary movement, high point of, 122n1
Western model of evangelizing, 183
Western model of the church, 219
Western pattern of prosperity, encouraging uncritical hermeneutics, 184
Western Pentecostalism, translated into Neo-Pentecostalism, 70
Western Pentecostals, emerging in the twentieth century, 123–24
Western scholars, 88, 199
Western theology, 115, 219n19
Western values, 107–11
Western ways, as no longer unique, superior, or unsurprised, 130
Western worldviews, 184
Westerners, learning from Africans, 211n4
Western-exported Christian expressions, resurgence of theological discourses in Africa and, 124
Westlind, Nils, 4n9
When Helping Hurts: How to Alleviate Poverty without Hurting the Poor and Yourself (Corbett), 100
"whole gospel for the whole person," 215
whole person, reaching, 195
wholeness of life, 2, 195
Whose Religion Is Christianity? The Gospel beyond the West (Sanneh), 58, 58n22
Wilkinson, Bruce, 124
Winner's Chapel, David Oyedepo's, 8
witchcraft, 192
woe, Jesus declaring against the rich, 170
woman of Endor, as a diviner, 54n10
women
    abuse and oppressive acts against by prosperity preachers, 211
    as activists, 194
    caught in adultery, 194
    Congolese as evangelists, 194
    enlarging of religious space for, 68

women (*continued*)
　ministered to Jesus and his disciples, 194
　as missionaries (Lydia, Phoebe, Chloe, and Rufus' mother), 193
　Neo-Pentecostalism and, 191–93
　participating in leadership positions, 71n58, 192
　required by healers to drink palm oil and became ill, 40
　as victims of false prophets, 230
Woodbridge, 171
word of faith force phenomenon, 18
Word of Faith Movement. *See* Word-Faith movement
"Word of Faith-Force," 18
Word of God, transforming people's lives in the DRC, 232
Word-Faith movement, 8n22, 17
works of mercy, 196
world evangelization, requiring the whole church, 10
worldview(s)
　ability to challenge human behavior, 156
　African, 1, 163
　animistic, 6
　Christian, 80, 156, 233
　Congolese, 6, 39, 62–70, 83–84
　contributing to the expansion of Neo-Pentecostalism, 46–47
　essential to communicating to gospel, 153n3
　mixing with traditional cultures or belief systems, 233
　Neo-Congolese Christian, 41
　shaping the gospel of Christ, 207
　spiritual, 203, 211n4
　syncretized religious, 49
　traditional, 2
　understanding, 152
　US cultural, 82
　Western, 184
Worldview (Sanchez), 152n3
Wright, Christopher J. H., 9, 42
"Writing African Christianity Perspectives from the History of the Historiography of African Christianity" (Bongmba), 156
"Writing the Pentecostal History of Africa, and Latin America" (Anderson), 183
written literature, with the Western observer's voice, 199
Wuthow, Robert, 90

Xakalashe, Zulu, 165, 165n39, 166n39

Yamamori, Tetsunao, 148n63–49n63, 149
yoga and other spiritual disciplines (gods), replaced God, 202
Yong, Amos, on the prosperity gospel, 12, 81
"Your Miracle Encounter," 110

Zaire, 4n9, 19n61, 41
zairianization, led to a return to African authenticity, 19n61
Zambian community, social lift in, 16
Zimbabwean theologians, using liberation theology, 134
Zionist churches, 28n2, 68
Zophar, 215

www.ingramcontent.com/pod-product-compliance
Lightning Source LLC
Chambersburg PA
CBHW071235230426
43668CB00011B/1443